FLEECED!

Telemarketing Rip-offs and How to Avoid Them

FRED SCHULTE

Prometheus Books

59 John Glenn Drive
Amherst, NewYork 14228-2197

Published 1995 by Prometheus Books

99 98 97 96 95   5 4 3 2 1

Library of Congress Cataloging-in-Publication Data

Schulte, Fred.
    Fleeced : telemarketing rip-offs and how to avoid them / by Fred Schulte.
    p.   cm.
    Includes bibliographical references and index.
    ISBN 0-87975-963-1 (alk. paper)
    1. Telemarketing—United States—Corrupt practices. 2. Fraud—United
States. 3. Consumer protection—United States. I. Title.
HF5415.1265.S38   1995
364.1'68—dc20   95-5629
                                                                        CIP

Printed in the United States of America on acid-free paper.

To My Mother and Father

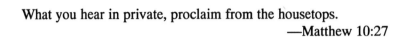

What you hear in private, proclaim from the housetops.

—Matthew 10:27

Contents

9

Introduction

Without a doubt you've been stalked by scam bandits, maybe not face to face, but over the phone, through the mail, or while scanning newspaper ads hoping to find a bargain.

Telemarketing, mail-order, or high-stakes investment swindlers have targeted eight of ten American households in recent years. They rob millions of people every year, hauling off loot that likely exceeds $40 billion.

This problem will only get worse. Scammers are extraordinarily adept at devising new and more sophisticated rip-offs, tapping into computer data banks to alert them to customers' buying habits and credit ratings. And before long, new computer technology will make them even harder to track down and prosecute.

Yet scam artists often use tactics that are fairly easy for a wary consumer to spot, practices that will become clear in these pages.

This book is divided into three sections to help you better understand and protect yourself from telemarketing rip-offs. Three appendices list nearly three dozen scams and help define many of the terms and sales tactics common to con schemes. Part one outlines the dimensions of this massive fraud, pegging some of the people behind the phone rooms along with the devices they rely on to ply their trade.

Part two shows how con artists use these tools to craft a seemingly endless array of bogus products, with an emphasis on how to protect yourself or your loved ones from falling victim.

Part three investigates why illicit telemarketing remains a menace despite years of efforts to wipe it out. I have tried to zero in on legal loopholes and other flaws in the justice system that conspire to keep these cons a few paces ahead of police or other regulators. These criticisms are not meant to disparage the efforts of thousands of law officers and attorneys general and other regulators who fight to protect consumers, sometimes from their own greed, and often with little political support or funding.

I have taken the position—a view shared by many regulators nationwide—that destructive telemarketing persists largely because the perpetrators face light penalties and small civil fines when caught. Nothing short of lengthy prison sentences is likely to deter these criminals. Consumers can only hope lawmakers are listening.

Some care should be taken not to confuse con artists with legitimate merchants who use the telephone to sell their wares. Legal telemarketing concerns boast more than $600 billion in annual sales and employ millions of people. Many of these businesses conduct their affairs honorably, though many people may find them far more of a nuisance than a novel or expedient means of buying goods.

The "phone pros" profiled here are a sinister breed. They peddle products no sensible person would buy if the item could be viewed, either because the prices charged are grossly inflated or the quality of the articles is shoddy. These unscrupulous telemarketers lie grandly or omit pertinent details that would give any prudent person pause. Some terrorize their victims, calling dozens of times in a week or threaten the elderly unless they agree to buy. Court cases reveal that some have gone so far as to threaten physical harm to the families of customers who spurn their offers.

All of the con artists described in this volume, and their prey, are real. While trying to keep unnamed sources to a minimum, I have deleted the names of some victims to spare them embarrassment. Similarly, I have honored requests to withhold the names of a few telemarketers who provided incriminating material.

While a tiny group of these scammers have landed in jail, thousands like them still pillage pocketbooks from coast to coast. Their histories have been pieced together from court documents, law enforcement surveillance videotapes, transcripts and other public records, and personal interviews. In all, tens of thousands of pages of files were reviewed, including legal briefs from more than thirty-five states and several federal agencies.

My research into telemarketing fraud began with a series of articles in the Fort Lauderdale *Sun-Sentinel* about boiler rooms that sold cheap certificates good for vacations in Florida and the Bahamas.

I quickly found that South Florida, while a hotbed of phone scams, was by no means alone. More than 6,000 phone and mail schemes have sprung up in more than forty states since 1989, representing everything from phony charities to ostrich farms. The owners of many of these shady enterprises have skipped from state to state, and scam to scam, for years without detection.

Florida and other Sunbelt states remain the reluctant hosts for far too many telemarketing frauds that prey on residents of other regions. We can only hope that the lawmakers in states that have housed this rip-off rabble wise up and enact laws to send them packing.

I am indebted to many hard-working consumer advocates who have struggled to halt these cancerous con games, and, to that end, gave freely of their time to help make this book possible. Some assisted with the cooperation of their superiors, others did not.

Special thanks to Carol Colen and Rosemarie Bonta of the Better Business Bureaus of Las Vegas and South Florida, respectively.

Many police and law enforcement officials also shared information, advice, and informed opinions. Charlie Donaldson of the New York State Attorney General's Office and Rene Champagne of the Florida Comptroller's Office come to mind. Thanks also to John Barker of the National Consumer's League.

I also owe a debt to former *Sun-Sentinel* editor Gene Cryer, who for many years gave me the time to pursue lengthy reporting projects, and to his successor, Earl Maucker, another strong believer in investigative journalism. Most of all, I must thank Jenni, whose support made this project possible.

Finally, a word to readers: judge harshly when it comes to phone salespeople with offers that seem too good to be true. Chances are they are. Hardly a day goes by at our newspaper that we don't hear from some unfortunate soul somewhere in the country hoping against hope that the firm to which he or she has sent a bundle of money is on the level. It's no fun telling these callers that they were cheated simply because they could not believe that the soothing voice on the other end of the line could belong to a thief.

The phone pirates know who they are. I have written this book so that you will, too.

Fred Schulte
Fort Lauderdale, Florida

Part One

Dollars in the Air

1

Prize Fever

Elsie Barcalow huddled in a corner of her bedroom. She buried her head in her hands and prayed she might find peace from the ringing that tormented her.

In her final year of life, Elsie was afraid to pick up the telephone. Phone salespeople invaded her home several nights a week, leaving her distraught and numb. They called from thousands of miles away to sucker her into buying junk products.

Time after time, they promised grand prizes to wear down her resistance. When she balked, they bombarded her with hard-sell pitches, part flattery, part mockery, part threats and verbal abuse. They pestered her until she surrendered her credit card account numbers, which they billed for $25,000 in one year alone.

Elsie didn't know her attackers. She could recognize some of their voices, but they used fake names to conceal their true identities. She could never pick them out in a police lineup, or even recall which voice sold her which goods. And she was too embarrassed to admit that she couldn't control the problem.

Once again, pirate telemarketers got away with the near-perfect crime. They swindled an aging widow out of her life's savings and left almost no evidence of their deeds. While they didn't intend to do so, they also stole her self-esteem and caused stress and heartache that may well have hastened her death.

Nobody held a gun to Elsie's head and forced her to buy. She could have slammed down the receiver, threatened to call the police, or fought back in some other manner. But she stood by helplessly while the bandits robbed her.

Elsie Barcalow is a classic victim of the telemarketing scam, the nation's fastest growing consumer fraud menace. Like so many elderly people, she had a tough time explaining why she fell victim. Barcalow worked as a legal secretary into her seventies. She was an honest, caring woman, who volunteered her time to work for her local Red Cross and other charities.

"I guess I'm just a sucker," she offered, rather feebly, when asked to explain how she let the con artists drain her bank accounts. "I really got myself into a jam," the seventy-four-year-old widow said.

The words came hard as the rail-thin woman, whose parched skin showed years of exposure to subtropical sun, raked her hands over thousands of pens and other useless products that littered her small apartment.

She had kept neat files full of the offers from telemarketers, at least in the beginning. One file folder that held her cancer insurance policy was commandeered to hold the overflow of gobbledygook letters from the prize promoters. Gradually, she lost count of the purchases, became confused, and fell further into debt.

While the elderly are often targets of the telephone scam, young people aren't safe either. Working-age individuals struggling to break free from debt, hoping to land a great job overseas, start a new business, or find a cheap family vacation get taken as well.

Not all phone offers are swindles. Telemarketing, legal and upright, brings in hundreds of billions of dollars a year to businesses, charities, and even political candidates. But telemarketing has a seamy underside of hucksters whose rule is to dial up as many suckers as possible and never give any of them a break.

Phone-scam gangs steal somewhere between $10 billion and $40 billion a year over the phone lines. Career "phone pros" skip from state to state and from scam to scam with little fear of landing in jail.

Crooked telemarketing comes in many shapes, though most arrive bearing gifts or sales offers or investments that are too good to be true. The operators also are a diverse group. Some are crude racketeers with organized crime ties and a relentless drive to raid every pocketbook within reach.

Others are jolly investment brokers who pick their victims meticulously and employ a string of lawyers to keep out of jail.

Sadly, others are recent high school and college graduates, gifted at gab but deeply deficient in any sense of business ethics. These chatty boiler-room soldiers love the quick cash, power, and revved-up lifestyle —the "glitz" they call it—that comes from outtalking, outearning, and outspending their young peers.

Whatever their origins, phone-scam artists are a growing pestilence, according to government officials who have battled for years to wipe them out. "Telemarketing fraud is probably the fastest growing illegal activity in this country. Attorneys general offices around the country are being besieged by telephone calls from citizens who have been defrauded of hundreds, thousands, even tens of thousands of dollars," said Maryland Attorney General J. Joseph Curran, Jr., in declaring war on telephone fraud in May 1994.*

Curran joined a number of law enforcement groups in Washington, D.C., in demanding tougher laws and public education campaigns to wipe out "this fraudulent virus."

That virus struck Elsie Barcalow and she became a chronic sufferer. The first symptom of the telemarketing malady appeared after a postcard arrived in her mailbox. Its message was upbeat and urgent:

> Congratulations! Your name appears on a list of first round winners of CASH in [a] $1 million publicity sweepstakes. As of now, your first round cash check is *uncollected* and *unrequested*. Many of the first round winners have *already* claimed their money. . . . Not a Hoax. . . . Not a joke!

While it might not have been a joke, it was not exactly a great deal either. The "cash" turned out to be play-money coupons good for discounts on junk products.

The more Elsie Barcalow began to respond to the offers, the more new enticements arrived. Most of the contests dangled four prizes, such as a pound of gold, a Lincoln Continental, a pendant, or a certificate good for a dream vacation in the cool waters off the Bahama Islands.

Each new sweepstakes offered more exciting prizes, and, as the months went by, Elsie bought health and fitness products, environmentally safe trashbags, a water purifier, even antidrug bumper stickers, all at shamelessly inflated prices, and all goods for which she had absolutely no use. At various points, she hoped to win a mink coat; a home appliance package of refrigerator, range, and washer-dryer; a Ford Thunderbird; a video camcorder; and other cars and prizes, just to name a few.

But the prizes she snared for spending $1,000 or more on her Visa card always turned out to be the ugly duckling, and least expensive, of the four. She wound up with a cheap pendant, or the vacation certificate, nearly worthless because of its many restrictions and hidden fees. Meanwhile, the products that arrived in crates from parcel post were either useless or worth far less than she paid.

---

*National Fraud Information Center news conference, Washington, D.C., May 12, 1994.

The auto bumper stickers bearing the slogan "Say No to Drugs" were hardly the sort of thing a widow would need, even if the telemarketer said most of his customers donated them to local police or a school.

Barcalow paid $2,500 for 1,200 blue-over-white bumper stickers; half bore the inscription "Say No to Drugs," the other half pleaded "Save the Earth."

The sales package came with a cheery inscription: "Thank you for your help in the community…and thank you for helping to keep our earth a clean and drug-free environment for our children." Added abruptly was the note: "All sales final."

Each deal led to bigger and more costly deals. Some promised bonus awards, often in stilted phrasing written to sound official and lawyer-like and hard for Barcalow to decipher, like this offer, for instance:

> Congratulations! This is your legal letter of guarantee for participating in our "Save the Earth" and "Say No to Drugs" promotion. As a thank you for purchasing our bumper stickers you have been chosen to receive an award and some bonus gifts.

The gifts included: $20,000 in cash, a ski boat and trailer, $5,000 cash bond, a six-by-nine Oriental style Belgian rug, and $3,500 in cash.

The fine print states the dismal odds of taking home the cash, boat, or bonds (one in 30,000). The flyer listed the chances of getting the cheaply made rug as 29,996 out of 30,000! But many customers such as Barcalow relied more on the chatter of the telemarketer than the fine print.

Unlike a state lottery, there's no guarantee that any of the prizes exist. Prize promoters often renege on their promises, as witnessed by consumer-protection lawsuits on file across the country.

In a conversation a year before her death, Barcalow tried to explain her weakness for the phone-sales schemes. She struggled with her thoughts as her kitten stared intently from a perch on her desk. "I thought some of the prizes might make good Christmas gifts," she offered, obviously unsure of her motivations.

Barcalow said she knew she was sinking further into debt through her impulsive late-night purchases. She wanted to tell her family about her misery, but feared they would deem her unfit to manage her finances, a shattering loss of self-esteem.

Some nights she took the phone off the hook to escape the onslaught of sales calls. She hated to do that because she thought it might worry family members in the event that they called her apartment to check on her.

Why did she fall for it over and over? Was it partly greed? Not likely. Barcalow was careful with her money and content with her station in life. She was also honest and giving. On a fishing trip to the Bahamas, in which eighteen people roughed it on bunks, she decided she could not afford a fifteen-dollar entry fee for a pool to be awarded to the person who caught the biggest fish. A man over thirty years her junior paid her entry fee so nobody would be left out. Elsie took first place that day, reeling in a twenty-one-pound grouper. Her first thought: give the man back his money out of her winnings.

He wouldn't take it. While greed did not motivate her, the telemarketer tapped other needs. While the phone must have seemed like a vile conveyance some evenings, the voice on the line also offered solace from loneliness.

Many older people feel the same, according to consumer officials, who estimate that ninety-two million Americans, often the elderly, have been caught off guard by nighttime telemarketing.

The risks of getting fleeced increase with age. The American Association of Retired Persons (AARP), in a study published in March 1994, found that one in four people over age sixty-five is vulnerable to fraud schemes. That's millions of people in the United States alone. Once they hit age seventy-five, the number climbs to 34 percent, mostly because older people tend to be unsuspecting and have little idea of where to complain.

"No amount of law enforcement is going to change this," said one phone pro who has worked all over the country, but asked to remain anonymous. "People are so lonely, so tired of life, they can't wait for the phone to ring. It's worth three hundred to four hundred dollars to them to think that they got a friend. That's what you play on." This comment reinforces FBI crime data which shows that the elderly are targets in about a third of telemarketing fraud schemes. The AARP's study found that the prize bait worked on 18 percent of people over age seventy-five, many of whom considered it impolite to hang up on a telemarketer. Not surprisingly, three of four people disliked the prize they received.

Many elderly people succumb because they are lonely, depressed, and simply cannot believe that the voice on the line could belong to a thief. Other senior citizens admit being flattered with the attentions of the phone marketers, who know just when to catch them during the day to cheer them up with well-delivered stock lines such as "I'm going to make you the happiest woman in (add city)." If the elderly can take solace in sales calls, it comes at a steep price both in cash and, perhaps even more devastating, lost self-esteem.

Barcalow's secret came to light after she asked a daughter to lend her $1,000 so that she could pay off mounting Visa card bills. "She was too embarrassed to tell me what was happening," said her son, Stewart, a veterinarian in Hollywood, Florida.

Barcalow found that his mother, who he thought had $30,000 in stocks and bonds, had frittered most of it away on purchases pushed on her by telemarketers from at least twenty-six companies in seven states.

Combing through her financial records, he tried to unravel the tangle of telemarketing transactions, and was shocked by what he found. He saw more than a dozen receipts for Federal Express showing the overnight delivery service had been out to her apartment time after time to pick up checks and credit card authorizations for delivery to boiler rooms in Utah, upstate New York, Nevada, and California. So vague were the sales receipts that he was unable to figure out if much of the hodgepodge of merchandise she ordered—from skin care products to a silver gift box—had been delivered. He quickly gave up in despair.

Barcalow's son tore up his mother's credit cards and changed her phone number. A few of the marketers found her anyway. She recognized the voice of one telemarketer who tracked her down despite her efforts to evade him.

Stewart Barcalow moved his mother into a retirement home to shield her from the shysters who kept trying to take another crack at her dwindling bank balance. Her health deteriorated rapidly and she died in January 1994.

"I can't say for sure that this ordeal caused her death, but it did disturb her terribly that she fell for this," Stewart Barcalow said. "The last two years of her life were difficult."

Getting refunds from the crooks has been an ordeal in itself. The best he could do was get his mother's name on a list of class action plaintiffs in a lawsuit against one of the giant telemarketing houses in Las Vegas from which she purchased items. He got seventy dollars as his part of the settlement, even though he's certain his mother lost thousands of dollars to the company.

It has been all but impossible for Stewart Barcalow to forget his mother's struggle with the phone pirates. New offers of fabulous prize deals and promotions, each more elaborate than the next, still show up, forwarded from his mother's old address, more than a year after her death."I recognize some of them as the same outfits that ripped Mother off," he said. "As soon as I see this stuff come in I heave it in the trash."

But he didn't throw away one letter that raised his hopes, at least temporarily, of getting some of her money back. The letter, addressed to his mother, exuded sincerity. It arrived unsolicited from a firm that said it specialized in getting refunds for victims of phony prize schemes. Here's part of the pitch:

> We have a tremendous success rate in recovering funds. We work very confidentially, and unlike others, we do all the work for you—without you spending huge sums of money in advance. . . . We work on a percentage of the funds we recover for you, payable when you actually receive refunds.

The company said its agents found Elsie Barcalow's name "numerous times" as a customer of telemarketing promotional companies. Stewart didn't think to ask the firm's representatives how they knew about his mother's losses or his own efforts to get some of the money back. Later, authorities told him that the firm probably purchased the names from a defunct telemarketer.

But Stewart Barcalow felt he finally had a chance to get even. Frustrated by the failure of state agencies to get refunds, he made the call. Within a few days a contract arrived that asked for a two-hundred-dollar retainer fee. The company also wanted 25 percent of any money it recovered.

Barcalow balked after the local Better Business Bureau raised some doubts. The bureau noted that "recovery" companies often do little more than write letters to state agencies, something consumers can do themselves. The bureau report also noted: "Letters demanding refunds are often sent to companies that have gone out of business, making such efforts useless." And while the bureau report didn't come right out and say it, the "recovery" rooms were simply the latest scam fad to hit Las Vegas.

Barcalow felt he'd suffered the lowest blow of all, a scam directed at people desperate to get back money taken from them by scam artists. But the experience drove home an essential truth of illegal telemarketing. Suckers will get hit over and over unless they learn to say no.

The telephone first became a mass marketing tool in the 1920s when brokers began to call clients and give them daily, even hourly stock updates. During World War II, with most of the men drafted into uniform, there was an acute shortage of salespeople. Many industries reacted by hiring women to handle the duties over the phone. After the war, the telephone banks proved an efficient way to handle sales, such as renewals of magazine subscriptions. The applications soared a few years after the advent of the 800 toll-free number in the 1960s. Citing this business bonanza, an exuberant supporter of the concept in 1967 coined the term "telemarketing." Twenty years after introducing the service nationally in the late 1960s, one hotel chain handled nine million calls annually on 800 lines.

The word "telemarketing" didn't debut in the *Webster's New International Dictionary* until 1986. It now carries the rather bland definition of "to market goods or services by telephone."

Of course, there is nothing illegal, or even unseemly, about using the phone for commerce. More than 3.5 million Americans make their living that way. They inject billions of dollars a year into the national economy, running sales campaigns ranging from newspaper circulation drives to fund raising for charities.

Telemarketing magazine, considered the authoritative source on the state of the industry, estimates that legitimate telephone sales gross more than $600 billion each year, while one marketing survey found that 184 million Americans purchased goods or services over the phone in 1992.

Many phone marketers shun sales tactics that annoy, harass, or cheat the public. They abide by a code of ethics and etiquette and limit irritating practices such as late-night calling. Phone marketers say they provide a critical service to residents of rural areas, the homebound, and millions of Americans who simply prefer to pick up the receiver rather than rummage through retail stores.

Judy Lanier, a former president of the American Telemarketing Association, pleaded the industry's case in a 1992 article published by the Direct Selling Education Foundation. She spoke of the convenience of shopping by phone and said telephone marketing was a profession.

> In fact, today consumers are purchasing virtually every type of product and service via the telephone, from prescriptions to travel services, to hand-made sweaters and lap-top computers. Who, then, is being exploited? In all cases, the consumer has the opportunity to consider and decline the offer. As with any other marketing medium, the individual can say "No thank you." It is his or her choice. As it happens, many consumers are saying "Yes, please," because by shopping by telephone they are saving time, avoiding stress, and (since telemarketing is more cost-effective to the supplier company) getting better values.*

---

*"Telemarketing: Exploiting a Good Idea," *At Home with Consumers,* vol. 13, no. 2, August 1992.

But even unabashed defenders of telemarketing admit that cheats and scam artists have invaded the industry and show no signs of letting up. While nobody knows exactly how many underground phone-sales shops have been set up in recent years, or how their numbers compare with legitimate marketers, it is clear that fraud artists have infiltrated nearly every state.

Since 1989, more than 6,500 deceptive phone schemes drew scrutiny from government regulators, at least a third of them for employing the type of phony prize deal that robbed Elsie Barcalow of her life's savings. Phone con artists targeted 92 percent of adult Americans in recent years, according to national consumer experts.

Some phone-sales rooms pop up in Sunbelt locales where murders and drug-trafficking crimes overtax police, leaving them little time, or desire, to corral con artists. Other scams favor remote areas or rust-belt towns where community leaders are happy to lure high-paying jobs, , happy they tend to ask few probing questions. If these outfits don't botl er residents of their host state, which they rarely do, local law enforce ment feels little pressure to shut them down.

"I can open a (telephone boiler) room anywhere. I mean give me ar office and parachute me into any city you want," said Bill Clark, a veteran of more than fourteen years in illegal telemarketing in Las Vegas and South Florida, both hotbeds of the phone hustle. "I can start a room anywhere."* From rented hotel rooms to offshore roosts beyond the reach of U.S. authorities, wherever they run the game, phone racketeers share one trait: huge pay-offs for bosses. Less than twenty phones manned in a small office can gross $25,000 to $30,000 in a week.

The soldiers, those who actually do the dialing, can earn up to $100,000 a year in commissions if they can stand the frantic pressure to produce sales. Their jobs are made easier by the fact that millions of people have little idea of what phone fraud is, and how to spot it before they fall victim.

Generally speaking, phone fraud occurs when sales agents misrepresent their product, or fail to deliver it. Related problems include the misuse of a customer's credit cards or bank accounts. The deception can range from overstating the dollar value or benefits of a product to implying that the buyer has won a contest to falsely claiming that a product has the endorsement of the federal government—just about any lie that causes a customer to purchase.

---

*Clark's comments were captured on an FBI surveillance tape, March 31, 1992.

Some examples:

• One Texas telemarketing company told buyers that the National Aeronautics and Space Administration used its tap-water processors on the space shuttle and the U.S. Environmental Protection Agency recommended the devices. It also said that the U.S. Congress was passing a law requiring the devices, so prices soon would rise. All lies, said the U.S. government, which won a court order banning the false claims, but not until the products had been sold all over the country.

• A telephone investment dealer claimed that its commodities were a sure bet to make money, even though 90 percent of the firm's clients had lost their money and the owners had repeatedly been sued for consumer fraud under a variety of different company names in state after state. Clients who asked the dealer about the firm's past were not told about the run-ins with the law.

• A southern California-based rare stamp dealer's telemarketers claimed the stamps that they sold were an excellent, low-risk investment and were priced below market value. In fact, customers purchased the stamps at two to ten times their real value.

Authorities refer to these enterprises as "boiler rooms," a term of uncertain heritage. Some say the name originates from phony stock-sales rooms that were hidden in basements to escape detection. Others insist the term refers to the intense pressure to make sales regardless of the tactics.

Lawmakers in Florida, a state overrun with the species, have defined a boiler room as:

> an enterprise in which two or more persons engage in telephone communications with members of the public using two or more telephones at one location, or at more than one location, in a common scheme or enterprise which sold or offered for sale a security or investment through fraud, falsification or concealment of facts.*

The risks of getting caught and sent to jail for running such an enterprise almost anywhere in the country are small. The telemarketers know they have the upper hand because more than 90 percent of law enforcement actions against them are civil rather than criminal. That means the phone firms, at worst, get slapped with lawsuits filed by state agencies on behalf of aggrieved consumers. These cases usually net the rip-off artists small fines, which they can make up in less than a week on the phones.

---

*Florida Statute F.S. 517.312.

Many state cases are settled when the company agrees to make refunds to the small number of victims who file complaints with the state.

Many never even get sued because regulators feel they require substantial proof—dozens of sworn affidavits from victims, for example—before they feel confident of winning a court battle to close down a con scheme. By the time law enforcers collect victim statements, boiler rooms often have moved, or closed down and reopened under a new name.

While boiler-room owners often seek to reassure novice telemarketers that their operations are legal, many phone sales pitches do in fact violate the law. Owners could be prosecuted for violations of state fraud statutes or federal wire fraud laws, which make it a crime to cheat customers over the phone lines.

Typically, cases are handled as civil matters either by state attorneys general or federal authorities. These cases tend to net small fines, so boiler-room kingpins know they usually have little to fear from state authorities. Even if they get convicted, most telemarketers receive only probation or short jail sentences.

While the punishment tends to be slight, the damage done to victims can be staggering. File cabinets kept by attorneys general and consumer regulators in dozens of states bulge with complaints from victims, often people who can least afford the loss.

The National Fraud Information Center in Washington, D.C., logged more than 30,000 complaints of telemarketing fraud during 1993, its first year. Callers included a Japanese-American fabric store owner in Southern California who said a telemarketer threatened to burn down her store unless she gave one hundred dollars to an antidrug campaign, and an elderly man in York, Pennsylvania, who transferred more than $105,000 in assets to telemarketers before his death in March 1994.

Few states are able to produce files showing the numbers and types of telemarketing fraud complaints received. But the experience of Florida's main consumer agency is telling. The agency logged nearly 15,000 telemarketing fraud complaints between 1985 and 1992. As a rule of thumb, regulators figure that just one of 100 victims takes the trouble to fill out complaint forms, mostly because they feel nobody will take action. Many phone rooms that handle hundreds of complaints from angry buyers in a week will show only a few dozen complaints with state regulators in a year's time.

So how do ordinary folks get trapped and how can people free themselves from this costly scourge? Take a few words of warning from another longtime telemarketer, who hawked products from phony precious metals to fake cable television franchises. "I can take anybody's money. It's just a matter of matching the right pitch to the right person," the marketer boasted.

The wild success of phony prize schemes shows that millions of people don't take a whole lot of persuading, despite years of warnings from consumer agencies to steer clear of green postcards that arrive in the mail with a zippy message that screams "Congratulations!"

This phenomenon is worth exploring in detail because it can be a channel to financial ruin. The card lists an 800 number to call, and many recipients figure, why not? How can you lose anything by calling a toll-free number?

Common sense dictates that no company will stay afloat handing out money for nothing. But the scammers know that millions of Americans hunger for any sort of jackpot and will roll the dice if they think it won't cost them anything.

Many people are inclined to believe they are lucky enough to be singled out for some faraway firm's largess. They do so, perhaps, because they are unaware of a few simple facts of the selling life. They don't know, for example, that anyone can buy sales leads from hundreds of brokers who compile marketing lists from sources such as phone books and voter registration files, even magazine subscribers. Anyone who dials back the 800 exchange gives the marketer a chance to capture his or her phone numbers with a caller identification device. At the very least, the marketer can match the phone number with an address and sell the information. Dozens of companies pay premium prices for leads on people gullible enough to respond to a prize pitch.

Too often, the initial sales contact bears even more fruit for con artists. They talk customers into buying something and pressure them to pay for it in advance by giving a credit card number.

Millions of people wind up regretting their first telephone transaction. A purchase made in a moment of weakness all but guarantees a flood of new sales calls and mail pitches as the hyenas scramble to feast on this new-found prey.

A customer's credit card numbers may wind up for sale on a black market to more con artists who tap the card for large sums hoping that the cardholder fails to notice, or is unaware of how to fight bogus billings. Credit card frauds go hand in hand with telemarketing schemes. Visa and MasterCard alone estimate annual losses of $200 million to improper use of credit cards by phone marketers. The only sure way to avoid straying into this marketing minefield is to *never* give out a credit card number over the phone, unless booking a hotel or other reservation, or buying from a known business.

The levels of deceit phony prize companies employ vary depending on whether they have any respect for the law or want to stay in business any length of time. Almost all telemarketers, legitimate or not, write scripts that salespeople read to potential buyers. Legitimate marketers use scripts to guard against overzealous workers who might be tempted to stretch the truth to make a sale. Fly-by-night phone rooms, by contrast, use scripts merely as a starting point for a sale. They expect sales agents to stray from the text and say anything it takes to close a sale. For this reason, customers should beware of sales callers who ask personal questions or try to get too familiar. Chances are it's a con artist fishing for an opening hook.

Ginger Ellis, then a twenty-one-year-old college student in Sacramento, California, recalled one such encounter with a friendly female telemarketer for one of the giant Las Vegas prize rooms. The caller implied Ellis would win a Lincoln, one of six prizes highlighted in a letter mailed to her home. Excited at the prospect of winning the luxury car, she called the toll-free phone number on the letterhead. The friendly voice said all Ellis had to do was purchase some high-potency vitamins for $719, including shipping and handling.

Ellis doubted the deal at first. She asked to speak to the phone agent's supervisor who assured her the promotion was legal under Nevada law. The supervisor praised her intelligence for asking questions, a tactic that allayed her concerns. By dropping her guard, Ellis was hooked. She bit on further sales calls with new offers of prizes, continuing to buy despite her disappointment that each prize she received was far less than the telemarketer had promised.

Looking back, Ellis admitted what few victims of the telemarketing scam will concede: her greed got in the way of good judgment. In the end she did not get something for nothing.

"She was very polite and nice," Ellis said. "We talked about her family and joked about her coming here to see me in order to rub the prize in my roommate's face if I were to win the Town Car." Ellis got taken for nearly $3,000, and the only award she got was a cheap tote bag and a lithograph.*

Many of the Las Vegas sweepstakes promoters stay in business for

---

*Ginger Ellis's complaint is cited in a July 20, 1992, court document filed by U.S. Postal Inspector Christopher Carillo to obtain a search warrant of Pioneer Enterprises in Las Vegas.

years fudging the truth through elaborate ruses. Marketers who plan to pick up stakes before the law catches up to them lie more boldly, and more often. They come right out and say the customer has won a prize—$100,000 in cash, or a luxury car—which gets forfeited if they don't call a toll-free number immediately.

Customers who take the bait get connected to a telephone boiler room, a place they would never send a nickel if they could see its furnishings and frenetic pace. The sales agents pressure them to send cash, money order, or a bank check to pay the "taxes" to release the money or the gift. Often these companies will send a courier or overnight mail service to pick up the customer's payment. Of course, there are no taxes, just as there is no prize. The company's address turns out to be a commercial mail drop where anyone can rent a box for as little as fifty dollars a month. Southern Florida, where shady telephone enterprises have flourished for years, has more than four hundred mail receipt centers. The scam artists simply breeze in and pick up the mail; convert the checks wherever they can, often through check-cashing services; and skip to a new location before police get a fix on them.

The fly-by-night phone dealers often demand bank checks for payment because, unlike personal checks, they cannot be canceled if the victim comes to his or her senses. Those foolish enough to fall for this offer almost never get a refund, even if they complain to police.

These common schemes are the unsafe sex of the telemarketing racket. While they may pose great thrills and quick cash, they violate federal wire fraud statutes by promising a nonexistent prize across state lines. While these con artists tend to use overnight couriers to avoid mail fraud charges, sending the prize message by postcard through the U.S. mail may alert postal inspectors and also risk criminal proceedings.

For consumers the important point to remember is this: any such firm is most assuredly a scam and any money sent for such an offer is gone for good.

While telemarketing rooms that sell for a few weeks before shutting down have been a problem for years in a variety of Sun Belt cities, longevity hardly assures customers they won't be cheated. More and more, sophisticated boiler-room operators play the racket for the long run. They know they have the advantage over customers who are thousands of miles away and can't drop by to demand their money back. So they stay put, counting on assistance from lawyers and other allies to keep their activities in the gray area of the law. In these cases, the scam becomes more subtle and difficult to recognize. Many high-volume prize dealers don't claim the recipient has won the prize, only that he or she has been "selected" to participate in a "promotion." They try to deliver at least some of what the buyer orders to avoid criminal liability for fraud.

Changing a few words in the sales pitch here and there has not dissuaded millions of Americans from taking the bait, and it has kept many phone marketers on the safe side of state consumer fraud and lottery laws.

The telemarketing pitch—most veterans say the product makes little difference—is built around three themes, which we will see over and over in the pages that follow. The first strategy is to find a means to make the victim feel special. This is why so many phone offers use a prize gimmick or other come-on that keeps the customer on the line. Many people respond well or drop their guard if they think they will get something for nothing.

Stage two quickly follows and it is simple enough: make the mind work. The marketer misleads the buyer into thinking the product is first-rate. A third-rate liner becomes a "luxury cruise"; a room barely the size of a closet with no windows is a "studio suite."

A phone pro, in answer to a buyer's question about the quality and value of a piece of jewelry, retorts: "It's a one-quarter carat diamond necklace. I don't know what one carat's worth but I just bought my wife, about a month ago, a three-quarter carat and it cost me $1,400." In a flash the customer is led to believe that a cheap necklace, which the telemarketer knows is worth less than $50, has a value in excess of $1,400.

The third ingredient of the telemarketing sale is urgency. The deal is "always good this day only," or "only a few are left and they soon will be gone." A wide range of telemarketing scams, from investment opportunities to bogus employment agencies, stress urgency. The telltale sign is the mention of an overnight courier to pick up payment in the form of a cashier's check.

Why would an honest business pay ten dollars to have a courier come and pick up a check? The only reason is to capitalize on the buyer's impulse. At best, this tactic suggests that the sale is final, given the fact that the cashier's check cannot be rescinded and is as good as cash. Even if you try to cancel there is no assurance the company will agree to refund your money. Why buy something sight unseen knowing you can't get a refund?

The United States Postal Inspection Service has assembled a few common-sense safeguards to follow when dealing with telephone merchants.

- Take your time.

- Don't buy something merely because you are being told you'll get a "free gift."

- Get all information in writing before you agree to buy. Beware of any caller who refuses to send further sales literature or put claims in writing.

- If possible, check out the caller's record with the attorney general's office or the Better Business Bureau. (See appendix for phone numbers.)

- Don't give your credit card account number to anyone who calls or sends you a postcard.

- Be extremely cautious about investing or purchasing anything from an unknown caller who insists that you must make up your mind on the spot.

- Don't send money or bank checks by messenger or overnight mail.

- Don't be afraid to hang up the phone if you feel pressured to buy.

- If it sounds too good to be true, it probably is.

2

50 States

Nevada's key industries are easy to find or remember from the history books. The glitzy strip of casinos that crowd Las Vegas and help bring more than thirty million tourists a year are clearly number one, though profits have been sagging in recent years.

Next comes mining, the attraction that first lured settlers to the desert state in droves during the 1850s. Miners tapped the fabled Comstock lode for more than $350 million in silver until they exhausted it in the 1920s. Nevada still boasts the nation's richest veins of silver and gold, and mining remains a major industry, but it's often boom or bust.

Another of Nevada's top industries is tougher to spot, mostly because it keeps a fairly low profile. There is little, if any, mention of it in tourist guides or history books, nor does it prompt much in the way of civic pride. It goes on in fairly dreary office suites far from the tourist traps, but never dares to sell its wares to Nevada residents. It is the telemarketing trade, an estimated $700-million-a-year powerhouse said to employ more than three thousand South Nevadans in dozens of outlets, mainly in the Las Vegas area.

The telephone trade takes many of its cues from its big brothers, gaming and mining. Like early miners, telephone pros are voracious and determined. They dig deeply into the pocketbooks of customers and rarely quit until the stocks, cash, or credit cards are used up. The phone force takes other hints from casinos, playing on greed and the seemingly endless supply of suckers waiting for a jackpot.

Insiders call the Vegas telemarketing style "reloading," the targeting of a set of buyers who are sold products over and over until they can pay no more, often the elderly who lose thousands of dollars in savings.

"We are trying to stop this, but it's so damn lucrative it's hard for people to quit," says Jerry Steiner, a Federal Trade Commission attorney in

San Francisco. "We're not talking about young people stung for a few hundred dollars. These are people from their sixties to their eighties, hit two or three or more times. It dwarfs other telemarketing losses."*

Las Vegas wants no credit for giving birth to the telemarketing scam, but take some credit it must. It dates to the early 1970s when mail-order "advertising specialty" outlets sprang up, paying more than one million dollars a year in postage in Las Vegas alone.

Many legitimate companies sell these products, which include everything from the "Do Not Disturb" signs hotel guests place on doorknobs to ice scrapers or pens bearing the name of a business and given away to its clients for goodwill. But some of the Las Vegas dealers got greedy. They saw enormous profits in hiring banks of salespeople to call new business owners and promise them pricey gifts—then not deliver.

Many of their customers (victims) also had a few drops of larceny in their blood. The business owners figured that they could deduct the cost of the goods as a business expense on their income taxes and pocket the gift premium with nobody at the Internal Revenue Service being the wiser.

The mail-order houses sent their wares using the U.S. Post Office C.O.D., or cash on delivery system. Postmasters became middlemen, issuing credit to the mail-order houses for the goods and collecting from the customer. While postal authorities began to worry about the growing incidence of fraud, they were not able to curb it.

Nobody plundered the public with the panache of 50 State Distributing, Inc., of Las Vegas, the granddaddy of boiler rooms. Fifty State Distributing opened in 1974 and grew into a massive operation with more than three hundred employees in satellite offices in two other states. Its sales agents promised gifts such as a diamond money clip, perfume, or a videocassette recorder for those who purchased advertising items. But the merchandise was "in fact shoddy quality and the gifts either did not materialize or were substantially worthless," court records state.

After sending an investigator to take the 50 State Distributing training course, U.S. Postal Service authorities obtained a broad search warrant and raided the room. More than forty postal inspectors swooped down on 50 State at about 9 a.m. on October 20, 1981. Sales agents were ordered to freeze at their desks. No one could visit the restroom without an escort. Police blocked the exits and said nobody could leave until they submitted proper identification and were photographed. A female agent took one woman who did not have identification into a restroom and searched her slip and bra.

*Interview with Jerry Steiner, March 16, 1994.

Unable to find a key, postal inspectors smashed down the door to a locked records room. They carted away vans full of sales vouchers, and even toys and gifts brought in for an employees' Christmas party. Postal officials said that in past boiler-room raids, workers had managed to leave with incriminating evidence, such as sales tallies and complaint forms.

The search of 50 State Distributing made legal history after a federal judge ruled that the action violated the civil rights of the company's workers. The judge ordered the government to return the seized evidence, but an appeals court overturned the ruling. The case now is routinely cited to justify search warrants in criminal cases.

But the 50 State Distributing ruling had other consequences that hardly pleased authorities: it created a massive new crime problem—national telemarketing. This telemarketing group served as training ground for hundreds of boiler-room racketeers, many of whom left Vegas after the raid and set up operations in other states. More than fifteen years later the graduates of 50 State Distributing remain stalwarts of the telemarketing con.

"When we shut down 50 State we created a monster," says Christopher Carillo, a postal inspector in Las Vegas. "They had eight hundred employees who they trained there who all created their own firms. These people got away scot-free. They were like a close-knit family and for years they were showing up all over the country going into business with each other."*

Authorities also were disappointed with the prosecution of the case. Fifty State executive Ronald T. Schroeder was indicted for mail fraud in 1984, but the charges were dismissed. The 50 State corporation pleaded guilty to wire fraud and paid a small fine.

The "crime-pays" message sent by the outcome of the 50 State case emboldened countless other scammers, who began using telephone rooms to sell other vastly overpriced products, junk nobody would purchase if they could see it first.

One fifteen-year veteran of the racket grinned as he recalled one phone scam that traded on the popularity of Winnebago mobile homes for family vacations.

They called him up and they said he had won the Winnebago. And they said, "You can go to the mountains; you can go to the ocean. You can go to the parks. Wherever you want to go your home is with you." So he

---

*Interview with Christopher Carillo, June 24, 1994.

sent them $2,900. About seven or eight weeks later, UPS came up and left a box and it was a Winnebago tent. For $3,000 he got a tent.*

The rapid spread of the new racket overwhelmed law enforcement. It was an enterprise anybody could learn just by working in a Vegas phone room for a few weeks. Afterward, it could be transported to any city.

Many of the early scammers set prices at a few hundred dollars or less per sale, knowing that modest prices would greatly boost their volume. Small losses, they reasoned, would make victims less likely to complain.

The notorious rubber boat deal, which emerged from boiler rooms of southern California in the mid-1980s, picked up on the 50 State spiel. A Culver City firm told customers across the country that they were among the "lucky few" chosen to take part in a "nationwide test marketing survey" of a power motorboat.

Thousands of people sent $129 to $199 to get a boat, which turned out to be a cheap rubber raft that could be had from a discount store for under $20, according to the North Dakota State Attorney General's Office. The North Dakota agency got the firm banned from the state for ten years starting in 1988 and collected a $3,316 fine.†

The rubber dinghy scheme served as a model for endless spin-offs as new generations of telemarketers applied its techniques to the sale of cheap Florida vacation "certificates," bogus campground rentals, and nonexistent overseas jobs, to name just a few.

One Maryland firm raked in as much as $10 million in two months after persuading 200,000 people to pay up to fifty dollars each for low-interest credit cards. The people either got nothing for their money or a kit of paper credit cards good for discounts on cheap gold jewelry peddled by the company.

In one early 1980s count, when postal authorities estimated sixty-four boiler rooms were selling nationwide, almost 80 percent of the owners had been schooled in the phone scam at 50 State. While some 50 State refugees fanned out across the country, many remained right in Las Vegas, where they refined the rip-off pitch.

They began to change as postal authorities cut off their access to C.O.D. through public education campaigns. One Las Vegas dealer in 1984 complained to associates that postmasters were ruining his business by handing out booklets warning of the mail fraud problem to people who

---

*FBI surveillance tape, Fort Lauderdale, Florida, April 1, 1992.

†State of North Dakota v. National Businessman's Corporation, County of Burleigh, No. 40535, July 19, 1988.

picked up their prizes. As a result, half the customers refused to accept the packages, cutting deeply into profits.

The ever adaptable scammers sensed that the days of getting paid through postal orders were rapidly coming to an end. They then turned to a new method of payment—credit cards—which were even more vulnerable to their frauds.

By mid-1984, several of the Vegas advertising specialties rooms began offering discounts or other incentives to buyers who paid by credit card.

Taking credit card numbers over the phone created a whole new set of problems. Some salesmen kept poor records, so often the same accounts were charged over and over by mistake. Yet one sales room's problem was another's bonanza.

It didn't take the schemers long to realize that they could bill a customer's credit card several times with little fear of any consequences, other than an angry purchaser, and that was no great concern to them. Before long, most boiler rooms had forsaken the post office for the credit card and a whole new apocalypse for consumers was unleashed.

By mid-1984, Visa officials estimated that fraud caused by telemarketers was costing $100 million a year, and causing nightmares for many consumers who innocently gave their credit card numbers to a telemarketer.

The 50 State crackdown had another far-reaching effect on the boiler-room racket. Operators began to use parcel delivery services and overnight couriers, which are not subject to the mail fraud statutes. They also began eyeing schemes that kept the value of individual sales below $300, the amount a sale must exceed to violate mail fraud statutes. Suddenly, many telemarketed products were costing $289 or $299.

Authorities began to see a pattern among the victims of these scams, namely, a shyness about coming forward that still hampers law enforcement. "Many dissatisfied customers feel that theirs is an isolated case, or they are embarrassed at having been taken in by the salesmen, or feel that there is nothing they can do and consequently fail to make formal complaints," Charles P. Jeronis, a Phoenix postal inspector wrote in an October 1984 court affidavit.

By the mid-1980s the Vegas operators seemed to be gaining ground and becoming more bold. They started selling directly to the general public using a spin-off of the trusty ad-specs line. They called it the "one-in-five," a phony prize scheme that unquestionably has reaped hundreds of millions of dollars nationwide. The telemarketer describes five awards and suggests that the buyer will win the costliest one by purchasing a water purifier or vitamins or some other junk products. "These guys pretty much gave up on the steak," said Phoenix Postal Inspector John Zemblidge. "They started to sell the sizzle. They went after the public with these water purifiers promising people big prizes. Gradually it got out of hand. It's all just a variation of the ad-specs routine. They reload the customer when they are still up in the ether thinking that they have won big. It's like a carney routine," he said in a 1994 interview.

When it came to selling sizzle nobody could beat Pioneer Enterprises founded by Christopher A. Easley, a California native, and Richard J. Secchiaroli, the son of a civil servant in Buffalo, New York. The pair joined forces in Las Vegas in 1983. Both were former sales managers at 50 State, the early master of the phony sweepstakes. Pioneer set a new standard for the prize routine, mushrooming into a telephone emporium of junk products that kept on selling despite repeated court challenges from scambusters all across the country. Pioneer boasted gross earnings of $102 million between 1988 and 1991. Regulators weren't able to harness the hucksters until early 1993 when the federal government won a court order fining Pioneer $1.5 million.*

In the meantime, Secchiaroli earned enough to collect eleven cars, including limousines and two Porsches, while taking up residence in a $1.2 million desert mansion equipped with a backyard waterslide. He spent $38,500 a month to maintain his family's lifestyle, court records state. That included $1,000 a month for landscaping and $500 a month for dry-cleaning bills, according to an investigation of his finances by the *Buffalo News.*†

Easley lived on a five-acre ranch with manicured green hills upon which buffalo and exotic bids roamed freely. He estimated his monthly housekeeping costs at $5,000.

Pioneer took off as the telephone community began to get a public personality in Las Vegas, a demeanor that hardly pleased everyone. In fall 1985 the *Las Vegas Sun* published a strident series of articles under the title "Fast Bucks in the Boiler Room." Estimating sales from just the ad-specs players at between $50 million and $100 million annually, the newspaper reported that at least fifty of the outfits remained.

While offering little documentation, the articles related a number of tawdry tales, including accusations of low-level female workers being forced to offer sexual favors to help their bosses lure top salesmen and

---

*FTC v. Pioneer Enterprises CV-S-92-615-LDG-RJJ.
†"The Telesharks," *Buffalo News,* June 27–July 2, 1993.

one yarn about an unnamed boiler room whose manager secretly laced the morning coffee with methamphetamine, or speed, in order to get the staff primed for work. A Florida telemarketer recalled the 1980s in Vegas as being "nuts" in a surveillance tape secretly recorded by the FBI nearly a decade later. He remembered open drug use in some of the phone rooms: "Walk around with three grand of coke in your pocket and sprinkle on the desk. It was nuts. It was crazy."

Tales of the high life among those working in Las Vegas's mighty boiler rooms are legion. One owner presented the head of customer service with a Rolls Royce as a Christmas bonus. In another case, a top phone salesman, having crashed his car on the way to work and fretting over having to leave his phones to shop for a replacement, got a generous fringe benefit. Worried over lost sales time, the room's manager delivered a new car that day, on the house. He attached a note, "We'll take it back if you don't like the color."

Las Vegas rooms roared through the late 1980s behind the one-in-five scam because few, if any, regulators in Nevada showed much interest in stamping it out. With all the victims living out of state, there was little local pressure on law enforcement to act.

Many state consumer protection officials from around the country gave up on Nevada's civil regulators, who seemed unresponsive to pleas to discipline the industry. Others wondered why the federal government, the ideal entity to attack a multi-state crime problem, seemed asleep at the switch.

State regulators directed much of their anger at the Federal Trade Commission (FTC) for failing to step in and halt the scam spree. The FTC is an independent federal agency with the duty to enforce laws prohibiting "unfair or deceptive" trade practices. It can file civil lawsuits in federal courts to halt illegal trade practices and win refunds for consumers.

But the agency's record when it comes to cracking down on telemarketing fraud is spotty at best. In the vast majority of its cases, telemarketers declare bankruptcy or go out of business before FTC lawyers can collect a court judgment to repay victims. In most cases, the agency settles for "consent decrees," in which telemarketers admit no wrongdoing but promise not to violate trade laws. Before the ink is dry many are back in business behind the phones.

Despite these impediments, regulators began to catch up. One by one state attorneys general started filing lawsuits against the boiler-room kingpins, hoping to at least stop them from ripping off residents of their states.

Other regulators started to make inroads. Twenty-eight Las Vegas prize marketers generated 1,223 formal complaints to the Better Business Bureau of Las Vegas between January 1990 and March 1992. The agency was able to win refunds for at least some of these victims.

Yet telephone firms kept on selling despite fifty-five law enforcement actions, mostly lawsuits filed by state attorneys general accusing them of consumer fraud. Each case represented hundreds, if not thousands, of cheated customers, some fleeced for $10,000 or more.

Fighting state regulators in court simply became a cost of doing business. Despite the lawsuits, the prize racket grew bigger and bigger; fourteen new houses opened in Las Vegas in 1990 alone, and others set up satellite phone rooms in Louisiana, Arkansas, and New York State.

Pioneer Enterprises rose to the top of the heap, despite complaints from all over the nation. The Pioneer nerve center was a two-story, light-brown brick structure with a red-tile roof and blue-on-white logo. It shipped its product from an adjoining warehouse, which also handled merchandise sold by an affiliate called 21st Century Marketing, an elaborate structure with smoke-colored lettering etched into the front windows.

Reviewing the company's record, it's a wonder the scheme lasted as long as it did. The U.S. Postal Service received 968 written complaints from all over the nation about Pioneer between October 1990 and July 1992, when postal inspectors sought a search warrant to raid the premises. The postal complaints mirrored more than 475 that had been filed with Nevada consumer officials alleging gross patterns of consumer fraud.

One elderly woman from Azle, Texas, said she gave her credit card number to a Pioneer salesman when he assured her nothing would be charged to it. She received a $398 water filter unit, which she returned, only to get a call from someone at Pioneer who said she was shipping the box right back, and would "call me every day until I agreed to buy something." She finally agreed to an offer by Pioneer to credit her charge card for $200, half of what she paid. She agreed, under duress, because the incident had upset her husband and she wanted to be done with it. She wrote in a complaint cited in a U.S. Postal Service affadavit:

> My husband has a heart condition and has already undergone bypass surgery and was obviously upset. . . . I was upset and concerned about him and feel I was forced into this agreement because I was so eager to get off the phone and attempt to calm my husband. I certainly did not want him to have a heart attack over a water filtration system.

Vermont's attorney general, in a suit settled in June 1992, accused Pioneer of charging "unconscionably high" prices (up to $598 for a supply of vitamins or water purifiers that cost the marketer between twenty dollars and fifty dollars). Pioneer paid a fine of $196,000 and agreed to stop selling in Vermont.*

The Federal Trade Commission also accused Pioneer of ripping off the public in a lawsuit filed in July 1992.† Pioneer telemarketers charged from several hundred dollars to several thousand dollars for items for which the company paid from two dollars to sixty dollars, prices the agency called "grossly inflated."

The agency also took aim at portions of Pioneer sales scripts that directed telemarketers to advise customers that the sales promotion was "not available to the general public," and the customer was fortunate to have been "selected" to participate—phrases right out of the 50 State playbook. Pioneer's marketers went on to raise a customer's hopes with lines such as: "You're definitely coming out as a major award recipient. I'm excited for you. I don't get to talk to a lot of major award recipients. . . . You were very lucky to have been selected from among thousands of people in your area. . . . When you receive everything you are going to be ecstatic."**

The FTC cited five more "entirely false and misleading" sales devices. Among them:

- You are in a win-win situation. You have done fantastic in this promotion.

- They are all very expensive awards. We're not dealing with microwave ovens, popcorn makers, things like that.

- I guarantee you, whichever award you get you're going to love. They're fantastic awards.

- I'll tell you something. You can't afford not to purchase. You know you hit a grand slam here. Why stop on third base?

One Pioneer telemarketer, when asked point blank about the price of the watch "won" by a victim, chimed in: "It's a genuine diamond watch. This is not an everyday watch. It's for special occasions. It's the kind you put under lock and key."

---

*The Vermont Attorney General's Office accused Pioneer Enterprises, Inc., of running a fraudulent prize promotion in a civil suit filed in December 1990.

†FTC v. Pioneer CV-S-92-615-LDG-RJJ.

**FTC court filings, July 20, 1992.

In fact, the watch was worth ten to fifteen dollars, according to two experts who appraised one for the FTC. One of the jewelers said the "diamond" shattered when he tried to determine its value. Pioneer paid about fifteen dollars for the watches, ten dollars for the cameras, and thirty-three to forty-three dollars for the fur coats. The FTC blasted the firm for charging as much as seven hundred dollars for vitamins that had cost the company $2.05 per order.

And what about the quality of the products? Opinions vary, but the water purifier, a mainstay of telemarketing houses, is at best grossly overpriced and at worst useless. A congressional study released in 1992 said that only fifty-four of six hundred manufacturers of the devices set quality controls, while no standards exist to determine if the units remove pollutants. Claims of wondrous results often are bogus, the study concluded.*

In December 1992 Pioneer agreed to pay $1.5 million to settle the civil fraud case brought against it by the FTC. The agency charged that beginning in 1988, Pioneer mailed postcards to consumers telling them they had won one of four prizes to induce them to purchase junk products.

While the company did not admit any wrongdoing, the fine was split among more than forty-six thousand Pioneer customers, who got back from five dollars to about six hundred dollars depending on how much they had spent. Most victims received only a fraction of the money they lost.

The lawsuit also disclosed what many consumer regulators nationwide had long suspected: the parent company worked under several corporate names and passed customers back and forth, thus snaring them in an ever-growing web of costly repeat purchases.

While customers often had the impression they were dealing with several different companies with varying product lines, Pioneer actually owned satellites, such as 21st Century Marketing, which sold "Say No to Drugs" bumper stickers among other products.

Postal authorities placed an undercover operative inside Pioneer who reported back to them that the company's customer service department was a sham. A second informant was told by a supervisor to keep complaint reports "clean" in order to mislead the state investigator who would come through periodically and inspect the records to see if grievances were resolved.

A copy of the quality control job description smuggled out of the Pioneer office showed the hard-sell nature of the telemarketing room and

---

*General Accounting Office Report to the House Energy and Commerce Committee, January 1992.

its contempt for customers, many of whom only bought in the first place because of the layer of promises that were made. The job description read:

> The main job of the quality control rep is to retain as much money as possible without the end result being a chargeback (credit card refund) and to satisfy the customer's needs as best as possible. This does not necessarily mean the customer will always be completely satisfied, but that they will agree to the terms the rep has set for them. . . . At times it may be necessary to bluff a customer and really hammer them so they will honor their original commitment.*

Many of the other Las Vegas prize rooms draped their sales pitch around a theme customers found hard to resist. For Virginia Lynch, the widow of a Chicago police officer, the subject was the scourge of narcotics.

The salesman from National Health Care Associates of Las Vegas, which Lynch assumed was in the health-care field, persuaded her that his firm led a national crusade to wipe out drug abuse. The toy flying disks she bought to aid the campaign—her arthritis would never let her heave one skyward—bore the slogan "Say No to Drugs."

"I thought it would be a nice thing to do for the kids, to keep them away from drugs," says Lynch, who volunteers her time to work with children at her parish church.†

And Lynch, well in her seventies, admits that the steady offers of prizes, a Lincoln Town Car and a big-screen television among them, made her purchases seem painless, a winning deal for everyone. "I thought it would be wonderful if I won." She planned to sell the luxury car and invest the proceeds. "The awards I got were terrible and cheap," Lynch says, holding up a dinky imitation Oriental rug, too thin to place anywhere but the trash.

National Health Care Associates did not have any ties to the war on drugs or any other worthy cause. It was simply a telephone boiler room, one of dozens guilty of bilking thousands of customers nationwide in recent years. The FTC won a court order in Nevada forbidding the company from engaging in deceptive sales in February 1993. Lynch lost $5,000 billed to her Visa card between late June and October 1992.

The telemarketers didn't go away. They next appealed to Lynch's sense of civic pride and concern about pollution. Why else would anyone

---

*Carillo affidavit, July 20, 1992.
†Interview with Virginia Lynch, October 2, 1992.

pay five dollars apiece for earth-toned, reusable nylon lunch bags stamped with antidrug messages?

Fifty of the lunchbags, pictured in an advertising flier alongside a schoolchild's lunch, cost $250. They were six dollars each if bought in smaller lots. "Why not be a hero in your neighborhood? Give them to your family, friends, school, or church group. . . . Instead of littering our country with trash, your children and grandchildren will be making a positive statement," the pitch went.

Lynch also bought three cases of a mix-it-yourself cleaning fluid, so strong that a capful had to be diluted with a cup of water. "By mixing your own cleansers, you SAVE MONEY & SAVE THE EARTH," according to promotional literature.

Lynch stored up more detergent in her garage than any homemaker could use in a decade, enough to turn a swimming pool into a giant soapy mop pail.

"Isn't this something," she says as she dodges the shipping crates that dominate her duplex home. "I could open up a store."

She bought other shoddy goods including cartons of a dozen cheap imitation perfumes and skin-care and beauty products, "more than I could use in years," she says. She couldn't eat in her dining room for all the products piled up. She didn't even have the strength to open most of the boxes, and had no idea what to do with the contents.

A quiet woman married more than forty years, Lynch frets over her purchases as she shows them off. She talks excitedly one minute and seems a bit glum, even solemn, the next. She seems to lose focus midway through a thought, and has trouble remembering everything she had bought. Widowed just a year, she says her late husband had warned her to be careful when he was gone, that she was too trusting—and a perfect mark. Many phone fraud victims struggle to explain why they were taken in repeatedly. Few are inclined to admit that greed played any sort of a role, even though it often is a motivating factor.

Lynch has no doubts that tough telemarketers were intimidating her, demanding that she drop whatever she was doing when they called and purchase products she did not want.

"He preys upon you," she says of one of her callers, who started out friendly but turned mean in a moment if she showed a hint of hesitation. "He called me over and over and he told me he knew when I didn't answer I was trying to avoid him. I was almost afraid not to buy it."

Lynch says she would try from time to time to cancel an order. When she did so, she got trapped in an elaborate "customer service" system that passed her from agent to agent, or put her on endless hold until she tired of waiting and gave up. When she could get through, a manager brushed aside her concerns, saying she could pay her bill a little at a time if need be.

"I should have had better sense than to get involved with these people," Lynch says.

Family friends came to her rescue and helped her get some money returned through the efforts of the Better Business Bureau of Las Vegas.

National Health Care Associates shut down after federal officials charged it, and several affiliates, with civil fraud in February 1993. Despite sales pitches that implied buyers would win a car, almost everyone received a cheap gift, the government alleged. One patron said the "big-screen projection system" she won turned out to be a large, clear sheet of plastic that was to be placed in front of her television to magnify the picture.

The lawsuit took note of the reload tactic. The government charged that some customers lost thousands of dollars because sales agents lied to them, saying that as they bought more and more products they would be eligible for "advanced" promotions that would yield even bigger prizes.

The investigation also bore out complaints from elderly citizens such as Virginia Lynch that they were called repeatedly to wear them down, in some cases several times an hour or once a day for weeks, court records show. As a clincher, some salesmen angrily threatened to sue customers who tried to cancel their orders, officials said.

Hardball sales tactics also defined the phone rooms operated by partners Steven Morris Rowe and Gary D. Hosman, owners of Sierra Pacific Marketing in Las Vegas. The owners lived the good life, despite lawsuits aimed at shutting them down.

Sierra Pacific dodged civil bullets fired by attorneys general across the country. Sierra Pacific signed a court order in April 1992 agreeing to pay a $42,500 fine and to halt sales in Idaho. The order also settled allegations that Sierra Pacific had failed to deliver prizes, according to then Idaho State Attorney General Larry EchoHawk.

The attorney general demanded an end to hardball sales tactics. He said a Sierra Pacific marketer had gone so far as to threaten to kill the children of a Idaho consumer if he complained about harassing phone calls.*

A federal judge in Las Vegas in February 1993 froze Sierra Pacific's assets after the FTC sued the company.† The charge: the firm "used a

---

*Echohawk news release, April 1992.
†FTC v. Sierra Pacific Marketing, Inc., CV-S-93-134-PMP (RJJ).

variety of misrepresentations" to get consumers to buy cosmetics, vitamins, "environmentally safe" cleaning products and other junk products.

One year later, Rowe and Hosman settled the FTC case by agreeing to pay a $1 million fine.* The deal with the government also barred both men from operating, or assisting others in running, any sort of prize sweepstakes, or selling the names of previous customers. By the time of the order, the business had expanded into nine offices, including satellites in Georgia, Arkansas, Oklahoma, and Arizona.

Supersalesmen Rowe and Hosman were not eager to answer any questions when a camera crew from the tabloid TV show "Inside Edition" came to town to seek them out.†

The show's investigative reporters said on the broadcast that they chased Rowe, a veteran sales agent with the prim look of a male model, "all over Las Vegas . . . and even when we knew he was home, he pretended he wasn't, and sent a security guard to remove us."

The reporters quickly found people willing to talk about Rowe's reputation as a big spender. Tammie Smith, an investigator with the Nevada Department of Consumer Affairs, said on camera that she believed Rowe had paid $750,000 in cash for a car. "I do know that he purchased an extremely expensive automobile not too very long ago, to the tune of $750,000, and he got a real deal on it because the car's worth a million or so," she said.

The reporters ambushed Hosman at the most expensive exotic car dealership in Las Vegas, where they shouted questions at him before he drove off in an $80,000 BMW. Asked if he felt guilty about victimizing senior citizens and taking their life's savings, Hosman replied: "I don't have victims, I have customers."

Hosman, a thickly built blond with a rough edge about him, discussed the finances of the sales room in a videotape deposition. He admitted that the firm, which operated from a second-story suite just off a busy thoroughfare, paid far less for its products than customers did. A year's supply of vitamins, sold by Sierra Pacific for $599, cost the firm about twenty-four dollars, he said. Some people bought ten years' worth because they hoped to have a shot at winning a car.

Hosman grew annoyed at questioning about the chances of driving home the car, saying the "odds are in black and white, one car in 50,000 participants." Asked if the public may be confused by the offer, he replied curtly: "They may be confused, but I'm not a mathematics teacher. I don't think it is my responsibility to educate America on mathematics."

---

*FTC news release, February 16, 1994.
†"Inside Edition," November 23, 1992.

Consumer regulators across the country watched the Pioneer and Sierra Pacific cases eagerly. They hoped the legal assault against two of the largest Las Vegas players would clean up the industry, or at least cause the dozens of similar sales rooms to rethink their sales tactics.

The Vegas telemarketers did retrench, but the result hardly pleased regulators. Just as they had done after the heat over 50 State cooled, the phone cons emerged with a third generation of the reload scam. They called it "telefunding." Its sales claims were even more outrageous than the past schemes—and now it is running wild.

Customers throughout the country donate as much as $3,500 each to a "charity" because Vegas telemarketers tell them they will win a prize whose value equals, or greatly exceeds, the amount of their donation.

As in the classic one-in-five sweepstakes promotion, the prizes—usually a luxury car or cash—never show up. Instead, contributors get a mass-produced Norman Rockwell lithograph, cheap Civil War memorabilia, or low-cost jewelry.

These telemarketers lie to clients, telling them their contributions are tax-deductible. They also say they have to contribute some money to win a prize, even though laws in many states prohibit a sweepstakes from requiring a purchase (or a "donation") to win.

And the charities are suspect, according to government officials. One sounded like a grab bag of good deeds. "Operation Life," the pitch went, helped flood victims, protected endangered species, assisted drug addicts, sheltered battered women and children, and helped the homeless. The FTC, in a lawsuit filed in Nevada in early 1994, asserted that the charity did none of those things.

The telefunders take advantage of loopholes in Nevada's telemarketing licensing law, which requires new phone rooms to pay a registration fee of six thousand dollars, and each telemarketer to shell out one hundred dollars for a license. Fearing flak from the state's legitimate charities, Nevada, like several other states, exempted charitable solicitations from the telemarketing registration law. And with authorities cracking down on the one-in-five palaces, fund-raising scams are a safe bet because they can so easily capitalize on the average person's goodwill.

The emergence of telefunders also worries many in the legitimate alms industry, who fear a drop in donations as word spreads that the scam artists have turned to fund raising and the schemes spread to other states.

Although the forms it takes vary, Las Vegas sweepstakes promotion seems unlikely to die. It lives on despite laws intended to regulate it out of existence.

Several states have enacted laws requiring that the promoters register, post bonds, and disclose a number of details about the awards, such as their value and the chances of winning them. But these records sit in a government office in the state capital, where nobody who might consider playing the sweepstakes is likely to find them.

Other states have outlawed sales schemes that require a purchase to win a prize and crack down on companies that insist on the entrant buying junk goods in order to receive the prize. But these claims are tough to verify, so most complaints of illegal pressure tactics by the sweepstakes promoters go unanswered.

And the prize peddlers, the descendants of 50 State Distributing, move on, mutate, and make millions.

3

Chosen People

You can't miss Tim O'Neil. He's the guy who looks like he just walked off the golf course talking hurriedly on the phone amid all the confusion at Cypress Creek Promotions in Fort Lauderdale, Florida. A spindly man with sandy-gray hair and a ruddy complexion, O'Neil sits in a private office just within earshot of his dozen noisy telemarketers. He is a volatile, profane man who flies into swearing fits at anyone who scorns his sales pitch. But he can also sound conciliatory, even gentle, when he senses trouble on the line.

At this moment, O'Neil needs to be polite and calm. He is returning a "hot call." It came from an elderly Philadelphia woman, a "five digit customer" taken for $10,000 or more by O'Neil's telemarketers. She summoned police detectives to her home and O'Neil knows he can expect trouble if she swears out a fraud complaint against his company, which is, after all, engaged in a $2.5 million telephone swindle.*

Warding off approaching visitors like a traffic cop, O'Neil takes charge. He knows the drill well from years spent working his way up through the boiler-room hierarchy in Nevada and Florida. As the owner of Cypress Creek Promotions, he's eager to quiet the disturbance and awe his guests with his prowess. He speaks with a firm, though sandpapery voice, folksy and with no hint of condescension.

> My personal reason for calling you is to find out what the problem is so we can rectify this. We've sent you out some lovely collectibles from (a gallery) in Bal Harbour, Florida. I trust you've received those. . . .
>
> The Gettysburg collectible. Those are actual bullets excavated from the Civil War. . . . Well my point is if anybody should question you on

---

*FBI agents taped Cypress Creek Promotions employees including O'Neil between February 9, 1993, and April 1, 1993.

anything, and I know you've dealt with other companies, but I would at least like you to let them know that Cypress Creek Promotions has fulfilled their obligations to you. . . .

We're still gonna send you out something that's lovely. Do you wear pendants? This is a beautiful, is a diamond . . . it's absolutely gorgeous. Would you please call and let me know how much you like it? . . . I'm not gonna ask you to spend a penny. . . .

How old are you? God bless you. . . . 89. . . .

We're gonna get that out to you. . . . Look for it in the middle of next week, and then give us a call and then let us know how you like it. All right honey, you can call collect anytime, all righty. Well listen, you have a lovely day and I'll be looking forward to a call from you. . . .

Well I hope I put a little sunshine in your day. OK, honey and God bless you. Oh don't cry now, we're here to take care of you [laughing in the background]. We'll be here and if you need to talk to anybody at any time you give us a call, okay? Bye, bye, and God bless you.

Tim ends the call satisfied he has smoothed over any problems, then grins through nicotine-stained teeth. Turning to his visitors, he remarks: "Remember, always hang it up lightly."

At age fifty, O'Neil takes up four pages in the FBI's crime computer log. His criminal record dates to the early 1970s in New Jersey, where he was arrested four times for possession of marijuana, or other pot charges, and placed on probation.

O'Neil turned up in the late 1970s at 50 State Distributing, the Las Vegas scam school and granddaddy of phone rooms. Always the casual dresser, O'Neil cut quite a figure among the straight-laced veterans who stocked the 50 State office. He was the only salesman to show up for work without socks. Nobody would speak to him for weeks. But O'Neil did his talking on the phones where it counted, rising to a manager's job, which gave him stature in the burgeoning Nevada boiler-room community and fixed a career path that he has stayed on ever since.

He remained in town after postal inspectors shut down 50 State, landing with an upstart marketing house called M&W Specialties that used much the same pitch.

O'Neil managed the afternoon crew at M&W Specialties out of a two-story, sandy-colored warehouse. Known for his loud clothes, energetic sales strategies, and hard drinking, O'Neil presided over a menagerie of sales pros from a tiny man built like a bear cub who wore an unkempt salty-colored beard to a mustached colossus who resembled a bouncer on the Vegas strip.

The men had secretaries to do the dialing for them. The tactic helped build excitement and lend credibility to the pitch, in which each salesman claimed to be the company president bearing great gifts.

M&W drew dozens of complaints to postal inspectors for its phony sweepstakes. One man from upstate New York paid four hundred dollars for sixteen dollars worth of coffee cups. He never got the twenty-one-foot boat with trailer as promised. Another man from Wyoming who thought he had won a videocassette recorder instead found a "cheapo" camera and projector in his gift box. A Californian expecting a new television paid $350 and got just two hundred cheap pens. When he complained to M&W, whose sales brochures promised that any complaints would be promptly resolved, he was told the salesman he dealt with had been fired. Nobody else would take his calls.

M&W kept going for eleven months under the ownership of Mark Trainer, a crafty executive in his mid-twenties who rarely drove his black and maroon Lincoln Continental to the office. Trainer ran things from a white brick house in Las Vegas with security bars on the windows and doors, secreting his business and payroll records in a small safe tucked in a first-floor bedroom.

M&W was memorable for more than just its roguish and rude sales force. It pulled off a bold stunt in setting up a unique shill. An M&W salesman formed a corporation called the Better Business Bureau of America and used it as a reference. Many people felt they were dealing with the real Better Business Bureau, perhaps the best trusted name in commerce.

M&W stamped its delivery packages and other materials with large gold-colored stickers reading: "Gold Seal Member, Better Business Bureau of America, a Nevada Corporation. Inquiries toll-free 1-800-351-XXXX."

People who had doubts about M&W called the number where a woman recited a glowing report on the company that persuaded many customers to go ahead with the deal. Some who lost money later tipped off the genuine Las Vegas Better Business Bureau to the scam.

Authorities discovered that the 800 number for the "business bureau" rang at the M&W Specialties warehouse, where a young employee did the honors of reading the flattering reports to callers. So successful was the scheme that other phone rooms in need of good references were approached to join the "business bureau" for one thousand dollars in cash.

Trainer's salespeople ignored warnings from postal inspectors to tone down the pitch and thus found themselves indicted on mail fraud charges.

Trainer was found guilty and sentenced in November 1985 to three years in prison, but only had to serve six months. Manager O'Neil got three years, but served three months. Four other associates pled guilty to the mail fraud charge, as O'Neil did. At the time, the M&W case resulted in the largest number of criminal convictions for running an ad specialties boiler room in Las Vegas.*

O'Neil drifted to South Florida, remaining in the "ad-specs" racket, the sale of overpriced junk products with the promise the buyer will receive a prize, and getting into more scrapes with the law, some prompted by a severe drinking problem.†

Police arrested O'Neil in Florida in 1986 for unemployment compensation fraud, and again on the same charge in 1989.

O'Neil spent several years working for others in the racket, paying more dues, before he broke free and went into business for himself. When he opened up Cypress Creek Promotions late in 1991, he picked an industrial site in Fort Lauderdale, where even a small phone operation can gross more than $30,000 a week.

Police in South Florida call it "maggot mile." The term is a loose description for several clusters of telemarketing boiler rooms that stretch from downtown Miami to Fort Lauderdale, thirty miles to the north, and beyond into chic Boca Raton.

They are often cheap, decaying office suites that can be rented for under one thousand dollars a month with dozens of phone hook-ups in place. All new tenants need do is lease some phones, plug them in, and engage the cheapest long-distance carrier they can find.

The long-distance phone bill is one of their biggest single expenses, as much as twenty thousand dollars a month, because South Florida boiler rooms almost never call anyone locally. Once the phones are in, they simply tack up the sales script, rustle up some telemarketers through local newspaper classifieds, and begin dialing for dollars all over America.

Many of these shabby offices are in their sixth, tenth, even twenty-fifth generation, serving as quick corporate addresses for dozens of scams that each last a few months and then pick up and leave, with regulators in faraway states unable to find anyone to charge with fraud.

Skipping around South Florida in this manner, telemarketers make up a mature and resilient underworld that has largely defied years of efforts

---

*USA v. Mark Trainer, U.S. District Court of Nevada, 84-0246M.

†His several alcohol-related arrests include driving while intoxicated, for which the state of Florida suspended his driver's license in 1989.

by state and federal scambusters to wipe them out. Some companies are run by the sons and daughters of boiler-room pioneers who perfected the trade in the early 1980s. As savvy as they are mobile, phone scamsters stay afloat by making sure most of the people they swindle live in states that are slow to spot scams, file court action, or alert Florida police to their whereabouts.

Many phone-scam artists joust for years with state attorneys general and other consumer-protection regulators, each of whom sues only on behalf of consumers in his or her state. Getting kicked out of one state hardly stuns a nationwide sales operation. The sales manager simply sends a memo to the staff telling them to quit calling numbers in that area code.

While phone "pros" can connect with networks in almost any city and quickly find work, South Florida is overrun with the species. Working off prepared sales scripts, these highly skilled mercenaries can flatter, cajole, bully—and sell at prodigious pace.

Florida's main consumer agency logged nearly fifteen thousand tele-marketing fraud complaints between 1985 and 1992. As a rule of thumb, regulators figure that just one out of every one hundred victims takes the trouble to fill out complaint forms, mostly because they feel nobody will take action, or because they are embarrassed that they could have fallen for such a scam.

Nearly a third of the fifteen thousand complaints about Florida boiler rooms cited firms in the Fort Lauderdale area. No other county in the state came close to matching the swarm of phone swindlers in the one-time Spring Break capital.

While the hundreds of customers they call daily all over the nation have no way of knowing it, many sun-drenched telemarketers are felons. Most patrons no doubt would hang up immediately if they could see rap sheets showing arrests ranging from narcotics possession to grand theft.

Some of these "voices" are both drugged out and incorrigible cons, such as Nick Getty.

FBI agents arrested Getty in March 1993 on a federal charge of con-spiracy to commit wire fraud. A judge released him on a $50,000 bond cosigned by his mother, on the condition that he live with her, attend drug treatment, and submit to random urine tests. Getty's first three samples proved positive for cocaine, court records state. Getty had trouble keep-ing his larcenous ways under control as well.

Less than three months after his arrest, Getty got back on the phones and allegedly bilked an elderly Wisconsin woman out of nine thousand dollars. The woman "was a frequent and favorite victim" of telemarketing reloaders, court records show. Getty allegedly deposited her check in his bank account, but withdrew it within three weeks. A federal judge revoked his bond at the urging of prosecutors.

In a handwritten letter, Getty begged the judge to change her mind. He said he needed to be free to care for his girlfriend who was six months pregnant "and needs me very badly right now to be her lamas [sic] coach." The magistrate denied Getty's request. He later pleaded guilty.

At least one Florida phone-fraud artist got into the racket after federal authorities created a new identity for him. The man, who ran a phony overseas employment room near Fort Lauderdale, turned out to be in Uncle Sam's witness protection program, which uses tax dollars to build new lives for people, many of them criminals, who agree to testify against other criminals. The job broker panicked after government officials used his real name in a lawsuit seeking to shut his scam down. He asked a judge to seal the court pleadings because he feared some of his former associates might blow into town and kill him. The judge granted the motion.

By no means are all the fast-talkers who perform on South Florida's boiler-room circuit hoods, coke heads, or reprobates. Many ordinary people wind up behind the phones because it can be a calling card for quick cash, no experience necessary. Many workers who answer classified ads placed in newspapers by boiler-room operators are not aware they are doing anything illegal. Some who ask questions are assured the scheme is perfectly legal. Others aren't inclined to ask questions once commissions start rolling in. One working woman made two thousand dollars a week in sales commissions just long enough to afford a down payment on a new home with a swimming pool in the suburbs.

"It's high pressure, it's stressful, and it's stealing. I don't know of a legitimate phone room," said Barbara, a self-described yuppie, who chatted about her phone-sales life while putting her newborn baby to sleep.

She quit from guilt: "If you know your stuff some little old lady will believe you. I wouldn't want someone to be doing that to my mom."

Barbara admits to missing the excitement in the early days, the mid-1980s, when rooms used ringing bells and other means to stir up the sales staff. "I remember when they used to throw fifty or one hundred singles up in the air and shout that the next sale gets the cash," she said. "I'll never forget seeing all those dollars in the air." Despite the lure of quick cash, most who enter the telemarketing trade do not hit the jackpot and many wish they never applied.

One large South Florida health products boiler room ran through more than eight hundred salespeople in nine months. Most amateurs last a week or less because they can't make the sales quota, or feel guilty about reciting a rip-off sales pitch.

"We were buying sales leads and they were all old people," said one thirtyish woman who bailed out when the exploitation of the elderly sickened her. "You hit it big when one of the people you called was senile and would send you their money. It's sad how people will treat other people."

Larry Bonneville recalled his misery working in the customer service department of a telemarketing house, which he said often failed to ship products or give refunds. His statement sits in a thick police file on the phone room.

> These people would bombard me with these irate calls, saying, "You guys got my money. You guys got my money." It brought me down and it made me really feel bad because there were people calling up there who had to work for a living. Some people on welfare, some people on fixed income crying with three or four kids. You know, "I don't have my rent. I don't have my car payment. It's going to be repossessed and it's going to be foreclosed." I felt bad for some of these people. Some of these people were from another country. Some of these people were uneducated.*

Many other telemarketers become disgruntled when they learn there is little honor among thieves, a situation many feel has worsened in the 1990s. Many rooms do not deduct Social Security or payroll taxes from workers, considering them independent contractors. Nor do the marketers pay income taxes on their commissions. The workers bemoan that many owners often refuse to pay commissions or otherwise cheat sales agents out of money they are due.

"They feel there is an endless supply of workers. When they refuse to pay you, you have no recourse," said one old hand. "You can work an entire week without getting anything. The managers lie and tell you that the deals didn't go through or that the customer's check or credit card was declined." He added: "These people respond to classified ads thinking they will make thousands of dollars a week. But most of them can't handle the pressure and they go home fired with nothing. That's pitiful."

The efforts by phone-room managers to cheat workers make for lively conversations in various Boca Raton bars where boiler-roomers con-

---

*Taped statement, Boca Raton (Florida) Police Department Case 92–9012.

gregate to swap telemarketing tall tales. One operator acquired a bank's "bad check" stamp that printed "Returned Non-Sufficient Funds" over checks. He would photocopy checks before cashing them, then stamp the checks, recopy them, and keep them on file to persuade the salesperson that the buyer had written a bum check, and therefore no commission was due. Others simply shut down from time to time and tell unpaid workers the bank has frozen their accounts and they can't pay their debts until the thaw.

Operators of another large-scale South Florida phone-sales room were startled to learn that managers solicited kickbacks of up to two hundred dollars a week in order to pass hot leads to certain sales agents. Those who paid the kickbacks were known as "chosen people."

*   *   *

Tim O'Neil knew all the ups and downs of telemarketing in the 1990s and he set out to run a multi-million-dollar phone room where top sales talent would find a home and law enforcement would never cross the threshold. He started by having his new company register with the U.S. Securities and Exchange Commission (SEC) in Washington, which gave him the legal right to sell shares in the boiler room. O'Neil filed the SEC paperwork for Cypress Creek Marketing in August 1991, a few weeks before a Florida law requiring licensing and bonding of telemarketers went into effect. The law made it a crime to run an unlicensed telephone sales room and denied licenses to convicted felons such as O'Neil. But the registration law exempts companies regulated by the SEC in Washington.

"Hell, I'm a public company and I'm not governed by Florida telemarketing laws," O'Neil boasted after pulling off the coup. "I applied to become public and did all the lawyers and all the fuckin' scrutiny of the SEC and all the bullshit that had to be done."*

O'Neil's nine-page SEC registration, which allowed him to issue stock in the venture to friends and associates, was laughable, even if it was legal.

The documents list O'Neil's seventy-three-year-old mother, a Boca Raton resident, as president and chief executive officer of the telemarketing company, which said it would sell advertising specialties such as baseball caps, pens, business cards, and ice scrapers. Ms. O'Neil has "absolutely no experience" in telephone sales and has not been employed

---

*FBI surveillance tapes.

in the past five years, according to the filing. However, the SEC filing states that "preliminary" negotiations are under way to bring the president's son, Timothy O'Neil, on board as sales manager. The paperwork makes no mention of O'Neil's experience or criminal background.*

O'Neil said later that he planned to hold Cypress Creek stock for two years, when he projected annual earnings would near $5 million, then sell and retire to a life of golf and leisure, a millionaire.

Cypress Creek Promotions was a huge hit from the start. Started with a $5,000 loan, it had grossed $500,000 within six months. Things went so well that O'Neil branched out to two locations in other parts of town. He changed the firm's name and abandoned his old office when authorities in several states started asking questions.

O'Neil, who remarked that he had put into Cypress Creek everything he learned in the phone business, both good and bad, had "tremendous ability to motivate" his sales force, according to a former financial backer. "I've always said, ever since I've known Tim . . . if he could just channel his energy and keep on the straight and narrow, you could take that energy he used to spend chasing broads and drinking and put it into business and capture a Hoover Dam," he says.

O'Neil, who often gave his sales team advances against their commissions if they had a slow week, was proud of his bombers. Most were veterans, including two he knew from 50 State. But O'Neil discovered a few new phone talents. One was an English carpenter and handyman with an aching ambition to own a house on the ocean. Captivated by his accent, O'Neil urged the man to try the phone life. He resisted until a rainy spell sidelined him for two weeks and he needed some work. Within a month, he sold more than $11,000 worth of goods over the phone, keeping almost $4,000 as commission.

Federal court evidence would later show that there were plenty of other oddballs who "banged" the customers as O'Neil put it. Delores O'Keefe, a testy sixty-three-year-old woman with flaming red hair and a worn-out siren's face, worked out of her apartment using fake names such as "Linda Evans."

Sad-eyed Howie, with shaggy rumpled hair that stretched below his collar, spoke in a monotonous baritone that nearly squashed his Brooklyn accent. Divorced with two kids, one entering the teen years, he popped Prozac for bouts of depression.

Then there was Bill Clark, thirty-five, a live-wire veteran of fourte

---

*SEC Registration Number 0-19475, August 20, 1991.

years in the Las Vegas scam swirl. Slightly preppie in appearance with a moonish face, slack jaw, and foul mouth, he sold frantically. Clark had four customized sales pitches all of which he knew by heart and an endless supply of waspy-sounding aliases. "I can make two thousand in my sleep," he once told an associate. O'Neil quickly promoted Clark to a sales manager.

O'Neil had only the highest praise for his teenaged reloader, Carlos Bernal, who took one customer from Albuquerque for more than $40,000.

At nineteen, Bernal tooled around Fort Lauderdale in a vintage black Corvette, living the high life. He made $50,000 cash in eight months by joining the subculture of phone "pros" who skip from scam to scam.

Despite his youth, he was a seasoned scammer, starting at age fifteen as a summer job. He even gave new employees in one phone room lessons in the fine art of repeatedly ripping off the same clients.

Bernal hit his stride at Cypress Creek Promotions. He was one of the top reloaders, and he scammed people over and over until they had been stripped of thousands of dollars. Bernal earned 25 percent commissions on sales he made, and that came to more than $5,000 some weeks. He used a total of seven different phone names, and never his true one.

Tapes introduced as evidence in a federal court case have Carlos bragging of his skills to an inquisitive young sales rep with a Georgia telecommunications firm:

CARLOS: This is very simple to do ten of these (sales) a day.

REP: $399 is what you sold it for?

CARLOS: Yeah, I could have gotten anywhere from up to $700 out of her, yeah up to eight, yeah, easy, easy. I mean it was just a matter of saying it.

REP: What kind of time span do you guys wait to reload or call again?

Carlos: Ah . . . exactly about thirty days.

REP: Did they have any problems like disbelief or not thinking this was real?

Carlos: Well, the way I presented myself as head of the awards division, there was no doubt in their mind. (She) asked me how big the company is, if we're established and . . . I got around that because if I told her we only been around for a year you know, she wouldn't have bought that. . . . I told her . . . we're bonded with the . . . ah . . . gaming commission and that means we have to comply with the rules and regulations of the Florida State Lottery and that just shut her up. (Laughs)

REP: That is it, huh?

CARLOS: That was it. Just rebuttals, you know, shut them up, just talk.

REP: Just keep talking.

CARLOS: Yeah, not give them a chance to . . . think . . . I got her real excited. She was excited to begin with, but I made her believe.

The sales staff at Cypress Creek Promotions made many people believe. The company sold pens, keychains, magnetic business cards, and other gizmos, imprinted with the name of a business. The telemarketers used a variation of the "one-in-five," the venerable prize scheme that never seems to fall out of favor with people eager to win something for nothing. Cypress Creek guaranteed customers receipt of:

• A new Chevrolet Camaro

• A satellite dish

• A 14-karat gold ingot commemorating the 500th anniversary of Columbus's voyage to America

• A 2.5-carat diamond and sapphire pendant

• A 50-inch Hitachi big-screen television

The scheme aimed at small business owners and the elderly. Telemarketers told business owners that in order to win one of the prizes they would have to purchase the advertising items, for a minimum of $399. When they called ordinary citizens, they claimed an advance payment was needed to pay taxes, insurance, legal fees, or anything else that seemed reasonable to the customer.

They also claimed, falsely, that all of the awards greatly exceeded the amount of the payment, which buyers sent by cashier's check through an overnight delivery service.

Other lies used in the pitch included:

• The customer had a one-in-five chance of winning the car. In fact, the sales agents called as many people as possible in a day. O'Neil joked that he almost never gave away a car and the only buyers who received a vehicle spent far more than the car was worth.

• Cypress Creek selected the customer because he or she had attended a recent trade show. If the customer denied attending such a show, the sales agent apologized for the mistake and launched into the sales pitch. In fact, the boiler room bought sales leads from brokers, who compile lists based on applicants for occupational licenses and other records, including names of previous purchasers. Names cost as little as three cents each, more for reloads.

• Cypress Creek claimed that the promotion was being offered only twice a year and that it would end at the close of that day's business. In fact, the company hawked the same deal day after day. The telemarketers also claimed to be the firm's "promotions director" or "awards director."

• Corporations "donated" the prizes to Cypress Creek Promotions in exchange for free advertising in Cypress Creek's national catalog. No such catalog existed and O'Neil bought the prizes, mostly cheap jewelry, from wholesalers.

The more experienced members of the reload staff would go even further, creating any ruse they needed to close a sale. One agent went so far as to state that a spin-off company had been in business for twenty-eight years, when it had been open for just three months.

Cypress Creek Promotions had another trick that gave it an advantage over its competitors. It figured out how to hoodwink the Better Business Bureau of South Florida. While not as brazen as the "Better Business Bureau of America" scam that O'Neil had seen in his Vegas days, it worked.

O'Neil talked the Miami Better Business Bureau, which lacks the resources to check the backgrounds of its members carefully, into running a taped message that gave callers the impression that Cypress Creek Promotions ran an upstanding sweepstakes. The tape became a potent sales tool that the telemarketers drew on whenever a customer seemed suspicious. It gave buyers undue confidence in O'Neil, who wrote the text of the message.

The referral system also tipped O'Neil's sales force to customers who were close to falling for the scam, and would be good future prospects even if they chose not to buy after the first contact. "I think I'll nail this guy," Bill Clark said after giving a wavering customer the Better Business Bureau number.

Those who called the Miami Better Business Bureau number reached a recording that asked them to dial in the phone number of the firm they wanted information on. That done, the caller heard a favorable report on Cypress Creek's sweepstakes that recited the prizes to be awarded. O'Neil planned to have a lawyer write future taped reports to keep him out of trouble with the law.

O'Neil boasted of manipulating the Better Business Bureau to give him a good report. With characteristic bombast, he had this to say about the bureau: "They're bigger whores than we are."

O'Neil also plied his trade by using an old carnival barker's routine, the audience shill. Sometimes called a "shouter," or a "crier," the individual helps sell others by singing the praises of the promotion. Some are in the employ of the telemarketer, others are not. O'Neil used a small businessman from Missouri, who spent $399 for the products and got a $2,000 cash award. Before O'Neil sent him the cash, he required the man to sign a release giving O'Neil the right to let new customers contact him. The man readily agreed and became an unwitting sales tool. O'Neil wrote forty new deals off the man's reference. O'Neil made one big mistake, though. He let the FBI infiltrate his boiler room and as a consequence he and several of his key employees were convicted of wire fraud and sent to prison.

Many of O'Neil's strategies now are in use in dozens of boiler-room operations, especially in Las Vegas and South Florida. They're popular with the Florida folks because most customers are small businesses, which rarely write bad checks. More importantly, business operators are loathe to admit they were defrauded, which keeps complaints down. Those who do complain often find police not terribly sympathetic because they tend to view the matter as a dispute which should be handled in civil court.

Many of the ad-specs rooms in Florida regard their sales ruse as a recipe for quick cash. One placed ads to hire workers which said: "If you can walk, talk, and chew bubble gum at the same time and want to earn between $1,000 and $2,000 weekly, call."

But customers of these companies often got nothing for their money but cheap sales tricks. Some instructed the sales staff to build excitement by placing customers on hold while the sales agent "checks the computer" to verify the customer is a likely big winner. Coming back on the line after the pregnant pause, the sales agent tells the customer he or she "has the lowest (registration) number I've ever seen," thus greatly boosting their chances of winning a grand prize.

One long-time operator of the racket held hour-long sales sessions with new hires in which he bluntly explained: "We are selling greed." He also would storm through the sales room daily yelling at employees to close more sales and make him richer faster.

The soldiers in these scam brigades have their own language, code of conduct, and hierarchy. They refer to their customers with contempt, calling them "mooches," or people who deserve to get cheated because they tried to get something for nothing.

"People want money to fall out of the sky, and we make it sound easy and comfortable," says one master of the ad specs swindle who requested anonymity. "We don't care if they ever get their products or if they spend their last dime on it. They bought the story and they deserve what they get."

Life in an ad-specs sales room begins as "fronters," people with no experience attracted by the hyped-up classified ads promising huge earnings. Right away, they begin using sales scripts full of deceit and out-and-out lies. New hires often snicker at their work area, which often is covered with wall signs such as Misrepresentation Equals Termination. The signs hang for the benefit of regulators who might wander through the room to make sure everything is running clean.

While the sales agents tell buyers they had a one-in-four chance of winning a car, 41-inch color television, or cashier's check for $1,200, nobody sold by fronters ever got anything other than a cheap watch, tennis bracelet, pendant, or coin.

The fronters also talk customers into sending a picture of themselves for use in the company's nonexistent catalog along with their check.

In most phone-sales rooms, fronters are low-end salespeople who take the worst duties such as "cold calling," or simply dialing everybody whose name appears in a phone book or other mass lists. The chances of ringing up a sale from these tepid lists is one sale for every thirty calls. Often the fronter explains the sales promotion, then passes the victim to a "closer," a more experienced salesperson skilled in overcoming a buyer's reluctance. Closers sometimes call themselves the company "manager" in order to inspire the buyer's trust and cinch the sale. In turn, the closers often pass the buyer on to a third person, a "verifier," who is supposed to "clean up the pitch," or smooth over any untruths uttered by sales agents.

Many telemarketing rooms tape record the verification portion of the sale. These tapes can be used to quiet regulators and intimidate buyers who later ask for their money back. Because the tapes do not contain the sales pitch itself, it is difficult for law enforcement to prove whether deceit led the buyer to purchase the goods.

The verifiers play a pivotal role in pacifying customers, often months after a sale, when they fail to receive any merchandise or demand a refund once they see the goods are shoddy and worth far less than promised.

The ad-specs rooms rarely hand out anything other than a "gimme gift." A typical one-in-four scheme offers a Buick Regal or jeep, a Sony 40-inch big-screen television or $2,500 cash, a home entertainment center, and the "gimme gift," usually a set of his-and-her diamond watches for which the sales room pays twenty-five dollars each. Alternative gimme gifts: a Panda coin, which costs $125; a tennis bracelet that costs $40, diamond pendant ($25), and an electro-brand stereo ($40). The total price for an ad-specs promotion ranges from $398 to $898, including one hundred or so cheap pens or other advertising gimmicks, that are worth a few dollars or less.

The boiler room also uses a system to "pad" the value of the prize items. This tactic makes it appear to anyone auditing the books that prices are far less outlandish. Often when boiler-room operators are ordered to pay restitution, they will try to convince authorities that the products shipped to customers were worth the inflated value of the pad.

The difference can be enormous, reducing the amount of restitution one convicted telemarketer had to repay to victims by more than $200,000. The pad rates also greatly reduce sales commissions the owners must pay. For example, a customer paying $498 would get the $25 watch, which had a pad value of $168. The sales agent's commission is based on the difference between the sales price and the pad value, or $330. The agent gets 30 percent of that figure or $99 for the sale.

In most telephone operations the giant commissions go to members of the elite level of sales hierarchy, the reload room, which often takes in $20,000 to $30,000 a week in sales all from people who bought over and over vainly hoping to win the big prize.

Many sales rooms hire reloaders from outside the operation, but others let fronters work their way up based on sales volume. Almost all reloaders customize their sales pitch and trample the truth to fire up their customers to jump into the phony raffle over and over.

Once they have pounced on a customer so often he or she threatens to go to the police, some expensive gifts might actually appear. One large ad-specs room gave a car to a New Mexico resident who complained to state regulators. In another case a doctor who spent over $30,000 in promotions got a car worth less than $10,000. An Oklahoma resident who spent about the same amount as the doctor received a jeep worth less than a third of his investment.

Another sucker who spent more than $50,000 got a diamond bracelet, earrings, a television, and a VCR, all of which were purchased from department stores. A sampling of complaints shows that people who threatened to complain to the attorney general's office or to the Better Business Bureau, and followed through, had the best chance of getting satisfaction.

Once they get out of the "ether" phase of thinking they will get something for nothing, many buyers can explain why they fell for the scam. Often, they say telemarketers simply thought faster than they did and outmaneuvered them.

Telemarketers refer to that trait as the "rebuttal" or "objection," the pitch used to counter a customer's reluctance. Objections are a key element in telemarketing schemes and most rooms write them out and issue them to sales agents. In the ad-specs scheme, the catalog gimmick is the primary objection hurled by the hucksters.

Here's how it works: The company asks "prize winners" to send pictures of themselves for publication in a catalog, which makes them feel special. The catalog doesn't exist but many people mail in their pictures believing it does. The catalog rebuttal helps telemarketers explain why they can afford to give away terrific prizes. Sales agents simply tell customers that manufacturers donate the prizes in exchange for the free publicity of being featured in the catalog.

While it may sound corny, the catalog objection works because many people have seen television quiz shows that give away brand-name products obtained for free in exchange for a plug. The photograph ruse also mimics a technique used by some legitimate sweepstakes promoters and state lotteries that publicize winners' names to help spur sales.

Ad-specs executive O'Neil used most of these techniques to build Cypress Creek Promotions into a $2.5 million crooked business, with more than three thousand victims, in little more than a year. While he took pains to keep regulators at bay, he eventually ran into trouble with attorneys general in seven states who launched investigations.

The state of Oregon filed a civil suit against O'Neil in July 1992, charging him with telemarketing into the state without a license and deceiving customers about the value of gifts in his promotion. An Oregon judge in December 1993 found O'Neil and Cypress Creek Promotions had cheated at least eight state residents and imposed a fine of $129,284.

By that time, Cypress Creek Promotions had been out of business for more than six months.

When authorities showed up with a search warrant at Cypress Creek's office in March 1993, they found only a four-drawer file cabinet, papers and shipping documents strewn over the floor, ten boxes of documents, and mail that included a letter to O'Neil from the state attorney general of New Mexico.

But O'Neil can't count himself among the dozens of Florida telemarketing bosses who skip out of a scam or steal off to start up another, leaving attorneys general in distant states confused or in possession of court verdicts they can't enforce. O'Neil had left a legacy of hours of tapes secretly recorded by the FBI, records that provide a bird's-eye view of the boiler-room racket and enough evidence to get him convicted on federal wire fraud and conspiracy to commit wire fraud charges.

Federal criminal charges are just about the only enforcement action telemarketers truly fear. Wire fraud is punishable by five years in prison for each count, and indictments typically lob at least eight counts at a defendant. While convictions never bring the maximum sentence, the federal prison system also has no parole. Unlike state courts where white-collar criminals almost always draw light sentences and serve as little as a fifth of their time, the federal system is formidable, almost assuring a few years in prison if convicted.

Tim O'Neil donned a dark blue suit for his first appearance in U.S. District Court in downtown Fort Lauderdale. He wore a business-like red tie and spectacles and a ball pen clipped to his jacket. While waiting for his case to be called, O'Neil rushed to hold open a door for a female court clerk who arrived with a pitcher of ice water for a judge.

Inside the courtroom, O'Neil stood beside former sales manager Bill Clark, who was subdued and pensive and wore a blue blazer and gray slacks with a necktie tied unevenly. Also present was a dour Delores O'Keefe dressed in an unflattering blue pants suit and complaining bitterly that the courtroom was too cold.

The others among the dozen Cypress Creek Promotions workers rounded up by the FBI either had been granted immunity in exchange for their testimony or pleaded guilty. Fifty-year-old Howie, who told his mother after his arrest, "I knew these people were no good," pleaded guilty to a single count of wire fraud.

Teenage reloader Carlos Bernal, who had been working in a coin shop after his arrest, pleaded guilty to a count of conspiracy to commit wire fraud. He took responsibility for $428,548 worth of consumer losses, less the value of the prizes.

The two-week trial opened with an arduous jury selection process, itself a comment on the extent to which telemarketing has permeated South Florida. Several members of the jury pool were excused because they had worked in phone sales or were married to telemarketers.

As the trial progressed, it became clear that Cypress Creek Promotions crashed largely because of O'Neil's ego and greed.

The FBI infiltrated the firm with the help of a convicted telemarketer who knew O'Neil at 50 State Distributing. Unknown to O'Neil, his old buddy was on the FBI payroll and the company he claimed to represent, which sold automatic dialers that could greatly boost boiler-room profits, was an FBI sting operation.

O'Neil and Clark could not resist performing for the undercover FBI agents who asked them to strut their sales pitch—while hidden recorders ran. O'Neil bragged about manipulating the Better Business Bureau and the Securities and Exchange Commission, and even the eighty-nine-year-old woman who had lost more than $14,000 to Florida telemarketing scams. He also had to admit that the "Gettysburg collectible" he sent the Philadelphia woman cost him sixty dollars.

O'Keefe had problems, too, even though she did much of her selling for Cypress Creek Promotions from her home. One of the customers she called was an undercover FBI agent to whom she lied repeatedly to make a sale. And the inquisitive "sales rep" from Atlanta to whom Bernal had opened up also was an undercover FBI agent.

The tapes were tough for defense lawyers to overcome. While they tried to argue their clients did nothing more than stretch the truth, the recordings left little doubt that O'Neil and Clark were con artists.

On tape, Clark launched into several obscenity-laced tirades, calling his customers "fucking morons," and turned to FBI agents gleefully intoning, "What can I tell you, I learned from the best scammers in the business."

Jurors believed the three phone pros intended to violate the fraud statutes. The jury found all three guilty as charged on June 14, 1994. O'Neil, who had been working as a salesman for a local car dealer while awaiting his trial, received a ten-year sentence and was ordered to make $2.4 million in restitution. Sales manager Bill Clark drew a sentence of fifty-seven months and $1 million in restitution. The judge sentenced dour Delores O'Keefe to eighteen months. Carlos Bernal, the young reload whiz, received 21 months and an order to make $364,266 in restitution.

The trial left little doubt about the magnitude of telemarketing fraud, its insidious power to strike victims over and over, and the endless array of forms it can assume. Take it from Tim O'Neil: "My guys are lying . . . . You can't sell on the phone without lying," he remarked on tape. "[That's] the nature of the business, but it's also fuck 'em and make 'em like it. You know, that's what we're trying to do."

4

"Felony" Travel

Stan Cohen stares a visitor straight in the face and swears up and down his telephone travel agency is on the level.

Cohen, tall, balding, and dripping gold jewelry, gives off a heavy mix of sincerity and menace as he talks. Seated behind a paper-cluttered desk, he waves canceled checks in the air wildly, more than $3 million worth, by his count.

"This is obviously a profitable business," Cohen thunders. "I'm not taking people's money and skipping town."

Cohen insists his company, Omega Fun 'N' Travel, sends thousands of people on the cut-rate trips it peddles over the telephone. His fistful of bank paper proves it. Hotels in South Florida and the Bahamas cashed the checks after housing his travelers, most of whom enjoyed a great holiday, Cohen says. He pays about $44,000 weekly just for the day-cruise ship that carries Fun 'N' Travel vacationers to Freeport from Fort Lauderdale.*

Cohen knows his trade has critics. Since the mid-1980s consumer advocates nationwide have warned the public to steer clear of bargain travel "certificates" hawked by telemarketers. Many fail to deliver the trips, for which customers pay four hundred dollars or more well in advance. Others tack on hidden fees or stall departure dates for so long that the buyer can't ever take the vacation. While travel scams have flourished from Houston to Chicago, Florida is the undisputed leader of the pack.

"In most business, you find 85 to 95 percent of the people are good, and the rest are bad. Our industry is 85 to 95 percent bad apples. Most take the money and run," Cohen confides.

But not Omega, says Cohen, the company marketing director. Omega moves more tourists a year through Fort Lauderdale than any other travel agency. Setting aside the pile of checks, Cohen yanks a handful of service

---

*Interview with Stan Cohen, May 13, 1992.

contracts from a desk drawer. The contracts show the agency buys in bulk and pays as little as twenty-five dollars a night for beachfront hotel rooms, rates so low that Cohen can make a handsome profit. The contracts are added proof that Omega plans on growing. According to Cohen, business is so brisk the agency will soon launch a major expansion.

Cohen starts a tour of the travel depot with a disclaimer. The site, he concedes, is an unlikely spot for an agency boasting annual sales near $10 million. Most travel agencies search out busy commercial strip malls, so people can easily drop by on their lunch hours or after work to flip through glossy travel brochures and discuss their trips. Travel agents live off of commissions paid to them by airlines, hotels, and tour operators. Commissions paid for cruises in Florida are above 10 percent of the cost of the ticket. Cruise lines and tour operators often curry favor with large travel agencies that can assure them many bookings.

Omega is a different breed. It needs no high-overhead offices or walk-in clients because it sells by phone and most of its customers live thousands of miles away and will never see the front office.

It's a good thing they don't. While Omega maintains a Fort Lauderdale mailing address, the site lies miles from the beach in an aging industrial park on the city's shabby outskirts.

Omega runs from two goose-gray warehouses just beyond the barbed-wire perimeter and blue runway lights of Executive Airport, a city-owned airfield housing mostly private planes. Omega sits among an odd assortment of air cargo firms, factories, and repair shops in a storage zone whose former tenants include more than a few illegal telephone boiler rooms.

No signs point the way in. From the parking lot visitors must strain to see the corporate nameplate, the size of a bumper sticker, on the mirrored metal security door.

Easier to see and hear are Lear jets that whisk corporate titans in for some quick relaxation in Fort Lauderdale's fabled sunshine and yacht basins. On cool mid-winter nights the cheers of crowds at nearby Lockhart Stadium, spring training home of the New York Yankees, compete with the roar of air traffic.

Omega's 12,000-square-foot suites buzz day and night. Two dozen telemarketers, mainly young women, read scripts and take reservations for a "fabulous five-day trip to Florida and the Bahamas."

Travel-broker Cohen surveys his troops with obvious pride and ticks off their duties as he walks. He crosses rows of work stations, where telemarketers sit in orderly, open cubicles. They wear headsets with tiny boom microphones and barely look up to eye a stranger or their rather imposing boss. They stare intently at their scripts, and call after call, deliver a cheery sales message: "The most fabulous combination Florida and cruise vacation ever made available. Six sun-drenched days and five star-filled nights of Florida and Bahamas sun, fun, and surf."

Here's the deal:

- Two nights in a Fort Lauderdale hotel for two adults;
- A cruise package from Fort Lauderdale to Freeport, Grand Bahama, for two adults;
- Two nights accommodations in Freeport;
- A cruise from Freeport back to Fort Lauderdale;
- One night accommodations in Fort Lauderdale.

A steal at just under five hundred dollars, says Cohen as he steps toward the warehouse loading and shipping dock, a critical area of the operation. Stacked twenty feet high are thousands of bright yellow mailers, about the size of boxes used to gift-wrap a man's shirt. The cover photo is of a cruise ship sailing a smooth Caribbean passage with the enticing line "Come Cruise with Us."

The boxes are hollowed out inside to neatly fit a nine-minute network-quality videotape. The video gushes over the "world famous" hotels under contract with Omega and shows young couples frolicking in the islands, snorkeling, strolling white-sand beaches arm-in-arm, and bargaining with natives in the straw market.

The films thrill buyers eager to see what awaits them on their vacation, and for that reason they are a staple of the travel-voucher trade. Cohen ships the videos within three days of purchase of the travel package. He says the tapes, for which certificate dealers pay only two dollars or so apiece, including the mailing box, are a cheap investment in good public relations. He even slaps a notice on the box that the travel package includes a free "trip cancellation and interruption" insurance policy, giving his clients added assurance that they have made a smart purchase.

"A lot of the people we travel have never even seen water," Cohen explains. "You have to remember that this is a discounted trip. We are not traveling high rollers."

Cohen winds up his tour by showing off testimonials to Omega's clout in the travel industry. He hands over a half dozen letters from Fort

Lauderdale hotel operators grateful for Omega's bookings. One letter from the Grand Bahama Ministry of Tourism credits Omega for an upswing in visitors to the islands, which have suffered a drop in tourism as a result of problems ranging from rude help to decaying hotels. Omega, the tourism ministry writes, is a "true ambassador to the Bahamas."

Adds an anonymous reviewer writing in a travel newsletter: "Today you can procure a true, honest-to-goodness travel package that can deliver what it promises. . . . I repeatedly found nothing but happy, satisfied customers."

Yet Cohen's enthusiastic sales job omits a few details customers might like to know before they sign up for Omega's dream vacation.

For starters, Cohen is an alias. The man's real name is Ted Powder. He's a convicted felon with past ties to South Florida mobsters and a history of running travel schemes that collapse. Cohen's partner, David Wood, on medical leave this day as he recovers from a heart attack, also has a failed travel certificate firm and a half-dozen aliases in his past. Also a convicted fraud artist, his real name is James Cicero.

As Cohen brags of Fun 'N' Travel's plans for the future, the travel brokerage is a few months away from shutting its doors, leaving nearly one thousand customers demanding more than $400,000 in refunds, and Florida's state attorney general charging the firm with consumer fraud.

"We were starting to call this operation Felony Travel," said one South Florida police officer who has watched Powder wend his way from scam to scam, mostly without paying any penalty. "These guys are really something else."

The saga of Omega Fun 'N' Travel, and the men behind it, is worth telling because it shows why telephone fraud artists often win many rounds, even if they eventually outwit themselves and land in jail.

Powder and Cicero were partners in crime in 1985, a time when they sped around Fort Lauderdale in new Cadillacs, Ted's champagne-tinged, Jim's off-white.

In late spring, as the locals delighted in the annual ritual of taking back their town from snowbird residents, the Florida Department of Law Enforcement struggled to rid the county of unwanted visitors of another kind: mobsters.

So many organized crime figures turned up in the greater Fort Lauderdale area—many as year-round residents—that police couldn't recognize all of them. That worried the authorities. Fort Lauderdale had always been open territory for the mob and they feared that a turf battle to control local rackets could erupt into a bloody gangland war.

The crime fighters set out to crack open the secret gangland society. They did so with the help of wired informants who met gangsters at spots ranging from a mirrored noisy deli near the Pompano Harness Track in Pompano Beach to Joe Sonkin's Italian restaurant in oceanfront Hollywood, an eatery decked out in Chicago memorabilia and an alleged haunt for underworld types.

Before too long, agents honed in on Powder and Cicero, mostly because of the company they kept. Police listened in as a storm began to brew around a jewelry store the partners ran under aliases. Cicero called himself "Hy Goldberg." Powder was "Ted Post."

Sunshine Precious Metals, Inc. opened after Powder and Cicero paid a local man five hundred dollars to serve as a "front" owner. While the front man had no role in running the store, his name appeared on corporate documents setting up the company because Powder's two felony convictions on federal criminal charges might have attracted the attention of police.

Despite the precautions, the jewelry store appeared suspicious to any customer who wandered in. While its front room contained glass cases of jewelry for sale, the owners spent most of the time in the back room conferring with guys who looked like they walked off the set of the old "Untouchables" television show. Others who frequented the room included a three-hundred-pound bookie named "Wiggles" who turned up often. Sales people who asked the owners to advertise as a means of attracting walk-in business were told to "mind their own business," according to police records.

While paying little attention to retail sales, Sunshine was dealing in the back room. It began building up its credit line through cash purchases of gems and gold, which were later resold to other dealers. As they developed credit with a few suppliers, the proprietors made bigger and bigger buys on credit. When these purchases topped $400,000, the owners shut down and vanished, leaving creditors unable to collect a dime in a scam known as a credit "bust out."

Powder and Cicero might well have avoided prosecution for the jewelry escapade, as they did for later travel scams, except for one fact: the surveillance tapes. The gem store took center stage in the organized crime investigation as Genovese and Bonanno family figures bickered over how to divvy up the profits. Both Cicero and Powder had previous business ties to organized crime figures, although neither was a member of a mob family, Florida law enforcement records state. And each tried to call in friendly mob associates to mediate the dispute, without success.

While mobsters squabbled over their take, law enforcement agents taped their conversations. Powder boasts of paying seventy-five dollars for a genuine Rolex watch box and paperwork, then going and buying a cheap fake which he had a crooked craftsman known as "the Arab" stamp with a bogus plate reading "18 carat gold." Powder says he repacked the timepiece and sold it for $3,500. Powder recalls his jail time. He jokes about yelling "tough luck" to a bleeding inmate who begged for help after being stabbed in a Missouri prison.

Powder ducked under the covers, as did other inmates. Powder is less amused as he recalls getting scammed by a "kid" who took Powder's $22,000 to make an unspecified purchase, but pocketed the money instead. Outraged, Powder reported the theft to local police and demanded that justice be done. After police pulled Powder's rap sheet they decided he deserved it and refused to lift a finger to help.

Cicero and Powder also admitted a role in passing up to three hundred counterfeit bank checks. On tape, they fret about getting caught after police arrested their "gopher" using one of the checks to buy $68,000 in gold coins. Police concluded that artisans forged the checks at a Garfield, New Jersey, warehouse thought to be the site where a murdered Bonanno crime family boss was chopped in half and stuffed into two oil barrels for disposal.

The justice system caught up with Powder and Cicero because of the taped evidence. A state jury convicted them of grand theft and fraud charges in 1987 for their role in the jewelry store caper. Powder served three and a half months in prison. Cicero also spent a short time in jail.

By the time police arrested the jewelers on the theft and fraud charges, they had new aliases and a new business—travel certificates, which had become a hot new product line for Florida telemarketers.

Powder and Cicero opened Promotional Management Systems. Run out of a cheap office in Fort Lauderdale's suburban reaches, the company hawked four-day gambling junkets to Las Vegas for four hundred dollars, airfare included. The partners took the names Allen Sherman and Jack Levy for the venture, and sold the vouchers as fast as they could print them.

A travel club called Travel Centers of America bought three thousand vouchers for $297,000. The club's owner, an enormous man known in telemarketing circles as "the Whale," years later pleaded guilty to federal wire and mail fraud charges for running the company.

But at the time of the purchase, the travel club, which promised members "incredible savings of up to 50 percent on future travel needs," claimed it had been ripped off by Powder and Cicero. In May 1987, the firm charged that the Las Vegas certificates it purchased were useless because they contained so many restrictions.

While Powder and Cicero denied the charges, the lawsuit stalled in court. As so often happens in the phone trade, the owners walked away while their patrons paid the price.*

"We are not rich people. This was a lot of money to us," wrote victim Linda Gibson of Columbus, Georgia, who paid $350 to join the travel club. "We felt this was a chance for us to go somewhere we always wanted to but probably would never be able to, at a good price."

Powder and Cicero's Las Vegas jaunts also drew twelve hundred complaints to the Florida state attorney general's office, many from buyers who never got the trips or refunds. The state won a court order directing Cicero and Powder to make partial restitution to victims of about $100,000.

Before the state's suit even got a court hearing, Powder and Cicero had a new business name, two new aliases, and a fresh product. The company was Omega Fun 'N' Travel. The new names: Stan Cohen and David Wood. The commodity: the fabulous Bahamas vacation.

That the men pulled it off leaves little doubt that Florida regulators by the end of the 1980s had lost any hope of subduing the phone sharks.

Sticklers for detail that they were, both men filled out paperwork to register their aliases as required under state law. The papers giving legal standing to Stan Cohen and David Wood remain on file at Broward County's government center in Fort Lauderdale.

Cicero and Powder also found their way around obstacles imposed in 1989 by the Florida legislature to protect the public (mostly out-of-state residents) from travel predators. The new law required travel-certificate firms to register with the state and post a bond of $10,000 which could be used to repay buyers should the firm go out of business, as hundreds of such companies had done. The law also prohibited felons from owning a travel voucher company. But the statute turned enforcement over to the Florida Department of Agriculture and Consumer Services in Tallahassee, which had no investigative staff to pursue violators with vigor.

In any case, state officials had no idea David Wood, the man who signed Fun 'N' Travel corporate records, was the alias of a convicted con artist. Had they known, they would have barred him from doing business in Florida. Stan Cohen's prior felony convictions, including one for ship-

---

*Travel Centers of America v. Promotional Marketing Systems, Inc., Seventeenth Judicial Circuit, Broward County, Florida, CV 87-18297.

ping stolen goods and two others for securities fraud, also rendered him ineligible to hawk travel certificates.*

The felons at Fun 'N' Travel did not keep their secret for long once they started selling heavily. A jealous competitor blew the whistle by notifying state investigators that Cicero was steering Fun 'N' Travel. Based on the tip, state consumer officials tried to deny Fun 'N' Travel an operating license, but Cicero sued, arguing he was just the "manager," not the owner. He lost the case, appealed and lost again, but all the while he stayed in business.

While waiting for the court appeal, Fun 'N' Travel discovered a loophole in the law that would keep it alive for more than two more years: it became a full-scale, licensed travel agency, even though virtually all of its sales involved telemarketing.

Like so many laws designed to crack down on consumer fraud, the Florida travel law contained exemptions, in this case to appease the state's powerful travel industry, which did not want to burden its members with new government regulation. At the insistence of the travel lobby, the law exempted travel agencies bonded through an entity called the Airline Reporting Corporation.

A Virginia company, the Airline Reporting Corporation extends credit to about forty thousand travel agencies nationwide by guaranteeing payment to airlines for any plane tickets member agencies issue. The corporation requires members to carry a bond of as much as $70,000. Should an agency default, however, the bond money is used to repay airlines, not consumers, so the system does nothing to protect the public from errant travel agencies.

The airline corporation, known as ARC in the travel trade, has even less staff than the state of Florida to check out the backgrounds of travel agencies it takes on as members. Perhaps the lax standards help explain why more than 2,700 bonded travel agencies shut their doors or defaulted on their bonds in 1991 alone, causing more than $29 million in losses to ARC and perhaps even more to consumers.

As a private entity the airline corporation does not have to disclose why it accepted Fun 'N' Travel in the face of warnings from Florida officials to look into the history of the company's two main men. Fun 'N' Travel convinced the Airline Reporting Corporation to bond it, thus exempting the firm from state scrutiny. The giant warehouse maintained

---

*Powder was convicted of interstate transportation of stolen property on September 4, 1975, in U.S. District Court, Miami and sentenced to three years in prison. His record also shows convictions for transferring forged securities.

a tiny room with a few colorful posters on the walls and a machine to process airline tickets. It was staffed by a single agent, who worked part time.

Had the airline reporting corporation's examiners made even cursory checks of court files in South Florida, they might have doubted Fun 'N' Travel's integrity. In one 1992 federal lawsuit filed in Fort Lauderdale, a Michigan travel company sued Powder and Fun 'N' Travel alleging that the Florida firm counterfeited its discount airline coupons and sold them. In a court affidavit, a witness swore that Powder sold five thousand of the phony coupons for $20,000 to a local precious metals telemarketer with a history of consumer fraud judgments and arrests. Powder and Fun 'N' Travel settled the lawsuit by agreeing never to make or sell any counterfeit coupons in the future.*

Fun 'N' Travel also used the courts to its advantage. The company filed a number of lawsuits against the local Better Business Bureau, competitors and clients that kept regulators at bay while complaints mounted about the Bahamas package and telemarketing tactics.

After warning the Better Business Bureau of South Florida to stop telling the public that the firm had an "unsatisfactory record" of responding to customer grievances, Omega sued for defamation. It later dropped the suit, but the tactic clearly intimidated the business group, which at the time had become so fed up with rip-off tropical vacations that it was denying membership to new travel-certificate companies.

A theme quickly emerged in Omega's legal pleadings. While the company did not deny many travelers had hellish experiences, it sought to place the blame elsewhere.

One constant source of consumer gripes was the disrepair of Omega's Freeport hotel, the same spot described on the agency's color videotape as "a beautiful resort." Hotel guests arrived to find soiled linen on their beds; filthy bathrooms; and bugs, dead and alive, in the rooms.

Another problem was Fun 'N' Travel's repeated refusal to honor its certificates, in one case seven hundred of its travel packages sold by telemarketers around the country. Fun 'N' Travel insisted that a middleman had sold the certificates without paying for them and warned regulators to brace for an upswing in complaints from the public.

These novel tactics, along with frequent correspondence with the Florida state attorney general's office, went a long way toward keeping the sales operation a step ahead of regulators.

---

*Entertainment Publications, Inc., v. Ted Powder, U.S. District Court Fort Lauderdale, 92-6123-CIV-Gonzalez.

The state took no action against Fun 'N' Travel until after the Fort Lauderdale *Sun-Sentinel* disclosed the complaints building up in the state attorney general's files. In April 1992, the state attorney general's office in a civil suit accused the travel agency of cheating buyers by failing to honor requested travel dates or grant refunds, imposing hidden charges, and other "unfair and deceptive" trade practices.

The firm kept writing new business, however, mainly because the turnover-plagued attorney general's office failed to push its lawsuit forward. Instead, the state repeatedly handed the case to new assistant attorneys general and the matter stalled in the court system.

Rather than have to explain its business tactics to a judge, Fun 'N' Travel continued to fire off self-serving letters to regulators and business officials, always seeking to shift blame for consumer complaints. While accepting these lame excuses, the state had no idea how many certificates Omega was selling or whether the firm would ever be able to fulfill them.

Fun 'N' Travel outdid itself when it advised the Better Business Bureau in May 1992 that the Bahamas hotel the company had been using presented a "significant risk to the health and safety of any traveler." Sanitary conditions were at best "poor," stress cracks could be seen in columns, and railings were in danger of crumbling, according to a structural engineer hired by the company. Omega, which enclosed the engineer's written report, stated that it would cease using the hotel rather than "be responsible for innocent deaths."

Omega also sent a summary of the engineer's findings to clients who were a few weeks away from leaving on their trip. Omega cancelled the cruise and Freeport portion of the trip citing the dangers at the hotel, offering additional nights in Fort Lauderdale to compensate.

Omega never explained why it could not place its clients at other hotels in the Bahamas, and regulators didn't require the firm to do so. Instead, Omega brazenly advised regulators to brace themselves for a wave of complaints.

While telemarketing rooms all over the country kept selling Omega's certificates, bewildered government lawyers in Florida couldn't decide what to do about the company's string of excuses for not delivering trips. They did nothing and their indecisiveness let things get worse.

Within a few months, Omega began sending out computer-generated notices to travelers who were a week away from departing for Fort Lauderdale. As usual, these notices were striking for their absolute gall:

Due to circumstances beyond our control, which is a combination of several factors, we are unable to honor your reservation. Do not come to Fort Lauderdale.

Once again, the Florida state attorney general's office took no action, and the situation deteriorated. In September 1992 the firm sent its obituary to waiting travelers:

We are sorry to inform you that Fun 'N' Travel is unable to fulfill your travel request. As of this date, Fun 'N' Travel will cease to do business. This action is not of our choosing but we have no alternative.

After a few furious buyers forwarded the death notice to the Florida state attorney general's office, the state sought an emergency hearing to preserve any assets for distribution to customers. By then it was too late.

The end of Fun 'N' Travel didn't stop Powder from cashing checks and money orders from customers who had not been told of the firm's demise.

One buyer, Charles Cramer of Iberia, Ohio, who bought his Omega voucher through a Las Vegas telemarketer, wondered in a court affidavit: "How can they cash our check in December when their business closed in September?"

That question remains unanswered. As of March 1995, the list of buyers who filed notarized affidavits demanding refunds stood at 961 and their claims totaled $416,517.13. That's probably just a small fraction of the people who lost money. But chances are nobody will see a dime. Travel brokers Powder and Cicero haven't even paid off the $100,000 judgment entered against them for the sale of the Las Vegas certificates.

Powder, under the alias Stan Cohen, developed far more serious legal troubles. U.S. Secret Service officials arrested him in March 1993 for his role in the manufacture of counterfeit cashier's checks, the same sort of enterprise he had boasted about running on the Florida Department of Law Enforcement surveillance tapes recorded years earlier. Cicero had no connection to the 1993 case.

U.S. Secret Service agents nabbed Powder in the parking lot of his new business, Discount Premiums, Inc., after he took possession of a box of 350 counterfeit bank checks. Federal agents learned of the crime after the printer's partner tipped them off. On his arrest form Powder listed his occupation as a salesman. True to his word, Powder did not skip town. He pleaded guilty in June 1994 to a single count of counterfeiting securities. He was sentenced to eight months in prison.

Powder committed the counterfeiting offense after the travel agency closed down. But he discussed the operation of Fun 'N' Travel with a co-defendant in the counterfeiting case. Powder boasted of selling 120,000 of the travel "certs," mostly to telephone boiler rooms at wholesale prices of forty dollars to eighty dollars apiece. The telemarketers eventually resold the packages for about five hundred dollars each for a total take of $65 million.

Powder conceded that as many as forty thousand of the 120,000 buyers who paid for trips never took them. He had an explanation. Omega, Powder said, was "no different than an insurance company. You pay a premium to the insurance company, and then if you claim, they pay off. If you don't claim, they keep the money."

Telephone sales of certificates for low-cost Florida travel rope in customers all over the country, and give the state's legitimate tourism industry a black eye. "This is a very big problem in the state," warns Bob Crawford, Commissioner of the Florida Department of Agriculture and Consumer Services. "There is a tremendous amount of money in it and a lot of the profit is derived from failure to deliver the goods."

Every time Florida officials decide they have some of the most egregious dealers under control or that the public has wised up to the scam, a new wave of operators surfaces in a new corner of the state.

At least four hundred "cert" marketers came and went in the Sunshine State between 1989 and 1993. They used a combination of telephone lines, newspaper classified ads, and the U.S. mails to lure buyers.

This generation of sleazy sales rooms drew 4,500 complaints to Florida authorities, mostly buyers from all fifty states and as far away as England clamoring for refunds. Some Florida travel rooms even sold to in-state residents, a sign of contempt for regulators.

The vacation-voucher trade draws frowns from traditional travel agencies. The American Society of Travel Agents argues that these offers deceive travelers because they tend to spring unforeseen costs on them, either when they sign up or when they reach their destination and are powerless to do anything about it.

National consumer protection groups weigh in with annual bulletins warning of inflated "port charges" or other fees that buyers often overlook, such as frightful taxi fares to hotels which turn out to be ten miles or more from the beach.

Yet the travel-cert racket never goes away because the money is great and legal risks for most operators are low. In 1994 travel-certificate schemes began to turn up in advertisements in newspapers in the Soviet Union, where they are striking a whole new audience of victims.

The quick cash even tempts some ARC-bonded travel agencies to telemarket the coupons after hours. At least one South Florida travel agency spends the day booking cruises and writing airline tickets, then closes for an hour or so, draws the blinds, and reopens as a cert peddler from 6 P.M. to 11 P.M. It plugs in extra phones and targets buyers in Pacific time zones.

The scheme works year after year, deal after deal because nobody places any controls on the numbers of certificates printed. Nobody monitors outlets that sell them, or requires an issuer such as Fun 'N' Travel to prove it has the cash to make good on the trips.

Here's a quick look at the major pitfalls for customers who think they will get a bargain vacation.

Fulfillment

Cert companies sell their travel coupons to boiler rooms for from two dollars to sixty dollars each. Some have sold for as little as fifty cents. The telemarketers resell them at fantastic mark-ups, often by overstating their worth. One Florida firm sold 150 to 180 vouchers a day at $399 each, grossing more than $400,000 in a week. Some of the certificate issuers own a network of telemarketing rooms under an assortment of names, giving them control over wholesale and retail profits, and making it tough for authorities to follow the money flow. By using middlemen, the issuing companies make it much harder for consumers to get refunds.

Misrepresentations

Fraud occurs when the telemarketers lie about the vacation package or fail to mention certain fees, restrictions, or other facts that would lead a buyer to think twice. Buyers give the telemarketer their credit card numbers, which get billed for about two hundred dollars, what they are told is the full cost. After the buyer contacts the company that issued the certs to schedule the trip, he finds out that he must pay extra charges. The most common hidden fees are phony "port taxes" of nearly two hundred dollars and other advance charges that must be paid to take the trip.

All Sales Final

The certificate dealer tells buyers angered by the deceptive sales tactics that all sales are final and that he is "not responsible for any misrepresentations made by any independent agents or distributors." In fact, Florida law gives buyers seven days to cancel a trip and requires the firm to issue a refund. Desperate to salvage their trips, many buyers relent and throw good money after bad. They agree to pay the added charges, which jacks the cost of their vacation up to about $500 for the Fort Lauderdale/Bahamas jaunt.

Questionable Value

Can the package be a good deal? Almost never. The day cruise to the islands, including rooms at Freeport hotels, can be bought in Florida at deep discounts and since the certificate doesn't cover transportation to the state there is no real advantage to booking the day trip way in advance. Most of the Fort Lauderdale hotels offered are hardly top-notch, and are inexpensive out of season, when cert packages are likely to be honored. A skilled travel agent can find better values.

Long Stall

Nobody knows how many cert buyers wind up relaxing in the sunshine. But thousands of people who hope for a quick island getaway get an endless run-around instead. While cert dealers deny it, they stay afloat by selling far more coupons than they redeem, a concept known as "breakage" in the industry. How else can they sell their certificates so cheaply to boiler rooms? Some certificates state in the fine print that the issuer has up to two years to make good on the trip. In an industry as volatile as travel, two years is an eternity and chances are the firm will be closed well before the time limit expires.

Sorry, That Date's Full

Thousands of people have taken the trips, but it often took the patience of Job, and then some. Buyers often face a battery of brazen stall tactics when they try to redeem their travel vouchers. The companies tell them to submit three travel dates, knowing most people can go only on the dates they've previously signed up for at work. Often the company writes back, saying those dates are taken, please submit three more dates, which also turn out to be full, and so on.

Cert dealers sternly remind patrons who complain that the travel package is "subject to availability." Calling to protest further simply runs up a long distance bill because cert companies, like all telemarketers, delight in slapping complainers on extended hold.

Endless Forms

Some stall tactics are worse than others. A New Jersey bank manager tried to use a certificate for a trip to Orlando, airfare included. He received the voucher, said to be a $1,250 value, for sitting through a time-share spiel, in which investors buy shares in a vacation property giving them the right to occupy the property a set number of days per year, at a New England resort. The cert dealer billed him for $150 in service fees, before snowing him with paperwork. The letters said he would forfeit the trip if he did not respond to each inquiry in writing.

Over the next six months, the firm demanded that the man prove that he earned over $25,000 a year, which he did by mailing a copy of his W-2 form. Then they wanted proof that the woman he intended to take with him was his wife. He sent a copy of his marriage license. The company's "legal department" then demanded that he sign forms absolving the firm of any blame should he or his wife contract typhoid, be abducted, or be caught in a riot while in Orlando. A second notice made him swear he would not blame the travel firm should his plane crash or get hijacked. The banker fought back. He wrote to Florida consumer regulators, who managed to get the firm to return his $150. But it took a year and he never got the trip.

The Upgrade

Other cert dealers pressure buyers into paying for costly "upgrades" of Bahamas hotel rooms, a classic bait-and-switch sales maneuver. Many buyers readily agree after hearing a sales agent call the package hotel a "dump." A former Miami travel telemarketer testified in a court case that all dates were "sold out," unless the buyer agreed to pay extra money, sometimes as much as $1,500, for hotel upgrades. They got the same hotel anyway. Only ten of the sixty people sold trips daily got anything other than the cheap videotape showing suntanned tourists dancing in the Bahamas to a calypso beat, others testified.

Many people who pay for upgrades or receive other assurances that they are booked into first-class hotels are astounded when they arrive. Wrote one customer of her Florida hotel: "So dirty that we couldn't take a bath or walk in our bare feet. Moldy, smelly, dirty, so much black mold around the tub you didn't dare lay down your soap. *Thanks for the upgrade!*"

A Seattle woman found much fault with the cruise as well, writing: "The ship was so old and stunk so bad, people were getting sick everywhere on deck and below. The crew didn't clean it up. They just left it lay and served dinner." Her "upgraded" Bahamas hotel for which she paid $119 extra for two nights "smelled like the inside of an old shoe."

"Free" Airfare

A Ham Lake, Minnesota, couple fell for the $99 airfare-to-Hawaii package offered by Worldwide Travel and Tour, a telephone travel room housed behind an animal hospital in a Fort Lauderdale suburb. The couple read a small classified ad in the *Minneapolis Star-Tribune* placed under a bold-faced heading of "dream vacation," one of three such deals listed in that day's paper.

The "once in a lifetime" offer promised seven nights in the islands "staying in first-rate, luxury" rooms. "Why spend your money getting there, when you could spend it having fun?" the sales pitch went. The firm also guaranteed "the best hotel rates available."

The woman sent a cashier's check for the $99 vouchers, plus a $50 money order to cover a "reservations fee." Despite promises of low hotel rates, the agency billed the Minnesotans $281 a night for a very average hotel room, so average that police who called to inquire about the normal rate were quoted $70 a night. Many travel agents snagged rooms at the hotel for their clients for as little as $45 nightly.

Only a Few Left

Newspaper classified ads state that a corporation has "overbought" vacations and wants to unload them cheap. Callers to a toll-free number reach a polite, youthful-sounding voice eager to let them in on the great deal, so long as they hurry. Callers have no idea they are speaking with a boiler room where sales agents tell everyone they have only a few packages left. Buyers must decide to purchase on the spot and pay with a cashier's check, a sure sign that the deal is a scam.

The Phony Contest

The travel trap snares many others who make the mistake of filling out an entry blank to win a "free" vacation at a county fair, restaurant, or other gathering spot.

Many Americans grab these forms without a second's hesitation. They scribble in personal details such as marital status, family income, occupation, and, of course, phone number and address.

Phone marketers call this set-up a "drop box." Companies place them around the country on behalf of telemarketers who use the blanks as cheap sales leads. Phone marketers figure anyone dumb enough to readily give private family details to strangers is a fine sales prospect. Marketers pay from twenty cents to two dollars a slip, depending on how many details are provided.

The drop box operators empty the contents and send the slips to telemarketing rooms across the country, where sales agents call everyone excitedly and congratulate them on having been "selected" for the trip to the tropics. Many people think they have won the contest and drop their guard. Before too long they have bought a cert for five hundred dollars.

Credit Verification

The telemarketer claims he needs a prospective buyer's credit card number to verify credit ratings and determine whether the buyer can qualify for the travel award. The marketer promises to send some sales literature to help the customer reach a decision. He never sends literature, but uses the card numbers to bill the customer for the full cost of the package, a charge the buyer doesn't discover until the monthly credit card bill shows up. By that time, the telemarketing company has folded and the buyer must dispute the charge with a bank. Some phone rooms will use the credit card numbers to double bill, even triple bill, for the package, causing customers giant headaches in trying to get their bank to remove the bogus charges.

Overnight Payment

The demand for payment by bank check, cash, or money order sounds another warning. Never pay for a travel package way in advance with any sort of check. Federal law allows you to refuse payment for any service or product that is not delivered, but no such protection exists with a cashier's check, which is fully negotiable. A personal check is little better for if the travel agency cashes the check and goes out of business, a consumer has little recourse other than to get in line along with other creditors. Few customers realize that the sixty days allowed under federal law to dispute a credit card charge can begin with the date the trip was supposed to be taken.

When the deal must be paid for by bank check and the travel broker suggests that an overnight courier stop by and get the check, you can rest assured that the only thing traveling is your money, and it won't be returning.

Fly by Night

Some Florida travel telemarketers don't even bother setting up an office. Consider the case of Leo Paul Johnson, a cagey, de-licensed New York City stockbroker who struck out for the Sunbelt.

Using made-up corporate names like Travel Express and American Financial Systems, Johnson peddled cheap vacations to the Bahamas from a cramped apartment in the suburbs of Fort Lauderdale. Most of the buyers, who lived in tiny towns in Montana, Nevada, and Oregon, thought they had stumbled upon the deal of a lifetime when they spotted classified ads Johnson placed in weekly newspapers, for cruises for just two hundred dollars.

Johnson talked his customers into dispatching bank checks by overnight courier to a "suite" at what they thought was a major office building. The suite was Johnson's apartment. Johnson cashed the checks at a liquor store in a seedy section of town. He failed to send out any cruise tickets.

Police arrested Johnson after a number of buyers complained. He pleaded no contest to communications fraud and grand theft, got out of jail in less than a month, and got right back into the travel racket.

Arrested again on fraud charges, he fled Florida while awaiting trial. Police caught him in Atlanta, holed up in an apartment furnished with just a desk, a blanket, and a telephone with a toll-free number—all he needed to get back in the bargain-vacation scam. A Florida judge sent Johnson to prison for five years in 1992.

Johnson's odyssey shows how easily a phone scammer can drift into a town and set up shop. Some have made a career of doing just that, changing products almost as fast as they clear state lines.

5

The Baron of Breast Cream

All hail! The Baron of Breast Cream is here. Leonard Gregory Friedman doesn't look too regal, with his double chin, beltless black polyester slacks, and sloping belly. But he makes a royal impression on the small audience at a Midland, Texas hotel.

"My goal in life since I was fourteen was to become the richest man in the world," Friedman says. "I always thought I deserved to be a prince."*

Friedman is the big Kahuna of Hawaiian Secrets International, a start-up cosmetics company that bestows titles of royalty on its sales agents and turns an extract of plain old pineapple into wonder lotions imbued with the healing powers of the islands. The potions will pamper millions of women worldwide and churn fabulous wealth for everyone in the room, if they sign up to sell the health products through telemarketing rooms and door-to-door networks. Hear him: "You can go fishing for the rest of your life, go live in Tahiti or Hawaii for the rest of your life on a beach somewhere and every month in your mailbox from Hawaiian Secrets is going to be a check for twelve-and-a-half thousand dollars. That's 150 thousand bucks a year. Now that's retirement planning."

Friedman, a blue plastic lei around his neck and a papier-mâché pineapple prop at his side, wants to admit the faithful into his kingdom of quick cash. "I want to make $30 million a year. I also have the ability to pass a lot of that money on to other people," he asserts with a smirk that spreads across his rusty-brown moustache.

Donning spectacles, Friedman paces around the podium, stopping fitfully to pull a big gulp from a giant-size soft drink cup, or to catch his place in the sales pamphlet he and an associate have handed out. He gets distracted if anyone interrupts to pose a question, and bristles if he senses the query is impertinent.

---

*Friedman's presentation was recorded on videotape September 26, 1991.

His story opens on the mysterious Hawaiian island of Kauai, where he journeyed to marry his current wife (his sixth, though he didn't mention that fact to the Midland crowd) in a native ceremony.

His bride to be, lovely though she was, suffered from horrible psoriasis, for which the only remedy was smelly pine-tar baths that left her feeling like a "greased pig" at night. He says: "Some little old lady who ran an eelskin shop told my wife to rub pineapple on it, and it started to work. I knew I was on to one of the greatest scientific discoveries of modern times. I had a cure for a disease that nobody even knew what caused. . . . There were no more blotches on her arms and legs. I wouldn't have believed it if I hadn't seen it."

She had been to nine clinics and twenty dermatologists and nothing had worked, until now. "It was more than relief, it was a cure." Friedman's eyes light up as he recounts his reaction to the discovery. "I'm gonna make millions, maybe billions on this."

Friedman pauses, perhaps to make sure the Texans fathom the bigness of the numbers he's talking about. "A million seconds is twelve days. A billion seconds is thirty-two years. That's a big difference."

But even pitchman Friedman knew he could not sell simple pineapple, of which 625,000 tons are harvested in Hawaii every year. So he set out to discover the ingredient in pineapple that caused the miracle cure.

He sought out chemists, including one he calls a Nobel laureate, who told him to add other vitamins, including vitamin A, D_2, D_3, and a "proteolytic digestive enzyme" known as bromelin, discovered fifteen years prior but having no use, until now, to eat away dead skin.

Nobody breaks in to ask Friedman what he is talking about, but the respectful silence in the meeting room suggests that some people are confused by the chemistry buzzwords but are too shy to ask.

Friedman runs on. "The chemist came to me after we had the products developed for a short time and said, 'Lenn, you need to get this out to the public. You need to get this out so the public can learn about skin care. You can educate them the same way you were educated and people can finally use something healthy.' "

Pineapple had other quick benefits, he says, recalling the stinky pine-tar baths: "We could have a great romantic life for a change because she didn't feel like a greased pig anymore."

Friedman dreamed up twenty-two other lotions and potions, a few of which he has on hand in small sample jars for all to touch, rub, and smell.

There's also a pure white tanning lotion that turns a ghost into a "California beach bum" in nine hours and lasts for ten days, won't wash off, is harmless, and costs seventeen dollars for six ounces.

There's a hair revitalizer that will "almost triple hair in a matter of months," and a dandruff shampoo that cannot yet be shown, he says, because the product awaits Food and Drug Administration approval, plus a concoction that can remove stretch marks and surgical scars.

And this is just for starters. He plans to issue a perfume, dropping names of movie actresses dying to lend their name to the line. Next to debut: sportswear and bikini swimwear with "Hawaiian" printed over the cup and "Secrets" etched over the crotch. He promises a new product line every three months.

But the pride of his fleet is the breast cream, which he asserts is the "number one" cosmetic sold in Europe and Asia, a balm women need "to properly care for their breasts." The cost of the cream is twenty-six dollars an ounce, forty-four dollars for two ounces.

The fragrance—alluring, sensual, *fleur blanche*—"smells the way I want a woman to smell when I go to bed," and it lasts fourteen to sixteen hours.

Regular application will allow women to more quickly spot lumps, according to Friedman, which in turn could lead to earlier detection of breast cancer. Men will delight in applying this "fun product," he says, with a wink. Then he lobs the bombshell, coyly: "We can't make the claim but a number of women who have used this product have stated that it enlarged their breasts. . . . Women who are small breasted, real small breasted, will notice their breast size increasing. As a claim we can't make it, but it does happen." No doubt few, if any, women saw these results happen. A group of investors did see Friedman sent to prison in 1992 for violating a probation that forbad him from engaging in the sale of business opportunities.

Friedman's claims may seem outlandish, his bearing pompous, and his promises ridiculous, but they are not so terribly far from sales tactics that have earned millions of dollars for others. Cosmetics and other skin-care products, some of which come tagged with unsupported claims, are a more than $5 billion-a-year industry in the United States. And that does not include the telemarketing houses for whom suspect health products are a perennial favorite.

Cosmetics counters at upscale department stores carry skin-care products that range in price from $4.50 an ounce to $46.50 an ounce (with fancy French names and designer packaging) aimed at the aging skin of some thirty-seven million female baby boomers. Many of these products claim to shrink or ward off wrinkles and other signs of age, or imply benefits much the way Friedman does. Consider the fact that users may not be able to tell if one concoction yields better results than another, and the temptation to overstate claims in the packaging becomes clear.

One test conducted by the *Seattle Times* in 1994 seems telling. It concluded that few women can tell the difference between cosmetics, regardless of price, designer labels, or sales claims. The newspaper used thirty-six volunteers, aged thirty-eight to seventy, as testers and most could not tell the products or their effects apart.

Suspect products highly similar to Friedman's have sold furiously well in the past through mail-order advertisements in supermarket tabloids and women's magazines, and there is every reason to assume that they will continue to rack up sales.

In the early 1980s, a company called Robertson-Taylor claimed $2.2 million per month in sales of breast-enlargement creams, tanning tablets, and anti-aging products through mail order. The company czar, Mitchell Friedlander, who drove a Porsche and lounged around a plush Fort Lauderdale office complete with moving stock quotes, charged about eighteen dollars a jar for his concoctions. The entrepreneur fought off postal officials for years before they finally succeeded in shutting him down. In 1988 Friedlander pleaded no contest to state charges of operating a scheme to defraud. He entered his plea the day jury selection began for his trial. He was sentenced to a year in jail, which the judge suspended, a decision that disappointed prosecutors, who argued that the punishment was too lenient to deter others from setting out to scam the public. But the size of his earnings testifies better than anything to the allure of miracle cures—whatever the price.

Lenn Friedman hoped to build on previous sales schemes, a point he trades on to persuade people to sign up for the Hawaiian Secrets sales plan. The royalty scheme is based on other so-called multi-level marketing companies that rank their sales agents by volume.

Friedman's sales personnel will inherit royal titles based on the amount they sell and the number of new people they persuade to become distributors. The original distributors continue to draw commissions off sales from their "downline," the new generations of agents they bring into the company. That pyramid-like chain of sales commission is how associates who get in the company early on will wind up fishing in Tahiti, waiting for their monthly check to arrive.

Friedman adds other touches that set his scheme apart from others. He promises his subjects that they can get rich either by aggressively recruiting new sales people, by selling products themselves door-to-door, or through the company's fleet of telemarketers.

Friedman speaks so fast and sales tallies spill from his mouth so quickly that nobody seems able to keep up with or contradict him. And that fact, of course, is the secret to his success. Friedman is a veteran telemarketer and con artist who knows every facet of the fraudulent phone-sales racket. His visit to Midland concludes with his last-minute boarding of a flight to his home in Phoenix. He almost misses the plane because he can't stop spouting his sales pitch at the airport waiting lounge, trying to win over a single convert who is wavering in deciding whether to join Friedman's "palace guard" of investors.

A short time after his departure, at least six west Texans, working-class people, wish they never had heard of Lenn Friedman.

Two Arizona public servants were not present in the West Texas desert on the chilly December night Friedman arrived to pitch his skin products. Had they been there they might have let the folks listening to Friedman know a little about the man before his ascent to royalty. One is a probation officer, the other an assistant district attorney in Phoenix who had spent several years trying to bust Friedman.

"Friedman felt he deserved a certain lifestyle and he needed money to promote it," says probation officer David Wilcox. "He's one of these guys who comes across very well if you're looking to make a little bit of money, but he will separate the money from your wallet."

Adds Assistant State Attorney General Sheila Sundlof: "I don't know him to have ever done an honest day's work in his life. He has total delusions of grandeur and he's famous for name dropping. He takes on the trappings of people who sound impressive."

She must admit that Friedman's jabberings can be endearing, though he is a scoundrel who sidles up to the unaware and steals their dreams of quick riches. "He's the consummate salesman, very bright, and can sell anybody anything."

Truth is an early casualty in Friedman's sales campaign, a layer of lies that become bolder and bolder as he gets revved up.

While he opened his Midland speech by relating a harrowing tale of being captured by the North Vietnamese regular army and tortured alongside a Texan, he never saw anything like that kind of action. He did spend three years in the U.S. Army, where he served in the medical corps. At other times he has boasted of working as a CIA operative in Central America—poppycock according to authorities.

If he spent any amount of time in the Hawaiian Islands and traveling Europe on his breast-cream mission, he did so in violation of a strict probation that barred him from leaving Arizona following his guilty plea on state fraud charges. Then again, Friedman admitted violating his probation by traveling to Idaho. On another occasion he was detained by authorities in South Florida as he prepared to board a flight for the Bahamas.

Contrary to what an associate told the Midland crowd, Friedman did not spend much of his youth bedridden by a rare disease that ate away at the bone in his leg and left him unable to get any schooling until age nine. Nor did he race through grades kindergarten through twelve in three years and graduate at age thirteen, as he claimed. He spent only three weeks in traction, according to family members.

Friedman was born in Huntingburg, Indiana, on May 2, 1951, according to a pre-sentencing report in the Arizona fraud case. He dropped out of high school in the eleventh grade. He received a high-school equivalency certificate in the army, but never completed college, despite his claims to have done so. While Friedman says he attended a number of college classes in accounting, low self-esteem made him drop out. He blames his lack of self-worth on being the adult child of alcoholics.

Friedman claims to have been raised amid other family troubles, including child abuse. Yet his own brother says he is a liar who once stole his credit card and ran up a $4,000 bill on it, according to court papers. Friedman admits other problems, such as habitual use of at least five prescription drugs, Valium among them. He also takes Percocet, a narcotic painkiller, for treatment of carpal-tunnel syndrome, a condition caused by use of the arms and hands for repetitive tasks.

Friedman's court papers also disclose that he has been married to six women, two of whom took the trouble to write letters on his behalf to beg a judge to keep him out of jail. One wife called him a "true pacifist" while another said she had "never known him to intentionally break the law."

His criminal record dates to his early twenties. Arrested in Jasper, Indiana, in July 1976 on a misdemeanor charge of theft, he paid restitution. Extradited in December 1981 from Kentucky to Arizona to face a felony theft charge, he was placed on probation for five years and, once again, ordered to make restitution to his victims.*

Ironically, Friedman's probation report suggests that keeping him out of jail might be a good idea, even though he is described as a major risk to "re-offend." The report's author based his conclusion on the belief that

---

*State of Arizona v. Leonard Gregory Friedman, CR 90-00381, Pre-sentence investigation, May 16, 1991.

the criminal justice system's primary goal should be to win restitution for Friedman's victims. Soon-to-be victims of L. G. Friedman and Associates, of Phoenix, one of several scams that bear his imprint, might wish the judge had sent Friedman to jail in the early 1980s.

L. G. Friedman and Associates opened in August 1986, according to Friedman, as an outgrowth of his volunteer work helping the poor in South Phoenix fill out their income tax returns. While Friedman possesses no formal training in tax matters, he has from time to time represented that he has, once telling associates that he was a tax attorney, according to law enforcement files.

One of his tax clients won millions of dollars in a personal injury lawsuit filed after one of the man's daughters died and another was crippled. Friedman became the family advisor, and persuaded the patriarch to sign a power of attorney giving Friedman control over the family finances. Friedman said his motives were to save the family from frittering away its entire fortune. He also helped family members get drivers' licenses, resolve squabbles, and kept them from drinking to excess. He described the parents as "very heavy alcoholics, violent, abusive, and functionally illiterate," in court papers Friedman filed on his behalf.

Friedman took more than $100,000 from the family's savings and invested it in his new enterprise, L. G. Friedman & Associates. He told the family he planned to become an investment counselor to other litigants in civil cases who were awaiting large jury verdicts, but needed money to tide them over until they received their awards. Friedman decided to lend his clients money at 14.1 percent interest and bill them for his counseling time, as well as hiring social workers to manage human problems.

Friedman quickly built on the $100,000. Just before Christmas 1986, he met a woman about to receive a hefty divorce settlement; she was eager to invest.

L. G. Friedman eventually brought in more than $300,000 from investors, including the first couple for whom he had power of attorney. But he loaned out only $53,000. Friedman squandered the rest on vacations, payments on a Jaguar and Corvette for company officers, and a waterbed for Friedman's apartment.

Friedman pleaded guilty in April 1991 to a single felony count of "fraudulent schemes and artifices," a violation of Arizona law. Sentenced to seven years probation and ordered to make restitution of $180,273 to victims, he began making payments of $275 a month. He also was ordered to do five hundred hours of community service, and was forbidden from telemarketing, selling investments, or managing the finances of others, court records state. In a twelve-page, single-spaced plea to an Arizona judge, Friedman admitted misusing investors' money, but he insisted his intentions were noble. "I really did start this company with the belief that I could do a lot of good for people in need and make money for everyone involved, including a good profit for my company and myself," he wrote.

But the venture left him in the red financially. By the time Friedman told the crowds in Midland of his travels throughout the Orient and huddles with Nobel Prize winners in pursuit of wonder cosmetics, he actually was behind in the rent on his Phoenix apartment and about to have his electricity shut off, according to probation officer Wilcox. He claimed monthly expenses of $2,400 and an income of $500 from doing odd jobs.

While describing himself all over Midland as the "owner" of the cosmetics company, his probation report is more modest. In it, he pins his prospects for repaying victims of previous scams on Hawaiian Secrets, a cosmetic marketing firm in which he "hopes to obtain an executive position."

How could anyone fall for Friedman's yarns and half-cooked sales concepts? Easy. Friedman is a master of what telemarketers call "weaving the dream." He knows how to manipulate people who are desperate to become upwardly mobile, and suspicious of a system they feel has cheated them out of the fruits of the American dream.

Crippled by self-doubt, his victims are ripe for the plucking. Friedman seems to sense the right tactic to make people buy. When he picks up that his group is hostile to "the establishment," he lets fly a quick joke: "How do you tell when a lawyer is lying? When his lips are moving." He gets a knowing laugh. But one woman who eagerly invested in Friedman's scheme now fails to see the humor. She had doubts and visited a local lawyer. After listening to her describe Friedman's scheme for about five minutes, the lawyer blurted out: "This sounds like a con scheme to me."

Friedman takes quick advantage of other emotions. When he hears a woman voice anti-abortion sentiments, he denounces with fury cosmetics that contain human placenta, apparently from aborted fetuses. He is not above dropping the comment "I have accepted Christ as my savior" amid religious people.

When he senses the need to answer a sales objection, he lets fly a totally new concept without as much as a moment's stumble. After a potential investor wonders how working people who are in between weekly paychecks will be able to pay cash for their cosmetics order,

Friedman unveils a Hawaiian Secrets "credit card" for customers. It comes with a $1,500 limit, leaving the customer with no reason not to reorder.

"John Doe can't tell you to come back on Friday when he gets paid," Friedman says, adding that the credit cards have no interest. "We want them to buy our products, not pay interest. If they don't pay in thirty days, then we send them to a collection agency."

Friedman sells on his feet, making up persuasive rebuttals as he moves along. It's a trait that sets him apart from many telemarketers who rely on scripted objections. It serves him well in Midland.

When a working man worries that the cosmetic company may be too good to be true, he shyly approaches Friedman, who presses him to let out his concerns. He does. The man wonders why Friedman, who claims to be such a bigshot sales executive, would turn up in west Texas.

Friedman explains with yet another yarn.

While hobnobbing with the likes of movie stars in Hawaii, Friedman made the acquaintance of a star-struck Austin man, who, unlike Friedman, needed to wait hours to get a shot at a celebrity autograph. Ever outgoing and generous, Friedman struck up a conversation with the commoner and let slip that he was in the cosmetics business. Bowled over by the grandness of Friedman's vision, the Texan introduced Friedman to a friend in Midland, who in turn brought in more of her friends. And that's how the salesman extraordinaire came to be sitting in a Midland investor's living room amid whining children and hopeful chatter.

But some remain uneasy. Friedman, who is claiming to have made $800,000 a month in multi-level sales, sure is short on trappings. He takes cabs around Midland, holds sales meetings at the airport while the public address system calls commuter flights, and dresses in unfashionable polyester. But he has a quick retort, finishing sentences for an investor who is both giddy at the prospects and wary at the same time. Here is a sample of Friedman's objections offered not so much to understand him as to show how he and like-minded schemers work and how to spot their tactics.*

How come you don't look rich?

"Some people say I do things wrong. They say I should get a very expensive office with a big desk and a big comfortable chair and a beautiful sec-

---

*Source: audio and videotapes recorded by investors, who turned them over to the Arizona Attorney General's Office.

retary and a huge telephone and just sit there in my office and talk to people all day long, while thirty or forty floors below me people are working. Maybe that's the way other people like to do business. . . . I know a lot of other people in a lot of other companies that had founded the companies and became their presidents and CEOs like to act that way, and maybe that's the way they want to be, and that's ok. I can't die for anyone so I'm not gonna tell them how to live. But equal to that they can't die for me, so I'm not gonna let them tell me how to live."

Is he one of us?

Friedman adjusts the pitch for the humble roots audience. The move exploits the sense of insecurity in the audience as well as the Horatio Alger nature of marketing and his man-of-the-people personality.

"I enjoy being with people, OK. I'm not any better than anyone else. I'm not any worse than anyone else. Yes, I've made as much as $800,000 a month in a partnership in my life before. I've also panhandled on street corners because I didn't have a place to live when I was living in my car. I was lucky to have the car. It was a 1972 Gremlin, so it wasn't even a very nice car, but I had it—at least it was a roof over my head, at least the back seat reclined so I could have some place to stretch out and sleep at night in the parking lot and not get picked up as a homeless person."

As he gets revved up, Friedman throws in a touch of the prodigal son. Nobody interrupts.

"And I was that way back in the 1970s. So, I mean, I've been a bum, I don't mean literally a negative bum, but I've been down on my luck. I got out of college and I did some good things. I made some money. I went out and I blew my money. I impressed more women than Carter's got liver pills. I blew more money on women than most guys would ever dream about in their life. I had a great time while I did it. But the money ran out and I ended up broke. I didn't know how to act for a couple of months so I ended up panhandling. So I've been down and I've been up, and I'll tell you what. I enjoyed the up a lot more than I did the down. But I also know that building a good multi-level company means that the top and the bottom must always be together. . . . That's the philosophy that founded this company. You get successful by making other people successful. You don't make them successful from sitting in an office somewhere and talking to them by phone. You get off your butt and meet the people. Jeez! that's the way you do it. If there's another way to do it, teach me! This is the only way I know."

Are we doing the right thing?

Friedman takes his pitch a step further, beginning to portray his venture as not only a sales opportunity but also a moral crusade and a chance to help one's fellow man, at least materially.

"Money doesn't impress me anymore, suits don't impress me anymore, what impresses me is honesty and quality of life. Those are the things that impress me. . . . Don't sign up unless you're willing to help other people. Let's make a lot of people happy!"

Are these products approved?

Others wonder whether Friedman has government approval for his products. They hear an outlandish story that telemarketers often drag out to imply that a government agency has blessed their project. Friedman skillfully rolls the line right off his tongue with barely a shrug and segues right back into the wonders of his breast cream. The Federal Trade Commission does not have any role in approving the sale of a product. It regulates only "unfair and deceptive" trade practices, and the agency frowns on anyone who implies that his product is endorsed by the government. Friedman doesn't seem to mind.

"We are approved by the Federal Trade Commission, which gives us permission to operate in all fifty states. We're also approved to sell in nineteen foreign countries right now. Japan is one of them. . . . The ladies in Japan are going nuts over the breast cream. (Laughs) They really are. You wanna know the funny part about it. Our suggested retail price is $44 for a 2-ounce jar. Now we men think that sounds like a lot of money, but I think you'll agree with me that most women don't think that's a lot of money. You know what this guy is selling it for in Japan, $219, and he can't keep it in stock. . . . There's no cost to join Hawaiian Secrets. That will keep us out of trouble with the attorneys general in all states."

Are we treating Mother Nature right?

Friedman repeatedly recycles popular telemarketing pitches. His products are all natural, contain no filler from animal fats, eschew animal testing, and protect the environment. He hammers the point home, once again showing his conviction and moral outrage.

"Who are we to take poor, unwilling, innocent animals just because their body parts make great filler for our cosmetics and skin-care products, and butcher them? We condemn Hitler and yet none of us stand any better with our animal rights records. That makes us hypocrites, doesn't it?"

Then comes the "save-the-earth" theme, so common because it works time after time on a wide variety of audiences.

"We also are very conscious about being earth friendly. . . . You can eat, I don't recommend it, any of our products. You can take it internally because all of the ingredients—almost all of them in every one of our products—are used as preservatives in many cases by the U.S. Department of Agriculture."

So devoted to saving the earth is Hawaiian Secrets that the company plans to use royal blue plastic bottles for their products and charge a ninety-cent deposit fee. Customers who send the bottle back for a refill will get back one dollar.

"Plastic is the worst pollutant in our entire environment. Plastic really kills more animals than anything else we got on this planet. I mean it is just killing them left and right. We're big on animal rights, no animal testing, no animal by-products, no animal fillers, no anything like that. We're really big on animals' rights and the ecology. We'll be the first company in the history of this country ever to pay you back more money than you paid in a deposit, and it's all to promote earth friendly and animal rights."

That said, the baron excuses himself to go outside and have a cigarette.

Why is this plan better?

The people gathered to hear Friedman in Midland know that multi-level schemes can collapse once the market gets saturated by too many distributors. In 1988 alone, U.S. postal inspectors shut down nearly a dozen of these schemes, which often closely resemble pyramid sales in which continued success occurs only as new entrants come into the program and pay a fee. Friedman says his policy of letting new franchise agents in for free will minimize the problem as well as keep his company on the right side of the law.

Friedman stresses that for early entrants multi-level marketing can mean awesome earnings. "This is not a ground floor opportunity," he says over and over, "it's subterranean." That's another common ploy of rip-off marketing schemes, playing both on greed and desire for exclusivity, the "mine-all-mine" syndrome. It's a variation of the "negative swelling" tactic mentioned previously in which sales agents make buyers feel they are special and privileged to be offered the opportunity ahead of others.

Friedman says the Midlanders will be among the first fifty investors in what promises to be a true cosmetics empire. Here's how sales agents ascend into the highest reaches of royalty and titles they earn along the way. Baron Friedman plans to move up fast by proving he is as good at selling cosmetics as investments. This is the commission structure, based on a concept known as "generations." The investor in the scheme is the first generation; people he or she persuades to enter the sales operation are the second generation, and so on.

Baron/Baroness: $500 a month in group sales. Six percent commission on self and first generation sales, 5 percent on remaining.

Count/Countess: $1,000 a month. Seven percent on first generation, 6 percent on second, 5 percent on remaining.

Duke/Duchess: $3,000 a month. Eight percent on self, 8 percent on first generation, 7 percent on second, 6 percent on third.

Prince/Princess: $12,000 a month. Twelve percent on first generation, 10 percent on second, 8 percent on third, 7 percent on fourth, 6 percent on fifth, 7 percent on others.

King/Queen: $50,000 a month. Fourteen percent on self and first generation, 12 percent on second, 10 percent on third, 8 percent on fourth, 7 percent on fifth, 6 percent on sixth.

Friedman says that the way the company will be structured, agents who do $50,000 a month in sales, by themselves or through the efforts of others, get back $7,000 a month in commission.

Once affiliates become kings/queens, they also are known as "ruling monarchs." If people they brought into the company reach that level of sales, they "break away," but the monarch still gets 5 percent commission off their sales.

The monarch is also a member of the "royal palace guard" that will govern the realm, and make all business decisions. These people will take as much as $12,500 a month from the labor of sales serfs who market the skin products across the country.

Will the product sell?

Hawaiian Secrets product jars come printed with a toll-free number: (1-800-X-X-A-L-O-H-A) that customers can use to reorder. The telemarketers will dispatch the order via overnight mail and credit the distributor with the sales commission.

Friedman's scheme at first glance appears to be a much better deal for the sales force, the group he is hoping to enlist at his Midland meeting, than similar companies selling cosmetics door-to-door. Later on, he will set up national telemarketing of his products, for telemarketing is the sales medium he knows best, and telephone sales promise to boost sales agents' incomes even more.

For now, his distributors will buy the products at 40 percent below the retail price, but their sales commissions will be figured on the retail price, giving them a substantial mark-up, far better than competitors offer.

The end result: while many multi-level marketing companies have a 52 percent profit margin, which means key executives and owners walk away with the lion's share of the proceeds, Hawaiian Secrets will be showing a profit of 18 percent for corporate. The difference, according to Friedman, will wind up in the pockets of the sales force, including himself, the top salesman. "To borrow a quote from our former President Abraham Lincoln, and God excuse me, Abe, for doing this, but this is a company of distributors, for distributors, and by distributors."

But the $20,000 generated by Friedman on behalf of Hawaiian Secrets during his swing through Midland ended up in his pocket. While Friedman claimed to have contracts with laboratories to manufacture the products, there is no evidence that anything other than the samples he brought to show off at the sales meetings ever was produced.

The money Friedman collected came from about a half-dozen citizens, would-be members of his "palace guard" who hoped to get in on the ground-floor opportunity and wind up fishing in Tahiti, just like Friedman promised. None of the money, which Friedman used for his expenses, was recovered.

"We should have asked a whole lot more questions," one investor later remarked in the session she taped with her lawyer.

Fortunately for the Midland residents, they video-recorded a number of sales dealings with Friedman, with the baron's full consent and even his appreciation. Friedman said he expected the videos to serve as a rough starting point for professionals who would be hired to film training sessions as the firm expanded.

Armed with several hours of taped evidence, the investors applied some of their determination to get rich quick to making sure Friedman paid a high price for ripping them off.

Once they learned of Friedman's past, they pressured Arizona authorities to take action against Friedman, whose sales activities were in apparent violation of his probation order. A Phoenix judge found he had violated his probation and sent him to prison to serve his seven-year sentence in July 1992.

"I think we saved a number of people from being victimized," says probation officer Wilcox.

Friedman walked out of the Arizona state prison at Perryville in August 1994, on parole and determined, he says, to steer clear of the scam life. "You need to realize I'm not getting involved in anything any more. Two years in prison has regimented my life for me and I'm not getting back into the 200-mile-per-hour lane," he says. "I've done some foolish things. I'm glad it's over and the debt is paid. I'm not going to get back into that lifestyle," he said in an interview within days of his release.

While Friedman admits to making mistakes in the cosmetics venture and telling some "tall tales," he insists the beauty potions were real and the marketing plan sound. The cosmetics would have been developed had the company been better financed, he says, though he is vague on key details. For instance, asked the name of the "Nobel laureate" chemist who assisted him in developing the creams, Friedman draws a blank. At the same time, he claims that "one of the largest labs in the Southwest," which he does not name, had endorsed the project.

Friedman, who says he will drive a cab if need be to earn an honest living, gets defensive about some parts of his sales yarn. One is his wife's vanishing psoriasis, after a native Hawaiian woman applied green pineapple to her skin.

"All of the story was very true," he insists. "In my mind, there was never any intent to deceive anybody. I stumbled across something that was a very viable product that could do a lot of people a lot of good."

He bristles at the suggestion that the cosmetics caper was simply a con job, then recovers and softens slightly, more hurt than offended. "If I look back on all the things I thought were scams, I see some that turned out to be successful products."

Friedman falls back on a defense employed by many health-product entrepreneurs when asked about documentation of the curative claims, in his case the purported magic powers of his breast-enlargement cream. In essence, someone had said they were true. Friedman does not say whether the people making these claims were paid to endorse the products or whether any scientific research sought to support the assertions.

"Those were the manufacturer's statements made directly to me. I called over to there and they sent me affidavits from women who said they had wonderful results," says Friedman. "How real they are I don't know, but they said they had wonderful results. Did I verify the information? No. But there was no need to doubt it."

Only Friedman knows whether he accepts responsibility for his actions, the first step, many believe, in going straight. He seems ambivalent. "I have never considered myself a criminal, though I know I have been one," he says, quickly talking on. "I never wanted to live this life, but we end up having to suffer the consequences of our actions. The important thing is that I have been able to stop that life and refuse to go back to it. I'm going to live by the rules. The price to pay was too expensive."

No doubt Friedman has reached that conclusion because he was caught and sent to prison for schemes related to the telephone trade. Others who have remained free have a different view, he points out.

"Telemarketing rooms are cash cows and people like to see the cash flow," Friedman says. "The majority play in as gray an area of the law as they possibly can. Anyone can get into the business for fifty dollars, and when there is that much money to be made that quick everybody becomes a whore."

Says Phoenix prosecutor Sundlof, who saw him rise to prosperity thanks to the telephone sales racket: "One day he had no money at all, and the next thing you know he's taking in money hand over fist in telemarketing," she said in an interview.

While Friedman says he has forsaken the phone life, he has left a legacy of legal cases that reveal a good deal about the inner workings of these racketeers.

Friedman's ill-fated swing through Midland was just another stop in a career that reveals many facets of illegal telemarketing, from vacation vouchers to low-interest credit cards. Tracking his movements across several states provides a rare look at how con artists get into the telemarketing racket and why they stay there.

Along the way, Friedman was able to tap into an underground network of list brokers, shady financiers, and low-level sales operatives ready to assist his ventures with few questions.

6

Helping Hands

On his first visit to an office suite in Scottsdale, Arizona in 1989, Leonard Friedman saw the way of his future as his host showed off $132,000 in cash, the proceeds from a newly born telemarketing boiler room.

Friedman took a good look around the three-room office complex. He saw more than a dozen young adults talking into telephones with energy, purpose, and results. They talked gullible people, mostly their peers, into paying $96 for a list of banks that offered low-interest credit cards, a list worth at most a dollar or two.

Open just two weeks, the boiler room posted impressive profits. A bulletin board listed 250 sales for the day, all by "kids" paid just four dollars an hour. The "kids" sounded like pros when it came to conning people out of their money. Friedman heard the youthful telemarketers falsely claim to be working for a local bank or major credit card company, lies that made their pitch believable.

The credit card scheme tends to target young working people who don't know that many banks are eager to issue new credit cards and charge unusually low interest rates to bring in new accounts. Nor do victims know that many newspapers routinely print the names of banks offering the lowest interest rates for credit cards. Some consumer groups also will provide the names for a small charge, usually a couple of dollars or less.

Friedman chanced into a hot new scam, one that still bedevils regulators every time the economy takes a dip. How many people fall prey to the credit card scam is hard to assess, but at least sixty companies in more than two dozen states have ripped off people for millions of dollars in recent years by peddling the product.

Sales tactics vary. Many sales rooms send out postcards to people with poor credit ratings, or a history of being denied credit. Here's one such pitch, similar to the one Friedman heard in Arizona:

I am pleased to notify you that due to your excellent credit history you are eligible to receive a MasterCard or Visa with an annual interest rate as low as 11.8%, *the lowest interest rate in the nation!!!* I am authorized to hold this rate offering for only 48 hours from the receipt of this notice, so call me immediately at (an 800 number).

The 800 number patched callers through to telemarketers who ticked off advantages such as "no annual fee" at most of "our banking institutions," a twenty-five-day grace period before bills came due and "cash advances" from automated teller machines. Many banks already offered some if not all of these "advantages," but customers believed they would get a new, cheaper credit card in exchange for paying a "processing" fee. The hard sell went on:

You may obtain both (a) low-rate Visa and MasterCard, you still will only pay a one-time processing fee . . . what we do is work with a variety of banks throughout the country that offer Visa and MasterCard to preferred customers like yourself at a lower rate.

Visa, based in San Francisco, won a federal court order in 1991 prohibiting an Alabama company from infringing on its trademark and from telling falsehoods, such as that the boiler rooms "work with" banks. The court also forbad telemarketers from calling customers "preferred" when they recited the same pitch to every person they called.

In court papers, Visa asserted that thousands of people paid from $79 to $200 for the list or a credit card application, if they got anything at all. Sometimes telemarketers threw in a short pamphlet on financial planning. A final insult: many of the telemarketers billed the customer's existing Visa card for the processing fee.

While the number of people who fall for these deals is not known, the Alabama company claimed to be able to generate more than fifty thousand orders a month, court records state. The company used a database of people who had been denied credit within the last month as a customer list.

The sales tactics used by the Scottsdale firm Friedman visited weren't much different, though the operation did not appear to be tied to the Alabama concern. The venture appealed to Friedman, who had met the company's owner through a former girlfriend. He had no ownership interest in the boiler room, but in the best traditions of the telemarketing hustle, he copied what he saw and went into business for himself.

In August 1989 Friedman set up American Bank Services in Phoenix.

That was less than six months before his indictment for scamming investors in L. G. Friedman & Associates, the venture in which Friedman promised to loan money to accident victims awaiting personal-injury awards for which he was convicted and sentenced to seven years' probation.

While he copied the credit card caper in most details, he added a few Friedman touches, such as throwing in tips on where to get the lowest car loans. He charged ninety-eight dollars for the package, two dollars more than the phone room that inspired him.

Despite his zeal, Friedman could not get American Bank Services running on his own. He didn't have to. He found plenty of help from a network of businesses, some legitimate and some not, which teach new telemarketers the tricks of the trade.

These firms are the "helping hands," a cluster of telemarketing allies whose role is little known to the public even though they are a major reason why phone fraud plagues the nation.

Hundreds of companies provide phone rooms with services they need to stay a few steps ahead of police and other regulators. The services include: sales scripts, mail and telephone lists, product shipping, and perhaps most important, a means to manipulate the banking system to launder the dirty money that rolls in.

Few of these firms see themselves as aiding or abetting a criminal enterprise, and many bristle at the suggestion that they do so. In fact, many allied businesses have a number of legitimate clients who need shipping and handling services. But others are fully aware that the materials they provide are being used to help defraud the public.

"It's sort of like going into a sports store to buy a gun," says Mark Moran of the Wyoming state attorney general's office. "The owner hopes you don't use the gun at a 7-Eleven in a holdup. Some of these people are selling loaded pistols and the question is what duty do they as suppliers have to protect the public?" Moran said in an interview.

Some helping hands boldly offer one-stop shopping for anyone who wants to set up a shady telemarketing scheme. One advertised in marketing journals "a complete range of professional capabilities" to help new boiler-room operators insure an "optimum return" on their investment.

These companies, called "turnkeys" in the telemarketing trade, do everything but dial the phones and recite the sales pitch; they design, print and mail postcards to drum up business, help hire telemarketers; furnish scripts; even find brokers willing to launder credit card receipts. Some of the firms charge hefty consulting fees or take a percentage of the earnings as commission.

It's hard to overstate the importance of mailers to the telemarketing racket. A May 1992 Louis Harris and Associates poll found that 92 percent of Americans had picked a prize-solicitation postcard from their mail. While two of three people threw the offers away, 31 percent responded, which projects to 53.6 million people. As public suspicion of cheesy prize offers increases, creators of these sales gimmicks churn out ever more elaborate—and deceptive—mailers.

The fact that telemarketers such as Friedman have easy access to these sales tools has long frustrated regulators, both state and federal. Yet only in the last few years have officials begun to crack down on copywriters and sales promoters who look the other way while supplying telemarketers with materials used to swindle the public.

The Federal Trade Commission fired a warning shot on behalf of the U.S. government in April 1990, as telemarketing fraud complaints were reaching epidemic levels. Barry J. Cutler, then director of the FTC's Bureau of Consumer Protection, in a speech delivered to credit industry officials in Washington said:

> We are also taking a closer look at the companies that supply and provide assistance to telemarketing boiler rooms. One of the problems of dealing with boiler rooms is their fly-by-night nature. Since they need only a few leased telephone lines to go into business, in many instances by the time we bring an enforcement action they have either moved or dispersed their assets. Some of these boiler rooms are set up and supplied by more established companies who profit from the underlying fraud. If these firms are held responsible for their own participation in the fraud, they will undoubtedly give more care to the decision whether and on what terms to deal with telemarketers. While we may not be able to eradicate boiler rooms, we can certainly make it harder for them to get going and to stay in business.

Cutler urged the credit industry to join in the fight against telemarketing fraud. And the federal agency, which has only civil powers and often gets criticized for taking too long to build cases against con artists, took some action.

Two cases show the change in enforcement strategy that began in the 1990s, though many critics still wonder whether the FTC lawsuits, which typically yield fines, can make a dent in the multi-billion dollar business.

The FTC in July 1991 settled a lawsuit filed against Promotion

Specialists, Inc., of Port Orange, Florida, charging the firm with telemarketing fraud for providing sales literature, phone sales scripts, and prizes used in a telemarketing promotion. The FTC charged that the firm's owners knew their materials were used to deceive the public.* The owners agreed to pay $200,000 to reimburse consumers as part of the settlement, in which they did not admit wrongdoing. They said they settled the suit to avoid a protracted and costly legal battle.

Precision Mailers of Bloomington, Minnesota, agreed in February 1993 to pay a $75,000 fine to settle an FTC lawsuit alleging the firm's postcards were deceptive. The FTC alleged that the company mailed as many as 8 million postcards a year beginning in 1984, promising prizes for attending sales presentations at two hundred time-share resorts.

The postcards, according to the FTC, puffed the value of awards, falsely claiming that recipients "will definitely receive either an S-10 Chevy Blazer or $5,000 CASH for attending a sales presentation." The visitors got a 35-mm camera worth about ten dollars; earrings worth a few dollars; or a certificate for a 45-inch widescreen projection system, which turned out to be a plywood box with mirrors, according to the suit.† The company did not admit wrongdoing.

Neither suit nor several others filed to crack down on affiliated businesses has come close to short-circuiting the telemarketing network's vast nerve center. State attorneys general have had even less success, mostly because many of the helping hands operate in several states at once.

Some telemarketers conduct business, from shipping products to calling customers, in as many as five states at once. Using a company in a distant state to distribute products, for example, allows the telemarketer to spread the blame when the goods don't arrive. It often takes regulators months to connect the dots.

Grand Marketing, a Houston outfit which has since closed, serves as an example. The Missouri state attorney general won a $14,000 fine and barred Grand Marketing from doing business in the state in 1992. Here's how it worked, based on state files.

1. As many as 5,000 people a week received postcards from a *Tarpon Springs, Florida,* mailing house, cards with a familiar refrain: "Congratulations. You have been selected to receive one of four gifts, a Chrysler LeBaron, $15,000 worth of vacation holidays, a cashier's check for $2,500, or a choice of a Sony music center with color television and $1,500 in cash."

---

*FTC v. Promotion Specialists, Inc., 00-479-CIV-ORL-19.
†FTC news release, February 1, 1993.

2. The phone number customers called to claim their prize rang in a *Houston* boiler room. Up to twenty operators pressured callers into paying $400-$500 for skin-care products or a 3D camera. Grand Marketing claimed it had paid fifty dollars for the skin products and $124 for the cameras. Sales agents took home fifty dollars a sale; the company got the rest.

3. Customers paid for their products by giving telemarketers their credit card or bank account numbers. Grand Marketing funneled the numbers through brokers in *Dallas* and *Las Vegas* to a *Chicago* company that processed the billings in exchange for 20 percent of the gross. The Chicago processor assumed part of the risk that many customers would later dispute the charges and demand their money back. Grand Marketing used credit card processors as far away as *England.*

4. Grand Marketing mailed its goods from a warehouse in *New Orleans.* Nobody won the car, stereo system, or the cash. All got the "$15,000 vacation holidays," which turned out to be a travel voucher that Grand Marketing purchased for forty dollars. To use the voucher, the customer had to buy two airline tickets at sky-high prices from a *California* firm.

When dealing with a company that spreads its various departments over five states, and perhaps a foreign country, the customer can have a tough time figuring out where to call to complain if merchandise fails to arrive or falls short of expectations, as it often does. The customer's long-distance phone bills can rival the cost of the product. It's such a problem that many consumer advocates advise the public to steer clear of any firm that operates portions of its business in several states.

Friedman was one of many telemarketers who tapped into the network of helping hands, moving across several states in the process. His first service: a list of who to call.

List brokers are another boiler-room ally because sales leads are the lifeblood of any telemarketing room, the main way to keep the phones ringing.

Selling names and phone numbers is legal, though some may question the ethics of certain types of sales. The sellers range from underworld brokers who prey upon elderly and senile "reload" victims to corporations that provide instant lists of elite groups such as wine connoisseurs, time-share owners, public relations executives, or just about any other groups targeted for sales or political campaigns.

Regulators argue that list brokering can condemn people who bought from a telemarketer in a weak moment to incessant calls from even more telemarketers. Exploitation seems certain when lists are sold naming elderly people who have purchased water purifiers or other suspect products. One company charged five cents a name for a list of 6.1 million Americans who were often late in paying their bills—good candidates for a loan or credit-repair scam.

An ad in a marketing trade journal for the list of forty thousand people who filled out entry forms to win a $500 sweepstakes promoted by a Las Vegas firm in late 1990 puts the issue in perspective. A broker offered the list to new marketers at eight cents a name at the same time at least one state attorney general was demanding refunds for consumers ripped off by the sweepstakes scheme.

Friedman, in setting up American Bank Services, tapped into lists of previous telemarketing victims. He turned to a Las Vegas businessman to buy the names and phone numbers of five thousand people taken in by the water purifier scam in the past. He paid twenty cents for each name.

Friedman also bought from a Fort Lauderdale company called Hot Lists, located in the same building as Fun 'N' Travel, the travel-certificate company operated by felons Stan Cohen and David Wood. In fact, Wood acted as a broker for Hot Lists when he sold Friedman nine lead sheets, each with five thousand names, for fifteen cents a name, according to statements Wood gave to Arizona authorities.

Police raids on boiler rooms often yield colorful lead sheets, many containing scrawled notations to help telemarketers remember key points about suckers they will attempt to re-sell at a later date. Sometimes they reveal something about the personalities of phone pros. Lead sheets seized from an Alabama telemarketer clued cops in to the salesman's bad intent. Handwritten notes next to one elderly woman's name and number: "lady good for $1,500 to $2,000 a call." Another read: "I sold this guy three quarter-ounce gold coins for $6,000. Some fucking genius."

But the telemarketer's biggest challenge remains finding a steady means to convert credit card numbers to cash, in other words, a back door into the nation's banking system.

Banks have a secret they don't much like to talk about: they can be deceived, easily and often, by telemarketers and their allies.

The vulnerability of banks to telemarketing fraud, both through misuse of credit cards and checking accounts, stems largely from the financial industry's desire to keep money moving through them. Banks would rather sustain occasional frauds than accept new laws that would slow down the movement of money, which might inhibit commerce and put a dent into profits.

Companies from hotel chains to airlines to catalog-sales outfits would have a tough time staying in business without taking customers' credit-card numbers over the telephone and presenting them for payment to a bank, even though nothing exists in writing to prove that the consumer authorized the purchase. Similarly, banks accepting checking account debit slips without the account holder's signature rely on the integrity of the merchant.

"Banks perpetuate the myth that people's money is safe," says John Barker, head of the Alliance Against Fraud in Telemarketing in Washington, a consumer-advocacy group. Barker says his agency has tried without success to persuade the industry to crack down on abuse of customer accounts by telemarketers.

Nobody knows the full extent of credit card frauds in the nation, but it appears to be "quite prevalent," according to a 1992 Louis Harris and Associates poll, which concluded that 7 percent of past and present credit card holders, 9.2 million people, had been the victims of credit card fraud.

Visa and MasterCard alone estimate annual losses of $300 million to improper use of credit cards by phone marketers, most of which is shouldered by banks, which then pass the charges on to the public through higher fees.

The schemes telemarketers set up to bypass the banking industry's security devices are legion. But they almost always begin in the same manner: telemarketers talk customers into reading their credit card numbers over the phone. Ruses vary, especially since consumer groups have been warning the public for years to *never* give out their credit card numbers to someone who calls them peddling a product.

The warnings seem to be having some effect. The 1992 Louis Harris poll found that only about 2 percent of American adults said they were "very likely" or "somewhat likely" to give out their credit card number to callers who stated they needed the number for identification or to prove the cardholder's financial reliability. But the percentage willing to recite their card number doubled among adults with less than a high-school education and incomes below $15,000, the poll found.

Once telemarketers have the credit card numbers they can use them to bill the customer's charge account repeatedly. Customers often are billed twice for products, such as vacation certificates. Telemarketers who engage in this fraud know that customers won't discover the overbilling until they receive their monthly statement. Some will contest the charge, but others won't, either because they don't know that federal law gives them 60 days to dispute a credit card charge, or because they don't want to bother or they are too embarrassed.

Some boiler rooms shut down before the credit card companies can catch up with them, or a customer's credit card numbers may wind up for sale on a black market to more con artists who tap the card for large sums.

"Once in possession of consumers' credit card numbers, some telemarketers turn around months and years later and use these account numbers to submit unauthorized charges whenever their businesses need an infusion of cash," says Federal Trade Commission official Cutler.

The only sure way to avoid straying into this marketing minefield is to *never* give out a credit card number over the phone, unless booking a hotel or other reservation, or buying from a known business. Even then, a consumer is not safe from credit card fraud or other misuse of the banking system.

Bank account debit drafts, called a "demand draft," also cause big problems for consumers. Telemarketers get customers to read off the numbers of their checking account, then fill out a draft and present it for payment, without the customer's signature.

"Under no circumstances should you give information about your bank accounts to phone solicitors," warns former Washington Attorney General Ken Eikenberry. Many prize telemarketers, according to Eikenberry, will try to talk the numbers out of their victims. "Fortunately, consumers can order their banks to stop payment on these drafts. But the bad news is that banks charge a fee for this service," he says.*

And many consumers find that their banks try to talk them out of canceling a demand draft because the bank will lose money it has already paid out to a telemarketer.

One South Carolina firm, Mandy Enterprises, offered people help in finding new credit cards by joining its "Credit Today" program. Members paid $98 to $128 by reading off the numbers of their checking accounts, which the firm used to prepare an auto debit. The FTC dragged the firm into court in 1991, asserting that the sales pitch misled consumers because it failed to advise them that the credit cards they received must be secured with a minimum deposit of $350 in a New Jersey bank.

But the processing of credit card sales remains the method of choice for laundering telemarketing receipts, largely because the charge card is so pervasive and its misuse next to impossible to police adequately.

Customers demand the convenience of slapping down plastic to pay

---

*Ken Eikenberry, "Consumer Alert," April 24, 1991.

a dinner tab, department store purchase, even a fill-up at the gas station, and so many businesses must honor charge cards.

Here's how the system works. Businesses apply to banks to open merchant accounts allowing them to accept credit cards. The banks charge the merchant about 1 to 3 percent of the transaction's value as a service fee. When merchants present credit card slips to the bank, the bank immediately credits their account, minus the service charge. This gives the business a ready means to convert credit card receipts to cash.

The system works well most of the time. Visa, which boasted worldwide sales of $259 billion in 1989, the year Friedman started up his phone room, reported fraud rates of about one-tenth of 1 percent of total sales. Yet that figure amounts to $259 million. The system can be thwarted by con artists—telemarketers are among the worst offenders—who sell under false pretenses and obtain payment far in advance of the receipt of merchandise.

Telemarketers are notorious for failing to send merchandise they bill for, for sending shoddy goods, or for double and even triple billing customers. Banks discover the fraud when large numbers of customers demand a refund, but that often does not occur for at least a month after the purchase date, giving telemarketers plenty of time to rack up a huge volume of sales, get paid for them by their bank, shut down and skip town, or reopen under a new name.

If the bank cannot collect from the telemarketer it winds up taking a loss because federal law requires banks to reimburse consumers who dispute a fraudulent transaction billed to their card.

Banks call these demands for refunds "chargebacks." Most monitor their accounts to make sure the level of refunds stays less than 1 percent of sales. Some boiler-room operators have posted chargeback rates of 50 percent or higher.

Banks generally won't divulge losses due to telemarketing fraud, but at least one Arizona bank failed because it signed up too many phone-sales firms. The Gateway National Bank in Phoenix began processing credit card receipts for telemarketers in January 1989. By September of that year it was in such deep trouble that the Comptroller of the Currency, the nation's top bank regulator, ordered the bank to get rid of its "high risk" clients.*

The bank failed to listen, according to government officials, and went under. Government records cite losses of at least $1.5 million. In February

---

*Comptroller of the Currency news release, Washington, D.C., February 10, 1992.

1992 the Comptroller of the Currency announced that three of the bank's officers had signed an agreement with the government permanently banning them from banking. None of the executives, who also paid fines of $5,000 to $15,000, admitted wrongdoing. Neither did five of the bank's outside directors, who consented to fines of $5,000 each for failing to make sure the bank complied with the government's order to quit handling the high-risk accounts.

As is nearly always the case with a bank failure, U.S. taxpayers wound up footing the bill. The Gateway National Bank failure also prompted the Federal Deposit Insurance Corporation to warn banks that while the "profit potential to banks can be very attractive," from processing credit cards, lax monitoring of merchants can be devastating.*

Many banks protect themselves from phone frauds by refusing to open merchant accounts for any business that derives 25 percent or more of its revenues from telemarketing or mail-order sales.

For its part, Visa tracks more than 3.5 million merchants authorized to accept its credit cards by identifying companies with chargeback rates that are above 1 percent of total sales.

Companies that exceed the 1-percent threshold, twelve times the norm for Visa merchants, get a chance to clean up their act. If they don't, they can be barred from opening future Visa merchant accounts. Visa officials in 1992 reported finding two hundred merchants with excessive chargeback rates. While the numbers were small, each merchant manipulating the system could cause millions of dollars in losses.

But the lure of quick profits from credit card processing hooks banks, and despite growing wariness, they still toy with telemarketers, often using intermediaries.

Called independent-service organizations, these outfits approach banks on behalf of telemarketers and others unable to obtain merchant accounts. The service organization promises to cover any chargebacks and the bank goes along, believing it can't lose.

In turn, the service organization requires the telemarketer to escrow large cash reserves to cover demands for refunds. FTC official Cutler in the April 1990 speech alleged the service organizations often are "the middlemen in the fraudulent telemarketing scheme," adding:

> Unfortunately, when the telemarketer is engaged in fraud, the consumer may not realize that he or she has been duped until weeks or months after the sale has been processed. The chargebacks mushroom at breath-

---

*Advisory, Comptroller of the Currency, March 29, 1990.

taking speed to catastrophic levels. The reserve is quickly depleted . . . .
Our investigations have shown again and again that it only takes one bad
merchant to cause a real financial catastrophe.

Cutler concluded his speech to the credit-industry executives by
threatening to file lawsuits against banks or service organizations that
knowingly profited from telemarketing fraud, or failed to warn other
financial institutions of fraud schemes. He cited an example:

> In one case, a bank accepted sales drafts from a fraudulent merchant
> that, over a six-month period, generated chargebacks and returns at rates
> ranging from 43 to 53 percent. When the bank finally had enough and
> told the merchant it was closing its account, it passed the merchant on
> to another unsuspecting bank with a glowing letter of reference from an
> officer of the bank. The second bank subsequently sustained losses well
> into the hundreds of thousands of dollars on the account.

The Federal Trade Commission did take action against one service
organization which had processed credit card receipts from several of Las
Vegas's premier prize rooms.

In December 1993, Electronic Clearing House, Inc. (ECHO), of Las
Vegas and Agoura Hills, California, settled FTC charges that it aided and
abetted deceptive prize promotions telemarketers, including mega-mar-
keter Pioneer Enterprises, by processing credit card transactions. The
agreement barred ECHO from ever dealing with prize telemarketers or
from assisting any telemarketer who it knows employs a misleading sales
pitch.*

ECHO did not admit any wrongdoing. Under the agreement ECHO
must conduct monthly audits of any telemarketers it contracts with whose
monthly sales exceed $30,000 and sever ties with any marketers its audi-
tors find to be engaged in deceptive sales practices.

The FTC struck again in 1992 at companies that profit off suspect
telemarketing transactions, this time suing a subsidiary of Citicorp.

The FTC charged Citicorp Credit Services, of Long Island City, New
York, with aiding and abetting deceptive telemarketing by processing
credit card slips for a travel club. The FTC claimed the processor knew
that the travel club billed customers after they canceled their member-
ships, failed to issue refunds, and "was subject to continuing investigation
by government agencies."

---

*FTC v. Electronic Clearing House, Inc., U.S. District Court, District of Nevada, No. CV-S-
93-01218-LDG.

The FTC alleged that Citicorp Credit Services officials knew that one of four travel-club members had demanded refunds, more than twenty times the industry average for credit card refund requests. In a settlement agreement announced in November 1992, the processor agreed in future to more closely monitor refund rates for companies it contracts with.* The company paid no fine or other penalty. Citicorp has since sold the processing company.

Many telemarketers never bother to seek out a service organization to process their credit charges because they don't want to post cash reserves. They turn to a dirtier set of helping hands, brokers who are expert in deceiving banks and credit card companies through a laundering system called "factoring."

The practice, illegal in about a dozen states, is another reason why unlawful telemarketing flourishes. Many consumer advocates feel that phone fraud will persist until Congress bans the practice nationwide and imposes tough criminal penalties on violators. But efforts to do that have died repeatedly amid lobbying by special interests. However, the FTC won new power to ban the practice through regulations in a telemarketing reform law signed by President Clinton in August 1994. The regulations should be written some time in 1995, but nobody is certain whether civil penalties will deter the large-scale factors, particularly ones with international connections.

In the meantime, wily marketers have devised a number of means to get around the factoring laws of many states, some of which are so vague they seem unenforceable. Other factors are looking to become international, hoping to put themselves outside the reach of U.S. authorities.

Factoring occurs when someone possessing a merchant account agrees to process credit card receipts from another entity, in exchange for a hefty percentage of the gross. In effect the merchant buys credit card sales slips at a discount and launders them through his account. Consumers can recognize factoring when they purchase goods using their credit card from one firm, only to see a different company name appear on their monthly bill.

Credit card companies argue that factoring provides telemarketers another back door into the financial system, allowing them to loot banks. Increasingly, they worry about international factoring operations that can take months to become apparent to banks.

---

*FTC news release, November 19, 1992, FTC File Number 892 3033.

Visa, which has issued more than 286 million credit cards worldwide, argued its case against a Culver City, California, company called National Approval Center. Visa won a federal court injunction in 1992 preventing the firm from using merchants in Europe and Asia to launder at least $2.75 million in sales receipts from American telemarketers.*

National Approval Center placed advertisements in international publications, including the *International Herald Tribune,* for foreign merchants willing to launder Visa slips for 9 percent of the gross, Visa alleged in its lawsuit. One British bookseller in a two-week period processed $295,000 worth of credit card receipts for American telemarketers, only to see 578 of the 650 sales disputed by cardholders as fraudulent, a chargeback rate of 89 percent. Another company in the United Arab Emirates laundered $417,700 in phone sales of luggage and travel packages, two-thirds of which later were disputed.

Factors in this country generally charge higher rates than their international counterparts.

The Arizona boiler room copied by Friedman paid 30 percent of gross value for factoring of credit card slips. The phone room used a Phoenix man who specialized in setting up merchant accounts and had accounts open at banks in California, Nevada, Arizona, Utah, and Florida, according to Friedman.

Friedman got a better deal. He found a broker in Utah who agreed to factor the Visa slips from the American Bank Services scheme, taking 20 percent of the gross. Friedman's telemarketers filled in customers' credit card numbers on blank slips, which Friedman forwarded to the broker via private courier. After cashing the slips at his bank, the broker returned cashier's checks to Friedman, minus the service charge.

The bank caught onto the scheme after a few months because of the high number of chargebacks. It froze the broker's accounts to recover some of the losses. Friedman said he referred other telemarketers to factors. All told, his referrals led to the laundering of about $700,000 a week in credit cards through the underground banking network.

Friedman also became embroiled in allegations of factoring in Illinois when he set up a travel agency called VESA Travel Services outside Chicago in 1990. At the time, Friedman was under indictment in Arizona. The modest travel agency hawked the familiar Omega Fun 'N' Travel Bahamas vacation vouchers, making about three hundred sales in three weeks. Friedman charged $429 for the travel package.

*Visa International Service Association v. Sheldon Katz, et al., U.S. District Court Central District of California, 92-4953.

Friedman said he accepted personal checks for the packages while waiting to get approved for a merchant account. But an Illinois businesswoman said Friedman stung her with bad credit card slips. She met Friedman after she listed her travel agency for sale.

Friedman said he wanted to buy the agency and, as part of the deal, persuaded her to deposit $25,787 worth of credit card slips from sales of the Bahamas cruise package in her merchant account. She kept 8 percent for processing the receipts and gave Friedman a cashier's check for the difference. She drowned in chargebacks from Friedman's sales, and lost her merchant account as a result. The woman detailed her accusations in a letter to the Arizona judge who sentenced Friedman in the accident-victims case.

Friedman never faced any charges as a result of the alleged factoring. Nor did his low-cost credit card telemarketing operation draw any jail time. Under his plea agreement on the 1990 Arizona fraud charges, the Arizona state attorney general's office reserved the right to bring charges against Friedman for American Bank Services. But no charges were brought in the case. Friedman moved on to become the breast-cream baron.

Even telemarketers with merchant accounts, or easy access to processors, worry about the time lag between sales and chargebacks. They know the system encourages their sales agents, all of whom work on commissions, to lie or overstate the product to cinch a deal. When commissions are paid out weekly, the telemarketing-room owner can lose money if chargeholders dispute the charges and void the sale a month later. By that time the agents who made the sale can be long gone. Some phone rooms hold commissions in reserve to cover "bad" sales. Others try to rely on checks— the last part of the banking system that telemarketers have learned to manipulate.

As we know, many telemarketers try to persuade clients to send them bank cashier's checks, which are as good as cash and cannot be canceled. One boiler-room veteran estimated that $50,000 in sales a week via checks delivered through overnight mail equals out to $70,000 to $80,000 in credit cards, because so many credit card holders exercise their rights to dispute the charges at a later date.

But regulators worry that more and more boiler-room operators are taking advantage of the personal checking account, which they can tap to steal money without the account holder even knowing about it. With 79 percent of American adults having checking accounts, the system is a potential gold mine.

"There is this myth that the checking account is sacred," says Barker, of the Alliance Against Fraud in Telemarketing. "That's bull. There is so much paper in the system that nobody takes the time to look at it."

The major problems stem from automatic debiting. About one of four checking account holders have some payment automatically deducted from their accounts, according to the 1992 Harris poll. Of this group, 2 percent said they had money withdrawn from their account without their permission.

Telemarketers who obtain checking account numbers are coming up with new ruses, which often seem reasonable, such as saying the numbers are needed to verify that the customer is "qualified to participate in the sales promotion."

Once the phone agents get the numbers, and present an electronic debit at the bank, the account-holder many not learn about the draft for a month and may inadvertently overdraw the account, resulting in bad-check charges.

As with credit cards, the banks would rather not delay the movement of money by requiring a signature for every check transaction. But many consumer advocates believe something must be done to prevent a person's credit rating from being damaged because of a bogus bank draft, especially when the customer did not know the draft occurred.

Take one Florida diet-pill company, which advertised nationwide with an 800 number on television. In June 1992 Bob Crawford, Commissioner of the Florida Department of Agriculture and Consumer Services, warned against automatic debiting by the Boca Raton marketer called Choice Diet Products. Consumers, Crawford said in a news media release, thought they were authorizing a charge of $9.95 plus $3 shipping for the product, only to find out their checking accounts had been debited for as much as $300. He cited twenty-six complaints against the company, noting that some had been resolved. The company blamed the problem on an affiliate.

"Consumers should not reveal their bank account numbers over the telephone," Crawford warned. "Divulging this information provides an opportunity for someone to make a withdrawal without the account holder's knowledge or authorization."

Many victims of automatic debiting need to take some advice from the National Consumer's League, which worries that victims often get talked out of contesting the charges by managers at their banks who want to avoid taking a loss.

"The big problem is that most consumers don't have any idea of their rights to dispute these charges. People don't know that if they gave out an account number they can go to the bank and stop payment on the check," says John Barker. Barker says that few people realize that the bank has the obligation to "restore funds" if done in a timely fashion when the bank has paid a draft from the account holder's account without a signature.

Says Barker: "We tell people that if the bank stonewalls, they must be brazen and demand their rights."

Barker relays the story of a sixteen-year-old girl who had authorized sixty dollars a month from her checking account through the year 2007 to purchase magazines from a telemarketer. "We hope that one of them is *Modern Maturity.*"

Many consumer advocates agree that the helping hands extended to the illicit telemarketing community must be withdrawn to protect the public. As it now stands, the network supports an endless array of rip-offs, leaving regulators in the uncomfortable role of sitting and waiting to see where the phone pirates will strike next.

Part Two

Words to the Wise

7

Voices in the Sky

Trusting and full of hope for life in a new country, Soviet immigrant Vulf Ikhlov made a perfect victim. An engineer who settled in Skokie, Illinois, Ikhlov needed a job and knew little about how to secure one in his new country. Coming from the Soviet Union, he had never heard of telemarketing fraud.

Ikhlov is wiser now, after losing $395 to a telephone-employment scam that promised him a job, but gave him only a run around.

"I got nothing but letters and excuses," said Ikhlov, now a manager at a Chicago warehouse. "People who had been living here longer told me not to send them money, but when you have just come here, you want to believe people."*

Ikhlov fell for one of the telemarketing racket's meanest dirty tricks—the overseas job hustle. It's one of three perennials that tend to hit people least able to afford it. The others are work-at-home scams and credit-repair and loan services. While the pitch varies year to year, the results never change: desperate people take another hard knock.

Personal finance is a good place to begin examining the many ways telemarketers draw on deceptive sales tactics, allied businesses, and weak consumer-protection laws to ply their trade.

Overseas Employment

Engineer Ikhlov hoped to land a skilled job that would fit his qualifications, but could not find one in Chicago. He was willing to go back overseas if need be. Ikhlov saw a chance with a newspaper classified ad.

---

*Interview with Vulf Ikhlov. Ikhlov lodged a written complaint with the Broward County Sheriff's Office Economic Crime Unit, Fort Lauderdale, Florida, on July 8, 1992.

Construction
Site Workers
18 mos. contract in Europe
$39.70-$66.50/hr.
HVC Group, Inc.
800-xxx-xxxx
Equal Opportunity Employer

Ikhlov made the call. While he did not know it, the number rang in a boiler room in Pompano Beach, Florida, which placed ads in big-city newspapers all over the country. A friendly voice on the line promised him a job. He agreed to send a bank check for $395 to the company via overnight delivery service to lock in his job. The voice called the payment an "application fee."

Six days later, a letter arrived asking Ikhlov to fill out an application for the position, a Superintendent II. The letter promised him a 7.75 percent hardship-pay allowance, fully paid accommodations for himself and his family, medical insurance, and a $25,000 life-insurance policy with his new job.

Excited that the benefits seemed so much better than those available in this country, Ikhlov felt lucky. But a week after lifting his spirits, the company brought them crashing down. Addressed "Dear Valued Client," the letter cut to the disturbing news quickly. The employer did not need more workers after all and so there was no job for Ikhlov. There also was no refund.

Despite his limited command of English, Ikhlov fought back. He demanded that the firm hold up its end of the bargain, writing: "If you are the honest people and really concern about what you are doing, and how you are doing, you have to send my money back. Otherwise it's look like you are deceiving people and hoping to get away with it."

Short of traveling more than one thousand miles to Florida, there was nothing else Ikhlov could do. Had he made the trip he would have found the employment agency to be nothing more than a phone bank on the maggot mile, the strip of sleazy phone shops where deceit and underhanded deals are standard operating procedure.

Ikhlov followed his letter with a phone call, only to learn that the employment broker's phones had been disconnected. His next call went to the fraud division of the Broward County Sheriff's Office. A detective filed the complaint, the sixteenth Fort Lauderdale-based overseas-employment scam to draw fire from customers across the country in 1992.

Oddly, Ikhlov felt better when he learned from police that the overseas racket rips off millions of dollars and turns up in at least a half-dozen other states every time the economy turns sour.

"I was not the only one who was so stupid," Ikhlov said.

Overseas-employment phone rooms are not to be confused with employment agencies. The legitimate companies that match candidates with jobs almost always collect from the employer, or require that the candidate and employer split the fee after the job is secured. Good job agencies keep in constant touch with prospective employers and secure up-to-date lists of jobs.

By contrast, the phone rooms require payment of $300 to $700 upfront, and many guarantee candidates a specific job, which often does not exist.

Many of the phone rooms call themselves "resume services" in order to avoid the need for state licenses. Trouble often comes, as it did for Ikhlov, when the phone room sends a written contract several weeks after taking the customer's money. Reading the fine print, the customer realizes the contract makes no guarantees of job placement and grants no refunds. In other cases, the firm does type up a resume, but never circulates it to employers. No matter how it gets expressed, the bottom line is the same: the customer gets no job.

The overseas-employment scam is perfectly suited to the South Florida boiler room, as dozens of such successful operations amply demonstrate. One set up shop in a hotel room in the chic Art Deco district of South Miami Beach. South Florida's reputation as a gateway to Latin America and the Caribbean adds veracity.

The room managers and verifiers play a key role in stalling callers who complain about not getting jobs. While the operators get their money from the customer via overnight mail, it often takes months before customers realize they have been taken.

Even when complaints begin flowing in, authorities often do little.

Angry callers who phone the local police must first figure out which city has jurisdiction. While many of the rooms use a Miami or Fort Lauderdale address, they are in fact situated within the limits of smaller cities, with small police departments.

More than fifty police agencies enforce the law in the honeycomb of cities and towns housing South Florida's 4.5 million people. Many small police departments are less than responsive to out-of-state complaints lodged against a local business. With few exceptions, police fraud units tend to view a dispute over a telephone employment opportunity as a civil matter, not criminal fraud. Police don't investigate civil matters and so the complaint can be filed away as part of what police call "intelligence files."

"We don't always catch on to what these boiler-room guys are doing and a lot of complaints about them get written off as a bad business deal," says Fort Lauderdale prosecutor Scott Dressler. "Police need to start seeing these complaints as crimes and that there are probably five hundred more victims out there. But too often these cases go uninvestigated."

While few cops will admit it, they have their hands full trying to solve crimes against local residents; they aren't terribly worried about the plight of someone living halfway across the country.

Others tempted by the overseas employment scheme have turned to the Better Business Bureau for guidance, or tried to. In South Florida, the lines were nearly always busy, a fact that the scam community banked on for years. Even if a caller managed to get through and obtain a "report" on a company, chances are it would be bland and not much help. Better Business Bureaus won't recommend or condemn a business. The most a caller will hear is that the bureau "advises caution" in dealing with any sort of advance-fee employment business.

That leaves the Florida state attorney general's office, housed in an enormous black stone edifice in the aging city of Hollywood, the hometown of Attorney General Bob Butterworth and his political stronghold.

That office's attorneys are so overwhelmed they can barely count the numbers of bogus agencies that crop up, and perhaps file a case against one or two of them, hoping others will turn and run. They almost never do.

"There are half a dozen telemarketing offers for every case we file," concedes Butterworth assistant Kent Perez.

The late 1980s were hothouse years for the overseas-employment scam, which appeared to drop off, then rebound when hard times hit in the early 1990s.

Racking up hundreds of complaints from aggrieved buyers, the employment scamsters had little to fear from the state of Florida. In the rare cases in which Butterworth filed suit and won a judgment, it was far from a victory for consumers.

Little has changed. The state often accumulates fifty or more sworn affidavits from victims prior to filing a lawsuit. Months go by as the attorney general's office waits for victims to return notarized affidavits. Scammers use that time to bilk several hundred thousand dollars from customers, then shut down. Some telemarketers don't even bother to answer a state lawsuit.

In many cases, it hardly seems to matter. The judgments go unpaid because by then the firm has long since disposed of any assets or its owners cannot be located.

The records of Universal Placement, one of the few overseas rooms whose principals faced criminal fraud charges, shows why the state needs to crack down.

The firm charged $675 for its services, far higher than most, and failed to deliver anything to buyers.

While the pitch might seem in hindsight to be too good to be true, it targeted people who had lost their jobs and were desperate to get back on their feet. The unemployed often are such easy marks that owners will hire rookie telemarketers to do their selling. The sales script passed out to new agents at Universal came with a phonetic pronunciation of "dossier," just in case they weren't familiar with the word. Many practiced telemarketers can handle the sales scripts easily, but not the remorse.

From the Universal script:

> We work in about 180 countries all over the free world along with 500 different companies. Our technical writing staff will prepare your international dossier (pronounced da-z-a) which is forwarded to the companies. And as soon as the company receives your dossier they will contact you or us directly to set up an interview. . . .
>
> The company will fly you to the nearest major city and discuss the length of your contract, departure date and benefits, which are normally 50-60 percent more than you make here in the U.S. They will also pay for your roundtrip airfare and hotel accommodations from Friday to Sunday, as most of the interviews take place on Sunday. . . .
>
> Also, you are exempt from taxes when you work overseas, you can earn $70,000 before you are taxed. Other benefits are free medical, free food, free housing, and free transportation. . . .
>
> Plus you get 2 weeks vacation in the nearest country free (and you can choose the country). After one year they give you 30 days vacation. They offer bonuses of 10-15 percent over your salary at the end of the year (which is extra thousands for you so you will stay with the company). . . .
>
> Now . . . we charge an advance processing fee of $675 which is reimbursed to you when you are overseas with the company. We guarantee you immediate overseas exposure. If you are not employed overseas within 12 months we will refund your entire annual dues and the processing fee is tax deductible on your income tax. There are a lot of positions available overseas through major American companies throughout the world. . . .

Do you have a resume? Go ahead and send me a copy of it. If you don't have one just send me a letter explaining your skills and work experience. In the meantime, I'll send you some information about our company, resume form, and information about overseas jobs and tax information. . . .

When you receive our information call us and we will arrange our courier to pick up all of the paperwork along with the processing fee of $675, a cashier's check made out to Universal Placement. If you have any questions feel free to call me. . . . We have a job waiting for you. Call us back when you can.

Universal slipped in a few clever clauses, such as giving itself a year to get a job for the customer at the same time its telemarketers intoned, "We have a job waiting for you." Tactics such as this forestall consumer complaints allowing the operation to sell undetected by authorities.

Universal's sales people also told customers to go out and get passports, and "wind down their affairs because they would soon be heading out." While making those claims, employees who compiled dossiers threw them into massive file cabinets, not even placed in alphabetical order. Police wondered how Universal could even find clients' records, let alone land them a job.

Being unable to afford the $675 fee did not always rule out a customer, at least when sales went slack. Some days telemarketers would accept a down payment in order to keep a sale from falling through. They also encouraged couples to apply together, saying it was "more economical" for Universal to place couples. Universal even gave couples a fifty dollar discount for signing up, so long as they sent their money by overnight delivery to avoid "lost opportunities."

Other false claims, according to prosecutors included:

• Australia, New Zealand, Britain, and France were "wide open" for construction with "lots of construction projects ongoing employing thousands of U.S. workers." The company also falsely claimed access to new projects in the Circular Quay area around Sydney and its surrounding harbor.

• One-year contracts could be renewed for a big bonus if workers agreed to stay on the job and workers would be flown to a large American city for interviews.

• Clients would have to be ready to go within six weeks. Many were told to dispose of cars, guns, furniture, and other personal possessions since their new employers would not pay to transport these items.

A federal grand jury in Miami indicted thirteen owners and associates of Universal Placement in March 1993 on fifty-five counts of mail fraud, wire fraud, and conspiracy. The indictment cited four hundred victims defrauded out of $200,000 in a six-month period, including victims from California, Utah, South Carolina, and Kansas, among other states.

None got a job for their money. One of the men indicted had already been indicted for running a second overseas employment room he modeled on Universal Placement. Those who pleaded guilty drew sentences ranging from four years' probation to two years in prison.

Other companies in the racket build credibility by dropping names of large-scale construction projects in tiny Caribbean islands, sending out letters bearing overseas return addresses, or claiming to be representatives of prominent employers.

Many potential clients fall for the ruse because they don't realize how easy it is to set up. The scammers simply scan the business-news sections of newspapers or trade journals to learn of large offshore projects, such as the building of a new resort on a tropical island. One Texas engineering company got drawn into the scam after placing ads in professional journals for a project in St. Croix, Virgin Islands. A Florida phone room caught sight of the ad and began telling clients it had secured them jobs with the Texas firm in St. Croix at salaries far higher than anything the company paid. The Texas company learned of the scam when a couple of suspicious clients called its executive offices. But most customers are not likely to call and the scam artists know it.

Like most telemarketing scams, Universal had a clever set of written "objections" to keep sales from falling through once clients heard the cost. The room went so far as to order telemarketers to write down any new objections thrown at them. The shift manager in the phone room pored over these lists to issue new comebacks. Universal's closing statement ended with these objections.

Objection: It's too much money.

Answer: With these terms we are taking the chance. Compare us to an employment agency's fees, they take up to 40 percent of first year's income.

Objection: How do I know it's not a scam?

Answer: Would we give credit, make phone calls, pay for all these faxes and preparation? Our cost far exceeds the money that was paid.

Objection: Why can't you send literature?

Answer: We get over 150 calls per day and we want to work with people who are serious and committed. We process two hundred resumes a day!

While the unemployed are considered easy targets by boiler-room veterans, some exhibit a peculiar disgust for the racket.

"I'm a telemarketer and I didn't have the stomach to stay," says Mickey, who quit a Florida jobs scam. "We were taking people's last dollars. Some guy told me that his mortgage was past due but he was sending the money to us because we were his last hope."

Many others stay, though. They begin their sales with a businesslike set of questions, the "qualify" phase of a telemarketing deal. Marketers seed the customer with several mundane questions such as "Do you have a current passport?" or "Are you willing to work for at least a year in the job?" The answers determine whether they continue or hang up. Phone sales agents won't spend time talking to a caller who is merely curious and has no real interest in working overseas or doesn't have the money to send in.

"I ask people a set of questions and the first bad answer I'm off the phone," says Marcia, who admits to working more than a few telemarketing rackets. "I got to think about my time because I'm here to sell. If it's a guy, sometimes I have to crawl into bed with him. Then there is negative selling, telling a guy he can't have it, that we are going to choose the best person to have this."

Marcia and others who ply the trade are masters of quickly seguing into the "build excitement" phase once their caller clears the early hurdles. It's what telemarketers call the "voice in the sky," the deal that is so good it truly is a godsend. Who are more vulnerable than people with families to support who get laid off and can't find work?

Sometimes the overseas rooms raise suspicions by making a pitch a little too precise.

Joel Eggart, who lives in South Carolina, sent $295 to a Florida jobs broker that promised him a job in Bermuda as a refrigerator technician with a major U.S. company. The deal: guaranteed annual salary of $75,000; free medical care; four to six weeks vacation; a furnished one-bedroom apartment in the island's American community; free meals and groceries in a commissary; and cars for his use.

Eggart's wife questioned the generosity of the employer. She asked the firm's name. The voice on the line wouldn't tell her, claiming if they gave names out, some clients would contact the firms directly and the agency would lose its fee.

The voice also said that American firms have a tough time getting workers to leave the mainland and thus the terrific benefits. Once the couple sent the check by overnight mail, they were told the job was "taken out of the computer" and was slated for Eggart.

As time passed the couple became uneasy. Calls to Bermuda contradicted the voice from Florida. Bermuda officials knew of no major new resort, or an American community outside of a naval base, and said that visitors are not permitted to drive cars on the island's narrow roads. Worried, they began calling the Florida company, only to be placed on hold or hung up on. The couple became one of hundreds who fill out affidavits demanding refunds.

Work at Home

Another cruel hoax preys upon low-income people, often housewives with children and few job skills, who get conned into thinking they can earn fat salaries by working out of their homes.

Work-at-home schemes were among the top items drawing inquiries to Better Business Bureaus across the country, according to figures released in May 1994. Others in the top five also revolved around personal finance, such as loan and credit brokers and mortgage financing. But the work-at-home schemes topped the list, everything from stuffing envelopes to business opportunities.

Few people would answer these ads if they knew some of the sultans of the scheme, such as the father-and-son Dinzler team.

Thomas Dinzler has a history of arrests in his native New York and Florida. He is tough, intimidating, a regular at the race track, and has a penchant for collecting license plates. His son, Randy, is dapper, preppie, and a huge hit with women investors. Together they formed a telemarketing twosome that eluded authorities for years. But father and son recently found themselves facing wire fraud charges.

Randy Dinzler first showed up on the scam circuit for an inventive work-at-home scheme that U.S. Postal Service inspectors targeted.

Dinzler ran a firm called Data Bank Industries in Lighthouse Point, Florida, which ran this classified ad in daily newspapers across the country:

> Customer Service
>
> Multi-national company
> now hiring customer service
> representatives in (Name of
> City) and surrounding areas.
> $12-15/hour depending on
> qualifications. No experience
> necessary. Full Training
> provided. Call Thursday & Friday
> only 305 783-XXXX

People who called the number were connected to a boiler room operating in the back of a storefront office, where telemarketers read a script that was memorable for its boldness.

I will need some background information, but first let me explain the position to you. Would you be able to start from your home? Good. The name of the company is Data Bank Industries. What we do is help people obtain MasterCard or Visa. Our customers call in to apply for the service. Your job would be to take their calls. You would screen through their backgrounds and credit history, fill out their computer entry form and explain our service in complete detail. Does this sound like something you would like to be doing? Great!

Have you worked with peoples' credit in the past? Then I assume you have not been licensed with the National Credit Licensing Board? Well ——— you would have to be licensed with the National Board if we were to hire you. That would run you $49.00 once you were hired. I could start you between $11 and $14 an hour depending on your qualifications. Is that the salary range you were working for? (*Take down work history*)

You sound good on the phone. I like your qualifications. I will be able to start you at $12.50 per hour which is our company-based set rate of pay. Can you live on that? Good. Now I need some basic information for the license.

A. Have you ever been convicted of credit card fraud?

B. How about securities fraud?

I don't see a problem. Give me your social security number and date of birth and I will call the licensing board and they will run a quick background search to see if you qualify for the license. Hold the line and I'll be right back with that information.

OK. They've cleared you for the license. How quickly can you start with us? Great! How quickly can you activate your license (*must be immediately*)? To activate your license you must go and get a money order for $49 and make it payable to N.C.L.B. Then you must call (305) 946-XXXX and ask for Mr. Cole. He is the person that cleared you for licensing. . . .

You will give him the money order number and he will start processing your license. I will send out all the training materials and start you working immediately. Any questions? Welcome aboard! Good, take care of your license today and I will talk with you tomorrow.

(Wait for dial tone before hanging up)

Authorities did not determine how much money Dinzler netted with the phony licensing board, but the postal services delivered twenty to thirty letters per day containing checks, which would amount to about $1,500 a day. Local police became aware of the scheme—as they do with so many—when a former employee with a grudge against the owner blew the whistle. They alerted postal inspectors who stopped delivering Dinzler's mail and won a court order shutting him down.*

Dinzler simply moved the phone room a few blocks up the street, began using the name National Defense Products and changed the product line.

The new firm hawked home-based franchises selling tear gas for personal protection. Once again, people who responded to newspaper ads were hired as "customer service" representatives. But before coming on board they had to send Dinzler eighty-nine dollars, which he promised to reimburse after they spent two weeks on the job. Also promised were full medical and dental benefits, all phony.

The fake "certification" board has been used by other work-at-home, or employment training schemes, including a Philadelphia company that collected sixty-nine dollars from people who answered a newspaper ad offering jobs as telephone operators. They were told they must send the money to be certified by the "Northeastern Certification and Credit Bureau" in Valley Forge, Pennsylvania.

Pennsylvania Attorney General Ernie Preate, Jr., said the certifying board was a phony, set up by the owners of the Philadelphia company. "Based on our investigation, we determined that this was a cruel, costly con specifically aimed at those who can least afford to be ripped off—the unemployed," said Preate. He won $7,200 in restitution for victims in 1991, so at least some victims got partial refunds.†

---

*U.S. Postal Service v. Randall Dinzler, U.S. District Court for the Southern District of Florida, 90-6751.

†Preate news release, September 25, 1991.

But Dinzler's victims seldom fared so well. In another room on the premises of his Fort Lauderdale office, Dinzler sold franchises for routes to sell tear gas cartridges for self-protection to local residents for as much as $4,000 each. Police tried to give Dinzler a break. They came by several times and warned him to get his company registered as a business opportunity under state law. Dinzler promised at least twice to get registered, but never did.

Meanwhile, complaints kept pouring in. At least thirty-nine people filed sworn affidavits claiming Dinzler cheated them. He pleaded no contest to fraud charges and received three years' probation in February 1992.

Randy Dinzler did not stay out of trouble. While still on probation from the earlier offenses, he moved on to a series of bogus companies based in Boca Raton. The office housed eight different companies and thirty different phone lines in six months, including a home-shopping club and travel-certificate offer.

FBI agents arrested Dinzler, his father, and several others for the travel operation, Orion Productions, which offered round-trip airfares for $599 for two anywhere in the country. The firm had a mail-receipt station in Florida, with a phone forwarding the calls to an office in Atlanta, as well as a Chicago outlet.

Randy Dinzler blamed his involvement in the scam game on his father, whom his lawyer accused of influencing him to "pursue a life of fraud and deceit." His lawyer told a judge in September 1993 that Randy had "turned his life around and has tried to make amends for his past misdeeds."

Randy, born in 1965, cooperated with prosecutors. His testimony before a federal grand jury supplied details that led to several indictments, including that of his father. Randy pleaded guilty to conspiracy to commit wire fraud on June 29, 1993. His father, Thomas Dinzler, pleaded guilty to the same charge on February 7, 1995.

While Dinzler insisted he has straightened out his life, at least one woman entering middle age is not ready to forget. She wanted to have her own business, but after losing $5,000 to Randy Dinzler's promises of easy success she learned that "you can't depend on anybody for success but yourself."

She said: "He is so convincing. If he put his energies into a legitimate business he would be a millionaire. He's the type who walks you to the elevator, treats you courteously. He's so convincing. It's terrible how they take advantage of people."

*   *   *

Alongside phony jobs, telemarketers often pitch schemes that falsely promise to secure loans or clean up poor credit ratings.

These schemes ran rampant in South Florida—at one point authorities estimated nearly ninety existed—until the summer of 1991 when a new state law went into effect outlawing advance-fee loans. Better Business Bureau officials in West Palm Beach reported about ten thousand complaints a year about the phone loan programs at their peak. And several telemarketing rooms responded to the new law by quitting the loan business and turning to overseas employment.

Only a handful faced criminal charges for the loan scams. One operator, Joseph Lanigan, fled after the U.S. attorney's office charged him in 1992 with conspiracy to commit mail fraud in the operation of Medford Credit, of Pompano Beach, Florida. The company placed ads in newspapers promising to obtain loans at 12 to 13 percent interest in exchange for an advance payment of $299, according to the government, which charges that customers received nothing for their money. Lanigan is a federal fugitive.

Other states continued to have problems with the loan brokers even after they began to drift away from Florida operations.

In 1991, Virginia State Attorney General Mary Sue Terry won a court judgment against United Members Loan Association, which had convinced at least 6,300 people to become members of a loan bank that promised them assistance.

All paid a thirty-five-dollar processing fee, expecting guaranteed, interest-free loans of up to $5,000 each, as well as twenty-five dollars in monthly dues. But the state's investigation found that the company had made just 125 loans after taking in millions of dollars. More than two thousand people stopped making the monthly payments and thus forfeited all previous contributions into the plan.

Saying the firm would never be able to honor its commitments, the state attorney general won a $2 million judgment to distribute to victims.*

But in most "advance-fee loan" schemes, nobody gets a refund. One such operation, Worldwide Credit, Inc., of Dallas, collected $250 through newspaper classifieds. When customers returned the call to an 800 number they were told that the company would locate a lender for them, and if they were unsuccessful, customers would receive their money back. By the time the FTC took action against the firm, it had folded.

Colorado was another state that found itself overrun by telephone loan brokers, and it took action to kick them out. Colorado State Attorney

---

*Terry news release, June 6, 1991.

General Gale A. Norton shut down Information Services of America, which in 1992 used an automatic dialer to promise consumers they had been guaranteed to receive a credit card, so long as they called a 900 number and paid forty-nine dollars for the call. They received nothing other than materials explaining how to apply for credit cards.

Colorado found itself hosting other such businesses, such as Rocky Mountain Financial Services, which got fifty- to fifty-five-dollar money orders from customers, despite a state law prohibiting advance fee loans. The company harnessed more than $1 million in just three months in Colorado. It also used checking account debits and a 900 number to collect fees, apparently from more than ten thousand people across the country. The state won a $763,000 judgment against the company, based in Aurora, Colorado, on October 3, 1991.

In August 1991, another of these firms sprung up, this one using overnight couriers to get people to send in bank checks for $279 for loans. "Consumers should be particularly wary of offers tailored to tough economic times, such as loan and credit card scams, advance-fee employment promises, and 'get-rich-quick' prize offers," said Colorado State Attorney General Norton.

Other states also have hosted variations of the loan scam, such as deals that throw in a fifty-cent vacation certificate. And in Ohio, State Attorney General Lee Fisher found that a telemarketer with a previous history had segued into the loan business. "Advance-fee credit card scams and advance-fee loans scams are becoming a national epidemic. My office has seen a dramatic rise in the number of advance-fee scams with the onset of hard economic times," Fisher announced. He suggested consumers could best recognize the scams if they understood that no company can magically "repair" a poor credit rating.

Fisher said firms charging from fifty dollars to one thousand dollars in many cases "do little or nothing to improve credit ratings," and often "take the (customer's) money and vanish."

Credit histories, he noted, are compiled by credit bureaus from banks, mortgage companies, department stores, and others who loan money or issue charge cards. Accurate items, such as a history of making payments late, cannot be erased by any company, no matter what it advertises it can do.

"If you have a poor credit record, time is the only thing that will heal it," Fisher said. "The only information which can be changed in your credit report are items which are wrong and you can do that yourself."

*   *   *

The possibilities for fraud against people of limited means are endless, between the work-at-home and credit-improvement rackets. While most of these schemes flare up in poor economic times, they never really disappear. The Federal Trade Commission settled a lawsuit in late 1993 against four work-at-home companies that claimed people could make solid wages assembling products at home, from potholders to mohair pillows and Christmas ornaments. The FTC, on December 22, 1993, announced settlement of civil charges against Homespun Products, Suisin, California; New Mexico Custom Designs, Inc., Albuquerque; Hairbow Company, Danville, California; and Sandcastle Creations, Newport, Oregon. The FTC had charged each company with misrepresenting the weekly earnings from working at home.

"Turn your sewing skills into significant income. We pay up to $627.00 a week sewing pillows at home," such ads often read. But only a fraction of the workers, if any, can expect that rate of pay. Many people end up paying out money, ending up worse off for trying to better their lives. Authorities report many such scams seek at-home assemblers in Spanish-speaking neighborhoods in California, New Mexico, and other states.

But the racket can also aim at hobbyists or anyone seeking to pick up some extra income. Another firm sued by the FTC sold guides telling consumers how to buy government-seized cars at "giveaway prices," paying twenty dollars to fifty dollars for one of the guides to "druglord cars." The booklets claimed souped-up vehicles could be had for under one hundred dollars, a claim the FTC scoffed at.

This same firm also published a guide called "How to Stay at Home and Get Paid $100 or more for Every Book You Read," purportedly by publishers and film studios. Not true, said the FTC.*

While job and credit-related scams drop off from time to time, they always spring back when the economy takes a dip and people are desperate for work or new sources of income.

---

*The FTC announced the suit against U.S. Hotline, Inc., Ads Across America and Jay Peterson, all of Lindon, Utah, on May 14, 1993.

8

Gimme Gifts

The Feed the Children Foundation's message, if true, would alarm even the most cold-hearted tightwad: babies are starving because of federal budget cuts.

Utah officials said the foundation, a telephone charity run from downtown Salt Lake City, promised to rescue one of the government's largest feeding programs for the poor.

Among its claims:

- The federal Women's, Infants and Children's (WIC) Program was tottering because its budget had been slashed in half.

- 600 children a month were being dropped from the rolls and many would starve without aid.

- A $38 donation would feed a child for a month.

- In one week the foundation sent $2,000 to help the government pay for the WIC feeding program in Utah.

All lies, according to the Utah Department of Commerce. The agency accused Feed the Children Foundation officer Lanny Gray of collecting funds through deception. Gray did not admit any wrongdoing, but he agreed to a court order placing his solicitor's license on probation for five years. He also agreed to a $5,000 fine, to be paid only if he violated the probation.

That action ended the state's case, although officials had no idea how much Gray collected. It's the way these cases almost always end, with no punishment for telemarketers who pose as do-gooders to tap into the public's sympathy for the downtrodden.

The pitch rarely is a total lie. The WIC program exists, though many Americans might never have heard of it or realize its support comes from federal tax dollars, not private donations. An arm of the U.S. Department of Agriculture, it projects a 1995 budget of about $3.5 billion. While WIC fails to care for everyone needy, it serves about 6.5 million low-income pregnant women, new mothers, and children. It accepts no money from the public or charities.

State regulators did not require Gray to explain his intentions in setting up the WIC charity. He did admit twisting the truth in a second fundraising effort he set up in Utah called Grayco Disadvantaged Work Program. Grayco began collecting money for Salt Lake City charities in February 1992, after Gray agreed to halt the campaign to save babies from starving.*

Its telemarketers, who implied they were handicapped or disadvantaged, sold lightbulbs and trashbags over the phone. Grayco came under suspicion after an undercover state investigator who was in fine health applied for a job there. He got hired, no questions asked, by a manager who joked that needing a job was a "disadvantage." The investigator listened to able-bodied workers hawk a "special" deal on lightbulbs, good only that day. The special ran day after day.

Confronted by state officials, Gray said that terms such as disabled "appealed to people's sympathy and got them to listen to a pitch they probably would not listen to otherwise."

Not seeming at all contrite, Gray defined disadvantaged as:

- long-term unemployment

- laid off

- homeless

- single parent unemployed

- single parent underpaid

- underpaid at present job

- unemployable

- on public assistance

- handicapped

- lacking experience or training.

*In the matter of the Investigation of Lanny Gray d/b/a Feed the Children Foundation before the Division of Consumer Protection of the Department of Commerce of the State of Utah, CP-7538-90, Settlement Agreement and Order, October 23, 1990.

Gray claimed that one telemarketer suffered from legal blindness, while another had a tough time walking. A third man had to wear a breathing device when he climbed stairs; another was a recovering substance abuser; another overweight and next to destitute.

Checking Gray's claims, officials discovered the "blind" woman had been issued a driver's license. She passed the vision test without the need of eyeglasses. The only person working in the phone room with anything close to a handicap was a man with a slight stutter.

Nor did Gray's telemarketers have a tough time making ends meet. A seventeen-year-old girl earned about $20,000 in a year selling by phone, while another sales agent took home more than $50,000. Meanwhile, only 10 percent of the money collected found its way to charities, state officials alleged in a lawsuit.*

The Utah state attorney general's office shut Gray down in the summer of 1992. He was not the only problem phone operator preying on the generosity of the public in Utah. That same year the state refused to license a charity promoter with an arrest record spreading over forty years, including armed robbery and assault with intent to murder.

"These guys are criminals with no conscience and nothing to deter them," says James Paine, chief investigator with the Utah Department of Commerce Division of Consumer Protection. "They need to be locked up, but all they ever get are administrative fines. Why should they be afraid of a fine?" he said in an interview.

Gray never spent any time in jail for his telemarketing schemes. But the state's mercy didn't prompt him to mend his ways. In June 1994 he pleaded guilty to a misdemeanor charge of telemarketing without a license in Salt Lake City. The case, strictly small-time stuff, involved the sale of a children's book over the phone. Because of his past involvement with suspect telemarketing, the state prosecuted, and Gray wound up with eighteen months probation. Another slip-up and he could wind up in jail. Prosecutors said he has learned his lesson and lost his lust for telephone fundraising.

Many others have not.

America's charities are awash in cash, taking in some $120 billion every year, more than 80 percent of it from the public, and much of that through aggressive mailings and telemarketing.

Many charities are run by dedicated folks who labor to hold down

---

*The State of Utah, Division of Consumer Protection v. Lanny Gray, District Court, Salt Lake City, Utah, No. 920903349, June 12, 1992.

office expenses and shun costly perks for chief executives. But the number of alms merchants has grown so vast that nobody—not even the experts—can keep track of them, or offer any guarantee that a donation will be well spent.

The National Charities Information Bureau, a private watchdog agency in New York City, lists nearly four hundred charities soliciting around the country for everything from American sharecroppers to overseas development. The group sets nine standards a charity should meet, from spending at least 60 percent of its expenses on program activities to supplying financial statements upon request. Just over half of the charities listed in the bureau's March 1994 "Wise Giving Guide" met all of the standards. The others came up short, often because they failed to provide the bureau with information about their finances and other aspects of their operations, despite repeated requests.

In the March 1994 guide, retiring National Charities Information Bureau president Kenneth L. Albrecht wrote that some charities mislead donors by hiding direct-mail and telemarketing costs under the guise of "public education" campaigns. He also chided charities for their growing reliance on mail and phone pitches, which have "attracted an increasing number of individuals more concerned with for-profit motives than the charitable mandates central to the public trust."

The Philanthropic Advisory Service in Arlington, Virginia, an arm of the Council of Better Business Bureaus, also offers a sobering view. The service, which keeps files on thousands of charities, publishes a bimonthly list of charities that generate the greatest numbers of inquiries. The report judges whether the charities properly account for their money. Most often, the bulletin names new charities that have failed to provide information despite three written requests to do so; it instructs readers to draw their own conclusions about why a charity refuses to let the public peek at its financial records.

While the watchdog groups help consumers to a point, many people don't read their newsletters. Instead, they are swayed by the pitch that arrives in the mail or over the phone.

The number of these calls is astonishing, judging from a 1993 survey by the American Association of Retired Persons. The study found that two-thirds of the American public in the last six months prior to an interview had been called by an organization seeking a contribution, and about a third received five or more calls.

The study noted that about a third of all consumers cannot name any organization that can help them check out a charity. Most who did have a source said they would contact the Better Business Bureau, which almost always comes out in surveys as the most trusted name in commerce. Only 13 percent said they would check with the attorney general's office in their state, suggesting, as have several other studies, that these law enforcers badly need to raise their profiles.

In the absence of tough standards, the donor must take a charity's good intentions largely on faith. While members of the alms industry decry dwindling public confidence in their drives, they have not imposed uniform reporting standards that might restore public trust. Many also have remained silent on revelations of scandalous salaries and perks paid to executives. In some areas of the country, major charities refuse to show a walk-in visitor a copy of tax returns, even though federal law requires that these records be kept on the premises and made available to anyone who wants to look.

Many charities provide only the most basic financial information, such as a single figure for all employee salaries, which makes it difficult for the potential donor to judge whether executives are living high off contributions.

The Better Business Bureau reviewers who took a look at the salary issue did not return with entirely comforting results. The bureau requested the salaries of the top two hundred charities receiving the greatest number of inquiries. Of the 183 that responded, 43 percent reported paying their chief executive more than $100,000 in 1991.

Other fundraising professionals have been disheartened in recent years by what they perceive as plunging public confidence in charities. Many cite a July 1993 Gallup poll showing that half the respondents felt that charities had become less trustworthy in the past decade. The poll was no doubt influenced by press reports of scandalous compensation and other indiscreet spending at United Way of America, conditions since cleaned up.

Not only does the public seem suspicious; sentiment for reform appears to be building. In September 1993, the Council of Better Business Bureaus released a survey showing that half the people polled were "very concerned" about the amount of money collected by charities that did not find its way to people in need. In addition, three of four people polled supported standards for the percent of contributions to be spent on direct services, rather than promotions and fundraising.

Not surprisingly, complaints are on the rise in the mid-1990s, according to the Better Business Bureaus. Most complaints concern the telemarketer's failure to explain his or her relationship to the charity and excessive pressure to donate. Others cite "vague descriptions of the nature of the charity's program service efforts to exaggerations about the amount the charity spends on its programs, as compared to fundraising and administration expenses," according to Better Business Bureau officials.

If the public has doubts about the trustworthiness of some of the nation's charities, those concerns play right into the hands of the quick-buck artists.

The scammers often do their best work in a climate of suspicion and doubt. They call it the "sympathy pitch," and it works well on people who are fearful of giving, perhaps because they have been burned before, just as it succeeds with people saddled with a crummy water purifier and cheap watch instead of the Lincoln Town Car they thought they were winning.

Many telemarketers who employ the technique don't expect to be around long enough to draw scrutiny from watchdog groups or regulators. They go straight for the gut-level appeal, hoping donors won't quiz them about how they plan to use the money. They may conclude a high-pressure sales pitch by sending a runner around to pick up a donor's check, collect money through wire, or get cash contributions, any way that gives victims no time to change their minds.

Some of these marketers claim to be advocates for the downtrodden, others for overworked civil servants such as police and firefighters. Some work all sides. Many exploit major news events, from natural disasters to violent social unrest, or fears of dreaded diseases, from cancer to AIDS.

Here are some of the perennials, worthy of attention because they pop up over and over, in state after state. While there seldom is any clear connection between the operators of these scams, their pitches tend to be remarkably similar.

Disaster Relief

Within days of the 1994 Los Angeles earthquake or Hurricane Andrew's devastation in South Florida in 1992, disaster relief scams appeared. Some perpetrators got caught, but most did not.

Taking advantage of the post-disaster chaos, these scammers set up, collected their money, and moved on. Two who overstayed their welcome ended up facing criminal charges. Police busted a Colorado employment scam that promised nonexistent jobs helping to clean up the hurricane devastation, while postal inspectors arrested a Los Angeles man who sent out four thousand letters asking for tax-deductible donations for riot relief in the wake of motorist Rodney King's beating in 1992.

Mindful of its hurricane scam toll, Florida officials dispatched a squad of fraudbusters to shackle the shysters who flowed into Mississippi River front towns under water from the great flood of 1993.

Testifying before a U.S. Senate hearing in October 1993, Collette Rausch, a Nevada deputy state attorney general, said the smash-and-grab style of charity con is tough for law enforcement to halt.

> Unfortunately, some of these people just simply set up shop, make phone calls, get the money through Western Union, and skip town. I don't know what anybody can do about that. You may get a handle on them if you are lucky, you may get tips, maybe the same people that you have seen before that you can track down.*

While calamities often spark quick-shot scams, chronic social ills also are prime targets. News coverage of "deadbeat dads," men who fail to pay child support, apparently spawned a Mississippi marketer's phone offer to help women collect delinquent payments. Hoping for assistance, many poor clients paid forty dollars to the firm, but got little for their money.

A few schemes are so bold as to tap into a national consciousness, such as the Voices of Freedom, whose telemarketers talked thousands of patriotic Americans into buying nickel-plated copper bracelets bearing the inscription "Operation Desert Shield. A Call for Freedom."

The group changed the inscription to "Operation Desert Storm" as the United States embarked on the war in the Persian Gulf. Voices of Freedom claimed that proceeds from the sale of bracelets, which cost $9.95 to $11.45, would support a message center for American troops. Voices of Freedom even had obtained tax-exempt status from the Internal Revenue Service.

But the Federal Trade Commission sued the enterprise, alleging that most of the money went into the pockets of the promoters. Voices of Freedom settled the suit in July 1992 without admitting fault. But its officers agreed to pay $120,000 in refunds and stop misrepresenting that the business was non-profit.†

---

*U.S. Senate Subcommittee on Consumer of the Committee on Commerce, Science and Transportation, October 11, 1993, Las Vegas, Nevada.

†Civil No. 91-1542-A (E.D. Va., July 13, 1992 [consent decree entered]).

Handicapped Sales

"Handicapped sales rooms" can be homegrown or franchises that creep into town from other states. Former Iowa State Attorney General Bonnie J. Campbell filed suit in the summer of 1992 against an Arizona company that had set up just such an office in Des Moines. Telemarketers sold garbage bags, cleaning solution, and light bulbs for $4.99 apiece, pricey because they supposedly burned for five years.

The telemarketers' "handicaps" included psoriasis, high blood pressure, asthma, pregnancy, and felony convictions, according to the suit. The court settlement ordered the company to issue refunds, halt the promotion, and pay an $18,000 fine.

"These kinds of claims are not only deceptive to consumers, they are unfair to legitimate charities who are forced to compete with con artists for charitable donations," Campbell said.*

Neighboring Minnesota became an unwilling host to a similar scheme after the business got kicked out of North Dakota and decided to find a new home in the Gopher State.

Minnesota State Attorney General Hubert H. Humphrey III found out that the charity assigned new telemarketers a handicap and put them to work. Outraged, Humphrey sent the phone pirates packing. "This company considers anyone who wears eyeglasses, has a bad back or a police record is handicapped," Humphrey said, noting that the solicitors made only minimal wages while the owners pocketed huge profits. "This is fraud, pure and simple. It is a cynical manipulation of peoples' willingness to support charities."†

Tactics in other states have been even more brazen. Florida State Attorney General Bob Butterworth sued a Sunshine State "handicapped" phone sales firm that went so far as to direct telemarketers to feign stutters and speak in slow and muffled tones to hoodwink customers. The firm paid a $1,000 fine.

Don L., a career furniture salesman, discovered how the racket works. Restless in semi-retirement, Don thought he would try telemarketing. He landed in a "handicapped" sales room making five to seven dollars an hour, one of twenty people of mixed ages working the phones.

"I was offered a job almost every place I went. No great tribute to my skills, personality or experience," says Don, sixty-eight. "These people

---

*Campbell news release, July 9, 1992.
†Humphrey news release, July 20, 1990.

will hire anyone who is breathing, speaks English, and can find his way to work without a compass," he said in a 1994 interview.

Using *Yellow Pages* books from cities all over the country, Don coaxed small companies into buying high-priced trinkets and cheap pens to help the handicapped. Tacked up in front of him was a list of area codes, time zones, and prices. Some of the "recallers," the equivalent of the reloaders in other types of telemarketing rooms, took home commissions as high as 10 percent of the sales they generated.

"I looked at the people all about me busily talking into their telephones, and wondered where the handicapped people were," Don says.

He later saw at least some handicapped workers laboring in the shipping room, where they packed the ballpoint pens, thin plastic trash bags, Christmas cards, and other items the company sold. Other backshop workers, he said, had no obvious affliction, although two or three were deaf.

"It was not actually a charity, it was a business. They like people to get the idea it is a charity, and these places select names that sound like charitable organizations, but they are for-profit," he says. "They sell the merchandise at an outrageous price, and can do a heck of a volume selling five pens for fifty-five dollars."

Don says most people would hang up or claim they had given to other charities, the old "I gave at the office" line. But many others were happy to help, thinking they were bettering the lives of the disadvantaged.

"People said, 'I'm more than happy to help,'" Don recalls with a half-laugh. "They thought they were helping humanity. We would say that we really needed some help this year, and end the pitch by saying 'the handicapped folks really thank you.' It's kind of nauseating. I started to hear it in my sleep."

The Benefit

Police-affiliated groups often turn to professional fundraisers or ticket sellers who sponsor charitable events such as a circus or benefit concert to fight gangs or drug abuse. Sometimes the fundraisers claim to aid charities when they don't, as officials discovered in Ohio.

"These companies have abused the goodwill and reputation of charities and deceived Ohio consumers while conducting a very profitable business, but returning only a very small amount to charity," said then-Ohio State Attorney General Anthony J. Celebrezze, Jr.*

---

*Celebrezze news release, January 19, 1990.

He claimed that one fundraiser falsely claimed proceeds from a "children's magic circus" held in Toledo would greatly benefit the Special Olympics, which sponsors competitive athletics for the handicapped. The Special Olympics, which had not consented to the use of its name, received nothing. Only about 2 percent of the proceeds from the sales went to the sponsoring charities even though they were supposed to get half, officials said.

By the time the court accepted a settlement in the matter in 1991, the state had a new attorney general, Lee Fisher. He announced that the fundraiser agreed to give refunds to fifteen hundred people who bought tickets to the event expecting to help the Special Olympics. "It is important that legal action be pursued in these cases to punish deceptive behavior and to protect honest charitable fundraising campaigns," Fisher said.

In Washington State, benefit shows purportedly aimed at fighting drug abuse instead enriched the solicitors. Telemarketers claimed to represent a "crime education task force," and said they were off-duty state troopers. Calling businesses, they said they were agents of the Internal Revenue Service and that 80 percent to 100 percent of the donations went to charity. Despite the sponsor's claims, just 15 percent of about $400,000 collected ended up with a charity.

Law enforcement groups often show regrettable tolerance when it comes to hiring telemarketers to collect for their causes. Police and firefighter organizations for years have drawn the most complaints to Better Business Bureau charity watchdogs.

The fact that these telephone solicitation companies pocket most of the donations has been frequent fodder for newspaper investigative reporters at least since the 1980s. And yet little seems to change.

The *Chicago Sun-Times* in a 1989 series studying Illinois charities ranging from police benevolent associations to handicapped-support groups found that as much as ninety-two cents of every dollar donated went to the telemarketers.*

Using an Illinois state law that requires charities employing telephone solicitors to advise the state how much of the money they collect goes to charities, reporters found that one third of thirty-three charities sent less than twenty cents of each dollar to help the disadvantaged.

In 1992, the *Kansas City Star* documented similar situations by professional fundraisers acting on behalf of police organizations. In another case, an Atlanta television station reported that a "sheriff's association"

---

*"Cashing in on Charity," *Chicago Sun Times,* March 5, 1989.

had set up telephone boiler rooms all over Georgia that were pressuring people to give to police groups.*

Veteran Groups

Second to police and firefighters in drawing complaints are veterans associations. While many veterans organizations do good work, others use professional fundraisers that take the lion's share of the donations. No less than twenty charities claiming to represent veterans collect nationally, and a number of them have run into problems with state regulators, often for failing to report where the money is being spent.

Many veterans organizations that give telemarketers 90 percent of the proceeds collected on their behalf defend the system, saying they lack the resources to set up their own fundraising systems. But the abuses have become so common that regulators advise consumers to resist any patriotic pitch from a purported veterans' group unless it is backed with written documentation of the organization's goals and finances.

The Big C

Health-related charities drew more inquiries than any other type during 1992, according to the Better Business Bureau charities watchdog agency. Of these, cancer perhaps inspires the most fear, particularly in the elderly. Although many other diseases may cost more out of pocket to treat, the fight against cancer remains a strong solicitation tool, and a battleground among rivals.

The combatants in the crusade against cancer are the mammoth American Cancer Society and dozens of unrelated organizations that the cancer society sometimes accuses of trading on its name and reputation.

While the American Cancer Society provides reasonably full disclosure of its activities, it accuses its competitors of concealing their finances in order to confuse and deceive the public.

In comments typical of the skirmish, Judith Mitchell, executive vice president of the American Cancer Society's Nevada division, gave testimony at a U.S. Senate committee hearing in 1993:

---

*WXIA-TV, Atlanta.

Organizations entering the cancer field today are willing to exploit the good name and reputation of the American Cancer Society and other worthwhile, legitimate health organizations to raise money for questionable use. For example, in 1989, according to one organization's own audit, of every dollar they spent fifty-nine cents was used for management and fundraising, thirty-five cents for education, three cents surplus, one cent research, and one cent for patient services. This by the way only totals ninety-nine cents.

Mitchell said the consumer must dig deeper to get a full understanding of the finances of this sort of operation. She continued:

Here is what they considered education—eleven cents for postage, eight cents for printing, six cents for mailing lists, three cents for mailing house, two cents for computer, two cents for counting the money, and three cents for other. Use of donor dollars in this way is making it increasingly difficult for organizations who are trying to be stewards of the public trust to secure support for their programs.

One frequent target of the cancer society—and government regulators—is a cloud of companies run by an Alexandria, Virginia, public relations company called Watson & Hughey. One of the charities, Pacific West Cancer Fund, has been the subject of a number of civil suits from regulators who attack its fundraising techniques. The company bombarded the nation in 1989 with letters from Robert Stone, attorney-at-law, whose office was a mail drop in downtown Washington.

Stone told the public he had been "retained" by the Pacific West Cancer Fund to advise persons they were among the many winners of a cash prize in the cancer fund's five-thousand-dollar sweepstakes. Stone asked recipients to return the form which would automatically enter them in a seventy-five-thousand-dollar sweepstakes. There was no obligation. But Stone's letter ended with the pitch:

You are not obligated to make a contribution to Pacific West Cancer Fund in order to claim your cash prize, but since this is a "charity" sweepstakes, we do hope that you will wish to contribute at least $5. As the number of new cases of most major forms of cancer continues to increase each year, PWCF's efforts to educate Americans about early detection and prevention become all the more important. Regardless of whether you contribute your sweepstakes cash prize remains yours to keep no matter what.

The same pitch turned up in Cancer Fund of America, Cancer Association of Tennessee, and Walker Cancer Research Institute, all clients of a Virginia advertising agency that created the promotion.

The U.S. Postal Service sued the Pacific West Cancer Fund and its affiliates in March 1989, alleging most of the prizes were worth less than the postage to receive them. In June 1989 the postal service won an administrative order forcing the charity to tell people the value of any prizes. That prompted a new letter:*

> It has been brought to our attention by the U.S. Postal Service that the mailing may have been misleading. While we do not agree, we want to make you aware of several facts. The . . . mailing was mass mailed to millions of people and the cash prizes awarded were between $100 and $.10, with most of the prizes being $.40. No person receives a check for $5,000. That is the total amount distributed to all who respond.

After admitting that most of the entrants in the $5,000 sweepstakes actually won forty cents or less, the letter went on to detail several "worthwhile" projects, including a scholarship program for college students who are victims of cancer, and a brochure on how to lower cancer risks, then concluded:

> If after receiving this information, you do not believe we were a proper steward of your funds, we will be happy to refund your contribution. . . . Those funds that were received as a result of the Stone mailing that are not being refunded will be used by Pacific West Cancer Fund to pay the expenses of the mailing, the awarding of prizes with the proceeds from this mailing going to our many worthwhile projects.

Attorneys general of more than ten states stepped in and came after the cancer fund and in January 1991 they won a $2.1 million settlement, believed to be the biggest ever in a charitable solicitations case. They stated that the use of a nonexistent law office in Washington, D.C., reinforced the customer's belief that he or she had won a prize.

The Pacific West Cancer Fund remains on the lists of unapproved charities by two watchdog agencies because of its failure to provide financial information that substantiates its claims. While the companies have acknowledged not sending full financial reports, they have repeatedly

---

*In the Matter of the Pacific West Cancer Fund, Cease and Desist Order No. CD-2597, June 28, 1989.

defended their fundraising efforts by stating that the money they collect gets used for "public education in conjunction with fund-raising appeals."

Telefunding

When federal and state investigators shut down or clipped back a few of the largest sweepstakes promoters in Las Vegas in 1993, employees scattered. But many did not seek out a new line of work. Just as the fateful U.S. Postal Service raid on 50 State Distributing in 1981 sent telephone con men scurrying all over the nation to open their own boiler rooms, the sweepstakes parlors recouped.

Some came back as phony charities and saw a chance to move up and set up their own phone rooms, using the same "one-in-five" prize lure.

The progression is logical. A major tactic of the one-in-five pitch was to appeal to the public's desire to fight drug abuse or help the environment. But the telefunders, as they became known, took advantage of another loophole in state law. Nevada's telemarketing licensing law exempts charitable solicitors. Telefunders typically take 90 percent to 95 percent of monies raised. As one regulator put it, it's the "new name, same game."

"My office is witnessing players from the traditional telemarketing industry moving into the charitable solicitation business," Nevada State Attorney General Frankie Sue Del Papa warned just before Christmas of 1993.*

She cited Baby Aid, Inc., of Las Vegas. Del Papa later won a court injunction in 1994 to halt the company from stretching the truth in its appeals. Among its claims:

- Three thousand babies in Nevada have AIDS (the actual number was sixteen).

- Donations will only be used to assist babies who got AIDS because of a blood transfusion their parents received and "not drug use or lewd practices."

- People who donated as much as three thousand dollars would win valuable prizes, awards worth more than their donation. Most telefunders simply hand out new varieties of the "gimme gift" worth ten dollars or so.

---

*Del Papa news release, December 10, 1993.

- The appeal is sponsored by casinos and large corporations, and had the blessing of the state attorney general. It didn't.

The emergence of the telefunding threat, which prompted Nevada Senator Richard H. Bryan to hold a pair of hearings, energized the Federal Trade Commission, ushering in what state and federal authorities called a new era of cooperation in eradicating telemarketing fraud.

Usually criticized for sloth in moving against new telemarketing threats, the FTC got out front on this go round. The FTC won an injunction in March 1994 against National Clearing House, of Las Vegas, which had joined with two charities in a sweepstakes scheme.* Telemarketers told contacts they would win a $50,000 annuity; $25,000 in gold, jewelry, or government bonds, or other cash prizes. But no prize could be sent until customers sent a "registration or acquisition" fee of $1,000 to $9,999. The customers sent their checks to Las Vegas via overnight courier. Instead of the cash surprises, many who sent in money received flowers or jewelry worth fifty dollars or less, according to the FTC.

Another of the operations sued by authorities dealt strictly with reloads, customers who had previously been suckered in the phony sweepstakes. They were hit for between $500 and $3,500 by telemarketers who told them that most of the money went to helping people in need all over the nation, such as Midwest flood victims, homeless people, and battered women.

The sales pitch used in a second scheme attacked by the FTC in 1994 went even further. It said that a charity called AWARE was working in the customer's community and that the prizes had been donated by major corporations such as AT&T and IBM. Neither claim was true, according to the FTC.†

Just hanging up on the charity callers didn't seem to work for some elderly victims. The telemarketers called over and over until they scored. One Colorado woman complained to the Better Business Bureau of Las Vegas of the harassment and losses she faced even after trying to say no.

The telemarketer who called her forged together the sweepstakes and the sympathy pitch until he found a formula that would defraud the trusting woman, whose name he most probably purchased from a list of previous victims.**

---

*Civil Action No. CV-S-94-00138-LDG (LRL), U.S. District Court for the District of Nevada.
†Civil Action No. CV-S-94-00138-LDG (LRL), U.S. District Court for the District of Nevada.
**William Henderson, Director of the Better Business Bureau, Southern Nevada, testimony before the U.S. Senate Subcommittee on Consumer of the Committee on Commerce, Science and Transportation, October 11, 1993, Las Vegas, Nevada.

I had about five calls from this organization, it is a charity organization, and hung up every time. Each time someone different called back. Then I received another call and I said I had already been called and hung up. He called right back and said, "How come you hung up when I am trying to give you the top prize?" He knew all about my problems with other Las Vegas marketing outfits and said they were not about to allow me to be taken again. If I donated $1,562 to this charity they would give me the top prize, and up it from $30,000 to $50,000.

Excited, the woman wired the money by Western Union, only to receive a thank-you letter and another call, saying that she had to pay "taxes" of $2,000 before the company could send out her winnings of $50,000. She complied.

The next day they called to say they had a meeting and had upped the prize to $80,000, so I would need to pay an additional $1,396. . . . They said to expect my prize check in about three to five days. After the five days I realized I had been taken again.

I am sure everyone wonders how anyone could be so gullible, but when you are in a desperate financial situation and see a chance of light at the end of the tunnel—it is obvious that we are easy for them.

Attorneys general in many states have wrestled with how to crack down on telephone charities that abuse the public trust. In Washington State, then State Attorney General Ken Eikenberry opened fire around Christmas 1991, announcing that the industry was "out of control" and urging sweeping new laws.

He cited horror stories, mostly traceable to telemarketers, some of whom posed as police officers and threatened to cut off emergency services to people who refused to donate. Nearly all the money went to the fundraisers, not the charity they represented. Things became so bad that one elderly woman received more than two hundred solicitation letters in a three-week period.

The state attorney general called existing financial disclosure laws "nearly useless" in helping the public decide whether donations were spent prudently. Even charities that reported their finances could manipulate the system to mislead the public, he said.

Eikenberry stated that paid solicitors should be required to identify themselves as such, and charities should be held responsible for the misdeeds of their solicitors. He also advocated tougher enforcement and improved financial disclosure, including publishing a reliable list showing exactly how much money collected went to charity.

To make his point, he filed a lawsuit against a West Seattle charity that used fourteen different names to raise funds for groups ranging from veterans to senior citizens.* The charity pooled its donations into a single bank account, which the executive director plundered to pay personal expenses: rent, personal jewelry, day-care services, private elementary school tuition, car payments, utility bills, interest-free loans to his "spousal equivalent," and payment of a $380 fine for drunk driving.

While the outfit claimed to funnel 32 to 70 percent of its money to charity, the attorney general claimed that only about 4 percent went to help the disadvantaged. The suit led to a court settlement in which the charity agreed to shut down.

"In quashing this charity's fraudulent activities, we have taken a small step toward bringing some unsavory elements in the charitable fundraising industry under control," Eikenberry said.†

Another charity that Eikenberry shut down in 1991 raised $440,000 for a homeless shelter but used none of the money for any charitable purpose. He won an $84,000 judgment against the owners but they were given ten years to pay it.

"I continue to be outraged by people who rip off generous, trusting members of the public by masquerading as legitimate charities. I am determined to do whatever it takes to clear the state of bogus charities and make it possible for honest charities to compete openly and fairly for the dollars of Washington donors," he said in announcing his agency had won a court judgment shutting down the homeless shelter "Helping Hands" on August 29, 1991.

Ohio's attorney general used the incident with the suspect circus charity to campaign for tighter laws to regulate professional fundraisers, including a $25,000 bond and fines of up to $10,000 for any violations and making repeat violations a felony crime.

Yet other states can't even figure out what types of laws are needed to crack down. In Florida, for example, consumer groups and charities split over changes in the law that dropped a requirement for charities to provide detailed financial statements. National advocates of tougher reporting condemned the law, calling it a step backward. Others said that it was an improvement because it stepped up penalties for violators.

Others argued that no law could convince con artists to register. They cited the case of a man facing fraud charges in Nevada who moved to Fort Lauderdale and hired kids to stand at street corners asking for donations. He left town when police began to wonder where the money was going.

---

*Eikenberry announced the lawsuit December 3, 1991.

†Eikenberry news release, December 11, 1991.

*   *   *

Laws that would force charities to spend a certain amount of their money on direct services to the disadvantaged are not likely, regardless of growing public sentiment for them. The reason is that the U.S. Supreme Court has struck down such laws and generally courts have held that restrictions on charitable appeals violate free speech.*

Even if the states enact laws requiring charities to register, their attorneys general are pretty much limited to regulating organizations operating in, and soliciting donations from, residents of their states. While many states have numerous "home-grown" charities which employ questionable tactics, most of the worst offenders are likely to be calling from out-of-state. By the time state authorities can bring a court action against a fraudulent, out-of-state charity it is likely to be out of business.

Voluntary regulation doesn't seem to work well either. Efforts by industry groups to standardize reporting so that donors can judge how much money *really* goes to help the disadvantaged seem doomed by the refusal of some organizations to participate and the tendency of others to engage in accounting tricks to subvert the process.

The bottom line is that the public will have to rely on the integrity of the charity's managers to make sure donations are well spent. And when the call for a donation is coming from hundreds, maybe thousands of miles away, those conditions are not likely to be met. A safe bet is not to donate over the phone.

Asked at the October 1993 U.S. Senate hearing what steps to take to avoid telefunding con jobs, William Henderson, the Better Business Bureau executive director in Las Vegas, replied:

> First of all, I don't think they should give by phone. I think they should ask the organization to send them something in writing. And that usually gets rid of those organizations that perhaps are here today and gone tomorrow. After you talk to some of the people I do, you just want to tell them to hang up and do not give.

Citing the case of a persistent victim of the telefunder, Henderson went even further: "I told somebody the other day that had been taken for $125,000 his best choice would be to call the phone company and have his phone disconnected. He said, 'You know, that is a good idea.' "

---

*The U.S. Supreme Court in Riley v. National Federation of the Blind of North Carolina (487 U.S. 781, 1988) struck down a state law that required a charity to prove the reasonableness of using 35 percent of the money it collected for fundraising purposes.

Short of ripping out the phone to evade rip-off artists, there are other steps to take to avoid becoming a victim of charities telemarketers. These hints are derived from Better Business Bureaus, law enforcement agencies, and other sources:

• Remember that the charities phone pros, like all telemarketers, have handy a glib set of "objections" they will use to overcome reluctance. Stand firm.

• Demand written material describing the charity's activities, including an annual report and financial statement. Any organization that discounts the need to review such paperwork, or refuses, is probably not legitimate.

• Never give a charity credit card or checking account numbers, or agree to have a runner come and pick up your check. Some legitimate charities have contracted with telemarketers who use this pressure tactic. The best way to encourage them to change is to refuse any such offer. More likely than not, however, the charity that demands money immediately is a scam.

• Be wary of the prize offer. People don't usually win sweepstakes they have not entered and any such offer arriving in bulk mail is suspect. If a sweepstakes asks for money to enter, or requires purchase of a prize or a donation to win, it is not legitimate.

• Pay attention to the board of directors of the charity. While the presence of celebrities or influential people does not guarantee money is well spent, it helps at least somewhat. While they may not be legally liable, board members in recent years have come under new pressures to police the fund managers and many are doing so.

• Check with the Better Business Bureau or state regulators to find out whether a charity has drawn complaints from consumers. Obtain copies of any licensing records or registration statements, including IRS Form 990s. Some of these filings give a reasonably detailed picture of what the charity does with its money, i.e., what part of a donation goes for its intended purpose.

• Make sure before giving to any police or firefighters organization that you understand what the organization does. Some might be using donations to support causes donors might disapprove of, such as to defend police officers accused of brutality, or to file a costly legal challenge to an effort by the city to force police officers to undergo routine drug tests.

• If the organization passes donations on to other groups or programs, such as a specific women's shelter or drug program, ask what audits the parent agency conducts to make sure its grantees are effective.

• Ask if the caller is a professional telemarketer or volunteer. If a professional, ask how much of the proceeds the telemarketer gets. The more questions asked of the pro, the more likely he or she is to hang up and go bother someone else.

Some people may choose to spurn all offers from charities as a protest to force the alms industry to sit down and work out its problems. It seems reasonable to put the burden on a charity to prove itself worthy. Maybe that stance will give the industry some incentive to weed out sleazy telemarketers once and for all.

9

Telephone Tag

Jack Dalton wanted to see the factory for himself before he shelled out $25,000 for pay telephones. So he flew East from California for the inspection, like a man who kicks the tires to make sure a car he buys is no lemon. Dalton couldn't afford to be wrong about his new business opportunity. Unfortunately, he was.

The misadventure began when Dalton answered a small classified ad in a newspaper for the business opportunity in the coin telephone trade. He dialed an 800 number where a friendly voice took his name and address and within a day a batch of sales literature arrived at his home via an overnight mail service. Dalton was intrigued. After two phone discussions with the company's owner, he felt the venture was a sure bet. Dalton agreed to fly to Florida at his own expense to discuss the exciting venture.

There were no signs of trouble when the real-estate broker stepped off the plane and into bright Fort Lauderdale sunshine on September 29, 1993. At the airport was Jim Brown, owner of Consolidated Payphone Corporation, a large and jolly Santa figure who led Dalton on a tour through his sales and manufacturing wonderland.

Brown showed him a set of bright suites in a tropical office park alive with freshly cut fern. The corporate nameplate in gold lettering adorned the wall behind a cozy reception area, where more ferns and a plucky office secretary greeted out-of-town arrivals.

The visitors saw a dedicated sales force working out of a cozy room, some twenty of them, mostly men, in white shirts and patterned ties, ultra-formal attire in the telephone trade. They worked split shifts from 9 A.M. to 3 P.M., then 6 P.M. to 9 P.M. The guys stuck to the written sales script and did very well by it, earning $200 a week plus 8 percent commission. They made sales in an orderly, but steady fashion; one room manager sold one in four "qualified" clients, a very high rate. The sales manager brought bagels and candy for the staff and near the end of November, one executive's daughter dropped by to help put up Christmas decorations.

Consolidated's manufacturing arm also looked alive, at least to visitors. The metal-and-wire insides of payphones lay on work benches as a handful of technicians finished up assembly and quality-control checks prior to shipping. Some used a computer terminal which sat connected to a small electric pencil used to test the phone's dialing pads, a final quality check. Some days no technicians were around. Visitors were told they went home early that day because they were caught up on their duties.

The inventory room, near a back loading dock, gave the impression of a whopping sales volume. Some fifty massive sealed cartons stood ready for shipping to new coin phone owners all over the country.

Dalton sat with Brown for three hours that day after taking the tour and getting answers to all his questions. Before he left, he handed Brown a cashier's check for $14,000, a partial payment for ten pay phones. His contract promised delivery within thirty days.

Dalton, forty-six at the time, thought Brown's pitch made good sense. He still believes that if handled honestly it might have earned him some profits.

Dalton planned to have a staff run the coin-phone operation. One company would scout out good locations to place the phones, and his staff would develop a regular route to empty the machines. He also expected to split commissions off long-distance numbers called from the pay phones, and to expand the size of his operation greatly through Consolidated Payphone's easy credit terms.

But shortly after handing over his check and returning to California, he could no longer reach Brown on the phone. He called fifteen times and left messages, hoping for a callback. None came. Three days before Christmas, no coin phones in sight, Dalton swore in an affidavit that he was the victim of a fraud.

His total loss was $29,000: the $14,000 he left in Fort Lauderdale, $11,000 more he mailed to Brown to complete the purchase, $3,000 that was supposed to be paid to a company that would scout out locations for the pay phones, and $1,000 he paid to visit Florida.

"I was hoping for the American Dream," said Dalton. "This looked like a legitimate business and it was logical and very convincing. But it turned out to be lies at every turn of the road. Nobody has any phones that are working as far as I know."

Dalton walked into the Florida "Fly and Buy," one of the oldest and most persistent scams in the Sunshine State. It also is one of the most costly because victims often lose a minimum of $15,000 but losses often top $100,000.

Florida officials have tried for years to regulate sales of these "biz opps," as they're called in the illicit phone-sales trade. The problem is not one of inadequate laws. During the 1980s, Florida lawmakers enacted tough registration and financial disclosure laws for sellers of business opportunities, who often advertise their wares in the nation's most respected daily newspapers.

But the state's strict law making failure to register a felony punishable by jail time has failed to halt the hucksters. Police say they just don't have enough officers to corral every crook who takes up the scam.

Nobody is sure how many such offers are extended, but statistics from the Better Business Bureau of South Florida give a hint. "Biz opps" are the top source of "inquiries" to the bureau. The queries also frustrate the bureau's staff, who often have little information to impart. They see the same people offering franchises and other opportunities over and over, and yet they keep mum on the off chance that the deal in question could be legitimate.

Every year the Florida Department of Agriculture and Consumer Services gets about 1,400 complaints from buyers all over the nation about deals ranging from vending machines to greyhound racing dogs.

"Business opportunities are a real problem right now and they are growing," says Eileen Harrington, associate director for marketing practices of the Federal Trade Commission in Washington. "These are the big dollars. They don't change much from year to year, but we are seeing them sold more and more through boiler rooms. This is a new twist."

Consolidated Payphone Corporation is one business authorities no longer need to worry about, thanks largely to Fort Lauderdale Police Detective Kevin Allen. He is a cop so by-the-book he once arrested a young woman on Fort Lauderdale beach for pinching his backside: Allen charged her with battery on a law enforcement officer.

Fraud detective Allen charged Consolidated owner Jim Brown with failing to register his company as a business opportunity. Allen, who has spent years dealing with deceitful boiler-room salesmen, was tired of dropping by Consolidated with new complaints.

Police also charged Brown with organized fraud, allegedly for failing to deliver phones to victims and misrepresenting the product. Prosecutors are holding Brown accountable to refund more than $500,000 to twenty-nine customers. Brown pleaded guilty on November 30, 1994, to one felony count of organized fraud. His sentence: six years probation with an order to make restitution of $447,400 to his victims. If Brown fails to make quarterly restitution statements over the years of his probation, he can be sent to prison.*

In a separate action, Florida's attorney general won a court order prohibiting Brown from engaging in deceptive trade practices such as promising investors fantastic and unrealistic profits.

Consolidated Payphone Corporation customers and former employees have testified that the company was a sham despite the sophisticated sales pitch and factory.

In sworn statements and other court papers filed in the Florida attorney general's suit, they said:

• Despite his claims to manufacture "Ma-Bell-style" coin phones at his Fort Lauderdale plant, Brown bought the few phones he possessed from a company in Georgia for a few hundred dollars each. The disassembled phones in the "manufacturing center" were strictly window dressing for the benefit of fly-in customers. The reason why visitors often didn't see technicians was because there were hardly any.

• The computer that Consolidated claimed to be using in testing dialing pads and phone ringers was a dummy programmed to show a test pattern and to blink knowingly on cue. Few people who viewed the phony demonstration looked closely or knew enough about computers to realize the hoax.

• The inventory room packed with shipping crates was perhaps the boldest part of the scam. The boxes were packed with cinder blocks used to build homes in South Florida, the company's former executive vice president testified.

Martin Cohen, Consolidated's executive vice president until he left in a dispute with Brown, testified that the owner wanted to be able to show fly-in customers that Consolidated sent out product—lots of it.†

> He wanted to make believe that we had a lot of phones on the floor. So he bought empty boxes and hired two people from the labor pool and he picked them up and he drove over to pick up cinder blocks. . . . And he had them put the cinder blocks in these cartons and seal them up and put them on the floor like there were phones in them.

---

*State of Florida v. Jim W. Brown, Seventeenth Judicial Circuit, Broward County, Florida, 94-7740CFB.

†Sworn statement, Martin Cohen, Fort Lauderdale Police Case 93-191678, January 1994.

The steady and business-like pose of the fellows in the phone room was not exactly the full picture. One Consolidated employee allegedly parked a van outside and retreated there to smoke crack cocaine, leading a sales manager to demand drug testing for the entire shop. Another worker filed a sexual harassment lawsuit against a manager, accusing him of threatening to withhold her commissions unless she submitted to his sexual advances. The manager also boasted of underworld ties in New York, threatening anyone who crossed him would be "taken care of" by his underworld associates. He allegedly assaulted another worker who had stopped for a bite to eat at a local deli. All of the events, sworn to in a civil case, left Consolidated employees "unable to function normally" and "terrified of answering the phone, going to work (or) socializing."

None of this chaos came through to customers who took the tour. Nobody was taking the tour the day an angry man from Minnesota flew in unexpectedly, not to see the factory, but to demand his $50,000 back. He stormed in asking for a sales manager by name, telling the receptionist he wanted to "kick his ass." The man, who had grown impatient after nobody would return his phone calls or send him his equipment, left half an hour later, happy. He still didn't have any phones, but was assured they would be sent.

Although the Minnesotan's losses cannot be traced from available company records, chances are he didn't stay happy for long. "I haven't had one satisfied customer," former Consolidated executive Martin Cohen testified.

Cohen did not provide authorities with a precise figure of Consolidated's sales, but he said one Sunday alone he sent out contracts worth more than $200,000. Brown told customers he expected Consolidated to do as much as $6 million in annual sales. While authorities doubt the take was that high, they admit that the twenty-nine buyers who have contacted police are just a fraction of the total victims.

Many suspect business opportunities, from vending machines to shares in racing greyhound dogs, proceed through several stages before nailing the investor. Taking advantage of people's desire to be their own boss is a constant in the pitch. So is the reliance on sales literature and advertising that builds confidence quickly. Here are the stages.

First Pitch

Most biz-opps want to make the susceptible buyer seek them out. This sales tactic is far more efficient than rummaging through lead lists and "cold calling" people all over the country. So they aim for the people who scan the "Business Opportunity" classifieds of newspapers, and the more prestigious the paper the better. Newspapers typically argue that they have no business censoring advertising and should have no liability for accepting suspect ads.

Most buyers contact the boiler room after reading a newspaper ad such as this:

PAYPHONE ROUTES
No Money Down!Lowest, Factory
Direct Prices.
800-xxx-xxxx

The scammers send the ad to major metropolitan newspapers, which routinely run them with few, if any, questions asked. Typically, they send a bank check for as much as $1,000 with instructions to run the ad "until it burns out," or the charges exceed the payment. Many sales rooms run up to twenty of these ads at one time to ensure a steady stream of callers into the boiler room. Some also order their ads through advertising placement agencies, which further cloaks them.

The newspaper industry's failure to check up on these advertisers is a sore point with many regulators. Newspapers argue that they cannot be expected to judge the legitimacy of an ad they publish. Regulators argue that the papers should at least determine if a company has filed registration papers. At least one state does. A 1984 Indiana law requires Hoosier newspapers to verify that a seller of business opportunities is registered with the state before publishing its ads. But many states impose few if any restrictions.

"The newspapers don't care, they get the check and it doesn't bounce," says Bob James, an investigator with Florida's Department of Agriculture and Consumer Services. "The newspapers are the leak in the dam." James argues that newspapers should have a duty to find out if their advertisers are licensed. "Without the newspapers, this would dry up in a week."

But the boiler rooms would surely find another method to spread their message if forced to. One coin-phone opportunity solicited customers through a mailer, similar to so many others sent out by telemarketers.

HUGE PROFITS NOW!

Millions Made by Private Individuals Since De-Regulation.
Prime Locations Available Near You—Don't Miss Out!
$5K to $6K per week Cash Income. Zero Down if Qualified.
Factory Sponsored Loan Program. Low Overhead
Smart Phones Do All the Work for You
Guaranteed Lowest Factory Direct Prices
Recession Proof Business
Part time or Full Time—Detailed Package Available.
Free Info. 24 Hours. Call
1-800-XXX-XXXX.

Once the sales rooms have got the customers' attention they route them to a "lead girl," similar to a fronter or inexperienced worker. She takes basic information, such as the caller's name, address, and phone number; what time to call back, and where he saw the ad. The sales rooms like to keep track of the location of their customers, particularly if they are drawing "heat" from one state's attorney general.

The sales room tries to have someone return all calls within half an hour of receipt, and this is where the pitch begins, starting soft.

Telemarketers give an initial sales talk and try to overcome any objections or answer initial questions. They talk customers into paying for an overnight courier to receive sales literature. Those who won't agree to pay the freight (under fifteen dollars) are not considered serious and are disposed of.

The sales agents wait three to five days and then call back to judge whether a customer is interested.

Here's part of a written coin-phone sales pitch. It's typical of many business-opportunities offers, stirring the imagination of the would-be entrepreneur.*

A WONDERFUL OPPORTUNITY FOR THE $MALL INVESTOR

$ A quarter may seem like a small amount of money, yet many of the largest fortunes in this country have been built on individual sales with profits no more than a penny, nickel, or dime.

$ The next time you watch someone drop a quarter in a Pay Phone, multiply that person by the hundreds of thousands of others in this country

*Source: Maryland Attorney General's Office.

who do the same thing every day of the year. Then you will begin to realize how much money these little silent mechanical salesmen accumulate for their owners. Yet they are paid no salaries, they hand in no expense account, they work at their jobs night and day and never ask for holidays or vacations.

$ The operating of Pay Phone routes is not confined to large cities. The small investor has, in many cases, equal or better opportunities of making a greater profit. The small operator has the advantage of close personal supervision and minimum operating cost, using the home until he gets the business built up from its own earnings to a point where it demands larger quarters. This business, however, also interests persons with unlimited capital.

Other sales literature gets more specific and this is where the problems begin, usually because the marketers promise a specific rate of return such as 60 percent return on investment in the first year.

Puffing

Sellers call it "puffing" when they begin to step up the extravagant sales claims and exaggerate the benefits. Many also claim to have direct ties to factories, thus allowing buyers to bypass middlemen and make far higher profits. They often offer loans to help their affiliates expand rapidly or promise exclusive sales territories, which turn out to be sold over and over. Some offer to buy back any routes that prove to be unsuccessful. All such claims, of course, are designed to minimize the risks and appeal to the would-be entrepreneur's greed. So do grossly overstated claims of profits.

Consolidated Payphone persuaded many buyers by offering to finance the purchase of as many additional phones as affiliates could handle, charging only a 10 percent down payment. One company flyer read: "GET THE MOST FOR YOUR MONEY! Don't be a chump!"

Consolidated hit on many of the themes common to small-business scams. Here's a sample obtained from Fort Lauderdale police files:

DO YOU WANT TO BE SUCCESSFUL?

It's not difficult, but you must use your head. These are the rules which must be followed:

1. You must buy right. Deal directly with the factory—you simply can't afford to pay fat commissions out of your pocket to middlemen.

2. Hook up with a company that will back you with a genuine loan program and not some phoney baloney. It's not a big trick to make it in business if you have something in your back pocket.

3. Once you are in operation, conduct your affairs responsibly! Keep accurate records, file your taxes on time, keep your units operational, be honest with your location owners and if you really want to turn your business into something big, re-invest as much as you possibly can.

If you follow these simple rules, you can have it all and provide your family with the very best of everything that money can buy.

Sending buyers inspirational messages does not violate any laws. But when the puffing gets to the point, as it often does, of guaranteeing earnings levels, smart buyers bail out or do their homework carefully. Not-so-smart buyers often listen to testimonials from happy customers whose names they get from the company, not independent sources.

Singers

While many customers find it hard to believe, business-opportunities vendors often pay people to lie about their experience. They call them "singers" in the trade because they praise the product to an unsuspecting buyer. They also "paint the dream" to excite buyers. The shills are more sophisticated than the audience plant at a carnival, often snowing new buyers by mixing technical lingo they don't understand with old fashioned rags-to-riches yarns. The buyers may hang up a little confused about the precise details, but they are convinced they will cash in.

Martin Cohen, the former vice president at Consolidated Payphone, explained the procedure in a sworn statement to Fort Lauderdale police.

A singer is somebody . . . that has painted a dream for a customer. These people (investors) don't have a hundred thousand, two hundred thousand to invest. They may have twenty, twenty-five thousand and they believe in the dream. And the singer paints the dream, OK? And he tells you what you want to hear.

Sometimes the singers are the owners of the company, posing as satisfied buyers. Florida's attorney general, based in part on sworn statements taken from Cohen, accused Brown of singing his own song for Consolidated Payphone. He allegedly gave investors the name "Bob Page" and an 800 number to contact him. Each buyer was told "Page" lived in a neighboring state. When they called, "Page" gave a glowing assessment of Consolidated Payphone. He claimed to own more than one hundred phones and be raking in profits. One caller from the Kansas City area remembered his contacts with Page as uplifting and inspiring.* He thought Page lived in Omaha.

> Mr. Page returned my call and related that he had been terminated from his job, had invested in the phones three and a half years ago. He said he had started with fifteen phones prior to the currently advantageous financing program. He now owned three hundred phones and was doing so well that he had brought both his sons into the business. He invited me and my wife to get together for dinner if we visited Omaha. Mr. Page returned several calls and always had positive, business-like answers to all my questions.

The 800 number listed for Page was an answering service that forwarded calls to Fort Lauderdale. Cohen testified that Brown would get on the line and disguise his voice to begin touting the company. After one customer discovered the ruse and confronted Brown, he got a refund, records state.

Other singers are paid for their services, usually $150 a week and $50 for any sale that results. Some companies also have used paid references to deceive customers. One Fort Lauderdale phone biz-opp paid the seventy-two-year-old mother of an employee $300 a week to tell callers she had ten telephones and was very happy she had entered the business. She had two extra phone lines installed in her California home to handle the volume of calls from customers seeking her reference.

Some buyers also try to check independent references such as the local Better Business Bureaus, but many people find the results disappointing. No complaints is no indication that a company is on the up and up.

---

*Complaint affidavit, Florida Attorney General's Office, December 27, 1993.

For example, the Miami-based Better Business Bureau's report on Consolidated Payphone contained general cautions about dealing with a business opportunity, but with this "customer experience" record: "our file experience shows this company has one complaint which has been settled."

The bureau found itself hastily filing an update to that report which read: "On February 2, 1994, authorities seized the company's business records, equipment and bank accounts, and arrested the president on a felony charge of not being registered to sell business opportunities in Florida."

The Owner's Close

Once customers have heard the singers' song, are satisfied, ready to deal, and demonstrate that they have the money to follow through, they are set up for the owner's close. It may not actually be the owner who handles the transaction, but buyers feel better to know they are talking to the top dog. The owner gets a cashier's check from the buyer sent out by overnight mail or makes arrangements to have the customer visit the site, where the rest of the money is taken.

The Stall

Many customers begin to get nervous after plunking down thousands of dollars, money most of them cannot afford to lose. They call and want to know when their product will arrive so they can get started. This is the point when the scam artists get creative and invent stories to explain why the product has not arrived, often four months beyond the shipping date specified in the contract.

Some companies throw out excuses as fast as a major league pitcher. They claim:

• A selection committee must meet to approve a final sale. (There is no committee and everybody gets approved, but the tactic appeals to the buyer's desire for exclusivity and gives a handy excuse for nondelivery.) The key committee members are said to be out of town inspecting properties in other parts of the country and unable to meet until next month.

• The parts needed by the factory are made in Taiwan and are on back order, or were shipped to the wrong site, or lost in transit.

• The parent company is having financial problems and has applied for a loan. While buyers are told the loan won't affect their transaction, they still must wait until the bank gives the go ahead.

• Licenses must be obtained. Some coin-phone scams have told buyers that they would have to wait an additional four to six weeks to get delivery of their phones because the company had to apply for a license from the public service commission in the buyer's state. Often buyers never check this assertion.

Heat Calls

A biz-opp reaches a maturity stage when the excuses start to wear thin and anxious calls from customers turn into "heat calls," in which buyers are threatening to go to police. Experienced operators can calm many of these callers with a new round of excuses, but eventually the regulatory agencies begin coming around. At this point, some refunds must be given, or the owners shut down and reopen under a new name.

With checks for thousands of dollars arriving in overnight mail almost daily, con artists would appear to build up enormous reserves. But they also must pay out cash commissions to sales agents weekly in order to keep top telemarketers. And owners often bleed the company for personal expenses, leaving behind cash flow crunches.

Yet customers who receive merchandise after complaining long and loud still may not be happy. Consolidated Payphone customer John Baumgartner is not.

Baumgartner, of Milwaukee, has five pay phones sitting in his house, useless because he never received the software, instruction pads, and training materials he needed to get his business up and running. He is ringing mad.

"I'm sitting dead in the water," Baumgartner says in an interview from his job at a security hangar at an airport. "I am absolutely beside myself. I borrowed money to start my first business venture, but I guess I was naive. That $15,000 was a lot of money to me."

Many other victims of these schemes are first-time entrepreneurs. The pitch often targets men over forty, with some supervisory experience, who've been laid off from a job for some time and can't find anything comparable to what they used to earn.

"The guy is desperate and tries to go into business for himself," says Florida investigator Bob James. "The problem is he spends more time buying a color television than investigating the deal."

Not all of the victims fit a profile though. Two Fort Lauderdale men, who collected more than $500,000 from investors whom they picked up at the airport in a white stretch limo, suckered victims of all ages and income levels. Among them was a veteran who lost his legs in Vietnam, an engineering student from Texas A&M who borrowed $16,000 from a bank to invest in the phones, and a Kansas couple who used their retirement pay.

Even when they get their products, many of these aspiring entrepreneurs fail, James says, because they lack the "street smarts" to run their own business. Often, they are embarrassed to admit failure and won't report their experience to authorities, or they get talked into taking back a fraction of the money they invested.

"The smart operators never let the complaints get to us," says James. "When their customers demand refunds they offer them twenty-five cents on the dollar and they take the equipment back. In effect, they buy back their complaints." Getting the equipment back, the con artist simply resells it to another sucker.

There usually isn't much hope of refunds once one of these companies shuts its doors.

One South Florida payphone operation took hundreds of investors without delivering the phones or granting refunds. A New Jersey investor wrote to a newspaper reporter of his anguish. He asked not to be named.

> After numerous telephone conversations with this Florida based company, and exhaustive investigation, I flew down to Florida to explore this opportunity in greater detail at their Pompano Beach offices.
>
> After a lengthy meeting and demonstration, I gave this company approximately $25,000 for the purchase of 10 GTE Model #2225 computerized pay telephones. I subsequently spent additional money for a locating service to sign up suitable locations for my telephones.
>
> The Florida company then stole my money—and ran away! And they did the same thing to over 100 other people, as well, stealing several million dollars and not delivering the promised telephones. . . . Your help, please! We just can't afford to lose the $25,000.

The state tried to help. Florida's attorney general filed a lawsuit accusing the firm L+V Enterprises and its owners of consumer fraud.

The men who ran the payphone company didn't even hire lawyers to contest the charges. They gave a feeble defense on their own behalf, pleading poverty, as telemarketers often do when they get hauled into court.

The state won a judgment against them for $1.5 million in 1992 and an order barring the pair from setting up further vending schemes in the state. But that was the full extent of the punishment. And authorities have no idea whether they are back in business under different names, or using other individuals as fronts.

In answer to his pleas, the man from New Jersey got a letter trumpeting the state's win. But the letter added a somber sentence, once again words to the wise: "At this time, however, the businesses are closed and we have been unable to locate any money or other assets through which to collect on the award."*

The Florida fly-and-buy has a long and ignoble history. Many consumer advocates trace the concept to the General Development Corporation, the giant land swindle that flew mostly working-class people to out-of-the-way Florida locations to review properties. A key tactic, as emerged in court years later, was that they never let their prey escape, or shop around, until after they had signed a contract. They told buyers their purchases were investments. Only months, and sometimes years later, did the investors discover that the houses were priced far above their worth.

Four of General Development's top executives drew jail sentences in 1993 and were ordered to repay more than $2 million to consumers. Sentences on the federal fraud charges ranged from five years for a company vice president to ten years for its president, Robert Erlich. Prosecutors said the scheme caused damages topping $117 million, on the sale of about ten thousand homes from 1983 to 1989. An average home cost about $74,000.†

Many other associates of General Development, primarily sales agents schooled in the scheme through videotaped training sessions, never went to jail. They turned to telemarketing and added many of General Development's high-pressure techniques into their repertoire.

Then, as now, state laws wouldn't prevent recurrences of these swindles. As we've learned, most states require business opportunities to register, but nobody checks to make sure the information they provide is accurate. In Florida, registration costs three hundred dollars and requires a biography of the owner, a description of any past bankruptcies, felony

---

*Letter to investors, Florida Assistant Attorney General Jody E. Collins, December 30, 1992.
†In a highly unusual legal move, a Florida appeals court in March 1995 allowed the four chief defendants to go free while the judges considered their appeal.

convictions, or other background. Applicants also must provide copies of unaudited financial statements and sample contracts for review. In 1993, its first year administering the program, the state licensed nearly one thousand sellers of business opportunities.

Florida law also requires a business opportunity headquartered in the state or selling there to provide buyers with its registration statements three days before the purchase.

Violators often draw only small fines for failing to register or provide information to investors. The state Consumer Affairs Department levied $15,825 in fines in its first year of enforcement in nineteen actions, most involving firms that hawked their wares at trade shows. Officials admit these fines are pocket change.

Gloria Van Treese, of the Department of Agriculture and Consumer Services, says the agency has been aggressive in forcing businesses to register, but that ultimately the buyer must beware.

"Like with any kind of business, people need to be careful to do background checks and not get carried away by the puffing," she says. "People need to ask for financial records and check references. These are all the questions that people don't think to ask."*

Van Treese admits that her agency must rely on the goodwill of the registrants to honestly list their backgrounds. "We have no way of knowing if the information they provide is accurate. Our crystal ball is on the blink. If they don't tell us about their past, there is no way for us to know it."

The federal government seems to be picking up some of the slack from Florida and other states that have large numbers of biz-opps causing problems.

The Federal Trade Commission in 1994 shut down several vending-machine and franchise deals, including a titan of the industry, Indoor Amusement, and forty-one other corporations controlled by Boca Raton, Florida, resident Marvin Wolf, whose former sales agents have spread out and sold business opportunities throughout the state. Authorities also raided Wolf-controlled companies in New York; Phoenix; and Vienna, Virginia, outside of Washington.†

Wolf's companies sold pizza-vending machines, telling buyers they could gross up to $350 a week per machine and pay for their equipment in six months. They also promised exclusive territories, high-traffic loca-

---

*Interview, Gloria Van Treese, May 6, 1994.

†Civil Action No. 94-8119 CIV-Ferguson, U.S. District Court for the Southern District of Florida, West Palm Beach Division, March 2, 1994.

tions for the machines, using shills or singers to hype the products. The FTC charged the companies with violating the federal franchise rule that requires investors to be given financial statements and other information substantiating the company's profit claims.

FTC officials said they had documented 175 complaints from investors who put in between $2,000 and $135,000 each for the pizza machines. They estimated the total take from the ventures at more than $20 million.

But as government lawyers prepared the civil suit for trial in the fall of 1994, one thing seemed clear: very little of the money would be returned to the investors, perhaps as little as $150,000.

Not everyone believes that civil enforcement ever will clean up the biz-opps racket. Some feel that the operators can too easily evade court judgments and reopen under new names with a new telephone room.

Susan Keener, a former employee of one of the biz-opp telemarketing firms, said she received two hundred complaints in one month working in customer service. She used the shipping-delay excuse and several others before realizing she was working for a scam. About her bosses, she said: "They've just taken their savings, they've destroyed their dreams, they've destroyed their faith in humanity and I think they need to serve a little jail time and let them see that you just can't walk around squashing people alive and get away with it."*

Some sellers of biz-opps have truly hit on great new ideas that could well make their investors rich, maybe even overnight. But don't bet on it. Many of the people hawking chances of a lifetime to run one's own business have in fact failed at such endeavors, and left previous investors holding the bag.

Many of these entrepreneurs collect substantial amounts of money from investors, often on the condition that they have six months or so to deliver their product. With that kind of money collected up front, there is quite a temptation to turn and run, or go out of business, claiming problems that could not be foreseen.

Given this pattern, individuals seeking a business opportunity are foolish not to thoroughly check out the past of anyone offering such a scheme. Here are some suggestions for doing so:

---

*Sworn statement of Susan Keener, Fort Lauderdale Police Case FL 6339PB, December 31, 1993.

- Many states require that the companies register with the state and file financial disclosure statements prior to placing any advertising to sell a business opportunity. Others require that any buyer be given financial statements at least three days prior to the signing of the agreement. Federal regulations require financial statements to be produced ten days before any money can be collected. Any business opportunities that violate these provisions are not worthy of trust.

- Don't fall for offers that say to sign up now before prices go up. Sellers with good offers do not use these tactics.

- Ask for disclosure statements, but don't stop there in checking out the operators. Most states don't check to make sure the details provided in registration forms are accurate.

- Check corporate histories of the individuals with companies that collect credit information on businesses. If individuals have dozens of corporations listed, many of them defunct, run away.

- Ask participants at a trade show whether they are registered with all states, and get a copy of the registration statement. Don't be content with that filing. Make use of increasing on-line services through libraries to check out these individuals.

- Check lawsuits. Most can be found by calling the clerk's office of the civil division of the courthouse. Business credit reports will also help run down these cases. Many of these checks can be made by computer. If you can't do these checks, consider hiring a private investigator who can. While a clean record does not guarantee a firm is honest, a lawsuit filed by a state attorney general is a warning to back off.

- Call the newspaper that placed the ad for the business opportunity to make sure no complaints have been received against the company. Also check with the local Better Business Bureau. Try to get any information the bureau has on previous operations run by the seller of a business opportunity.

- Seek out on-line computer services, clubs of enthusiasts, and trade associations that have expertise in the sale of the product you are considering. Write them for information. Some of the associations representing legitimate businesses are appalled by the blatant con jobs that give their trade a black eye and will help you judge the validity of a sales offer.

• Don't be afraid to ask questions. Forget about taking a tour of the work site or factory unless you have some extra time to make a few other stops, such as the state attorney general's offices. Check for complaints there, if possible. Drop by the local newspaper and ask for information. The local police department fraud unit and consumer affairs department are also good sources. Check occupational licenses with the city, or "fictitious names" filings to verify owners of the business.

• Be leery of groups or trade associations that will license and offer a positive reference for anyone who pays a fee to join. Ask if in doubt.

Most of all, buyers must be psychologically prepared for a letdown if an investigation or background check turns up damning information. Many regulators find that victims of these sorts of scams support the company they have pinned their hopes on, ignoring the warning signs.

Remember: it's not enough to get the promises in writing if you are dealing with a telephone huckster intent on defrauding investors. While taking the above steps may seem like too much work, they will pay off. There's an old newspaper adage that applies well to business opportunities. It's advice often given to rookie reporters prone to accept statements at face value: "If your mother says she loves you, check it out."

10

Golden Eggs

The ostrich hardly seems like a terrific cash crop. After all, the birds are awkward at seven feet tall, weigh more than three hundred pounds, and can be meaner than a Texas tornado. But in the early 1990s the ostrich hit the front pages of newspapers, hyped as the newest farming and healthful-eating fad. News articles raved about the highly prized feathers, durable hides, and breeding potential. And the meat, much leaner and less caloric than beef, began landing on painted plates at the trendiest of urban eateries.

With all the hoopla, it didn't take long for the herd of investment telemarketers and other quick-buck breeders to hawk shares in ostrich farms.

"The easiest thing to do is to take something that is legitimate and run a scheme off of it," says one veteran of the craft. "You just play on people's greed. If you tell a good enough story, people will send you their money."

Plenty of people sent their money to U.S. Ostrich. The firm's telemarketers persuaded more than one thousand investors from 48 states to send $3 million to breed the big birds on a ranch in rural South Florida.

The plan seemed sound, promising 40 percent to 60 percent returns on investment within a year. U.S. Ostrich predicted its six breeding couples would produce 50 eggs. They figured 10 would be "nonfertile," and 8 would die, leaving 32 chicks per pair. Riding a bullish market, the company expected to sell the chicks at three or six months of age for an "estimated seasonal profit" of $1.3 million. The company even offered a money-back guarantee in the early stages of the venture.

None of the partners saw a dime from the golden eggs. Instead, U.S. Ostrich crashed in bankruptcy court. The top twenty investors alone dropped $800,625. A postal worker from Baltimore lost $247,500, a nest egg he built from years of savings and bonds. Many others lost a few thousand dollars or less, but some had to borrow to invest in the ostrich scheme.

The buyers purchased general partnerships in the venture. They ranged from ambitious working stiffs to retirees looking to occupy their leisure time. An X-ray technician at an Indiana hospital spent weekends pumping gas to buy some units. Three others had retired from substantial careers: a naval officer from Nashville, a finance manager for the state of Oregon, and a civil engineer who put in thirty years with the California Department of Transportation.

They fell victim to yet another destructive telemarketing deal, the sale of general partnerships to scores of investors. Phone rooms from southern California to South Florida pitch these deals, far faster than government regulators can step up to swat them down. Recent entries in the field range from wireless cable and radio waves to mining and mineral ventures.

While regulators argue that many of these offers are shams set up to evade securities laws and conceal risks, they often don't file court action until long after the money is gone. While the products change from year to year, the results too often are the same: big losses for small, unsophisticated investors who hoped they could get ahead of the game.

"These frauds are like a mosaic. There are lots of little pieces and almost all of them mislead an investor and separate them from their money," Gregory P. von Schaumburg, a U.S. Securities and Exchange Commission attorney in Chicago said in an interview in 1994. "It is like a minuet. They do a dance step and we try to counter it. They try to avoid securities laws because those laws make it much more difficult for them to be selling these things." Von Schaumburg said public education is the best way to halt these phone hucksters, many of whom run scam after scam despite civil prosecutions. "Some of these people make their living in securities fraud. It's sad but true. All we can do is enforce the statutes. We can't send them to Devil's Island," he says.

Many of the partnership deals post all the signs of the phone-sales scam seen in earlier chapters, tactics bona fide brokers will not employ.

Boiler rooms send out postcards or letters promising unrealistic rates of return, or telemarketers call previous investors whose names they purchase. One boiler room spent over $66,000 in less than a year simply to snag names and numbers of new suckers. Finally, these "investment counselors" ask the client to send a check, often a certified check (via the usual overnight delivery service) to make sure they get their units before all are sold.

After the sale, the companies may send cheap videotapes of the product, much like the vacation-certificate scams, to placate expectant buyers. Others send newspaper clippings that appear to tout the product, or suggest it will appreciate rapidly. Sometimes the buyers are invited to a faraway partnership meeting and sometimes the venture collapses without ever holding a caucus.

While the warning signs of these scams may seem hard to miss, many customers do. Perhaps some drop their guard believing, mistakenly, that investments sold over the phone cannot exact the same financial ruin as the sleazy offerings of Las Vegas "one-in-five" prize rooms. Or they may think, also wrongly, that government regulators are standing by to bail them out should they deal with a dishonest, or incompetent, telephone broker.

Others get taken because they deeply mistrust government "red tape," such as requirements to file disclosure forms prior to selling shares in a business deal. Some people love to hear pitchmen rail against useless bureaucrats who stand in the way of honest, hard-working entrepreneurs by making them comply with costly regulations such as filing financial disclosure forms.

The antigovernment pitch never fails to elicit knowing nods from a roomful of sales prospects, many of whom will later wish they had checked with their state's attorney general, or some other regulator, before opening their wallets.

U.S. Ostrich made its offer sound simple enough. It sold general partnerships at $625 a unit. Investors could purchase as many units as they wanted, but received only a single vote in the partnership. The euphoric first phase, which began in October 1992, sold so well that the company opened up Ostrich II, luring in even more contributors before any eggs had hatched.

Most partners didn't settle for a single unit and some bought dozens over the phone, even though they had little or no idea who set up the company and whether they were trustworthy.

It took hindsight for several ostrich investors to realize they were gullible, greedy, or ignorant of what they were buying and the tough times that lay ahead for their ranch.

Lambertus Vanderstrom, of Comstock Park, Michigan, a sixty-five-year-old retired postal employee, didn't know stocks from bonds from partnerships. He lost $2,500, more than he could afford. "Maybe we were kind of gullible. It was the first time I ever invested in anything," says Vanderstrom, an electronics technician who worked at automating mail operations in his thirty-seven-year postal career. "I feel like I got burned," he said in an interview.

Vanderstrom learned a quick lesson in the legal pitfalls of these offerings. He volunteered to become a managing partner along with seven others. The managing partners were supposed to decide policy matters, but Vanderstrom said that in reality, they had no say in the company's day-to-day affairs.

Vanderstrom didn't understand that a partner could be liable for debts even beyond the amount of money he invested. Lawyers call it "joint and several" liability, which means that each partner is on the hook for the full amount of the venture's debts if the others can't pay.

After the ostrich deal soured, government regulators served "managing partner" Vanderstrom with a legal complaint, leaving him frightened at the prospect of having to fight Uncle Sam in court. He filed a court affidavit in response: "I invested all my savings into (the ostrich deal). As a retiree I do not have any extra money to afford an attorney. I request that the court appoint one, in case one is needed."

Vanderstrom took his loss in stride. "I have a roof over my head and enough to eat. That's all I really need. Life must go on."

Vanderstrom and his partners first spotted signs of trouble in the fall of 1993, when the U.S. Securities and Exchange Commission (SEC) began snooping around and auditing the books. In December 1993, while awaiting an ostrich birth announcement, investors got alarming news instead.

The SEC, which regulates the sales of stocks nationwide, charged U.S. Ostrich and its key executives with civil fraud.* Within a month of the lawsuit, the company filed for bankruptcy.† The SEC accused the executives of misusing funds and deceiving buyers by failing to advise them of the extent of their legal duties and failing to disclose past brushes with the law.

The federal agency also charged that U.S. Ostrich and its directors "deliberately structured" the partnerships to avoid SEC registration, which would require disclosure of the company's past and finances. SEC registration cannot guarantee a company will prosper, as anyone who ever lost money in the stock market can readily attest. But registration gives investors a better view of the previous experience of the key executives, factors professionals often consider in deciding whether to invest.

To bolster their case against the ostrich scheme, SEC attorneys filed court affidavits from investors who said they would never have bought units had they known more about the ostrich promoters.

---

*SEC v. U.S. Ostrich, U.S. District Court for the Southern District of Florida, Civil Action No. 93-7082, December 22, 1993.

†U.S. Bankruptcy Court, Southern District of Florida, No. 94-30022-BLC-PGH.

While it helped persuade more than one thousand investors to buy in, the sales literature was little help in judging the fitness of the farmers, according to the SEC. The brochures didn't answer basic questions about the offer's sponsor, Junction Financial Corp., which billed itself as "a privately-owned Florida corporation which for years has developed and promoted innovative commercial programs for exploitation by massed-capital general partnerships."

Operating out of a six-thousand-square-foot warehouse in Hallandale, Florida, an oceanside retirement community south of Fort Lauderdale, Junction described the ostrich deal as a "unique, ground-floor opportunity." Here is what the company disclosed according to sales literature introduced as evidence in the 1994 bankruptcy case:

Junction Financial Corp. Q&A

Q: How long has Junction Financial Corp. been in business?

A: Junction Financial Corp. has been in business since 1985, and at its present facilities since 1989. Junction Financial Corp. is a Florida corporation in good standing, and holds all required state charters and local licenses and permits necessary for the conduct of its business.

Q. Are you licensed?

A: Yes. Junction Financial Corp. has posted a bond and is licensed with the Florida Department of Agriculture and Consumer Services.

Q. Has Junction Financial Corp. done this kind of thing before?

A. Yes. Junction Financial Corp. has helped organize and develop several successful general partnership programs since 1985.

Nothing in Junction's Q&A is false. Junction had secured a bond with the state of Florida. While such a bond can be drawn upon to cover minor losses, it offers no real protection for investors in a multimillion-dollar company.

At the time of the ostrich offering, Junction was in "good standing" with the state. But so is any corporation that files an annual report and pays its renewal fee. The action says nothing about the honesty or stability of the company.

Just as its literature said, Junction Financial Corp. had sold general partnerships before. But the company did not reveal that seven states in separate legal actions had issued orders for Junction to quit selling its wares within their borders.* Like the federal SEC, the states argued the partnerships were unregistered securities.

The sales papers also failed to mention that Junction's telemarketing included some suspect products, such as Florida travel certificates, an endeavor that has drawn fire from consumer regulators all over America and beyond.

In perhaps the most significant omission of all, sales pamphlets gave no details about the company's key executives or financial backers. Only one name appeared: Marcia Josowitz, a sixtyish woman listed as Junction's president. Her husband, a postal service pensioner, headed the second company that was to manage the ostrich partnership.

But investors who arrived at a general partnership meeting in April 1993 at a West Palm Beach hotel found Marcia Josowitz acting more like a recording secretary and bookkeeper than chief executive. Her husband, Stanley, said almost nothing, except to tell the crowd he was indeed the "head honcho" of the management outlet.

Both deferred to their "program coordinator," who did most of the talking. The man who took the reins at the partnership meeting was Stephen Tashman, a boiler-room veteran who put burrs in the backsides of several sets of government lawyers. Tashman's mother and Marcia Josowitz were the sole stockholders in Junction Financial Corp., SEC regulators said in court filings.

In the early 1980s, oil and gas leases dominated the big-dollar boiler-room racket in South Florida. Lawsuits against one such company, which defrauded investors out of $51 million, took almost a decade to unravel.

Steve Tashman helped create a different company that stung investors for more than $8 million in oil and gas, not leases but actual drilling of wells. Beginning in 1984, Atlantex Associates, of North Miami Beach, sold partnerships for wells in Texas. Tashman wrote telephone-sales scripts, paced the sales floor in the boiler room, hired and fired telemarketers, and helped run partnership gatherings, court filings allege.

Atlantex promised buyers steady monthly income, little or no risks, and earnings that would surpass their investment in a year. Many people committed $12,000 for eight units in an oil deal. Atlantex retained 35 percent to 40 percent of the money as "organizational fees and administrative costs." While the company did lease wells, the yields came up far short of the gushers promised by telemarketers.

*The SEC lawsuit names the states as: Wisconsin, Washington, Hawaii, Oregon, Kansas, North Dakota, and South Dakota.

Atlantex picked managing partners mostly from consumers who had not complained about measly dividends and sold many people more units by lying about profits that were about to come due, a federal judge ruled.*

Atlantex went under in much the same manner as the ostrich venture would nearly a decade later. It fell apart when the Federal Trade Commission sued, alleging deceptive sales tactics and fraud. A Miami judge halted Atlantex from puffing up sales figures, but the court order hardly mattered.

Atlantex filed for bankruptcy on January 21, 1987, just 10 days after the FTC lawsuit. In November 1987 a federal court judge barred Tashman and other Atlantex executives from engaging in the sale of partnerships for oil and gas leases.

The judge also slapped the defendants with a whopping judgment: $12,175,250, which was upheld on appeal. Each defendant was liable for the full amount if the others could not pay.

Nobody paid. After Atlantex filed for bankruptcy, FTC officials said they could not locate any assets to repay the investors.

Tashman continued to have other run-ins with the law, mostly securities regulators:

• Tashman pleaded no contest to a felony charge of fraud in Texas in 1988 for his role in selling the oil and gas offers, according to SEC court filings. He drew probation as a sentence.

• He was the subject of cease-and-desist orders in New Mexico, Kansas, Texas, Massachusetts, Florida, and Alabama for selling unregistered securities, according to SEC court filings.

• He sold $825,000 worth of partnerships in Teen Discos, nightclubs for the underage crowd, claiming almost no risk and that buyers would earn their investment back within a year. Tashman shut down after eleven months, a federal judge affirmed. The partners lost almost all of their investment.

• In May 1990 Tashman's Junction Financial Corp. sold vacation certificates using the trusty "one-in-five" prize formula, but with a new twist: the 900 number. Junction's automatic dialers rang millions of telephones with a voice mail pitch, telling them they had "won" a vacation, with "no strings attached . . . nothing to buy."

---

*FTC v. Atlantex Associates, U.S. District Court for the Southern District of Florida, Case No. 87-0045, November 25, 1987.

Callers ended up with fifteen dollars to twenty dollars for the toll-call stuck on their monthly phone bill, and many felt ripped off after they heard of restrictions and extra fees for the trip. Junction also promised "free" photographic film for life. Left unsaid: the customer got a "free" roll of film for every one brought in for processing.

"Make no mistake: We will eliminate 900-number fraud in New Jersey," incensed State Attorney General Robert J. Del Tufo said in filing a lawsuit against Junction Financial Group in May 1991.* "We intend to continue bringing these companies to justice. Potential violators will think twice before preying on New Jersey consumers." Junction President Josowitz agreed to halt the promotion and give refunds. The company did not admit wrongdoing.

In June 1991, then-New York Attorney General Robert Abrams sued Junction for fraud, alleging that fewer than one of one hundred people who called the 900 number got a vacation. In February 1993 Tashman signed a promise not to sell by phone into New York State without posting a bond of $500,000. He didn't admit wrongdoing. Junction also paid $12,000 in costs and agreed to make some refunds.†

By the time Tashman settled the civil suit against him in New York, U.S. Ostrich Corp., had hauled in more than $1 million and set up its partnership meeting.

The late spring weekend in West Palm Beach was a time of high excitement for the bird breeders. At the ostrich partnership meeting, most who stepped to the microphone to ask questions exuded high hopes and confidence. An accountant from northern Virginia rose to tell the group he had "wised up" and quit the federal government after 15 years to run his own show, including twenty-two partnerships.

While one investor cautioned that he was "wrapped up with a lot of people with stars in their eyes," few shared his skepticism.

Most of the 141 partners brought their spouses for the weekend outing. Visiting the ostrich ranch, they saw incubators, large clean pens, and computerized breeding equipment. A modern split-level home with a short chain link fence surrounded the property. The birds pushed up against the fence, their pipe-like necks protruding way over the enclosure, their demeanor far less than hospitable. The birds can be territorial and

---

*Del Tufo news release, May 21, 1991.

†The state of New York's case against Junction Financial Corp., was settled March 31, 1993. Tashman signed an "assurance of discontinuance" without admitting any violation of state law on February 26, 1994.

mean, especially during breeding season. Back at the hotel, outside the meeting room, colorful ostrich plumes were displayed.

While investors paid their own travel costs, Junction picked up everybody's hotel bill and bar and restaurant tabs. The business meeting began after a buffet lunch.

Flanked by a lawyer, accountant, and other members of the sales and management team, Tashman seemed very much in control and able to quash any doubts quickly. He presided over the election of the eight managing partners and talked up the soaring prices for the exotic birds and their offspring. "Who ever heard of an ostrich five months ago? All of a sudden you can't read a newspaper or you can't see TV or even listen to a radio show without somebody talking about ostriches," Tashman said. "It is hard to believe."

Tashman credited the publicity with fueling rapid rises in prices, jacking them up to the point that three-month-old chicks sold for $3,500, while six-month-olds commanded $4,500. Said Tashman: "The marketing strategy is to get as much cash out as we can as quickly as we can. Once we get our money out, once we get that money out, I don't care how many pair (of ostriches) we hold onto. I just want to get the money out first. That is all I am concerned about," he said at the meeting.

Tashman put off other inquiries about the finances of the project by suggesting that he assumed much risk and had paid in advance for expenses the partnership should have shouldered, including booking hotel rooms for his guests. And he talked on about it.

> You know, we try to live within a budget. We try to computer budget. It never worked for me, but I try to do it anyway. We do the best we can with the numbers. We are not 100 percent accurate with our numbers. I don't mean that in a negative sense. We don't like to overcharge, and in most cases I wind up undercharging. That is the nature of what happens. If you would like to sit down with me, I will sit down and show you some of the numbers of the expenses. You are not going to believe it. You will just not believe it. It is a very costly deal to raise money this way. Extremely costly.

Tashman also talked about an "after market," the slaughtering of the birds, which he said might make some of the investors cringe. At the time, experts estimated the ostrich population in the United States at 40,000. At least 250,000 would be needed to start up a slaughter market, which could take ten years.

I can't think that far away. I have to tell you, when we get to that point and there is an abundance of birds and there is an aftermarket and people want ostrich meat, and research wants the eyes for medical science and skins for the boats and belts, and you saw the feathers, they are beautiful and very expensive.

The audience skeptic, one of the few speakers who did not give his name, got nowhere with a question asking what would happen if earnings fell below forecast. Many investment professionals consider such questions both prudent and routine, especially in a high-risk venture such as animal breeding. His query brought this answer from Tashman: "Things could go bad. They can go bad. Anything can go wrong, but everything can't go wrong, I don't think. I am afraid to say it, I will knock on wood. Where is some wood?"

Meanwhile, back at the farm, the birds were behind schedule. While the ostriches were well cared for, with monthly check-ups from veterinarians, they were slow to show signs of reproducing. During the summer of 1993, the veterinarians said the birds showed signs of stress from being moved to the farm from their previous home in Oklahoma. It was all they could do to molt, or produce new feathers to help them adjust to the new environment. "This is a very stressful event that requires most of their bodily energy," one vet wrote in July. She added: "I doubt if they can produce eggs at the same time they are producing feathers." She recommended keeping up good nutrition and said "beyond that it's up to the birds."

In mid-August, a second vet agreed that breeding was unlikely until the molt finished. "Do not be disappointed, if in fact you do not get egg production for the next few months, due to the stress of the shipping and the reacclimation," she wrote.

Before the birds finished their molt, there were more immediate problems for investors to be fret about, namely, government auditors who wondered where all the money went.

While waiting for the birds to breed, ostrich telemarketers brought more and more investors into the fold. Junction Financial Corp. was selling its third ostrich partnership when a federal government auditor flew in from Chicago in mid-December 1993 to comb the company's books, such as they were.

By that time, 1,170 people had bought units at a total cost of about $3.2 million. Yet the company's books showed less than $3,000 in cash.

Just $381,000 of the proceeds went to buying ostriches, the SEC audit discerned.*

While little money went to the birds, huge sums drifted out the door in loans to Tashman ($218,000) and a company called Hotel Promotions ($450,000) owned by his ex-wife which had since gone out of business. Hotel Promotions was sued, along with Junction, by the New York attorney general in 1991 for running the 900-number vacation promotion.

Hundreds of thousands of dollars went to other loans to Tashman's mother, Marcia Josowitz, and others tied to Junction Financial Corp.

The audit confirmed that much of the money raised in a telemarketing operation didn't stay around long. The company's books showed salaries and commissions, mostly to telemarketers, of more than $660,000 in a ten-month period.

During the same time, records show the phone bill came to $141,000. The auditor noted that the company could not fulfill its promise to give investors their money back prior to the partnership meetings because it had so little cash on hand.

The SEC went on to lay out a complex legal argument that the partnership was a fraud because the investors did not have the expertise required by the law to set up a general partnership. Under the law, partners are assumed to have the knowledge and skill necessary to run the business. But the investors either were cold-called or appeared on purchased mailing lists and none was asked if he or she had any expertise.

U.S. Ostrich sales literature stated "every effort will be made" to avoid incurring costs that could expose partners to debts in excess of their investment. However, the leaflet also recommended that investors check with their attorney or other financial experts before signing up for the partnership. About the cease-and-desist orders, the company stated that the states "disagreed" with its contention that the ostrich deal was not a security requiring registration and financial disclosure.

Tashman never faced any real threat to his authority over the company. Many investors did not attend the partnership meeting but gave their proxies to Tashman to vote as he saw fit. Unlike a stock proxy, however, which directs a holder how to vote on specific questions before shareholders, Tashman's proxies gave him full control.

Companies offering general partnership schemes often take a number of steps to ensure that the operators retain proxy that will give them the power to outvote any upstart elements at a partnership meeting.

---

*Affidavit of William J. Gaynor, SEC v. Junction Financial Corp., December 22, 1993.

Tashman also took other steps that worried regulators who reviewed the company. He blocked the investors from visiting the ostrich ranch without first making an appointment through Junction. Many of Tashman's sales tactics were criticized by SEC lawyers in court filings.

The SEC said that action and efforts to prevent the other partners from contacting one another were evidence of Junction's efforts to withhold information. Tashman said that he didn't want to give out a list of investors, because he believed the list would fall into the hands of other telemarketers who would harass the ostrich partners with new deals.

Tashman adjourned the partnership meeting in high spirits. But some said they should have wondered as they left if the elaborate meeting had been draining off their resources.

Said Tashman:

> We wanted everyone to come down here and have a good time. We put no restrictions on anyone. We have tried to be good hosts and we want everybody to have a good time. Best of all we want everyone to come back again because we enjoyed having you. We really do. I get excited. I see what I put together and I am really excited about it and I am showing it off to every one of you. I am excited about it. . . . Would anybody like to buy me a drink in the bar and sign it to their check? . . . I have to tell you something before everybody leaves. I can tell you. I have run several of these meetings and this was the most enjoyable meeting I ever had. You folks are really a wonderful group of people.

The receiver appointed to handle the Junction Financial Corp. case held an auction on April 13, 1994. For sale: six pairs of breeder ostriches. About seventy-five people turned out and the birds went for about $160,000, less than half the price U.S. Ostrich had paid for them. Prior to the auction the birds produced one chick.

Others in the tight-knit ostrich breeding community say Junction had little chance to succeed because it was geared for a quick, short-term gain, when all indications are that the market would take time to develop.

"These guys gave a black eye to our industry. There are a whole lot of honest hard-working people at our farm," Walter Green, a spokesman for Pacesetter Ostrich Farm in Folsom, Louisiana, said in an interview during the summer of 1994. "Some investors have done quite well, but a whole lot of people saw the high prices and they got attracted like flies." While he notes prices are falling, Green remains optimistic about the ostrich market, mostly for slaughter. He says millions of pounds of the meat sells annually in Europe at a price slightly higher than beef. In this country, where the meat brings about thirty dollars a pound, only the trendiest restaurants are serving it, the sort of places that get forty dollars a plate and can make a pound stretch into three portions.

With only about 100,000 of the birds in the country, and strict regulations on importation of the meat, the industry is years away from challenging beef or making an appearance in fast-food chains, if it catches on at all. Green says the farmers would need eight million birds to produce one-tenth of 1 percent of the U.S. beef market.

He concedes that the birds are far more difficult to breed than many investors in this country have been led to believe. They must be watched carefully because they are not the brightest creatures. Green says one of the 1,400 birds on his farm ate a piece of a two-by-four and walked around with the board lodged in its throat as if bearing a cross. A veterinarian surgically removed the board. He also said they can't resist eating empty aluminum soda cans. While opinions differ, Green says the birds are not mean, just curious and a bit territorial. The uninitiated often mistake their curiosity for meanness, he says. But Green is not getting overly attached to his exotic birds. He expects to sell 90 percent of them for their meat.

Junction Financial Corp., meanwhile, sits in bankruptcy court, a process that could take years to resolve. Its investors apparently don't hold out much hope of getting their money back. Just one of the more than 1,100 partners showed up at a Miami bankruptcy hearing to learn more about the progress of the case.

What is the lesson here?

The deck is stacked against the investor who listens to a telemarketer's pitch to buy into a general partnership in some exotic field. Regardless of the product, this type of investment is suited for people who have the knowledge and experience to run the company in question.

Several of the ostrich investors said they were foolish not to ask more questions and demand better answers before they agreed to purchase. They said they had no idea about the backgrounds of the promoters, other than the sketchy information provided in the sales literature.

Perhaps worst of all, they said they reinvested as the enterprise expanded without ever getting adequate reports on how their initial investments were spent. They got caught up in the ether, put under by some masters of the telemarketing ruse.

11

Heavy Metals

Albert Drury, eighty-three years old, kept his assets in coins and Krugger-ands, at least $83,600 worth. One day in 1990, after an unexpected phone call from First American Trading Corporation, the coins were gone.

The elderly Californian sent his life savings to the Florida brokerage thinking he was dealing with a reputable company with a similar name that advertised on cable television.

First American never set the old man straight. Instead, the brokers used Drury's money to trade furiously in gold and other precious metals, without telling him. Within a few months, he had just $3,000 left. Brokers' commissions alone snatched up $33,000, court records allege.*

Albert Drury died within six months of the episode. He left a widow with a mortgage-free house, but little to live on, and relatives furious at a legal system that failed to protect an elderly man from phone bandits.

The Drury family's outrage pours off the twenty-page lawsuit the estate filed against First American and its sales agents, a counterattack they hoped would, in their words, "bring these defendants to justice."

Almost four years later, the lawsuit sits bogged down in a Florida court, mainly because First American has long since been liquidated and the chances of finding any money for Drury's widow are nil at best.

Family members have never disputed that investments in precious metals are highly risky in the best of hands. They also know that bad luck and poor timing can wipe anyone out. Throw in a lazy or unethical broker who "churns" accounts (sells stocks repeatedly to boost commissions), and the small investor can lose big.

But they feel Drury's case cannot be written off as a misadventure in which an elderly investor got in over his head, or a bad broker put com-

---

*Estate of Albert W. Drury v. First American Trading House, Inc., Seventeenth Judicial Circuit, Broward County, Florida, Case No. 91-12502 CF10A.

missions ahead of conscience. They assert Drury fell prey to a sophisticated telemarketing fraud that masqueraded as an investment house.

Their lawsuit accused First American Trading of putting Drury's
money in gold, silver, and foreign currencies "solely for the purpose of
generating exorbitant accounting fees and commissions." While trading
heavily in high-risk items, First American's agents told Drury they were
taking a "conservative" approach. They also said that if they were not able
to find a suitable investment, Drury's money would be placed in an inter-
est-bearing account or returned to him.

Drury's lawsuit also accused the firm of racketeering based on the
presence of a convicted boiler-room operator on the sales team. That man,
Greg Long, helped handle Drury's account, without telling the old man he
was venturing into a highly volatile market that could easily wipe him out,
according to the family's lawsuit.

Long's background, once they found out about it, further outraged
Drury's family. Long had been convicted twice on fraud charges stemming from the sale of precious metals in Florida boiler rooms. The two
cases, which caused losses of more than $52,000, netted Long a thirteen-
month sentence, but he served less time because of prison overcrowding.
While First American Trading had no connection to those cases, detectives arrested Long on one set of fraud charges while he was working at
First American Trading.

By the time of the arrest, Drury's money was gone, and the family
members were struggling to get justice. That the Drury family can't get
their day in court comes as no surprise to regulators in Florida.

Lies and obscenely high sales commissions are touchstones of investment telemarketing fraud. While it often results in financial ruin for
clients, its masters face few risks. Government regulators lag so far
behind that a top salesman can drift from room to room for years with little fear of getting thrown in jail, at least for any amount of time. Many
learn the racket from an accomplished pro, then open their own phone
room, often adopting corporate names that sound similar to well-known
institutions.

Owners savvy enough to hire top legal talent tie the government up in
court for years, filing endless motions that stall enforcement action until
the scam bleeds thousands of investors and shuts down.

"These guys know that the percentage of prosecutions is less than 5 percent. Some of them haven't stopped doing this in ten years and why should
they? They know fraud cases are horrible cases for prosecutors because
they take a long time to prepare and lots of time for a trial. In the meantime

everybody is clamoring to get drug dealers off the street," says Rene Champagne, a senior investigator with the Florida Comptroller's Office in Fort Lauderdale. "We have a massive problem with these boiler rooms."

Champagne needs only to flick a switch on his desktop computer for a reminder: up pop forty-two thousand entities, some boiler rooms that came and went since the mid-1980s, others still active in Florida or other states. Many descend from the same owners, still use the same illegal sales tactics, and still defy law enforcement every day.

Champagne, a rough-knuckled and slightly rumpled man with a fierce passion for tracking phone bandits, tells a true story with a gruff laugh that barely conceals his bitterness: A scam artist stands on the courthouse steps only minutes after being fined a small amount by a judge for defrauding investors all over the country. He turns to his attorney and boasts: "We'll make that fine up in one day."

Many won't even pay fines. They'll close down when consumer complaints to government agencies stack up, change their name and reopen. Champagne has seen it happen over and over, with the same result: investors such as Drury lose their life's savings because they trusted the voice on the phone line, knowing next to nothing about the people they dealt with, like the people behind First American Trading House, for instance.

While Drury was trading his coins for precious metals, James Settembrino managed First American Trading in Fort Lauderdale. His wife, Linda, was the president of the company. James Settembrino is a boiler-room gladiator with a past that would make any prudent investor cower. A business partner once accused him of forging her name on company checks and cashing some of them at the race track. Fraud charges against Settembrino were dropped. He once sued an investor who threatened to go to police unless Settembrino returned his money, accusing the former client of extortion for demanding a refund. The suit was later settled.

Settembrino's phone-sales career dates back to the early 1980s when he used the name Jim Setti and drew frequent complaints from investors and regulators. He was on board a 1983 oil-and-gas lease boiler room along with Steve Tashman, who went on to become the ostrich man.

The program operated by Settembrino and Tashman, among others, promised to secure clients a shot at winning a drilling lease on federal government land in Wyoming. While such offers do secure buyers a spot in line for a lease, government officials note that anyone can enter the lotteries for a small fee. One buyer said he mailed in a check for more than $9,000, then tried to cancel when his wife objected. Someone at the firm, not Settembrino, told the man "even Jesus Christ could not get your money back."*

Settembrino joined Tashman in Atlantex Associates, the oil-and-gas general partnership, against which the Federal Trade Commission won the $12.1 million judgment. Settembrino, who court records identify as the Atlantex head sales manager, also failed to pay the court judgment.

Like his partners, Settembrino has largely avoided criminal charges. A Missouri grand jury indicted him on charges of selling unregistered securities in 1986, but the disposition of the case is under seal.

He also avoided a court judgment for his role at Uni-Vest Financial Services in Deerfield Beach, Florida. The FTC in 1989 accused the precious-metals firm of misleading investors about the size of risks and sales commissions.† While the FTC identified Settembrino as a Uni-Vest salesman, he was not named in the FTC suit, which succeeded in shutting down the boiler room.

Settembrino and his wife opened First American Trading in 1989, right about the time the government shut down his previous employer.

First American Trading opened in an upscale corporate office park set among a cluster of aerospace and high-tech companies straddling Interstate 95 in Fort Lauderdale. The company rented a suite in a five-story, green glass structure, complete with tropical fountains and marbled vestibule, digs which stood out among telemarketing rooms, most of which have no need for fancy quarters because they spurn walk-in traffic.

First American didn't have many clients visit. It didn't sell to Florida investors, like most Sunshine State phone rooms, to avoid drawing heat from local authorities. But the suite, which sat among the offices of several well-known brokerages, projected an upscale image of the sort that helps keep regulators at bay. While First American did not serve local clients it conducted business all over the nation. The long-distance phone bill topped $12,000 some months.**

By the time federal officials won a court order freezing First American's assets in January 1992, they found little worth taking from the once-fancy office. The phones were silent; the company's fourteen sales brokers had scattered and dozens of lead cards, customer lists, and sales

---

*The allegation is contained in a civil suit filed by Gordon and Maxine Sewell against Settembrino and others alleging fraud in a gas lease lottery program, Dade County, Florida Circuit Court Case No. 87-34252.

†FTC v. Uni-Vest Financial Services, Inc., U.S. District Court Miami, No. 89-6382.

**FTC v. First American Trading House, Inc., U.S. District Court for the Southern District of Florida, No. 92-6049.

brochures lay strewn about the empty premises. The company even left a $53,000 phone bill unpaid.

Officials sent an office vending machine back to its owner, had the sales slips swept up and stored in an evidence vault and sold the desks and furnishings at auction for $4,500.*

Government auditors could not find any records amid the rubble to show how much First American's clients had invested, or whether they made or lost money. Other basic business records, such as a general ledger, also were not available, leaving a dim trail to follow the money. While the books were in a shambles, plenty of money went into the hands of the Settembrino family.

The auditor found more than $400,000 in First American checks payable to "cash," which meant anyone could have cashed them. People with the last name Settembrino did the honors on $100,000 worth of these checks, and $150,000 more made out to them directly. The First American corporation wrote at least $35,000 in checks to Florida race tracks, while Settembrino family members tapped the corporate credit cards to buy horses, jewelry, bicycles, and clothing, records state.

While federal investigators had a tough time figuring out where the money went, they had no difficulty finding witnesses who swore they were deceived by First American. Court papers filed by the Federal Trade Commission cited eleven people who lost 90 percent or more of their investment. Four senior citizens, including Albert Drury, lost more than $70,000 each.†

The FTC alleged that First American telemarketers preyed on retirees living on fixed incomes, in some cases telling them to mortgage their homes or borrow money to jump into precious metals.

Such charges serve as a reminder of the threat to the elderly from investment scams launched over the telephone. While the tendency to target seniors has been a constant in investment telemarketing, the threat seems to be growing.

In late May 1993 the U.S. Senate Aging Committee found that low-interest rates for certificates of deposit and the uncertain course of the nation's economy have made retirees and other people on fixed incomes insecure. Many reach for risky investments to stay ahead of the curve, opening up vast new opportunities for shady investment brokers and other get-rich-quick schemes.

---

*Final Report of Receiver, FTC v. First American Trading House, November 17, 1992.

†FTC v. First American Trading, FTC memorandum in support of a restraining order, January 17, 1993.

Polling data show that senior citizens are the most likely group to receive telephone investment calls. The 1992 Louis Harris and Associates poll found that 42 percent of Americans age fifty or older reported such a contact, and only 7 percent knew the person calling them. Overall, about one out of 33 "cold calls" yields a sale for the telemarketer, suggesting what the poll's authors called "a very large market for fraudulent investments."

The senior citizens who invested with First American Trading fit the profile outlined above, according to the government's court filings.

James T. Angelo, ninety, of Campobello, South Carolina, lost $80,000. Like many others, he had no prior contact with the company but simply picked up the phone one day and listened to a sales pitch that sounded great. Precious metals would earn him so much money he "wouldn't know what to do with it," the salesman said. Angelo perked up, hoping to make enough to buy a retirement home in Florida.

"Given the rosy picture that they painted of their program, I did not at the time consider the risk involved in the investment program," Angelo said in an affidavit. He said the salesmen told him the price of silver would rise and he would make a profit. They told him to sell his stocks and place his money at First American, where he "could expect to get a much bigger return."

Angelo stepped in cautiously with $3,000, but six days later, after another call from the brokers, he sank in $30,000, then $15,000, then another $15,000, each sent to Florida by bank wire transfer.

Reading the newspaper, Angelo saw the price of silver falling and feared he would lose money, though he had no idea how much. But when he tried to close his account, a salesman resisted, saying to do so would cause Angelo to "incur tremendous losses." When Angelo persisted, the broker passed him to another salesman who not only persuaded Angelo to stay, but talked him into investing about $20,000 more. When he closed his account four months after opening it, he received a check for $1,289.02, all that was left of his $80,000.

Some of the investors have hazy memories of exactly what the telemarketers said to win their confidence. But federal regulators caught on surveillance tape numerous false claims by First American's salesmen. Here are some remarks made to investors, all untrue, according to government regulators.

- The investment is almost a sure thing.

- There is no way to lose money in the investment.

- The investment is a can't lose proposition.

- The investment is similar in security to putting money in the bank.

- The risk is pretty much nil and the risk here is minimal.

- When you look at the risk to reward ratio, the risk is very minimum (compared) to the upside potential.

- If you went last year, you had a real rough year, 20 percent (return). That's real rough.

- The risk right now is like a little ant and the profit potential is . . . like an elephant.

- No investor has ever lost money who stayed with the company.

While downplaying any risks, the sales agents talked up profits with wild exaggerations, which the government also alleged were fraudulent. Here are some of the assurances tossed out over the telephone.

- The investor should quadruple his money within ninety days.

- The investor could easily expect to double or triple his money.

- The investor should come close to doubling his money by the end of the year.

- The investor will be making big, big money, enough so that he can be driving a Porsche.

- This is something that over a six-month period you should get a nice return, and I would say between 25 and 50 percent on your money.

Reviewing the evidence, the Federal Trade Commission concluded that First American had mounted an "egregious example" of an investment scheme that a congressional committee in 1990 called "inherently fraudulent and . . . usually unsuited for many of the consumers who invest."

First American arranged for its clients to enter into a five-year loan with a financial corporation in Newport Beach, California, another hotbed of investment scams.

The financier, called Uni-Met, loaned the customers 80 percent of the purchase price for the metals, leaving only 20 percent equity for the customers. The idea is that the customer will make a profit because the rapid rise in the price of the metals will more than offset the costs of taking out the loans. But other undisclosed fees deplete the investment rapidly.

Clients buying 1,000 ounces of silver and holding it for six months invested only 35 percent of the total value of the metal and received the rest as a loan from Uni-Met. Between the companies they were charged:

First American's commission: 15 percent of the total value of the metal, which amounts to 43 percent of the money they sent in.

The "spread": This fee amounted to 9 percent because rather than purchase metals at the market price, clients paid a commission for the service of obtaining and later selling the metals.

Uni-Met's "unit processing fee": This fee came to 7 percent of the investment because Uni-Met leveled a charge of five cents per ounce for every transaction, which amounts to 7 percent of the investment.

Uni-Met's interest charges: In November 1991 Uni-Met charged 10.5 percent interest per annum. Over a six-month period, the interest cost the client another 12 percent of the initial investment.

Sharpening their pencils, FTC staffers concluded that the fees ate up roughly 70 percent of the buyer's investment, if the price of silver stayed the same.

Uni-Met also presented buyers with a "grim choice," according to the FTC. The company sent statements known as an "equity call" after clients suffered a loss due to the market dropping. The investor either threw in more money or Uni-Met closed the account for insufficient collateral, meaning the client lost everything.

Angelo, the ninety-year-old man who hoped to buy a retirement home in Florida, got a telegram from Uni-Met stating his account would be liquidated unless he sent a bank wire or cashier's check for more than $3,000. Uni-Met gave him two days to come up with the money.

A government-hired expert gave a grim assessment of the odds of striking it rich; because of the charges and commissions slapped against their accounts, First American clients stood less than an 8 percent chance of breaking even if they held onto their silver for six months.

The FTC also accused First American of lying about the size of the commissions by saying they charged only a "one-time commission."

Not everyone who lost money through First American did so after getting an unexpected call. Others called the brokerage because an enticing postcard caught their eye. One such as this from evidence seized by federal regulators:

SAFE.SECURE.INSURED
Investments In Gold, Silver & Platinum

The Stock market is like a roller coaster. The Dollar continues to be unstable. Silver, Gold, and Platinum are your best hedge in an unstable Economy. Call or write today to find out how you can use the power of leverage to take advantage of this exciting investment opportunity! CALL US TODAY AT: 800-553-XXXX

The sales pitch, like most in telemarketing, proceeded in stages called the "front," the "drive," then tape verification—and then a tough time getting a refund or answer to a complaint.

The front script directed sales people to "make a friend" and "get on a first-name basis" with clients, and then make sure they have the money to spend. Here is an example from U.S. government evidence:

The Front:
How old of a gentleman are you? Are you married? What do you do for a living? How long have you been in business? What is your annual income? You know everyone is looking for a vehicle to protect themselves from inflation. Are you presently in any low yielding financial instruments such as CDs or money market funds? Stocks? Real estate? (What kind) Savings/checking? (Get ballpark figures) I'm going to have my secretary send out our brochure along with the bank papers to open your account. . . . Bye bye for now!

The Drive:
Hello ———. My name is ———. I am a senior account executive with First American Trading House. How are you today? Good. I'm glad I was able to reach you again. The leading economic indicators are now pointing to the silver market to make a move toward $7.00 an ounce, and when that happens, based on today's price of just ——— an ounce you will triple your money. At First American Trading House, we believe the wise investor understands the three keys to successful investing, which are: information, diversification, and timing. Our research department has put out an alert to get as many clients into this market as quickly as possible.

The drive, if successful, ends with the client sinking money into the silver market, thus starting the spiral downward, according to government officials.

First American also bought names and numbers of potential clients from list companies, often people who had invested in the past and returned a mailer from another company. These people received a different drive pitch. The sales agent would tell the client his or her name "came across my desk as someone who has inquired about or had been involved in various investments in the past."

Tape Verification

After any purchase, the sales agent transferred the client to a supervisor who taped the client's response to a set of questions designed to keep the trading house from being vulnerable to fraud charges.

The company sought to get buyers on tape acknowledging that they understood the risks in the metals market and that profits could not be guaranteed. But regulators alleged in court filings that the First American sales agent downplayed these sessions as mere formalities, which lasted less than two minutes, and the taped sessions failed to explain many of the costs and commissions.

The FTC also claimed that at least one investor said he had been promised specific income levels, leading the broker to tell him to change his answer for the taping, or he would be not be able to take advantage of the "once in a lifetime opportunity."

Aftermath

Several investors described the worst part of their ordeal as trying to get First American to respond to grievances or to refund money.

One working mother wrote to James Settembrino two days after Christmas 1990, a holiday she described as a "one-present affair" for her children because of her losses with First American.

> How naive can a woman be? I know I ought to have called the Florida
> State and Connecticut State Attorney's Office to see whether your com-
> mission rates were competitive. They would probably have advised me
> against dealing with volatile markets in which I could not afford to lose,
> and to find a company whose commission structure was less. . . . I actu-
> ally spoke with some houses subsequently that found your percentage
> outrageous. . . . I am sorry I am not a millionairess who can bear her loss-
> es with greater aplomb, but $20,790 was all I had, and I sent it to you. I
> know that you are a compassionate man, and I am counting on you.

Another letter arrived from a sixty-nine-year-old Kansas woman who borrowed money to invest in metals, she said, after a First American salesman lied to her about the risks. She said her losses, which she put at $170,000, had forced her to return to work to make ends meet. Attacking the salesman, she wrote:

> He told me so darn many lies just to convince me to invest. I told him I did not need a tax write off—this was my retirement money which I could not afford to lose. Far as I am concerned, he never did have me, his client's, interest at stake—only his commission. Far as I am concerned, people like him should be "hung from the highest tree." ... Ringing in my ears I keep hearing "I have been in this business for eight years and I know what I am doing. Trust me. I will never let you down. I keep up with what the super rich are doing and I will make you lots and lots of money. Trust me. I know what I am doing?" ... How can such people sleep at night by "sweet talking/promising" little ol' elderly widow women out of their last possessions and convincing them that they have to borrow more money in order to salvage what they have invested?

The FTC case against First American ended in October 1992 with no recovery for investors. The FTC decided not to ask the judge to award any damages because they would be "wholly uncollectible."

Once again, the telemarketers won, walking away from allegations of fraud, no fine, no time. Only the owners know how much money passed through the doors at First American Trading in nearly three years of wheeling and dealing.

Linda Settembrino, without admitting wrongdoing, agreed not to use deceptive sales tactics to market precious metals ever again. James Settembrino signed a promise not to deceive buyers in any type of telemarketing venture. The court agreement also banned him from investment telemarketing. He did not admit wrongdoing.

First American Trading was hardsell all the way, promising fantastic returns and employing a string of boiler-room veterans who bobbed and weaved around the truth to make sales.

The company put investors through hell to correct unauthorized trades that wound up losing them thousands of dollars. One investor gave the FTC taped conversations with the Settembrinos in which he tried to get back money from improper trades. Just getting either party on the phone proved tough enough. He never got a refund.

Yet not everyone who gets taken by investment telemarketing specialists encounters rough-hewn hucksters who evade a client's calls and dart from one deceptive sales room to another.

Dan Burkhead, of Fairfax County, Virginia, a twenty-year U.S. government employee, lost more than $100,000 in less than two years to a highly refined oil investment. Burkhead, a computer systems analyst with the Department of Commerce's census bureau, told his story in March 1993 to a U.S. Senate committee investigating telemarketing fraud.*

Pulling the microphone closer to make himself heard, Burkhead told the committee a horror story that warned of the dangers of investment telemarketing. He began by noting that he lost his life's savings, money he had earned on the job.

It began when a telemarketer, who apparently purchased his name from a list of investors in a defunct real-estate partnership, called to offer a new deal: oil exploration. When Burkhead balked, saying he knew nothing of oil drilling and sought only conservative investments, the Texas phone-broker said he understood. But he pressed on, offering the oil well as just the ticket to keep Burkhead riding ahead of inflation. The salesman was not at all pushy.

> He was friendly, low key, and patient in answering my questions. He asked me about my job, my family, and my hobbies. He stressed that his company was complying with Texas regulations. He told me that he was a supervisor of other salesmen and periodically monitored their phone calls to make sure that they were not making promises that they should not be. The investment which he described was not presented as a get-rich-quick scheme. It was, however, presented as an opportunity to get a return on my investment better than anything I was receiving at the time.

Burkhead tried to check out the company. He called the Better Business Bureau in Austin, the firm's headquarters, which listed no complaints. He checked with the author of a published article about the company's previous oil drilling who raved about the company. Reassured and happy with the earnings forecast in the firm's prospectus, he took the plunge.

About three months after Burkhead invested, the telemarketer called back to advise that the well had come in "almost a gusher." He predicted

---

*Subcommittee on Consumer of the Committee on Commerce and Transportation, U.S. Senate, Washington, D.C., March 18, 1993.

a yield of one hundred barrels a day and said Burkhead would recoup his entire investment within a few months. The telemarketer had a new investment plan, this time a five-well package he presented as a low-risk way to enter into oil production.

Thinking he was in good hands, Burkhead wired the Texans $62,500. Shortly after his money left Virginia, troubles began to surface.

His primary contact, his only lifeline to the company, got fired for reasons that remain unclear. He began dealing with a new agent, who soon departed. Burkhead dealt with a succession of new "voices," each of whom had a wealth of excuses for failing to meet drilling deadlines or to hit the gusher.

> When the drilling did not take place when they said it would or the number of wells that were supposed to be drilled within a certain time period did not materialize, these individuals always had an answer. And when a well did not produce, they always had a good reason. They would also explain why the next well yet to be drilled would always be an excellent one. They had some incentives to keep the investors involved. On two occasions when a well proved unproductive they gave the investors an interest in a future well at no charge.

Burkhead sent more money though he began to have doubts. Because of the telemarketing happy talk that the gusher would come any day, Burkhead took two years to come to the realization that he "would be left holding an empty bag."

Concluding his testimony before the Senate committee, Burkhead said he learned too late that much of the upbeat sales chatter was not true. He said the company had perhaps dug one successful well, despite claiming that it had hit it big repeatedly. Burkhead "bought the dream" from people he thought he knew through telephone sales contacts. He never met any of them face-to-face until it was too late and he was suing in a fruitless attempt to get some of his money back.

That lawsuit brought to light many documents he wishes he had seen before he accepted calls from the Texas telemarketer. His attorney, using the federal Freedom of Information Act, obtained a number of documents from securities regulators that would give any investor pause; the company president had been the target of cease-and-desist orders in a number of states.

"Although I suspect the chances of regaining my investment are minimal, perhaps my experience may be a lesson to others," Burkhead concluded. There are lessons galore for both investors and government agencies charged with regulating them.

Clearly, the deck is stacked against the small investor, not just because of volatile market conditions and other risks, but because the government cannot assure that brokers who handle these accounts are honest or competent.

Further, the fact that investment telemarketers bounce around from room to room with little oversight has been well known to regulators, though not the public, for years. The Commodities Futures Trading Commission, created by Congress in 1974 to protect investors from fraud, struggles to keep pace with the boiler-room operators.

The commission took until October 1992 to propose stepped up enforcement of brokers or "associated persons" who drift among troubled brokerages. Reviewing case histories of telemarketing investment houses shut down for fraud, the commission concluded that:

> One factor common to those firms and directly related to their sales practice problems was the employment history and training of their sales forces. In particular . . . a significant portion of their sales forces were previously employed and trained by one or more . . . [companies] closed for fraud.*

Considering these factors, the Commodities Futures Trading Commission proposed requiring problem-prone companies to tape record initial sales contacts and retain the tapes for one year, stating the practice would be a "strong deterrent" to sales abuses and other deceptive marketing tactics.

But the rule gave sleazy operators plenty of wiggle room. First, it only applied to companies that had previously been disciplined by the commission or ones which employed substantial numbers of brokers who had worked at disciplined houses. The rule did not specify who would be held accountable for knowing about a broker's past employment.

While the rule pertained to commodities, the commission's conclusions apply to a number of investments sold by telephone rooms. Disciplinary actions taken against investment telemarketers seldom stick. Filing lawsuits against them often neither gets investors any money back nor gets the broker out of the investment business. Often, the owners or key employees of a fraudulent telemarketing investment firm sign consent decrees with government agencies that ban them from selling a certain type of product.

---

*Proposed telemarketing regulations, Commodities Futures Trading Commission, Federal Register, Vol. 57, No. 205, October 22, 1992, page 48210.

Invariably, they pop up selling a new investment product using the same underhanded tactics. Some sign agreements banning them from telemarketing altogether, only to turn up running new phone rooms before the ink on the agreement has dried. Still others simply use fronts to set up new companies and remain in the background where regulators have a hard time spotting them.

The securities industry has proven adept time after time at fighting efforts by Congress to reel its members in under telemarketing-reform legislation. The industry argues that its members face tough regulation from both state and federal securities watchdogs. For example, a Securities Industry Association official in 1989 was "profoundly disturbed" by proposed legislation to empower consumers to sue in federal court to recover damages against a fraudulent telemarketer.*

Investment telemarketers may be due for some new regulation of their activities, but only maybe. The Consumer Protection Telemarketing Act, signed into law by President Clinton in August 1994, requires both the Commodities Futures Trading Commission and the Securities and Exchange Commission to consider adopting rules to crack down on telemarketing abuses. But the law does not require them to do so if the agencies conclude that such a rule "is not necessary or appropriate in the public interest or for the protection of investors, or would be inconsistent with the maintenance of fair and orderly markets." The agencies have eighteen months from the date of the law's enactment to decide the issue.

Whether protections such as these would spare people such as Burkhead from losing their life's savings is debatable. Industry officials argue that many investors who seek high returns offered by risky investments must be willing to gamble. But that view, while having some merit, ignores the simple fact that investment telemarketers who engage in fraud have yet to be faced with powerful incentives such as lengthy prison sentences to mend their ways.

Nor has anyone been able to solve a fundamental problem with buying an investment over the telephone: no matter how hard he tries, the average investor simply can't thoroughly check out the background of a company.

While most records of enforcement actions against companies are public, they are by no means easy to track down. Few investors have the

---

*Letter from Donald J. Crawford, Securities Industry Association Senior Vice President and Director of Government Relations to the Honorable Thomas A. Luken, Chairman, Subcommittee on Transportation and Hazardous Materials of the House Committee on Energy and Commerce, April 17, 1989.

time, skills, or money to do the digging necessary to trace enforcement actions in fifty states or by several different federal agencies.

Often, state and federal agencies that prosecute telemarketers are not aware of each other's actions, so a casual investor has little chance of discovering past allegations of securities fraud.

The telemarketers know that fact well. It is perhaps the single biggest reason they stay in business year after year and scam after scam.

Despite cracks in the system, there are steps investors can take to protect themselves. Here are some tips from the Commodities Futures Trading Commission, in Washington. The agency notes fraud artists often use similar pitches. The agency advises consumers to be suspicious when a salesman:

• Tells you to borrow money, take out a mortgage on your home, or cash in your IRA to invest in commodities.

• Tells you to invest immediately, and then sends an overnight courier service to pick up your checks and give you forms to sign.

• Says that you will double or triple your money quickly; profit is guaranteed, or you can't lose the money if you invest.

• Tells you to write false information on your account form; for example, to overstate your income.

• Downplays the risk disclosure statement as just a formality that you need not take seriously.

After you invest, be aware of the following warning signs of trouble:

• Account statements that appear to be home-made or printed on home computers. (They should be printed on letterhead stationery, without typographical errors.)

• Delays in receiving your money when you order the broker to close a trade and send you your balance.

If you are considering a commodity investment, take the time to check it out!

1. Victim Virginia Lynch with some of the merchandise she was conned into buying. She also lost $5,000 billed to her credit card by telemarketers. The American Association of Retired Persons found that one in four people over the age of sixty is vulnerable to fraud schemes. (See chapter 2.) Photo courtesy Jackie Bell, Fort Lauderdale *Sun-Sentinel*.

2. Ted Powder, alias "Stan Cohen," of Omega Fun 'N' Travel. (See chapter 4.) Photo courtesy Broward County Sheriff's Office.

3. Leonard Friedman, "The Baron of Breast Cream." (See chapter 5.) Photo courtesy Arizona Attorney General's Office.

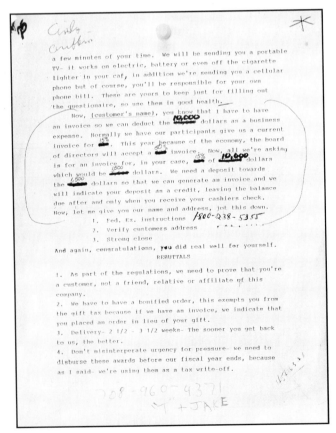

4. A boiler-room script. Note rebuttals. Photo courtesy Fort Lauderdale *Sun-Sentinel*.

5. Consolidated Payphone's boiler room. (See chapter 9.) Photo courtesy Fort Lauderdale Police Department.

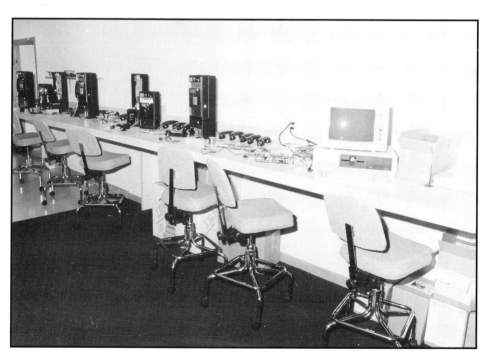

6. The work bench at Consolidated—all fake for "fly and buy." Visitors would see technicians busily at work assembling phones. Photo courtesy Fort Lauderdale Police Department.

7. Douglas Young arrested at Premium Ventures, an illegal prize-telemarketing room. (See chapter 14.) Photo courtesy Carl Seibert, Fort Lauderdale *Sun-Sentinel*.

8. "Operation Disconnect"—the FBI raids a boiler-room operation. (See chapter 17.) Photo courtesy Fort Lauderdale *Sun-Sentinel*.

12

The Family Jewels

In a world where so many people jump at a chance to get anything for free, Roland B. Clarke pitched an alluring offer. He told thousands of Americans that they might have money coming to them, funds left by long-lost relatives in New York State. Clarke said the money lay in the New York State treasury "where it is being held until the right (place name here) family claims it."

Thousands of people called a 900 number to hear how to claim their windfalls of forgotten tax refunds or abandoned bank accounts or even age-old stocks now worth a fortune. But the callers got little except some general advice and a ten-dollar phone bill—an annoying reminder of the many guises a telemarketing scheme can take.

The "Clarke, Winston & Hayes" caper took in as much as $100,000 in two months, according to U.S. Postal Service Inspectors. Its callers fell for a modern-age version of one of the oldest scams alive: the missing heir.

In days past, the scammer might pose as a rich man's cash-poor son, hit a victim up for a loan, and light out of town. He or she might claim to be a distant relative to gain the host's trust, then disappear with the family jewels.

These days, schemers have no need to visit homes in person: they simply mail out a batch of letters, set up a phone bank somewhere, and wait for the suckers to come to them.

Roland B. Clarke knew how to play the game. He sent out thousands of bulk-mail letters in the name of Clarke, Winston and Hayes, Ltd., of Phoenix, which appeared to be a law firm. Personal details such as the recipient's birth date, a "family file number," and the addressee's phone number were typed in at the top of the page.

Roland Clarke, who signed the letters with a deliberate hand, described his employer as a "private financial search company assisting people in the locating of unclaimed funds."

The letter told the addressee that the search firm had "identified an amount of money that may belong to you." The New York State Comptroller's Office held the money, Clarke said, for someone of the same last name. The letter gave a 900 number to call for details about how to claim the loot.

New York, like many states, does keep a list of people to whom money is due, mainly from tax refunds, unclaimed bank accounts, or money left in bank safe deposit boxes. But anyone can claim a list of these names for free. Some other states publish the list in newspapers annually.

For the average person, finding any money squirreled away in New York is about as likely as running into Roland Clarke at the supermarket. And that's not likely since he does not exist. Partners Randall G. Winston and David R. Hayes, listed on the letterhead, also are phantoms. The Phoenix office address, which provides a "suite" number, is a mail drop, according to the Iowa Attorney General's Office.

"This was pretty well designed," says Iowa Assistant Attorney General Pamela Griebel, who sued the firm in summer 1992 and won refunds for Iowa citizens who lost money. "We had more complaints about this than any other 900 number in history."*

While the scheme relied on an age-old human frailty—greed—it also displayed a keen grasp of information technology. The company rented massive lists of names and matched them to the names on the New York Comptroller's abandoned property list.

To assure a quick payoff, Clarke Winston & Hayes struck a deal with a Las Vegas telephone services company to answer the phone calls.

AT&T handled the billing, placing a ten-dollar charge on each customer's phone bill, at least until complaints began piling up. At that point, AT&T cut Clarke and company off. Shortly thereafter, the U.S. Postal Service inspectors and attorneys general from three states were pushing for refunds.

Thousands of people called the 900 number. They heard a recording telling them to write to New York State for a claim form. The callers got none of the assistance promised by the search firm, just a droning message that kept the caller on the line. Here's the script:

Thank you for calling the offices of Clarke, Winston, and Hayes. You may disconnect now and avoid a call charge of $4.95 per minute. Or,

---

*Interview with Pamela Griebel, March 25, 1994.

stay on the line and get information on how to claim money that could legally be yours. Please have a pen and paper handy so you can write down the important information you're about to hear. We have contacted you because someone with your exact last name had money belonging to them that was turned over to the New York State Comptroller's Office.

Their Unclaimed Funds Division is now trying to locate the rightful owner of that money. The money probably was left accidentally in a bank account, or it might have come from insurance policy payments, tax refunds, stock dividends, or other sources.

You could be the rightful owner or heir to this money. You may write to the following address: New York State Comptroller's Office, Unclaimed Funds Division, Smith Building, Albany, New York 12236.

When you write to them, please be sure to request they send you information on any funds held for people with your family name. They may have funds held in more than one account for people with your exact family name.

Please note that these funds definitely belong to someone with your family's last name. But they may not belong to you personally. We sincerely hope that when you contact New York, you discover these funds DO belong to you.

Thank you again for calling our office.

The call took more than two minutes and the billings were mostly for $9.90, according to the Iowa Attorney General's Office.

Iowa's lawsuit charged fraud. First of all, the company mailed the letters from Florida, and routed return calls to a Las Vegas telephone service bureau, not an office in Arizona. The company also made no effort to limit the mailing to people with some ties to New York, the agency alleged.* The U.S. Postal Service also signed an agreement with the operator of the scheme to cease and desist on April 15, 1993.

While citizens flooded the New York State Comptroller's Office with letters, the Iowa attorney general found that nobody made a successful claim as a result of hearing the prerecorded message.

In perhaps the most unusual twist to the short-lived telemarketing deal, authorities traced the scheme to a seventy-four-year-old retired musician who divides his time between upstate New York and South Florida.

Joseph Merman, who still plays piano on the Florida condo circuit

---

*State of Iowa v. Joseph Merman d/b/a Clarke, Winston & Hayes, Polk County, Iowa, Case No. CE-040-23174, June 17, 1992.

during the winter months, defends his role in the venture. He told an interviewer: "I thought the information we were selling was worth five or ten bucks." Asked how a retiree sets up this sort of venture, Merman said he was a "front man" for investors whom he declined to name. Merman said the deal lost money because so many people demanded refunds, adding, "I'm sorry my name got into it."

Authorities never found out how Merman managed to put Clarke, Winston & Hayes together; they settled for an order parceling out refunds to customers. While mum on the subject, Merman defended the firm's use of phony names. "There was nobody named General Motors either," he said.

In 1989, with little more than one thousand of the 900 numbers up and running, the industry earned about $1 billion, according to sales literature distributed by one Florida 900 promoter.

The 900-number promoters predicted sales would double in the coming year on phone gambits from "dial-a-prayer" to a "heavy women" exchange, in which overweight women describe themselves to male callers. But some of these lines raked in cash partly because many people—from children hoping to chat with a cartoon character to middle-aged job seekers—did not realize they would be billed for the calls.

In July 1990 the Federal Trade Commission won a court order freezing the assets of a Georgia firm that it said failed to disclose charges of fifteen to eighteen dollars to hear job listings or send job postings to many customers as promised.

Many states began to report problems involving these types of employment offers. New Jersey officials investigated ten such scams, closing down six of them, according to Emma Byrne, director of the New Jersey Department of Law and Public Safety's division of consumer affairs. "Marketing jobs through 900 lines is a fast-growing recession rip-off that preys on desperate people," she said in January 1991. The companies "target one of the most vulnerable groups in our society—the unemployed. These unregistered job services take money from the people who can least afford to lose it. And not only do they leave them at least twenty-five dollars poorer, the consumers are still without jobs."

The job schemes confirmed that some 900-number players took their cues from the telemarketing con, detail for detail. Ads appeared promoting "turnkey" firms that could get investors into the 900 market for as little as $5,000. These "service bureaus" supplied phone lines, mailers to advertise the service, a long-distance carrier, television ads, and anything else needed to fleece the public—even factoring the profits.

One telltale sign of trouble appeared: the phone companies began withholding a portion of revenues because of the high incidence of deceit or fraud. Many customers hotly disputed the 900 charges placed on their bills by phone companies, which acted as a collection agent for 900 operators.

As a goodwill gesture, many phone companies issued liberal credits to people who contested 900 charges. The credits became so common that phone companies began holding back part of the 900-number holder's receipts, or refusing to handle their accounts, much the same as banks shied away from credit-card transactions with telemarketers.

In December 1991 one national company told 900-number service bureaus that it would hold back 10 percent of their payments to cover bad debts due at least partly to problem sales. The company said "excessive caller credits" were "compromising the industry's profitability."

Federal regulators also worried about the growing fraud problem. Federal Trade Commission Chairman Janet D. Steiger in a May 1991 speech to a convention of direct marketers warned that fraud artists would tarnish the 900 industry unless legitimate business worked to weed them out. She said "it appears . . . that there is a direct connection emerging between conventional telemarketing fraud and 900-number fraud."*

Fraud or not, the 900 numbers quickly dangled some of telemarketing's best tested lures—the prize sweepstakes, for instance. And federal regulators pressed on trying to get the upper hand over the industry.

Two large firms agreed to settlements as public sentiments against the 900 industry began to mount. In May 1991 Audio Communications of Las Vegas and Teleline in Beverly Hills, CA, settled FTC charges that they had misled the public with 900 numbers that promised children prizes.† The Nevada company used television commercials that told children, "Call me now to get a free Easter Bunny gift, and help my favorite charity," or "There's a new story every day, and I'll help tell you how to get a free Christmas gift."

But the FTC said kids would have a tough time following rapid-fire instructions; they had to quickly jot down the firm's address and mail in a copy of their parents' phone bill to collect the prize. In settling the case, the FTC required the companies to add the following statement to their commercials: "Kids, you must ask your Mom or Dad and get their permission before you call." Also required: "This call costs money. If you do not have your Mom or Dad's permission, hang up now and there will be no charge for this call." Both companies denied wrongdoing.

---

*Steiger speech, Direct Marketing Association.

†The FTC announced the settlements May 8, 1991. Neither company admitted wrongdoing.

The FTC sued other firms using 900 numbers to sell an array of products, such as a Connecticut company that told people they could buy repossessed sports cars taken in drug stings for a few hundred dollars, or obtain low-interest credit cards despite having a poor credit history.

The callers didn't find out they were actually getting a secured credit card, which had to be backed by a deposit in the bank, or that they had to pay ninety-nine dollars to get it. The FTC alleged the twin schemes resulted in consumer losses of $13 million.

State attorneys general also struck back against a promotion that used a toll-free number to connect callers into a 900 line that charged them. Millions of Americans received letters from a Texas marketer telling them that they had won a prize, and giving an 800 number they could call for details. Many did thinking the call was free. But the toll-free number connected to a 900 exchange in a flash. A woman's voice told callers they could get "immediate notification" of their prize by staying on the line. Excited, many callers ignored the warning that they would be billed $3.90 a minute for about three minutes, officials said.

Attorneys general from Connecticut and other states cried foul in March 1992, arguing that the prize turned out to be a certificate good for two hundred dollars in discounts on the Texas company's products. The company agreed to halt the promotion and give Connecticut residents refunds.

Other types of schemes abused the new marketing tool. One scam sent postcards all of which gave a number to call for receipt of a package; the cards appeared to be sent by a private postal carrier or the U.S. Postal Service.

People who called, thinking they were calling a package delivery station, found a fifteen-dollar charge on their phone bill while their package turned out to be a worthless sales come-on.

One New Jersey enterprise showed how big the take could be using the new 900 technology. Using four lines, the company induced 66,135 people from all over the country to call over a three-month period for gross receipts of about $677,000. The firm's postcards said "Final Notice," or "Final attempt," as well as this message: "Unclaimed merchandise will be returned to the sender if not claimed within seven days." Many people thought the notices had been left by their mail carriers.

State regulators blamed the phone companies for acting as a conduit for the con schemes. After all, they did the billing for the 900 operators and in some cases had approved sales pitches. Other phone carriers asked no questions, but simply assumed if the 900 company signed papers saying the promotion was legal, it was.

Many state officials also groused that the phone companies were less than cooperative in helping them shut down 900-number con artists—actions that cut into the phone companies' profits.

Attorneys general in thirty states were at least partly satisfied in May 1992 when they signed an unusual agreement with three of the largest long-distance carriers to attack the 900-number rip-offs. Under the "voluntary procedures," the phone companies agreed to do a better job monitoring the industry, said Tennessee Attorney General Charles W. Burson, then chairman of the National Association of Attorneys General Consumer Protection Committee. He said:

> These procedures reflect a recognition by the carriers of their corporate responsibility to prevent the use of their legitimate services for unlawful purposes. This trend must be carried further to successfully combat telemarketing fraud. Along with the actions of Congress and the federal agencies, cooperative efforts such as these will go a long way to close off 900 services as an avenue to defraud consumers.*

While the state attorneys general hailed their agreement, others felt that consumers needed more protection, such as the threat of a class-action lawsuit.

George Sikes, a Georgia resident furious when his ten-year-old son ran up a $569 phone bill calling a 900 number, represented the class in one such suit. He took up the sword after Southern Bell refused to take the charges off his phone bill.

The ten-year-old called forty-eight times to a 900-number prize promotion he saw on television. It was promoted by Santa Claus, who said: "Ho-Ho-Ho! How'd you like to have $2,000 in your bank account tomorrow to use for your Christmas shopping? Here's a friend to tell you how you can," according to the suit.

A fine-print notice appeared on the screen saying that the call would cost $3.88 per minute for six minutes, as well as noting that players must be eighteen years old. But the lawsuit charged that the company prolonged the caller's time on the line by asking questions, such as the caller's area code. Time also is consumed as the caller answers inane questions such as "The Kennedy Space Center is named for which president?"†

---

*Burson announced the voluntary procedures at a Washington, D.C., news conference, May 20, 1992.

†Sikes v. Teleline, Inc., U.S. District Court Southern District of Georgia, Statesboro division, CV692-147. The case is pending as of March 1995.

Repeated warnings from consumer agencies to avoid 900 schemes have appeared to work, but not totally. An American Association of Retired Persons poll found in 1993 that about two-thirds of the public understood they could be billed for a 900 call. But among the elderly, only 44 percent knew, and awareness of the charges dropped even further in Americans over seventy-five years old.

Despite a flurry of lawsuits against those who operate 900 numbers, it took the federal government until March 1993 to regulate the 900 industry.

Under the rules, all 900 calls charging more than two dollars must begin with a preamble that states:

• The name of the company, the cost of the call, that anyone under eighteen must have a parent's permission, and when the charges begin. The caller must be given three seconds to hang up before incurring a charge.

• Any 900-sweepstakes promotion also must reveal the odds of winning, and companies may not use a toll-free number to connect buyers to a 900 number.

• Any 900 company that offers information about a government program must state that it is not affiliated or endorsed by the U.S. government.

The FTC rules also give consumers the right to dispute 900 billings, so long as the customer notifies the phone company within two months of the billing. A company must respond within forty days and correct the error within ninety days or explain its reason for not doing so.

While the FTC rules prohibit any phone company from cutting off service to a customer who refuses to pay a 900 bill, invoices may be turned over to debt collection agencies. In these cases, consumers can notify credit bureaus that the charge is in dispute, so it won't impact their credit rating. The best policy is still to avoid calling in the first place unless you are sure what service you will receive and the amount of the charges.

With the tighter regulations the bold abuses of 900 numbers have simmered down a bit, but they remain controversial.

Serial killer John Wayne Gacy earned thousands of dollars off a 900 number, causing Illinois Attorney General Roland W. Burris to sue Gacy in 1994 to recoup the costs of his incarceration, some $141,000.

Convicted in 1980 of murdering thirty-two young men and boys, and sentenced to death, Gacy professed his innocence at $1.99 a minute, in a twelve-minute interview set up by a Boca Raton, Florida, telemarketer. His appeals exhausted, Gacy died in May 1994 by lethal injection. The lawsuit lives on.

In another high-profile case, a 900 number shot up within days of the arrest of football star O. J. Simpson, charged with murdering his ex-wife and her male friend outside her Los Angeles condominium.

The 900 number, placed by a California company, sought to drum up grass-roots support with a $2.95-per-minute, two-minute pitch that said:

> Before the media totally distorts the O. J. Simpson travesty, voice your opinion, speak out. Do you feel you support O. J. Simpson? Results will be forwarded to O. J. Simpson's attorney.

While 900 numbers have some controls over them, many hawkers of products are finding they can get their message across unfiltered if they can afford the price of late-night television advertising runs or "infomercials."

The infomercial is a growing power in the advertising industry, accounting for $900 million in sales during 1993, according to an industry trade association. Political candidates have used them, as have diet gurus, hawkers of kitchen appliances, and many others. But these programs and similar television ads can also be a perfect forum for unscrupulous companies seeking to build trust using deceptive sales pitches that bulldoze consumer protection laws.

There is nothing illegal about the infomercial. Many of them present straightforward sales pitches that both entertain and sell. But the industry moves far faster than state regulators trying to assess whether any of the companies using this format are making deceptive claims about their products. And just like newspapers assume little responsibility for ads they print, television stations often take the stance that they cannot verify sales claims made in these programs. Once again, buyer beware!

More and more the hucksters seek common ground with their victims, much the same as the missing-heir scheme played upon everybody's hope to be remembered in a rich uncle's will. Victims often are members of "affinity" groups: the overweight, hobbyists, collectors, and people of similar religions or ethnic heritage.

There is no mistaking the target audience for the Mega Loss 1000 pill, hawked both on television and in some supermarket tabloids.

The ads promise fantastic weight loss with testimonials such as "I lost 32 pounds in only 9 days." One ad says:

> Now is the proper time . . . the turning point of your life . . . now you can shed your excess fat and have a firm, youthful looking body faster than you ever imagined possible. Regardless of the shape you are in now, the high-speed, fat-burning, doctor-recommended Mega Loss 1000™ rapid weight loss program not only can, but must accomplish amazing results for you. Satisfaction 100% guaranteed.

The message concludes: "Wake up slimmer the very next morning. Only $9.95."

The man behind the diet is William Santamaria, a large and commanding man who arrived at work in Boca Raton in a white limousine, when he didn't drive his red Corvette. Santamaria has chartered more than sixty different Florida corporations to hawk products, mostly through telemarketing, from bird seed to dating services that match single women to wealthy men.

Sold under names such as Choice Diet Products, Taleigh, Inc., and Tropix, his diet products are a big-ticket item. Using late-night television and the tabloids, the firms made twelve thousand sales a week, according to company statements to the local Better Business Bureau. And the buyers paid more than $9.95. Choice Diet telemarketers "upsell," sometimes for as much as three hundred dollars or more for diet products.

The diet firm's history testifies to the tough time regulators have presenting a united front against suspect sales claims pitched coast-to-coast to an affinity group, in this case clients desperate to lose weight.

Santamaria eventually got in trouble in Iowa, but the Iowa court judgment against him only applied in that state. In February 1989 he signed an agreement to quit advertising his weight-loss products in the state. Iowa's attorney general asserted that the diet pill's claims to "burn fat" were deceptive and false. The company denied the allegations, but agreed to pay $4,000 in costs.*

Santamaria kept selling in Iowa despite the court order, through magazines and on television, according to state officials. The court order directed him to place a notation on the ads reading, "No orders accepted from Iowa." When he failed to do so, Iowa officials sued again, winning another judgment against Santamaria in September 1993.

---

*State of Iowa v. Tropix Pharmacals and William Santamaria, Polk County, Equity No. CE 028 16280, consent judgment, February 7, 1989.

"Neither my office nor Iowa courts look kindly on con artists who ignore court orders to change their ways or stay out of Iowa," State Attorney General Bonnie Campbell said. The ruling granted refunds to 170 Iowans who spent $5,000 on the products, and fined Santamaria $40,000. Two of three Iowans who bought the product wanted their money back.*

Oregon scambusters also took aim at the diet kingpin and his pills. Oregon Attorney General Theodore R. Kulongoski signed an agreement with Santamaria in March 1994 in which the diet-pill promoter promised to alter his sales tactics.† The state attorney general alleged that the diet ads falsely claimed the products could "attack or shrink fat cells" and cause a "reduction of inches" without diet or exercise.

One concoction sold as "special for diabetics" contained sugar derivatives that could be hazardous to diabetics, Kulongoski said. Santamaria agreed to make refunds to Oregon buyers, to refrain from making any specific claims of weight loss that were not typical, and to pay a fine of $9,750.

"Americans spend an estimated $30 billion a year on all types of diet programs and products," Kulongoski said. "Trying to sort out all of the competing claims, which are often misleading, can be costly and confusing."**

Such court judgments give state law enforcers a chance to thump their chests in front of local media and voters. But they do little to slow the nationwide sale of products. Telemarketers take advantage of the void in federal law enforcement to sell using deceptive tactics. They take on one state at a time and pay paltry fines if they get hauled into court, or simply add a line to advertising saying the offer is not valid in any state that has kicked them out.

Choice Diet Products also came under attack for its business practices. In June 1992, Bob Crawford, Commissioner of the Florida Department of Agriculture and Consumer Services, accused Choice Diet Products of improperly debiting customers' checking accounts. Consumers thought they were authorizing a charge of $9.95 plus $3 shipping for the diet product, only to find their checking accounts debited for as much as $300, according to Crawford.

Like many telemarketers, Choice Diet Products had asked clients to

*Campbell news release, September 17, 1993.

†Santamaria signed an "assurance of voluntary compliance" with the state of Oregon in which he admitted no wrongdoing on December 30, 1993.

**Kulongoski news release, March 8, 1994.

read their checking account numbers over the phone to speed their purchases.

Crawford warned that consumers who gave their bank account numbers out to telemarketers were taking a big chance: their accounts could have been drained.*

The allegations of criminal conduct against the Boca Raton telemarketer caught the eyes of FBI agents and local police, who investigated but did not file criminal charges. The U.S. Attorney's Office in West Palm Beach, following a lengthy grand jury investigation, said the case did not meet the guidelines for a criminal prosecution.

Meanwhile, consumer complaints piled up. In June 1994 Better Business Bureau officials received more than two hundred calls about the firm. Many new complaints involved diet "patches" placed on the dieter's arm so that daily fat intake could be recorded. Another behavior modification device sold was Nicotain, a stop-smoking patch. These were not stuck to the skin, but were placed in a booklet to commemorate each day the customer went without a smoke. Regulators said many people thought they were purchasing a medicated product that would help them quit smoking.

The Better Business Bureau said the firm had an "unsatisfactory" record with the bureau due to a pattern of "no response to customer complaints." Many of those complaints will likely remain unresolved.

On June 20, 1994, the Better Business Bureau received a terse fax stating that the company was out of business. Said the Better Business Bureau: "Mail to the company has been returned as 'Not Deliverable As Addressed—Unable to Forward.' " On March 14, 1995, the FTC announced that William Santamaria had signed a consent decree in which he agreed to refrain from making any deceptive statements in the marketing of diet aids or stop-smoking products. Santamaria, who did not admit any wrongdoing, also agreed to post a $300,000 bond before marketing any such products in the future.

Choice Diet Products was not alone in making questionable claims for weight-loss aids. Several states have fought against suspect diet products or other fitness gimmicks, sometimes with success, sometimes not.

A court case argued in Iowa shows how high the stakes can be for telemarketers who hawk these types of products: nearly $400,000 in sales for one diet aid for 1988 and 1989 just in the state of Iowa alone.†

---

*Crawford cited the problems with Choice Diet Products in a news release, June 3, 1992.

†State of Iowa v. Health Care Products, Inc., Polk County, CE No. 30-17365, February 23, 1990. The company agreed to halt sales of its diet pill in Iowa, pay the state $20,000 to cover prosecution costs, and grant refunds to dissatisfied customers.

When big bucks are on the line, the industry amasses legal clout, which in turn crimps state enforcement actions.

One sales tactic regulators often try to curb is the use of testimonials from people who claim miracle results. In another Iowa case settled in 1994, a judge examined two women whose cases were cited by the maker of a weight-loss pill. The court found that one of the women, a nurse from Louisiana, had lost weight but that the connection to the product was "speculative." The judge also found that the company did little to substantiate the claims of its satisfied clients, other than talking to the woman on the phone and developing "a sense that she was telling the truth."*

Many other affinity groups become targets of telemarketing pros, who are adept at picking up on "ties that bind."

U.S. Sen. Richard H. Bryan (Nevada), at an October 1993 hearing, described some of the techniques overheard by undercover FBI agents who infiltrated telephone boiler rooms. Bryan said he was appalled by the tactics used to target groups:

> I mean, it was absolutely a shameless performance of human nature at its very worst. People would chuckle about how they were able to make a pitch based upon a religious argument that would be made to somebody who they happened to identify as being very active in a religious community. It was just incredible—pretty callous.

Ethnic groups have been hit by a number of affinity investment schemes, mostly in commodities, a high-risk area best left to professional investors.

The Commodities Futures Trading Commission filed eight civil suits in the early 1990s alleging fraudulent sales of commodities by companies that mainly targeted members of the Asian communities in New York and California. Officials said the sales pitches often "promise fantastic profits with little risk, and involve persistent, high-pressure contacts allowing no time for reflection or investigation by the investor."

Two such companies operating in California collected as much as $30 million from five thousand Asian investors before regulators raided the premises. For California regulators, accustomed to years of battling pyramid-investment schemes, the only new twist was the targets, who responded to ads for the investments in Chinese-language newspapers.

---

*State of Iowa v. National Dietary Research, Inc., Polk County, CE 38-22630 Judgment, January 7, 1994.

Many of these companies, while based in Hong Kong, hired sales agents from the local community to peddle precious metals and investments in foreign currencies to their neighbors and friends. In one of the first such cases filed, commodities regulators won a federal court order barring Sun Hing Bullion Investment Ltd. from selling futures contracts. In written documents outlining the case, officials wrote:

> Many investors were solicited by friends and relatives who had been recently hired by the firms, and who had themselves invested in the programs. Because of the preexisting relationships between the brokers and their customers, dissatisfied investors were reluctant to complain for fear of injuring their relatives and friends.*

Another case employed far more brazen tactics. A company called Goldex told customers that their money was being sent to Hong Kong for investment in foreign markets. Instead, company officials pocketed the money and wrote up phony invoices to make it appear they were trading the investments. They went so far as to pay an accomplice in Hong Kong to falsely confirm trades. The perpetrators got caught and sentenced to five years in a federal prison.†

Collectors also can be prime targets for affinity frauds. Some of these pastimes grow overnight into major investments that attract telemarketers who tarnish the industry for years.

One such pastime is coin collecting. In the summer of 1990 Barry Cutler, chairman of the FTC's bureau of consumer protection, had a stern lecture for coin dealers gathered at their annual convention in Seattle: clean up your act, or else.

Cutler said the coin industry had grown from "one of children looking for scarce dates in pocket change and visiting their corner hobby shops to an investment industry that has captured the imagination of Wall Street." According to Cutler, telemarketing con artists had invaded coin collecting, setting up boiler rooms all over the country to swindle hobbyists and investors alike.

Coins appealed to telemarketers because no standards existed for "grading" the condition and, therefore, the value of coins. The uncertainty over the worth of coins invited boiler-room operations which thrive on selling products at vastly inflated prices. When some big investors pre-

---

*"Backgrounder," Commodities Futures Trading Commission, May 26, 1992.
†"Backgrounder."

dicted a bullish market, the con artists found a cloak of legitimacy to drape over their racket. "Major brokers, relying on rosy reports . . . and the claims of rare-coin grading services about objectivity, liquidity, and the safety of rare-coin investments are making a major push into rare coins," Cutler said.

The Federal Trade Commission went on to spend years trying to weed crooks out of the coin business, with limited success.

The need for buyers to be wary became clear as far back as December 1986, when the FTC filed suit against William J. Ulrich of Minneapolis, one of the nation's biggest coin dealers and appraisers. Ulrich advertised "conservative" grading for his coins, which he sold through telemarketing and mail-order outlets. He said his grading process would "help assure . . . high quality in every purchase."

The FTC charged Ulrich with overstating the condition of inferior coins to mislead buyers and inflating the "value" of his coins by as much as 200 percent. While Ulrich claimed his coins would appreciate greatly in a few years, the FTC charged that his customers could only expect to lose money because of the grading scam. In 1990, the FTC won an $1.2 million judgment against Ulrich, which he did not pay, according to an FTC news release of March 3, 1993.

Other ruses quickly popped up, some obviously fraudulent. In December 1988 the FTC sued a Georgia company that sold rare coins to telemarketers for seventy-five dollars each, regardless of their condition. The telemarketers paid the company thirteen dollars more for a phony grading stamp that stated the coins were of investment-grade quality. With the stamps as a back up, the boiler rooms sold the coins to suckers for from $250 to $400 a coin. Typical investors in the scam, which went on for more than three years, lost from $1,500 to $5,000, FTC records state.

The FTC brought other cases against coin dealers in the states of New York, California, and Arizona, charging that dealers downplayed the risks of investing in the coin market or grossly overstated the value of their coins, sometimes pricing them two to four times their worth. Most of these dealers settled the fraud charges against them by paying fines, mostly far less than the profits they earned.

Liberty Financial of North America, in Scottsdale, Arizona, agreed to repay $224,000 to consumers to settle charges that it lied about risks and claimed it was approved by government agencies.* Liberty's coin prices were three to five times the market value, but the company used selling

---

*FTC news release, October 15, 1990.

slogans such as: "We feel a portfolio worth a million dollars in the next twelve years is not only possible but highly probable." Another pitch: "Yearly gains of 20 to 40 percent and more have become quite normal. . . . Our prices are consistently among the very lowest in the entire United States."

With these suits either settled or making their way through federal courts, FTC official Cutler lectured the coin industry once again in April 1991. He urged the honest dealers to crack down on crooked upstarts. "The industry has offered much talk, but little action, about self-regulation in the five years since the FTC became very active in the coin industry," he said. "What I see lacking is any genuine commitment to what the industry leaders say they do want—true consumer protection for investors and hobbyists alike." Cutler's words were borne out by more fraud lawsuits accusing even more coin dealers of phony grading schemes and wildly exaggerated claims.

U.S. Rarities in Miami, which routinely sold its coins for three to ten times their value, lured buyers by asserting that it used a grading service that applied the strictest standards, according to the FTC. From 1989 to early 1992, the firm claimed investors would reap huge dividends on its coins.

Not so, said the FTC, which charged that losses were "virtually inevitable" because of the inflated prices.* In May 1992 U.S. Rarities settled the case. The owners filed for bankruptcy leaving nothing for their investors.

The settlement required them to place on any future ads or invoices a warning that is good advice to anyone who decides to become a coin collector in today's climate:

> The investment value of a rare coin depends in large part on the price you pay. It is strongly recommended that before you purchase a rare coin as an investment, you seek to determine its current market value and liquidity by consulting a coin expert who is not affiliated with the person selling you the coin.

The FTC's campaign to clean up the coin industry is not over. It still has unfinished business with Ulrich, the Minnesota man whose phony grading kicked off the enforcement effort in 1986. The federal agency won an $11.1 million judgment against Ulrich in March 1990. The agency had asked for $20 million to repay victims of the fraud.

---

*FTC news release, April 16, 1991.

Ulrich never paid a dime. The agency is fighting to seize Ulrich's 30,000-square-foot home in Wazata, Minnesota, worth between $3 million and $6 million.

The Minnesotan agreed in 1991 to turn over the house as part of a complex plea bargain in which he would plead guilty to a single count of racketeering in exchange for a maximum penalty of six years in jail. Ulrich also was supposed to deliver $850,000 including cash and personal furnishings from his house, and to testify against others who allegedly helped him evade paying the FTC's judgment.

As that case stalled, the FTC took an unusual step of filing civil charges against one of Ulrich's lawyers and a Minneapolis bank, which the government contends conspired to assist Ulrich in hiding assets from the FTC.

The law firm allegedly helped Ulrich transfer millions of dollars into trusts in the names of his daughters, then siphon off money for his own use. A number of maneuverings by the bank and lawyers made Ulrich "judgment proof," the FTC said.

One law firm denied all the government's accusations but paid $35,000 to the FTC to settle the matter. It also agreed to hand over a $250,000 lien it holds on the Ulrich mansion.*

Nobody has much hope that any substantial amount of the money will be paid back to Ulrich's customers.

Has the industry cleaned its act up since the early 1990s? Perhaps, but the FTC and the American Numismatic Association continue to issue warnings to hobbyists and investors. They even issued a joint booklet that shows at least some degree of cooperation with the government to weed out fraud.

Although the recommendations discuss coins, they apply to numerous collectibles sold by telemarketers, ranging from objets d'art to stamps and lithographs:

• Do not rush into buying coins. People who make money do so after careful study of the types of coins they want to invest in. They also check the history of appreciation of the coins using independent sources.

• Make sure you know a dealer's reputation in the numismatic community. Before you buy, check how long a firm has been in business and verify any claims that a dealer belongs to professional organizations.

*FTC news release, March 3, 1993.

• Be wary of promises that the dealer will buy back the coins at a later date unless you are confident that the dealer has the money to stand behind such a claim. Many companies sued by the FTC through the years have made these claims, but have not done so.

• Before buying find out what the dealer's return policy is. Some will take back coins within thirty days, others give credit. After purchase, take the coins to another dealer for a second opinion. You may want to exercise the return policy based on getting a second opinion.

• Check with independent sources and be suspicious of grading certificates handed out by coin dealers. Because grading is not an exact science, it should not be done by the seller of coins.

The coin dealers association also warned about common telemarketing tricks that have swindled buyers over the years. These include:

• False claims of appreciation using a brokerage house report as support. One such report, which predicted 12 percent to 25 percent yearly gains, was widely circulated by telemarketers as a sales inducement. What was left unsaid was that the report based its findings on twenty very rare coins, not all coins sold by dealers.

• Even when coins are graded properly, they still may be no bargain. The association cited as an example a ten-dollar Indian gold piece with a market value of $1,750, which might be placed on sale for $5,000. Some dealers will claim their prices are in line with others, when in fact they are not. The booklet states: "Despite statements to the contrary, there is a great deal of risk in coin investments. If you are not knowledgeable about coins, you may lose all or most of your investment."

Part Three

The More Things Change

13

Busy Signals

Joan Johnson didn't set out to get ripped off by a telemarketer. She had doubts about the sales offer and tried to check with the only agency she could think of to call: the Better Business Bureau; in her case, the South Florida division. Johnson got nothing but a busy signal, time after time, hour after hour.

She went ahead and sent $599 to America's Clearing House in Fort Lauderdale for pens bearing the name of her small real-estate business The telemarketer shut down a few weeks later, without sending her a thing

"I got caught in a moment of weakness," says Johnson, who lives in Beach Park, Illinois. "They were very friendly on the phone. I guess I should have known better."

America's Clearing House "hit and ran" from a cheap office on Fort Lauderdale's "maggot mile," the warehouse zone where boiler rooms cluster like constellations in the summer sky.

Johnson, who knew nothing about the firm, said in an interview that she blames only herself for her loss. But she is annoyed that she had no place to turn for a quick, accurate report on the telemarketer.

That seemed only fair considering a boiler-room operator can buy almost anyone's name and phone number and invade their privacy at will. Yet short of refusing to do business over the phone with unknown callers, there's no way to be sure any offer is bona fide.

Just calling and checking put Johnson in an elite group, judging from a 1992 Harris poll, which found that two of three people had no idea how to inquire about a telemarketer, perhaps explaining why phone-fraud artists flourish year after year, deal after deal.

Among those who had an idea where to seek help, very few mentioned police or other law enforcement agencies such as their state's attorney general. Almost everyone picked the Better Business Bureau.

But some of these business groups admit they are having a tough time living up to expectations, especially when it comes to clamping down on telemarketers who pressure buyers to make quick decisions.

For starters, the Better Business Bureaus have no regulatory power. They are private, nonprofit agencies funded by dues collected from members, the businesses in their area. The bureaus provide the public with reports on member companies, including whether they resolve customer complaints. The bureaus also can help mediate disputes and boot out businesses that cheat the public. And they can refer complaints to law enforcement agencies.

But bureau standards vary widely nationwide. Some refuse to read reports over the phone. Others require callers to send a self-addressed stamped envelope to receive a report. Some will fax a report; others refuse. Some file reports that are timid or incomplete. An exception is the Las Vegas bureau, one of the few that goes out of its way to collect lawsuits and other derogatory information about Nevada companies—and will read it free of charge to anyone who calls.

The service is vitally needed given the simple fact that Nevada is crawling with phone cons. The bureau also has clout with some of the large Vegas telemarketing rooms, which tend to make refunds or adjustments to the small group of consumers who take the time and trouble to complain to the bureau.

But many other bureaus are caught unprepared when telemarketers creep into town, or become defensive of a local business when out-of-state callers request information.

In South Florida, also a crucial branch because of the warren of boiler rooms within its borders, callers for years had a tough time getting someone to answer the phone. The Miami-based bureau, bogged down by more than one thousand calls daily from all over the country, decided in 1994 to set up a 900 number and charge callers 95 cents a minute, an average of $3.80, to hear a report read by a computerized voice. The volume of calls dropped off by half.

The Miami bureau has had other problems that hardly boost consumer confidence. In the early 1980s, the bureau gave a favorable reference to Eagle Oil and Gas, a massive telemarketing swindle which promised thousands of buyers premium leases for oil and gas exploration on federal lands. Eagle filed sixty-six thousand applications for leases, but won just sixty, despite taking as much as $56 million from investors.*

---

*FTC news release, July 8, 1983, Civil Complaint No. 83-1702 WMH.

Former Better Business Bureau head Henry Scott Harris was convicted of conspiracy in 1985 after prosecutors charged he accepted eight hundred dollars a week in bribes from Eagle in exchange for giving the public a rosy report on the company. Saying Harris "violated the public trust," a federal judge sentenced him to four years in prison.*

Eagle kingpin Gurdon Wolfson fled the country following his conviction on mail and wire fraud charges that same year. He received a twenty-year sentence in absentia.

The bureau felt the stigma of the Wolfson case for years, often being left out of law enforcement gatherings for fear it could not be trusted. In 1991 the group and its national organization, the Council of Better Business Bureaus, agreed to pay $4.5 million to settle a suit brought by the Federal Trade Commission.† The lawsuit named a number of organizations, banks, and law firms that allegedly helped Eagle Oil keep the scam under wraps. The defendants in the suit kicked in $47 million, which the FTC intends to use to distribute to victims of Wolfson's scam.

That episode behind it, the bureau now enjoys an improved reputation among local law enforcement. But problems remain such as the scam run on the bureau by the irrepressible Tim O'Neil (see chapter 3), whose taped message about Cypress Creek Promotions gave callers the impression he was operating a legitimate sweepstakes. While O'Neil's scam has been smashed, there is no guarantee that some other operators won't be able to manipulate the system.

In its defense, the Better Business Bureau argues that it does not possess the law enforcement tools needed to investigate the backgrounds of business people. Other Better Business Bureaus are trying to balance their need to raise money against their duty to remain unbiased and free of conflicts of interest. In August 1994, the Better Business Bureau of New Jersey startled a number of its peer groups by sending out 600,000 mailers to state residents on behalf of advertisers ranging from siding companies to car dealers. The circulars included a six-paragraph letter on bureau stationery, which some took as an endorsement of the product. Answering critics, bureau officials said their letters contained the bureau's standard caution that it does not endorse any business.**

But doubters of the practice, which earned the bureau about $10,000 in its early stages, told the *New York Times* that they felt the action imper-

---

*"Ex BBB President Found Guilty of Conspiracy," *Sun Sentinel,* February 9, 1985.

†FTC File No. 812 3232. The FTC announced the settlements on April 30, 1991.

**"Watchdog's Deal Raises Revenue and Eyebrows," *New York Times,* August 10, 1994.

iled the business bureau's independence and integrity, allegations bureau officials reject.

At least many business bureaus provide information to the public upon demand. Many law enforcement agencies do the exact opposite: they hoard information and refuse to share it with their peers or the public. When the subjects are telemarketers, consumers badly need to know as much as possible about past exploits.

Too many law enforcement agencies would rather preserve the sanctity of their files and the secrecy of their activities than give people insights that could prevent them from being ripped off. Considering that few agencies recover money stolen from telemarketing fraud victims, the pro-secrecy stance seems ludicrous.

The federal government is best equipped to be a watchdog for the public and keep tabs on abusive telemarketers who sell across state lines. But it doesn't do that. Instead, officials have kept a lid on the data they collected, which, truth be told, is embarrassingly bad and incomplete.

The Federal Trade Commission has been the keeper of the government's telemarketing fraud database since the 1980s, collecting complaints from other law enforcement agencies and the public. The agency boasted to Congress in 1987 that its "automated data bank" let the agency learn about a telemarketer's past in a "matter of minutes." Officials also said that on-line complaint files would "allow us to put our cases together more quickly and more effectively."*

But the agency steadfastly refused to share any of this information with potential victims, and repeatedly opposed efforts in Congress to open up such data for public view. Testifying before Congress in March 1989, then FTC Chairman Daniel Oliver said:

> Based on our experience we believe that most persons who would make such inquiries would want information on whether a particular telemarketer is under investigation by the commission or whether any complaints have been made against the company. Disclosure of this information . . . would violate the commission's long-standing policy of protecting the confidentiality of its investigations. This confidentiality is indispensable to the success of our law enforcement efforts. Operators of telemarketing scams are likely to secrete their assets or disappear

---

*Hearing Before the Subcommittee on Transportation, Tourism, and Hazardous Materials, House Committee on Energy and Commerce, July 27, 1987, Washington, D.C.

overnight upon learning that they are the subject of a Commission investigation.*

Years later, the stance had softened, but not by much. Barry Cutler, director of the FTC's Bureau of Consumer Protection, stated the commission's position at a March 1993 U.S. Senate committee hearing. Under consideration by the committee was a telemarketing reform bill, which like many unsuccessful bills before it, created a clearinghouse to help consumers gain insights into the backgrounds of telemarketers.†

> Given the need for us to protect the confidentiality and integrity of our investigations . . . the commission reiterates its skepticism as to whether we could, in the normal course, provide consumers with meaningful information about many telemarketers with which they are dealing. In recent years, the commission has committed additional resources to the development of a database of nonpublic information to assist cooperative law enforcement efforts. In the context of this development, it seems doubtful that any benefits to consumers from such a clearinghouse would outweigh the substantial costs its administration would likely entail.

The FTC's opposition won out. The 1994 Consumer Protection Telemarketing Act, which evolved from years of failed bills that promised to crack down on the fraud menace, dropped the requirement that the FTC set up a clearinghouse to assist consumers.

The FTC's stance seemed self-protective to some people who believe the agency's enforcement record against telemarketing fraud has been slothful and spotty. In fact, many telemarketers could learn about an FTC inquiry because these cases often involve months of taking detailed depositions of marketers and reviewing company sales literature. In many other cases, the firms already have been sued for consumer fraud by state consumer regulators—information that should be widely available. State attorneys general, who must win re-election campaigns to stay in office, tend to be more forthcoming with the media and the public.

In one 1980s case, a single telemarketer had been sued by the attorneys general of fifteen states before the FTC stepped in. And in that case, as in almost every FTC case, there was no money available for consumers at the conclusion of the lawsuit.

---

*Subcommittee on Transportation Hearing, March 16, 1989.

†Hearing Subcommittee on Consumer, Committee on Commerce, Science, and Transportation, U.S. Senate, March 18, 1993.

The notion that the FTC struck fear in the hearts of telemarketers seemed almost delusional considering the fact that the agency has only civil powers and that few telemarketers worry about being sued. Most don't even bother to pay a fine.

So why not tell people before they get ripped off that they are dealing with a company that has a long history of lawsuits and judgments against them for consumer fraud? Because FTC bureaucrats don't want to.

I know this firsthand. Researching a series of newspaper articles on telemarketing that appeared in the *Sun-Sentinel* of Fort Lauderdale, I contacted every state's attorney general, asking them for records of enforcement actions against telemarketers. More than thirty attorneys general complied. Others refused, either citing privacy considerations or saying they were too busy.

The documents showed that many telemarketers had been sued repeatedly in a number of states, which often were not aware of legal actions taken by their peers. Using the reports, the newspaper confirmed that many telemarketing cons stay afloat for years by simply settling lawsuits state by state, usually for small fines. In a few instances, phone firms agreed to quit selling in a state rather than contest the charges. But most of the time the firm was out of business by the time the state got a court award, and nobody could be located to pay the fine.

But many states said they reported enforcement actions, mostly lawsuits which are matters of public record, to the Federal Trade Commission for entry into its national databank. Their intent was to alert law enforcement to individuals who hopped from scam to scam.

The FTC database seemed like a gold mine for consumers who for years have yearned for some sort of clearinghouse where they could get quick details on the trustworthiness of a telemarketer. One phone call sure beats calling every state, the only way to thoroughly check out a company's history.

In April 1992 I wrote to the FTC asking for the telemarketing data under terms of the Freedom of Information Act, a federal law which requires the government to release certain files to the public.

The request asked for the names of all telemarketers with enforcement actions against them, the types of products they sold, and the states they were located in. The request also asked for the number of complaints filed with the agency and the states victims resided in (but not their names). The idea was to discern which states had an abundance of sleazy marketers and which states they preyed upon.

The computer seemed ideally suited to such an analysis, which could identify states in need of stepped up enforcement action as well as areas in which consumer education campaigns should be focused.

The FTC did not agree. The agency had never sought to pull the numbers from its computers for any sort of analysis, and wasn't about to do so for a newspaper. The agency cited exemptions to the Freedom of Information Act that allows an agency to keep confidential records whose release could "reasonably be expected to interfere with enforcement proceedings."

The FTC refused to provide complaints because doing so would "reveal the targets of current nonpublic investigations or targets of investigations that are to be opened in the near future."

This stance is not unusual for law enforcement agencies which tend to regard their files as sacred ground, never to be trampled upon by press or public. Using the Freedom of Information Act to stall a requester, hoping he or she will give up in despair, also is a common strategy. (While the act contains provisions for sanctions against federal officials who abuse the law to unlawfully withhold public records, nobody has been sanctioned in nearly twenty years.)

In my case the FTC stonewalled through the end of 1992. The tactic left the newspaper no choice but to file a federal lawsuit in U.S. District Court in Fort Lauderdale to force the agency to release the data.

The lawsuit, filed in early 1993 just as a new administration arrived in Washington, seemed to get the agency's attention. The FTC proposed a settlement in which it agreed to hand over most of the data.*

When the material arrived, the reasons for attempting to conceal it seemed obvious: the computer system was a mess. The computer went on the blink continuously and gave programmers a tough time whenever they wanted to extract anything from it. It took agency lawyers and data managers numerous phone calls to explain how the system stored records. Agency officials were unsure what one code stood for, even though the code contained a large number of complaints.

The data held a few other surprises once pried loose and analyzed.

The largest single entry among the nine thousand complaints dealt with the fraudulent sale of toner for photocopying machines, many of them apparently forwarded by the National Office Business Machine Dealers Association in Chicago, a trade group that lobbies on behalf of its members and a regular contributor to the FTC database.

---

*Fred Schulte and Sun-Sentinel Company v. Federal Trade Commission, U.S. District Court, Fort Lauderdale, Florida, Case No. 93-6039.

The office toner scam is a chronic problem for businesses. Typically, an invoice arrives for an amount—often two hundred dollars—for office photocopying toner that was never received, in the hopes the company's accounting office will pay without asking any questions. In other cases, scammers actually send toner, but at astronomical prices.

While the toner scams should be stamped out, they are far removed from the daily needs of the vast majority of American consumers. The FTC filed several cases against California companies using the toner scam in the late 1980s, showing that it responded to groups with a strong lobbying arm to press their case.

Unfortunately, consumers lacked that potent lobby. The FTC did little else with its data and showed no interest in plucking it out to determine where its enforcement actions should be centered.

For the record, the FTC database, while flawed, seems to confirm many of the observations of law enforcement. It squares with complaints obtained from state regulators.

An analysis of FTC data showed that as of 1993:

• The largest single concentration of telemarketing fraud victims lived in Iowa, followed by California and Minnesota. The states of Iowa, Minnesota, and Illinois together accounted for one-fourth of the complaints. However, the numbers are far from scientific. Higher numbers in some states could be explained by more aggressive reporting of complaints to the data system.

• Two-thirds of the complaints centered on five telemarketing perennials. In addition to the toner scams, the top problems were advertising specialties and promotions, travel and recreation packages, coins, and vitamins.

• The telemarketers drawing complaints overwhelmingly operated from California, Florida, Texas, and Nevada. California racked up large numbers because of the toner scams which have been based in the Los Angeles area.

In Florida, travel and recreational offers topped the list along with advertising specialties. In Texas, the ad specs rooms and recreation products drew the most complaints, while in Nevada, grievances centered on ad-specs and promotions and vitamins.

The FTC data tended to support other contentions. Most of the states with large numbers of telemarketers drawing complaints had relatively few victims, suggesting that many problem operators feast on consumers in other states. This trend, long recognized by state law enforcers, points out the need for aggressive federal action against telemarketers.

The data has other limitations that could prevent the public from getting much use out of it.

In general, the complaint process takes way too much time and the longer it takes the more it favors the miscreant over the victim. Scam artists are adept at stalling buyers, sometimes for months, before they get fed up and file a complaint.

Boiler rooms often bilk hundreds of people before complaints start rolling in to state consumer agencies or state attorneys general. Some states slow things further by requiring victims to first send for a complaint form. Others demand notarized statements, which deter all but the most determined.

Once the state agency gets the complaint, more time passes while officials figure out what to do with it. Often they pass it on to the state where the telemarketer is located, which causes further delay. Once the complaint arrives at the second state, a clerk will prepare a letter to the telemarketer asking for a response. Many states lack the power to force a firm to refund a customer's money, but send letters hoping the company will try to stay on the right side of regulators. Often, the process takes so long that the letters are returned to the state agency marked "addressee unknown." And it is not likely that many of these complaints would find their way into a central, federal registry in time to do any good.

"By the time the state has accumulated enough complaints to understand that [a telemarketer] is a big problem, it is six months later and the firms are gone," Jerry Allred, a prosecutor in Florida's Panhandle said in a 1992 interview.

Few regulators like to admit it, but they simply are outclassed by telephone criminals. The marketers have computer technology at their fingertips, while many regulatory agencies still count complaints by hand. The telemarketers have something else regulators rarely show: good old-fashioned gumption.

Sleazy businesses seize the upper hand in negotiations with regulators, time after time. They demand the benefit of the doubt and almost always get it, usually through their lawyers. Some threaten to sue anyone who dares to suggest to the public they are running a scam; they keep the peace by offering a few refunds from time to time, or they pay law firms to offer quick settlements that discourage victims from cooperating with government investigators.

Telemarketers who cut prompt refund checks often have little to fear. Typically, regulators will fail to notice all of the consumers are alleging the same sales tactics, which if true, violate fraud statutes. And many agencies lack the staff to trot to court against every errant telemarketer.

Most agencies, from Better Business Bureaus to state attorneys general, are more eager to clear complaints, preferably with a consumer refund, than to match wits with top-dollar boiler-room lawyers in court.

Politics also hinder out-of-state consumers trying to get justice. Most states entrust consumer protection to elected attorneys general, some of whom view their jobs as a stepping stone to higher office. They tend to resolve complaints from voters who elected them, not people living thousands of miles away.

The proof of this bias: boiler rooms almost never sell to residents of the states they operate in. And they tend to nest in Sunbelt states known for lax enforcement of anti-fraud statutes.

Some problems are practical. Flying in victims to testify at telemarketing trials costs big money and these cases attract far less public attention than prosecuting violent criminals—or solving complaints from voters. "The feeling is why waste (Florida) taxpayers' money to represent people up north," says Will Harter, a complaint analyst with the Florida Department of Agriculture and Consumer Services in Tallahassee. "It's a tough situation for our state. We're looking worse and worse every year."*

Why doesn't government at all levels crack down on these frauds? The answer is special interests. So many legitimate businesses either make money off telemarketing or fear that new regulations to wipe out phone fraud would hurt their interests that a legislative paralysis sets in.

Dozens of states have tried to impose restrictions on telephone commerce as a means to curb fraud only to face fierce opposition from business groups, ranging from legitimate telemarketers to the banking lobby to local chambers of commerce. "Legitimate telemarketers scream bloody murder about restrictions on their business. It's tough to get laws passed to get at the scam guys," said Bob West, a U.S. Secret Service agent in Utah, in an interview.

Some of these powerful influences impede consumers seeking relief from phone fraud because they are too willing to rake in the profits. While the "helping hands"—those groups of businesses that profit handsomely

---

*Interview with Will Harter, November 13, 1992.

from selling phone hucksters the tools of their trade, are easily condemned, some others take no responsibility for being part of the problem.
They become indignant at the suggestion that they might be blinded by
the dollars to be made in extending hospitality to phone marketers.

Some cities are hopeful for the jobs that telemarketing might bring,
providing steady pay checks for workers and a steady tax base for their
host community.

Economic development officials in many areas—the Quad Cities in
the Midwest, for example—advertise in marketing journals in the hope of
luring telemarketing jobs. While no chamber of commerce willingly goes
out and solicits the con artist, chasing after phone-sales companies does
not put them in the strongest position to ask tough questions.

Being beholden to mammoth telephone rooms gives communities a
financial incentive to look the other way when some of the marketers who
mosey into town turn out to employ deceptive sales tactics as well as local
breadwinners.

Johnson City, Tennessee, is one area that has hotly pursued new telemarketers. In 1994 officials hawked the town as "a site for sore eyes" in
an advertisement placed in a marketing journal. They offered a former
discount store location with up to 77,000 square feet of space and 400+
parking spaces, close to highways, calling it a "perfect location for a telemarketing operation." The mountain community in northeast Tennessee
mentioned its advanced fiber optics, or phone service, "and experienced
work force, exceptional quality of life and a low cost of doing business."

The town's economic development board cites a number of satisfied
clients, including one which has drawn repeated complaints to consumer
officials across the country.

These telemarketing towns come and go as hotspots. The fate of
Sparta, a small town in White County, Tennessee, offers a lesson. Almost
overnight it became home to high-pressure boiler rooms that bilked the
public, mainly through the sale of vacation certificates. At one point in the
late 1980s, the industry employed over half of the county. But eventually
authorities caught up with it, and the boiler-room boys moved on, looking
for another community that would roll out the red carpet.

When it comes to assessing why phone fraud persists, there is plenty
of blame to go around.

Newspapers that carry indignant articles on the telemarketing menace
contribute to the problem. Many of the nation's mightiest newspapers
impose few restrictions on classified advertising, other than cash up front.

While the papers are loathe to admit it, many consumers are convinced a deal is bona fide if it appears in a big city daily.

Paula Kurtenbach of Overland Park, Kansas, felt that way. She said in an interview that she thinks her newspaper, the *Kansas City Star,* is partly to blame for her family losing $545 in a travel scam they learned about from reading a classified ad. She had to explain to her five excited children that their trip to the Bahamas was "stolen" by a telemarketer who folded shortly after she sent the money by courier. Kurtenbach said she expected the newspaper to do some checking before it accepted the ad. A *Star* executive said the paper does everything it can to police the ads, but in the end the buyer must check out any deal that seems too good to be true.

The episode could have occurred in any city. Travel ads in which companies list toll-free numbers and little else run in most Sunday travel sections of newspapers. Some are legitimate discounters, but others are phone rooms or travel agencies that will go out of business and strand travelers.

Some regulators urge newspapers to require advertisers—especially travel agencies—to provide addresses and other details in their ads so the public can get some sense of whom they are dealing with.

Many newspaper reporters and their editors might agree, but they rarely control advertising policies or other business matters. Some travel editors atone for some of the atrocious ads they run by publishing periodic articles warning the public to watch out for travel scams.

Some national newspapers claim they review company profiles before accepting an ad, but scammers evade these checks time after time, for everything from business opportunities to overseas employment.

Bob James, an investigator with Florida's Department of Agriculture and Consumer Services, said in two years only one newspaper had called him to check whether the advertiser of a business opportunity was licensed. Failure to register is a felony.[*] "Thousands of ads run every week in newspapers. They have the capacity to curtail these scams," says James.

Regulators agree that consumers often believe the ads they read or watch on television. "I think people expect an air of authenticity in the newspapers and on TV, especially elderly people," says Carmel Benton, an investigator with the Iowa Attorney General's Office. "People say, 'it would not have been in the paper if it was not legitimate.' "[†]

[*]Interview with Bob James, July 6, 1994.
[†]Interview with Carmel Benton, January 21, 1992.

Sometimes newspapers are the ones who get burned. One California paper near San Francisco was taken after it extended credit to a local woman who placed ads for a travel-certificate company. Only after billing the woman at the address she gave did the newspaper discover that the telemarketer had simply picked a name out of the phone book and used it to book the ad. Newspaper workers realized the mistake and called the 800 number in the ad. The line was disconnected. The newspaper was taken for about fifty dollars. Chances are its readers lost a good deal more.

Many newspapers also accept employment ads for telemarketing rooms that lure new employees into the field with deceptive promises of $100,000 salaries. Most end up earning only five dollars an hour, if that, because they cannot keep pace with the pros. Some of these ads, which almost never list the company's name, clearly are directed at the criminal underground of "phone pros," using street lingo such as "one-in-five" or "Fly and Buy Biz Opp," or "AD SPEC PROS/FRONTERS wanted. Call Mr. Money." Another ad in the *Sun-Sentinel* read:

> Telemarketers—If you're money hungry come see me. I'll stuff your pockets with cash. CALL CAPTAIN CASH!

In South Florida, fraud detectives read the want-ads to keep track of new boiler rooms.

Overnight mail services are another conduit for the telemarketing con. For years marketers have used them to evade mail fraud charges, but efforts to pass a federal law that would put the overnight services under the jurisdiction of U.S. Postal Service inspectors have failed, largely because of industry lobbying.

To its credit, at least one of the nation's large private mail carriers is trying to change things. While they cannot refuse pick-up, Federal Express drivers who suspect fraud can leave a warning brochure at the homes of people who call the service to arrange a pick up.

Even if the federal law is changed, con artists would simply use other services such as wire transfers and automatic debiting of checking accounts. But for now, payment by cashier's check, which is as good as cash, sent by overnight delivery service is an absolute bonanza for the telemarketing fraud artist.

The phone companies also have aggravated police and other regulators, who believe phone companies often are aware the operations that are setting up are fraudulent sales rooms.

Sgt. James Layman, an investigator with the Broward County

Sheriff's Office in Florida, has repeatedly tried to persuade private businesses to cooperate with police in investigations of boiler rooms. "They feel no responsibility as a good corporate citizen to tell us about problems. They are acting as a conduit for criminal enterprises."*

Federal regulators have the same problem. Testifying before Congress in June 1991, Kenneth M. Hearst, Assistant Chief Postal Inspector for Criminal Investigations, said:

> Our investigations have been hampered by telephone companies refusing to provide information concerning telemarketing operations using 800 numbers unless we first obtain a subpoena. Where our case has proceeded to the level of a grand jury, this is not a problem. However at the early stages, where we want to move quickly to detain the mail-in order to prevent the promoter from obtaining proceeds and "busting out," obtaining telephone subscription data without the delay inherent in obtaining a criminal subpoena would be invaluable.†

Phone company executives surely would be embarrassed by some of the goings on in the ultra-competitive long-distance service market if they could hear themselves tripping over each other to snare telemarketing-room accounts. One FBI surveillance tape of a Florida boiler-room owner meeting with undercover agents is interrupted by an unwelcome visit from a salesman from a long-distance carrier. The impatience with which the boiler-room operator brushes off the salesman, yelling at a secretary to send him on his way, gives a clear sign of the telemarketer's power as a major account. Even a small room can run up a long-distance bill of several thousand dollars a month.

Phone companies also will bill for almost any service provider, often without asking many questions about the nature or content, and shutting down the service only when the phone company doesn't get paid.

One company in New York State took more than $1 million in three months during 1993 by calling people and asking them to accept a collect phone call, then billing them for $49.95 for the call. The local telephone companies handled the billing for the suspect calls and kept a percentage as their fee, according to the New York Attorney General's Office.

Regulators argue that many customers are likely to pay bogus billings

---

*Interview with James Layman, November 16, 1992.

†House Joint Hearing Subcommittee on Regulation, Business Opportunities, and Energy; Committee on Small Business; and the Subcommittee on Health and Long-Term Care, Select Committee on Aging, June 21, 1991, Washington, D.C.

because they fear they might lose phone service if they refuse. While federal law protects customers against such an action, chances are consumers don't know that. The New York scheme tended to prey on the elderly and people who either did not speak English or had a poor command of the language. New York authorities believe the promoters of the scheme picked recent immigrants using census data, knowing many would not understand their rights to dispute billings.

All is not negative. Sometimes regulators and phone companies work together to keep the public from getting taken. One such incident in the Washington, D.C., area in January 1992 set the standards for private business and government cooperation. It involved a 900 phone number set up as the Washington Redskins were bound for the Super Bowl in Minneapolis, and many fans were desperate for tickets.

Two Coral Springs, Florida, telemarketers tried to cash in on the football frenzy with a 900-number lottery. They placed ads in the *Washington Post* sports section, claiming that for $3.30 a minute callers could enter a drawing to win two tickets and round-trip airfare to the "Big One" in Minneapolis. People who failed to read the fine print missed a key fact: the promotion was void in Maryland, the District of Columbia, and Virginia, the area where the *Post*'s readers live.

One day after the ad appeared, Maryland Attorney General J. Joseph Curran persuaded AT&T Communications to block all Maryland calls to the number and void charges.

"Even in the very unlikely event that you win this lottery, you couldn't collect the prize because the contest was void in Maryland," said Curran.* "This is nothing more than a cleverly worded ad that promises everything but produces nothing except a hefty phone bill. The irony here is that your chances of winning didn't improve by calling more often— you just lost more money," he said.

A few months later, the nation's state attorneys general announced an agreement with three large phone carriers for closer cooperation to regulate 900-number pitches.

Another legal business that often gets manipulated by fraud artists is the private mail-collection services. These mail drops—there are four hundred of them in the south Florida area alone—rent boxes to anyone.

Generally, these companies refuse to provide any information about the box holders to the public or authorities, but at least police can get a subpoena to force the firms to tell all. Members of the public are out of

---

*Curran news release, January 15, 1992.

luck. Many con artists turn to these services knowing that they will cover their identities, something the U.S. Postal Service will not do. After postal inspectors became aware that some companies used the anonymity of a post-office box to cheat the public, the agency adopted a rule allowing anyone to find out the identity of a box holder.

Local post offices also will give out forwarding addresses, although most require the person seeking the information to visit in person and pay a fee of one dollar for the address.

Other regulators get frustrated that as soon as they force through legislation to cut off the flow of money to the telemarketing con, the scammers find a new money line, such as check-cashing services. At a time when many South Florida telemarketers faced crackdowns on their use of credit card factors, the check cashers provided a new alternative. Some of these outlets launder checks, often for small-time con artists who don't want to bother to set up an office. Day after day, the same person can walk in with a bundle of checks from out of state, payments collected from a telemarketing scam, and get these checks cashed for a fee—no questions asked.

One check-cashing service handled more than $5.4 million in checks in about two years in Fort Lauderdale on behalf of telemarketers, according to prosecutors.

Sometimes regulators work against one another in embarrassing ways. For example, in 1992 U.S. Postal Service officials gave an award to a Texas mass-marketing firm that had been accused of using deceptive marketing tactics by the attorneys general of twenty-two states. The award for innovative use of bar-coding equipment, which Allied Marketing touted in a news release, alarmed some state regulators who had been clamoring to shut down the firm for allegedly running a phony sweepstakes.

Some state officials sensed a conflict. In 1990 the U.S. Postal Service delivered 63.7 billion pieces of third-class mail, nearly 40 percent of all the mail it carried. Revenues from junk mail amounted to $40.4 billion according to the Ohio Attorney General's Office. Postal executives insist that the profits do not influence them. They are lobbying for tough new laws to crack down on con artists who use the mails.

The flaws in enforcement of consumer-protection laws seem to be filtering through to the public, which is becoming more cynical and more likely to walk away from a bad business deal feeling that nobody can or will help them.

The American Association of Retired Persons found that less than a third of major-fraud victims who took complaints to Better Business Bureaus or other consumer offices were satisfied with the results.

Older people, the most likely victims of phone fraud, often feel less hopeful than younger people, with only about one in five people over age sixty-five believing that buyers who complain have their problems resolved. A Harris poll, conducted in April and May 1992, found that less than a third of people who felt they had been cheated reported the matter to anyone, and only 9 percent got a refund.

The most frequent reason that people failed to report theft was that they didn't feel it was worth the trouble or that they came to believe they should have used better sense. "Many people seem inclined to just put the matter behind them without giving thought to a civic responsibility to help prevent other people from getting cheated out of money by the same company," the poll concluded.

Once again, victory for the phone con.

14

Limits of the Law

Florida detectives thought they were raiding an illegal prize-telemarketing room called Premium Ventures. It sure looked the part. It occupied a scrubby set of offices tucked off the main road passing a decaying shopping mall. Inside, police found marked-up scripts and lead sheets strewn about, a board of sales tallies, and no state license.

The cops carted four men off to jail that day in October 1992, charging them with the felony of running an unlicensed phone room. They had been warned three months earlier to get a license or face arrest.

But Premium Ventures mounted a novel legal defense: the firm claimed to be selling for a church, which exempted it from the licensing law.

Prosecutors found very little of a spiritual nature in the Premium Ventures pitch: employees called people and told them they had won cash between $10,000 and $25,000. To qualify for the award they either had to send a check for $200 to $2,000 to cover "taxes" or order some merchandise. Police said many people did not get their prizes or products, or received "inferior" quality goods.

Premium Ventures produced a "marketing agreement" with the Inner Light Metaphysical Center, a storefront ministry registered as a church, to justify their position. Under the contract, Premium Ventures took 90 percent of the proceeds.

Citing the contract, Premium Ventures and its president, a chunky balding man named James Proietto, sued the state to void the arrests. The issue became moot after Proietto pled no contest to telemarketing without a license in January 1993.* Proietto was sentenced to eighteen months probation and made $18,750 in restitution payments. So did the other

---

*Premium Ventures, Inc., v. State of Florida, Seventeenth Judicial Circuit, Broward County, Case No. 92-29225.

three men arrested. In all, twenty-seven people living in eighteen states had filed sworn affidavits claiming Premium Ventures swindled them; one man from Fresno, California, lost $2,000.

The episode reminded police of the need to patch holes in the state's telemarketing licensing law, conceived as a major tool to combat illegal phone sales. Florida's experience offers a valuable lesson as more and more states turn to licensing as a means to crack down on the telemarketing-fraud menace.

After years of speeches in which members of the state legislature would rise to condemn Florida's reputation as a scam capital, lawmakers enacted the licensing law; it went into effect in September 1991. The law made it a felony to sell by phone from Florida without first obtaining a fifteen-hundred-dollar license and posting a fifty-thousand-dollar bond. The bond is intended to repay consumers should the company fold. Yet eighteen months after the effective date, state officials struggled to enforce it.

The problem was acute in the Fort Lauderdale area, the state's boiler-room hotspot. Nearly one third of fifteen thousand telemarketing complaints lodged with state officials between 1985 and late 1992 cited Fort Lauderdale firms. No other county in the state came close to matching the swarm of phone swindlers in the one-time Spring Break capital.

Meanwhile, new phone rooms were "springing up all over" in the Fort Lauderdale area, says Sgt. Ed Madge of the Broward County Sheriff's Office criminal investigations division. Madge calls the law "a joke."

While others are less candid in their criticisms, nobody disputes that the law got off to a shaky start. Initially, more than 95 percent of eight hundred known Florida telemarketing outfits failed to register. Half the firms had closed down or moved by the time state investigators asked them to register. And once they located them, most of the others claimed one of the law's twenty-six exemptions.

The law exempts charities, securities brokers, banks, churches, catalog-sales firms, record clubs, insurance agents, and people who sell subscriptions to newspapers and magazines by phone, to name a few.

Sgt. Madge blames "special interests" for watering down the law to protect their members from having to post a bond. The exemptions are so broad that many sleazy telemarketers can claim one. "The only way to change things is to get the legislature to change it," he says in an interview.

The glee with which telemarketers have sought loopholes in the law surprised nobody in law enforcement. It's a basic tenet of the con craft to do whatever it takes to outsmart authorities. "They would rather pay exorbitant legal expenses to fight us instead of getting a license. They don't want state control over them. They will go to great lengths," says Scott Dressler, chief of the Broward County State Attorney's Office economic crime unit in Fort Lauderdale. "Of course they hire lawyers using money from their victims."*

Dressler, who heads a telemarketing-fraud task force, has seen it all. Some telemarketers have rushed cheap, mimeographed "sale catalogs" into print to have on hand when the cops drop by. They claim they are a catalog-sales company. The law doesn't say they have to be a legitimate catalog-sales company.

Tim O'Neil, the owner of Cypress Creek Promotions, went so far as to register his boiler room with the U.S. Securities and Exchange Commission, using his elderly mother as president, to get around the state registration law. By avoiding registration, O'Neil cut off the state's primary means to keep tabs on his operation.

Many others frustrate police by taking advantage of the policy that gives a written warning to violators. By the time police return to check whether they have applied for a license, many have shut down and relocated.

Prosecutor Dressler, an engaging man with an ever-upbeat outlook, sees some good even in cases where the phone sharks steal away before they can be registered. The law gives police clear authority to enter a phone room and photograph salespeople and managers, and keep their pictures on file for future use. And the surprise visits have driven a number of phone scammers out of Dressler's jurisdiction. Unfortunately, most simply move a few miles up the Florida Gold Coast to Boca Raton, in the next county.

Florida splits telemarketing enforcement among three primary agencies, which have been known to stumble over one another, or fail to act in unison.

Telemarketers must register with the Florida Department of Agriculture and Consumer Services in Tallahassee, the state's primary consumer agency, which also receives the lion's share of fraud complaints about telemarketers. But the consumer agency has no authority to enforce the criminal provisions for failure to register or to force an errant telemarketer to make a refund. All Consumer Services does is write the marketer and ask it to handle the complaint. Most of these letters are returned because the business has folded by the time consumer affairs sends out the letters.

---

*Interview with Scott Dressler.

Consumer Services also lacks the power to enforce the criminal penalties for failing to get a telemarketing license. It must persuade criminal prosecutors in one of Florida's twenty judicial districts to file these charges. Many state attorneys regard telemarketing cases as a low priority in a court log jammed with violent crimes.

A third office, the Florida Attorney General, winds up handling most telemarketing enforcement. As in many states, the Attorney General monitors unfair and deceptive trade practices. But Florida's veteran Attorney General Bob Butterworth consistently favors civil lawsuits against telemarketers, even though his office has a statewide prosecutor's division that can file criminal charges. As we've seen, civil cases rarely alarm phone pros. To make matters worse, the Attorney General's Office and Department of Agriculture and Consumer Services often clash. Each accuses the other of inaction.

Both must plead guilty. The Florida Attorney General's lack of aggressive law enforcement has been noted repeatedly in these chapters. But consumer services also has more than its fair share of bungled casework that has left telemarketers toasting the night away instead of facing fines or jail time.

In late 1991, an informant advised the Consumer Services Department that a man, who a few months earlier had signed an order with the U.S. Postal Service to quit using deceptive tactics in the sale of water purifiers, was starting a new venture. The informant said the man's new firm promised people a chance to win a car or cash, then pressured them to pay about four hundred dollars for a vacation package that included airfare to Florida.

Regulators recognized the pitch as similar to the one used to peddle water purifiers. The state's tipster said the operation could be pulling in $400,000 a week selling through telemarketers nationwide and suggested few, if any, buyers were sent airline tickets.

The company set the prize drawing for the car for February 1992, but state officials didn't even bother to stop by the premises and ask a few questions or refer the case to other authorities for review. Instead, the investigator wrote a memo a few months before the drawing and filed it away with the warning: "Expect a flood of complaints."

State Attorney General Butterworth does not deny that telemarketers have bested his office for years. He once told an interviewer that every time he went to a national conference of his peers, he heard critics wonder aloud when his office would run the boiler rooms out. "There are half a dozen telemarketing offers for every case we file," concedes Butterworth assistant Kent Perez.

Butterworth has seen wave after wave of telemarketing frauds, vacation certificates, overseas employment, then vacation certificates again, and then overseas employment. When he has declared victory over the scammers he has learned to regret it.

Butterworth, a former sheriff in Fort Lauderdale and Florida Highway Patrol chief, in 1989 asserted that his office was "making strides" against the problem and had driven the "worst offenders" out of business. Yet hundreds more sprang up with nearly identical sales pitches and they remain a major consumer fraud problem.

These days Butterworth openly admits that his beloved state's reputation as a scam capital is well deserved, but he blames the Florida legislature, whose members are reluctant to pass laws that would help. Lawmakers, Butterworth says, are hard pressed to pass any restrictions on legitimate businesses that want to be free to collect up front for their service, such as some employment agencies. Why should they suffer for the actions of illegal outfits, they argue. Scam artists would be likely to ignore new laws in any event, they add. Lobbying by powerful business interests blocks legislation that would crack down on phone rooms, according to Butterworth.

Seeking to stave off needed government supervision, Butterworth asserts, places industry in the role of serving as an unwitting conduit for cons. "We are trying to regulate, but we can't get the laws we need," he says.*

Butterworth says the hardest laws to get on the books impose bonds that could be used to repay consumers, such as people taken by an employment agency, in the event the company shuts its doors without providing services. Legitimate job-placement agencies argue that bonding places too much of a financial burden on "mom and pop" operations, an argument that wins sympathy from lawmakers. "Every legislator has a 'mom and pop' operation in their district, so nothing gets done, and the consumers keep getting taken," says Butterworth.

Nevada is the nation's least populous state, but when it comes to telemarketers it often seems to be overrun. Like Florida, Nevada has left an embarrassing legacy when it comes to cracking down on the telemarketing con. Ever since the late 1970s, the state has been a hospitable host to telemarketers from the granddaddy of boiler rooms, 50 State Distributing, to a succession of phony charities and phone rooms that popped up in 1994 promising to recover money lost in previous scams.

---

*Interview with Bob Butterworth, December 3, 1992.

Through the years state officials have repeatedly said they had a handle on the problem, only to be humiliated by a whole new round of Las Vegas reload schemes.

In March 1989 then-Nevada Attorney General Brian McKay gave one of the periodic declarations that victory might well be on the horizon. Testifying before a subcommittee of the U.S. House Committee on Energy and Commerce, which was considering tougher laws on phone fraud, McKay said:

> Nevada, particularly southern Nevada, has been a center of boiler-room activity. Over 50 percent of the complaints received by the Nevada Consumer Affairs Division in 1987 concerned telemarketing. In 1988, over 54 percent of the complaints were related to telemarketing. In Nevada, consumer complaints about telemarketing are seven times greater than those concerning the sale of new and used cars. Almost all of these complaints are from nonresidents who are victimized by Nevada operations.*

It was a dramatic comment on the scope of the problem. Most states list auto repair and sales, not telemarketing, as their most serious consumer-fraud problem, although complaints of phone fraud have soared. But McKay suggested that his office had been breaking up boiler rooms right and left. He said forty boiler rooms were working out of the Las Vegas area, down from 120 in 1987. McKay said many phone firms forced out of Nevada had set up shop in other states. "In 1987, we were looked at by the fraudulent telemarketing industry as being a safe haven. That is no longer the case," he declared at the 1989 hearing.

McKay went on to advocate state licensing of telemarketers. Such laws, he said, had driven many shady firms out of California and Arizona and would work in Nevada.

Nevada passed a law in 1989 that required marketers to get licenses and adhere to standards of practice. The law gave the state the power to fine firms that violated the law. Much the same as Florida, the power rested with two different offices, the state's Consumer Affairs Division and the state attorney general.

The licensing scheme turned out to be something of a bust despite the build-up from its backers. Between October 1990 and July 1992 Pioneer Enterprises in Las Vegas alone drew 968 written complaints from all over

---

*Hearing House Subcommittee on Transportation and Hazardous Materials, Committee on Energy and Commerce, March 16, 1989, Washington, D.C.

the country to the U.S. Postal Inspection Service. The state's consumer division reported about 475 Pioneer complaints in roughly the same period.

The licensing division has registered more than fifteen thousand telemarketers and about sixty-eight companies with a staff of just three investigators. As of March 1993, the state had revoked just one license.

In 1993 a new state attorney general, Frankie Sue Del Papa, declared a need for further refinements in the law.*

> While the licensing scheme may have served as a deterrent, the need for improved enforcement became evident in light of numerous legal actions taken against Nevada licensees by other state and federal agencies and by the large number of consumer complaints continually filed against Nevada licensees. . . . The goal of the licensing system was to keep fraudulent operators out of Nevada while preserving a fair marketplace for honest companies. Unfortunately, this did not occur. Administrative law remedies were ineffectual against the increasing levels of fraud in the telemarketing industry.

In 1993 the state turned over enforcement to the state attorney general's office with a newly created telemarketing and consumer fraud unit having both civil and criminal powers. The unit employs three lawyers and three investigators, all experienced in handling telemarketing fraud. They watch over about twenty-five licensed telemarketing houses in Las Vegas.

This time, officials said, they mean business. Senior Deputy Attorney General Colette Rausch, a native of Reno, oversees the unit. She says she no longer must be embarrassed that her home state is a haven for the phone con. "Finally I can go to a national conference and not be holding my head down," she says. "We just didn't have the resources before to handle this problem."

The unit filed more cases, civil and criminal, in its first year than in the history of the state and saw a drop in complaints, down 16 percent in 1993 and projected to be down 40 percent in 1994. But those are complaints about the traditional, licensed telemarketers, who these days have settled down and become elder statesmen.

Nevada still struggles with upstart "telefunders," phone solicitors who claim to represent a charity. These groups are exempt from the licensing law, as in Florida. Also a threat are the recovery rooms which

---

*This analysis was released to the news media when Del Papa announced creation of the state's telemarketing fraud unit in 1993.

buy up lists of people victimized for thousands of dollars by defunct tele-marketing companies.

The fraud unit filed civil charges against one recovery room that had the audacity to tell customers it had been hired by the Nevada Attorney General's Office to locate funds for victims. The firm falsely claimed to be a federally funded office called the "Federal Consumer Protection Bureau," and said for a fee it could guarantee return of the victim's money. These firms usually obtain one thousand dollars or more from the client up front, as in so many scams, through a cashier's check sent to the boiler room by overnight courier.

Complaints about telefunding and recovery rooms soared in Nevada, from thirty-eight complaints during the last six months of 1993 to 412 for the first half of 1994. Many of the culprits were teenagers or young adults in their early twenties who worked for a while in a salesroom to learn the racket, then struck out on their own.

"We're getting better at this," says Rausch, "but there still is a lot of work to be done. We can't stamp out fraud, we can only get a handle on it to a degree." Like so many other regulators she believes only criminal prosecutions will act as a deterrent. "We don't want these people to just be able to pay a fine and move on."

Rausch knows that when the public gets the word to avoid the recov-ery companies, the phone pros will find a new racket.

"We have identified almost a dozen of these recovery companies. It's like treading water. We're holding steady, not sinking and with more resources we should be able to push back the tide," says Rausch.

Some other states have struggled to license the telemarketing indus-try into submission. Oregon passed a law in 1989 requiring any company, regardless of its location, to have an Oregon license to sell to Oregon res-idents. Violators are subject to a $25,000 fine for each violation. "Oregon has the toughest telemarketing laws in the country," says State Attorney General Charles S. Crookham. "We will not tolerate fraudulent telemar-keting in our state, and those who ignore our laws will pay where it hurts them the most—through the pocketbook."*

Oregon officials ask the companies to sign "assurances of voluntary compliance," a legal pledge not to sell in the state until they get a license. Those that refuse or ignore the state's demands face lawsuits. But a num-ber of the defendants in these cases have long since disappeared by the time the state wins a court judgment against them.

---

*Crookham news release, June 2, 1992.

Geoffrey J. Darling, an investigator with the financial fraud section of the Oregon Department of Justice, spoke of his frustrations before a House Select Committee on Aging in June 1991.*

> One of the greatest problems is merely locating and correctly identifying who these people are. . . . It is a very mobile, very transportable business. They use mail drops; they disguise their telephone numbers; they use names that give some type of official recognition or legitimacy to their operation. Yet they are very difficult to physically locate. This is very frustrating to me as an investigator. Often by the time we get to them through our judicial process, the money has dried up and has evaporated.

Darling noted that 40 percent of the state's closed cases against telemarketers were stamped "out of business." Some marketers located outside the state simply ignore demands to register. One legal demand sent by Oregon officials to an out- of-state phone room was returned with a cartoon figure of a mouse making an obscene gesture, according to Darling's testimony.

However, in other cases, telemarketers have not been able to duck the state. One such company was Federal Claim and Recovery Services, Inc., of Plantation, Florida. The firm told customers it was a "merchandise liquidator" for telemarketers who had either gone out of business or been shut down by authorities. The firm bought names of previous telemarketing customers who never received their prizes and offered them cellular phones or similar items for $750.

On June 2, 1992, Oregon officials won a court order fining the firm $25,000, one of seventeen out-of-state companies disciplined that day. None admitted any wrongdoing, but most agreed to give refunds to any Oregon residents who requested them.

While licensing laws can help some customers get their money back, other problems can arise. For one, many telemarketers trade on the license to give them credibility, telling victims they are "approved" by the state. Ever since the mid-1980s, telemarketers have tried to claim affiliations with government agencies to boost sales. And in some cases licensing laws may have the unintended effect of lending credibility to the pitch and giving the buyer a false sense of security.

Those fears are at least somewhat borne out by the fact that many

---

*House Joint Hearing Subcommittee on Regulation, Business Opportunities, and Energy; Committee on Small Business; and the Subcommittee on Health and Long-Term Care, Select Committee on Aging, June 21, 1991, Washington, D.C.

telemarketers who obtain licenses continue to draw consumer complaints alleging deceptive sales tactics and fraud.

Eileen Harrington, associate director for marketing practices at the Federal Trade Commission, said efforts to impose new laws or regulations are likely to yield mixed results. "I don't think more regulations are the answer. The telemarketers always figure out a way to skirt the regulations. If a federal regulation existed, legitimate businesses would comply and the bad guys would not," Harrington says.*

"These regulations would just impose costs on businesses which pass them on to consumers. When you are dealing with con men they don't comply with the law. We have to do a better job catching them and then deter them from doing it again."

The U.S. Postal Service, which has struggled ever since the days of 50 State Distributing in Las Vegas to get a handle on the fraud problem, notes that the ease with which young criminals can spend a few months learning the trade and apply their knowledge to open boiler rooms almost anywhere works against law enforcement. Kenneth Hearst, Assistant Chief Postal Inspector for Criminal Investigations, testified about the problem before Congress in June 1991.

> One of the most insidious aspects of boiler-room fraud is the ease with which owners and sales people move among the boiler rooms. After a "bust-out," or law enforcement action, the operators easily go back into business at other boiler rooms or under other names. We have seen a high degree of recidivism in boiler room scams and recognize that these schemes tend to operate as "training schools" where low-level employees learn the business and proceed to set up their own operation. Where possible, we seek to indict sales persons working in boiler rooms, as well as the promoters, in order to discourage them and others from starting additional boiler rooms. Often, however, it is difficult to prove the requisite intent to defraud where a salesperson merely reads a prepared script and has no ability to determine its truthfulness.†

While recognizing the limits of the law, some agencies are becoming more creative in applying laws and working with private business to combat the con artists.

---

*Interview with Eileen Harrington, June 1, 1994.
†House Joint Hearing Subcommittee on Regulation, Business Opportunities, and Energy; Committee on Small Business; and the Subcommittee on Health and Long-Term Care, Select Committee on Aging, June 21, 1991, Washington, D.C.

* * *

In Iowa, a state with one of the highest numbers of people age eighty-five or older, phone-fraud victims abound. Law enforcement officials resolved to do something about it. In late 1993 they unveiled a concept now called "victim venue," which means building a case against out-of-state telemarketers and hauling them into an Iowa courtroom where they must face a jury that might be hostile to the telephone trade.

The men behind First Financial Clearinghouse Services Corp., of Phoenix, hardly got a break in a Des Moines courtroom. The firm sold to previous big-ticket victims of telemarketing fraud, paying top dollar for leads, between ten and twenty dollars a name. They called mostly elderly people and told them they had won a prize, strongly implying the prize was worth $70,000 or more. In a well-worn scheme, they told clients they must pay "taxes and fees" in order to claim their prize. The amount varied depending on how much the customer had lost in previous scams, but often it approached $1,600. As usual, the victims sent checks or cash by overnight courier.

At trial, witnesses testified that several of the boiler-room operators, who referred to their victims as "mullets," took $70,000 in cash netted from the venture off to Las Vegas, where they made a number of $5,000 bets.

In June 1994 the Iowa jury convicted two Arizona men on felony charges of conspiracy to commit theft by deception. Another defendant pleaded guilty. All three drew prison sentences of up to five years.

The state's main innovation was taping the salesmen calling who they thought were elderly widows and bilking them—"very persuasive evidence at trial," said Iowa Attorney General Bonnie Campbell.*

Campbell's office set up a sting operation to catch the telemarketers. It played upon their tendency to reload their victims using sucker lists. When state officials learned of an elderly person victimized repeatedly, they knew her name would be sold to others and the calls would continue. So they gave a number of fraud victims new phone numbers and routed their old lines into a quiet section of the attorney general's office, where trained investigators answered the phones, posing as the victims and taping the entire transaction.

"This sting works because the same victims are targeted over and over. Their names are put on what are called 'mooch' lists and sold to other companies who contact the same victims again," said Campbell.

---

*Campbell news release, June 2, 1994.

Others in the state attorney general's office noted that the scam, unlike other undercover operations, gives the telemarketer no means to sniff out the trap. "There is nothing that the other side can do to avoid the problem," said Steve St. Clair, of the Iowa Attorney General's Office. "They are playing Russian roulette when they put the phone to their head. For all they know they could be talking to an agent of the attorney general. I think that these tapes are going to make a difference and help with criminal cases."*

St. Clair said the taped evidence strengthens cases because it leaves prosecutors with better evidence than the recollections of an elderly victim. That means a greater likelihood of criminal convictions instead of fines. "In the past, telemarketers had a risk that they might have to give some money back, and many people were more than willing to take that modest risk," he said. "But as the risks shift and people end up on trial in a state hundreds of miles away, I think it is going to get a little harder to populate so many of these boiler rooms."

U.S. Postal Service inspectors in Washington, D.C., wanted to prove a point about the bane of telemarketing fraud and poke a little fun at the public at the same time. They decided to use the same sort of salacious mailer that they have been trying to stamp out for years. They sent out a postcard which read:

YOU ARE A WINNER! CONGRATULATIONS

National Unclaimed Sweepstakes Prize Notification Bureau has great news for you today! You are a confirmed winner of one of the cash prizes listed below:

1. CASH MONEY . . . Could you use a $10,000 cashier's check?

2. FREE VACATION IN PARADISE . . . Would you be interested in Hawaii?

3. 1993 LUXURY AUTOMOBILE . . . Put yourself behind the wheel.

4. DIAMOND NECKLACE . . . A timeless treasure for the lady.

5. HOME ENTERTAINMENT CENTER OF YOUR DREAMS . . . 35" Stereo TV, VCR, and more.

---

*Interview with Steve St. Clair, August 2, 1994.

For important information about your FREE PRIZE OFFER, call . . .
1-800-XXX-XXXX Washington, D.C., residents call 202 268-5656.

The front side of the pink postcard bore the return address for a post office box in Columbus, Ohio. It stated: "This is your OFFICIAL PRIZE NOTIFICATION and it won't cost you a penny!" It added the cheery reminder, "Do not throw this notification away. THAT COULD COST YOU *PLENTY*!!"

People who returned the call heard a prerecorded message that said:

Thank you for calling our toll-free 800 number. Please take a minute to look carefully at that pink postcard in front of you. Take a hard look. It says you're a confirmed winner of a fantastic free prize and suggests that all you have to do to claim it is pick up the phone and call a toll-free number. Do you really think you're going to get off that cheap? Not likely.

The hard fact is that these kinds of postcards and letters usually require you to pay your hard-earned money before you receive anything. You may find that your prize is not what you expected, or you may not receive anything at all.

When you receive free prize notifications, sweepstakes entry forms, free travel offers or similar gimmicks, ask yourself a few tough questions before you part with your cash. Ask yourself:

"What do I know about this firm's reputation and honesty?"

"Do I have to pay money or buy something before I receive my 'free prize'?"

"Can I take my time to think this over? Or are they pressuring me to make a decision right away?"

"Why are they asking for my credit card number before I agree to buy anything?"

If you can't get satisfactory answers to these questions, throw that postcard or letter in the trash and save yourself money and grief.

Then came an explanation:

The pink postcard you received was mailed by the U.S. Postal Inspection Service. We investigate federal mail fraud violations and we want to warn people about questionable offers that come in the mail.

Postal Inspectors are using a fictitious company name and address and this pink postcard to attract attention to our 800 number. Why? Because we want to deliver an important warning to the innocent people most often victimized by these scams. We hope our efforts save you or someone you know from losing money to fraudulent promoters. To report a postal crime, or to receive a copy of this message, call our toll free Hotline number at 1-800-654-8896. Make a note of it.

Thank you.

Unfortunately, the pink-postcard stunt was a hit beyond all expectations. More than three hundred thousand people called the number, apparently thinking they would win a prize.

For postal regulators the experience reflects their frustration after years and years of issuing alerts and fighting for new laws to crack down on the problems. No matter what they do or say, many people don't seem to get the message to avoid these scams, and postal inspectors find themselves in the unenviable position of trying to regulate human greed.

Some private businesses are tired of being used as conduits for con artists and are taking tough action on their own to curb it.

Western Union is one of these businesses. Every year the company's eighteen thousand agents across the country process about twenty million transactions, only a tiny percent of which are fraudulent. Nothing goes wrong in most cases because the person wiring the money designates an individual to receive it. That person must present identification to get the money.

But problems can arise, for example, when someone loses their wallet in a robbery or has no identification. In these cases, Western Union sales agents are allowed to use a "test question" method. The question is placed in the computer and if the person answers correctly he or she gets the money. Many times the question is the recipient's mother's maiden name.

Con artists have learned to use the system to persuade people to wire them money using a test question or other means to evade security.

"Our agents tell customers to be sure they know the person they are wiring money to. If they don't it often turns out to be a scam. From all our indications this is a tiny percentage of the transactions, but we have seen people fall for it," Western Union spokesman Warren Bechtel said in an interview. Sales agents receive awards for talking people out of getting scammed.

* * *

One group in Washington, D.C., that wins high marks in the fight against phone fraud is the Alliance Against Fraud in Telemarketing, part of the National Consumer's League and a group that is among the most active advocates for consumers. A consortium of government and private business, it is far enough removed to get away with acting as an irritant and yet trusted enough to worm its way into the inner circle of law enforcement where key decisions tend to be made.

The alliance occupies part of the top floor of a sooty, columned building on 15th Street, a stark contrast to the innumerable chic Italian restaurants and cappuccino bars that have sprung up along the edges of Washington's old downtown, just a few blocks from the White House.

Inside the aged building, the alliance wages a high-tech war against telephone fraud. It is one place consumers can call and get a straight answer about the wisdom of accepting that great offer from a telemarketer. The phone room looks much like the boiler rooms described in this book. There are four computers in a front room, clocks on the wall showing the time zones. A row of operators talk into the phones, except they are trying—mostly with success—to talk people out of making the purchases that will get them fleeced by phone con artists.

Sponsored by a combination of consumer and government groups and funded by private industry, the alliance is the sort of shadow government operation that can have a dramatic effect on the war against telephone fraud. They can say the things that the government cannot, or will not, giving out advice on the operating procedures of scam artists.

It is the domain of John Barker, an affable former press secretary to then-Arkansas Governor Bill Clinton, and now executive director of the hotline against fraud by phone. "Fraud is a crime that doesn't create loss of life or destroy property, but it is invasive and very easily preventable," says Barker. "We can stop this if we can just get through to people and hit them over the head with education."*

He says the biggest single problem is the time lag encountered by law enforcement groups, which often do not even learn about a boiler room until after it has ripped off thousands of customers and has shut down.

Callers to the alliance get up-to-date, factual information and law enforcement gets grass-roots reports on emerging scams. The alliance forwards its complaints to federal and state law enforcement agencies, allow-

---

*Interview with John Barker, June 2, 1994.

ing them to identify new sales rooms immediately. More than six of ten callers are people who have not yet plunked down their money. "We say no. We just tell people not to do it," Barker says.

Founding sponsors of the antifraud network were Citibank, Master-Card/Visa, MCI Communications, AT&T, and Federal Express. The alliance has become the biggest single filer in the FTC's databases, turning the clunky and outmoded system, dominated by complaints about office-machine scams, into a center of complaint data. Fifty to one hundred new reports of telephone fraud are loaded into the system every day.

Between late fall of 1992 and early 1994, over 145,000 calls were answered. About thirty-five thousand of the calls resulted in complaints to the FTC. The FBI, U.S. Postal Service inspectors, U.S. attorneys, and most state attorneys general can access the files.

As of April 1994 the FTC has opened twenty-five investigations as a result of its tips. The alliance, knowing that many law enforcement agencies require a set number of complaints before taking action, follows up its referrals to see what progress is being made.

The tactic helps keep federal agencies responsive, says Barker. The atmosphere in his thickly carpeted enclave is calm and measured, not your ordinary phone room. The intent is to give sensible and informed advice in the hopes it will dissuade callers from falling under the spell of a telemarketer's sales pitch.

The system has a number of technical aspects that provide good data on the incidence of phone fraud. It has security features that identify calls from prisons and mental institutions. It can log cities by zip code and immediately identify known mail drops or answering services, when a caller wants to know if a business address is a legitimate office building. It also gives callers phone numbers for the appropriate attorneys general or consumer agencies in the person's state. And it has a security feature to prevent anyone from breaking in and tapping the names and numbers of callers, and selling their list of victims to telemarketers.

But there are limitations. "The problem is that there is no early warning system. Nobody is looking day by day and hour by hour trying to figure out what all of this means. That's where we come in," says Barker in the interview. "The time it takes to alert law enforcement about a new boiler room operation has now dropped from months to minutes. We can track down companies that change addresses."

They also have been able to pressure some of the overnight-mail services into handing out the alliance's business card when they arrive at someone's home to pick up a certified check. These efforts spawn many of their calls.

Finally, Barker feels that the agency has a check over the federal government enforcement bureaucracy because "we know what's being reported and we know what's been sent to them. We pressure them to get enforcement action. That's healthy." "I think at this point we are causing a little bit of concern in the boiler room community because of the growing numbers of people who are turning them down, but like everybody else says, we've got to get these people behind bars."

But some people have to realize that they need help. "Nothing is more frustrating than sitting at the phones with somebody who is being scammed for $5,000 and they won't listen to us or their family," Barker adds. "No matter what anybody says, they will go ahead and do it anyway."

15

The People's Court

Addison B. Murphy, of Willoughby Hills, Ohio, didn't set out to become a commando. But he began to feel that somebody had to fight back against the "miserable, inconsiderate, pushy, dishonest, telemarketing creeps."

Murph, as he is known to his friends, took up arms in his own way. At first, he simply hung up on marketers calling to try and sell him junk products he did not want. When they persisted, he began to stalk them, hoping to strike them first.

"I wrote [the telemarketer] and asked for some information and when the guy called I hung up on him!"

Murphy knows better than to buy vacation certificates or other suspect phone deals. While he took a chance by responding to the sales offer that his name would be sold to still more telemarketers, he felt it was worth it to get even.

Angry at having to fend off phone solicitors, he belongs to a great silent majority rarely heard in the long-running political debate to control telemarketing.

He numbers in his flock anyone who sits down to dinner and pours milk for the kids, only to be forced to jump up and answer a pesky sales call. He doesn't care whether it's a sleazy sweepstakes deal from Vegas or a bona fide bargain: he isn't interested.

Neither is one Florida woman, who also has come up with a novel approach to fight back.

Furious that her phone number and buying habits can be sold for a few dollars or less to any sales campaign, she gets revenge in her own way. She acts interested as the telemarketers launch into their spiel, and asks some questions to drag it out. After taking a few minutes of their time, she excuses herself saying somebody is at her front door and she must answer it.

263

"I leave the caller holding on the phone for five or ten minutes or until they get tired of waiting," said the woman who asked to remain anonymous. "They sometimes call back all upset or indignant, but I always feel great."

Disgruntled former telemarketers love to use this tactic; they know time is money in the phone-sales racket and nothing annoys phone pros worse than people who waste their time. They snicker, knowing that many of their ex-colleagues burst into roaring fits of obscenities when they get victimized by the people they try to sucker.

While nobody has any reliable statistics on the numbers of Americans who are annoyed by telemarketing, or find private means to strike back at unwanted callers, three databases provide a snapshot. They are "no-call" lists set up in Florida and Massachusetts and by a New York-based marketing trade group.

In 1990, Florida began allowing residents to join a state-run "no call" list. At least twenty-five thousand people have paid a ten-dollar fee and five dollars more a year to join, with very little prompting from state officials.

The Florida system exempts some phone callers, such as charities and newspapers, and is far from foolproof. Telemarketers can purchase the no-call list from the state, but are not required to do so. In three years of operation, state officials received 16,500 complaints from people who got unwanted calls despite paying to join. The state sued six companies for violating the law, but they received only small fines.

The system does nothing to deter fraudulent telemarketing artists who buy phone numbers from list brokers who may have no idea of the law.

Massachusetts, a state with about 3.5 million phone lines in 1991, allowed customers to choose not to receive calls from automatic dialers. About two hundred thousand customers did so. Using Massachusetts data, federal officials estimated in 1991 about 7 million Americans would opt not to receive such calls.*

The Direct Marketing Association, a trade group representing more than three thousand telemarketing and mail order businesses, has its own "no-call" list, which members of the association agree to respect. It contains the names of four hundred thousand people who have written to the association asking that their names be removed from marketing lists.

But the telemarketing lobby, and it is indeed a potent lobby, does not concede that its members often annoy the public. It hears telephones ring-

---

*This estimate is based on Federal Communications Commission data cited by the Direct Marketing Association in testimony before the House Subcommittee on Telecommunications and Finance of the Committee on Energy and Commerce, April 24, 1991.

ing up $600 billion a year in sales. In 1992, an estimated 184 million Americans bought something over the telephone, hardly evidence that telemarketers are a nuisance.

"We are under no illusions that telemarketing representatives would win popularity contests in every American household. Selling, by its nature, requires just a bit of persistence. Nonetheless . . . many families welcome telemarketing as a convenient means of shopping for goods and services," Amy N. Lipton, who represented the American Telemarketing Association, testified in a March 1989 congressional hearing.*

Such hearings became yearly events in the late 1980s, as Congress struggled to crack down on telemarketing fraud against fierce opposition from powerful business groups.

The Direct Marketing Association, with more than three thousand member companies, had this to say at a 1991 congressional hearing on a bill to battle telemarketing fraud.†

> The success that many businesses have enjoyed as the result of their telemarketing efforts confirms that large segments of the American people find telemarketing to be a convenient and inexpensive way to learn about or acquire goods or services that they need or want. We know of no empirical data demonstrating that American consumers are generally opposed to current "live operator telemarketing" practices. . . . Congress should not rush forward to burden a legitimate business practice with a technically complex and constitutionally suspect scheme of regulation on the basis of nothing more than the vague allegations that some people regard it as an annoyance.

Perhaps even more surprising, given the thousands of complaints of abusive phone-sales tactics and fraud piling up in the offices of regulators all over the country was that the industry refused to admit telemarketers can be troublesome.

At issue was a 1989 House of Representatives bill that prohibited telemarketers from engaging in conduct that would "harass, oppress, or abuse" any person. The bill directed the Federal Trade Commission to issue rules governing acceptable telemarketing procedures. The bill's language seemed reasonable enough considering that both the FTC and other

---

*Hearing House Subcommittee on Transportation and Hazardous Materials, Committee on Energy and Commerce, March 16, 1989.

†House Subcommittee on Telecommunications and Finance of the Committee on Energy and Commerce, April 24, 1991.

federal agencies had logged in hundreds of complaints of harassment by Las Vegas telemarketers alone in the late 1980s.

Early up, the National Retail Merchants Association took aim. First it showed off its guns, noting its members operated forty-five thousand leading department, chain, and other stores; employed more than 3 million people; and boasted sales volume of more than $175 billion.

> While we in no way support any form of telemarketing which could be reasonably described as "abusive," we are unaware of any record showing the need for . . . this legislation. We are not certain why this provision is contained in this legislation. Telemarketers are in business to sell goods and services to those whom they call. Engaging in harassing or abusing behavior simply does not sell products.

The marketers had an ally in the Federal Trade Commission, which seemed remarkably ignorant of the sales tactics employed by fraudulent telemarketers. In written testimony submitted at the 1989 hearing before the House Energy and Commerce Subcommittee, the agency stated:

> It is true that consumers who call scam operators seeking to rescind a fraudulent transaction or to seek performance of a money-back guarantee may sometimes be subjected to verbal abuse or other harassment. Such harassment can cause considerable emotional distress. In the typical case the heart of the problem is not harassment, but the telemarketer's fraudulent inducement to buy worthless goods and services and the consumer's loss of the purchase price. By focusing on a matter of lesser concern, this provision may have the unintended effect of drawing resources away from combatting hard-core telemarketing fraud.

The FTC's position on another matter in the 1989 bill—restrictions on the hours that telemarketers could call—also seemed closer to the industry's than to groups representing consumers.

The trade groups argued that any restrictions on calling hours could be disastrous for telemarketers and their customers. Several favored self-policing of the industry. Said the Direct Marketing Association, which urged its members to use "sound judgment" in deciding which times to make unsolicited calls:

> What consumers consider to be reasonable hours may vary greatly from region to region and differ even between urban and rural areas. . . . Most importantly, the adoption of national calling hours would not in any

respect combat fraud, but rather, merely restrict the calling hours of legitimate marketers, inconveniencing them and consumers.

Once again, the FTC, the federal government's chief telemarketing police, showed little enthusiasm for restricting calling hours. The commission's testimony stated:

> The provision would prohibit not only abusive calls, but also mere offerings of goods and services by honest telemarketers. It is our experience that the substance of the telephone call, rather than its timing, is the activity that causes significant consumer injury in telemarketing fraud cases. Thus it is doubtful that the proposed rule will significantly enhance the ability to prosecute telemarketing fraud. More fundamentally, in order for the commission to promulgate and enforce the proposed rule, it would have to divert resources from the principal task at hand—stopping fraud and the enormous losses suffered by consumers.

In a footnote the commission went on to cite "almost insurmountable problems" of deciding when is a good time to let telemarketers call, noting: "Although some may find it offensive to be called at night or on a Sunday, for example, others may find these to be the most convenient times to consider offerings by legitimate telemarketers."

The FTC also sided with the industry on the most controversial provision: the deal breaker that sent telemarketing fraud bills down in flames every year between 1988 and 1994. The issue was a power struggle between the FTC and the nation's state attorneys general who wanted the power to sue telemarketers in federal court.

The expanded powers could possibly bring an end to the pattern in which telemarketers face lawsuits state by state. One telemarketer was sued by fifteen states, each of which did its own investigation and won judgments.

Had one of those states been able to win that judgment in federal court it would have applied nationwide. But the FTC argued that giving new powers to the states could cause "inconsistent" decisions. The agency repeatedly testified that it was proud of its record of telemarketing enforcement and seemed irked at the criticism of its performance implicit in the move to award new powers to the state attorneys general.

The prospect of facing federal lawsuits from fifty different state agencies more than alarmed the telemarketing lobby and it was glad to have an ally in the FTC. Meanwhile consumer groups lobbied in vain to break the deadlock.

While powerful industries and regulators squabbled for seven years over who should rule the roost, consumers lost millions of dollars to telemarketing fraud. For most of that time, reforms were tied up in the stalemate.

Things began to change in the early 1990s as the FTC's opposition lessened and the industry began to sense that telemarketing abuses had become such a problem that it could no longer fight off the legislation.

The telemarketing reform bill that arrived on President Clinton's desk in August 1994 and was signed into law contained many provisions from the various bills that failed since 1989.

"Some legitimate telemarketers have been concerned that (greater state enforcement) would open up a Pandora's box," says Susan Grant, executive director of the National Association of Consumer Agency Administrators. "We pointed out that by and large the people we go after are not members of these trade groups, they are the fringe element," she said in an interview. "If we did sue their members it would be justified. If their members are doing nothing wrong they have nothing to fear."

Beside giving the state attorneys general new powers, the Telemarketing and Consumer Fraud and Abuse Prevention Act gave the FTC up to a year to define what constitutes abusive and deceptive telemarketing.

The law also states that the FTC must prohibit telemarketers from undertaking a "pattern of unsolicited calls which the reasonable consumer would consider coercive or abusive of such consumer's right to privacy." The FTC also must draw up restrictions on the hours of the day and night when unsolicited calls can be made and require any telemarketer to promptly disclose that the purpose of the call is to sell goods or services. Violations of these rules are punishable by fines.

Missing in political action were the provisions of early bills to create a clearinghouse of complaints about telemarketers, data the public could learn with a phone call to a toll-free number. That concept had never met with much favor among the federal law enforcement apparatus. However, supporters of an effort to battle the bane of telephone fraud rejoiced at finally getting something passed into law.

"It's been a long journey but we've done it," U.S. Sen. Richard Bryan of Nevada said in announcing passage of the telemarketing fraud bill on August 2, 1994. "Consumers of America deserve the protection this bill will bring. Untold billions will be saved from ending up in the hands of unscrupulous telemarketers. For senior citizens, who are most often the targets of telemarketing scam artists, this is especially good news. These criminals prey on senior citizens, ruthlessly attempting to steal their life savings through offers that sound too good to be true, and in most cases they are."

The nation's state attorneys general also hailed a great victory for consumers. "This sounds like gridlock breaking," said Tennessee Attorney General Charles W. Burson, also president of the National Association of Attorneys General in an interview two days after passage of the bill. "We have been fighting for this breakthrough legislation for more than five years and consumers have finally achieved a great victory for themselves throughout the country." Burson added: "This measure gives state attorneys general a new and powerful tool to help us effectively confront and combat fraudulent telemarketers. We are the guardians of the law and now we have even more ability to protect the public."

How well the states do with that new power will depend on how well the FTC stands up to tough industry lobbying to weaken the telemarketing rules and a growing hostility to federal regulations from the Republican-dominated Congress that sailed into power in 1994. On paper, the initial rules were promising. The FTC announced in February 1995 that it intended to ban dozens of practices that over the years have become hallmarks of the telemarketing con: from telling people they have won a prize to sending overnight mail services to pick up a customer's check.

Other provisions in the draft regulations would ban telemarketing tactics such as using phony references or shills to hawk products and forbid phone firms from calling more than once every three months to sell the same product. The regulations also seek to ban telemarketers from calling before 8 A.M. or after 9 P.M., and require them to declare upfront that the purpose of their call is to sell a product.*

The 1994 law also gives consumers a new power to sue telemarketers in federal court, but only if the amount of losses exceeds $50,000. While ballyhooed as another consumer protection, this provision is not likely to be of much use. Few individuals lose more than $50,000. Those who do most likely will have lost the money in some sort of investment deal, which is likely to have gone bankrupt.

Yet many provisions of the law offer the first real hope of putting some limits on annoying telemarketing tactics. Whether they will succeed in curbing the activities of phone-fraud artists remains to be seen.

Many consumers who are angry at telemarketers are not just upset at the invasion of their privacy. They have been cheated or misled and many

---

*The FTC is required to finalize its telemarketing rules by August 1995.

have been through hell trying to get a refund from the company, or trying to get state or federal regulators to take action.

That's no surprise. Technology sides with the telemarketer. Any marketer can pay less than one hundred dollars for a special softwear package that uses a caller-identification device to screen their complaint calls. With the device, a firm can direct its operators to answer certain calls, switch others to an answering machine, and forward all others to endless rings. Assume the telemarketing firm has the phone number of every person to whom it has sold goods. Once a sale is made the client's number can be stored in a database. The company can automatically recognize a call from the client's phone number, presumably a complaint. It can banish that call to the perpetual-ring mode. Customers can spend days or weeks calling to try and complain, never realizing they have been switched off into oblivion by a silent computer.

On the other hand, the phone numbers of the local state attorney general, Better Business Bureau, or other consumer regulators also can be programmed into the system. So when any of these agencies call with a complaint, their employees can get switched to a live operator immediately. Any regulator would be impressed with the firm's responsiveness.

Here are three cases of people who fought back against telemarketers either to get a refund, get some action, or for pure revenge—or all of the above. Following the cases are some tips on how to accomplish these goals.

Refund

Terry Heinz, of Cincinnati, had no idea what he was getting into when he booked a dream Bahamas vacation through Royal American Holidays. Formed in 1985, the vacation-certificate company had a history of run-ins with regulators. The firm ended a Florida Attorney General's Office investigation in 1986 by promising not to violate consumer-protection laws in the future. By March 1990, the state attorney general had amassed 120 written complaints of deceptive sales tactics, mostly from unhappy buyers alleging hidden fees and deceit. By January 1991, written complaints from 218 certificate buyers had been filed from twenty-eight states.

Then on New Year's Eve 1992 the firm made national headlines, stranding revelers on the dock in Fort Lauderdale when it failed to pay the cruise line that ferried its travelers to the Bahamas. Company officials said they had been away for the holidays and would straighten things out; instead, the company began bouncing checks. Other travelers found that the firm had failed to pay the hotels on the islands; they had to pay cash for their lodgings.

In April 1992 the Florida Attorney General's Office filed suit charging Royal American with fraud for failing to deliver its trips, false advertising, failing to advise buyers of their refund rights, and using illegal bait-and-switch tactics to sell customers upgrades. The firm remained open while the suit wound its way through the courts. In May 1992 a local judge ruled that the travel company had written nearly $25,000 in bad checks to a cruise line.

As is the norm in telemarketing cases, all of these actions occurred without Heinz or other travelers finding out about it. While the signs of the firm's near demise were evident in South Florida, telemarketers in more than two dozen states were happily hawking Royal American's certificates. All Heinz did was answer the phone and agree to buy what sounded like a great vacation deal.

Over the July 4 weekend in 1992, Heinz arrived in Florida for the cruise to Freeport. When he got to Port Everglades to board the day cruise ship *Sea Escape,* the ship's crew handed him a "Dear Passenger" letter:

> We regret to inform you that *Sea Escape* has stopped honoring travel vouchers issued by Royal American Holidays. We have taken this action because of Royal American Holidays' failure to pay *Sea Escape* for past sailings. We understand that you have planned your vacation for quite some time and we are prepared to help you continue with your plans.

The letter went on to offer a discounted fare to the islands, but Heinz would have to pay the cruise line directly and try to collect a refund from Royal American.

Heinz was among 132 people stranded on the dock at Port Everglades. Two days later, after complaints from the passengers, the Florida attorney general obtained a court order to shut down the travel agency.

Heinz had the presence of mind to collect the names and addresses of about seventy of the passengers, who had arrived from twenty-one states to take the trip: a simple deed, perhaps, but one that almost never happens. Instead, disgruntled buyers simply scatter, and few notify authorities. Heinz broke the mold and handed the Florida Attorney General's Office a list of victims, critical evidence in the court case against the company.*

---

*Unfortunately for the victims, the state lawsuit filed in April 1992 remained pending as of March 1995.

Get Action

California kit-car enthusiast Kurt Scott created a victim chain letter of consumers unhappy with their purchases that got so extensive authorities could not ignore it.

The target of his campaign was a Miami telemarketer called Classic Motor Carriages, which boasts more than $20 million in annual sales of car replicas ranging from a 1934 Ford truck to foreign roadsters.

Scott, who publishes a kit-car magazine, took up arms against Classic Motor Carriages in editorials and soon found himself serving as a clearinghouse for hundreds of complaints about the telemarketer's sales techniques.

The kit-car manufacturer is something of an anomaly in the phone business. First of all, the product is costly, about $10,000 on average. The kits are fiberglass-bodied replicas of classic roadsters, which the company advertises as "easy to build . . . for the person of average mechanical skills using ordinary tools." The buyer must supply the engine and drive train.

The company, which also has maintained an office in Minneapolis, has a history of running into problems with state regulators. In 1985, Classic signed an agreement with the Florida attorney general promising not to violate consumer-protection laws. Complaints did not stop. Between 1990 and 1992, the state received at least fifty written complaints asserting new sales abuses, ranging from high-pressure sales tactics, to failure to deliver parts on time, to imposing hidden charges.

In November 1992 the company signed another promise to refrain from violating the same law. The agreement settled thirty-four consumer complaints, and required the company to pay $20,000 to the state to cover the cost of the investigation. Classic did not admit wrongdoing.

"The agreement we signed finds no fault and no admission of liability," Classic attorney David Elder told newspapers at the time. He said that the firm sold about one thousand of the kits each year, adding: "Classic sells a lot of cars. Nobody is looking at how many kits are sold and how many people don't complain."

But the state's tolerance of Classic—familiar to motorists driving on one of Miami's main expressways for the antique car that sits atop its corporate offices—angered Scott. Scott supplied the state with sworn statements from customers, repeated in court papers filed by Florida's attorney general asserting that many customers never received their parts, could not obtain refunds, or concluded that the quality of the kits fell well below expectations. Many buyers complained that they were persuaded to buy after the telemarketer told them that an order had just been canceled, freeing up a small number of cars which they could buy at a reduced price if they acted quickly. The attorney general later stated in court papers that these sale assertions were false.

A complaint filed in June 1994 by Ronald McCoury, of Oxford, Pennsylvania, was typical. He saw an ad on television for a 1934 Ford convertible replica and could not resist. He called the 800 number and asked to be sent some literature on the kit. What happened next is in dispute.

As McCoury tells it:

> After several days I received a phone call from Fiberfab asking me to purchase one of these kits. I was told they had just two or three kits at a special price and I should make up my mind fast because these kits would not last long at this price. So I agreed to think about it overnight and he would call back the next night. He did, and to make it more interesting, he offered me a lot of extra parts if I went ahead and filled out the order form as he led me through it. I did go through the form filling it out as suggested. I gave him my Visa number and two days later Federal Express picked up my form.*

McCoury paid $1,500 as a deposit on the car. He was supposed to pay the remainder of the $9,345 price over twelve months. McCoury said he asked if he could get a refund because he suffered from a heart condition and might need to cancel the deal. According to McCoury, the telemarketer said he could get his deposit back. Two months later, his health worsened and he tried to get a refund, only to receive a letter from Classic refusing his request. The letter read in part:

> If purchasers could undo purchase agreements without financial and legal consequences, our business would be jeopardized by the mere whim of a purchaser simply deciding to do something else. . . . We hope you will continue with the purchase of your kit.

Scott put McCoury into his chain-letter system, sending off his story to about thirty media, law enforcers, advertisers, and politicians, many of whom at the very least feel compelled to respond.

While government agencies won't readily admit it, this sort of chain letter gets results. Scott's crusade, though at times strident and exaggerat-

---

*Complaint files, Florida Attorney General's Office, Hollywood, Florida.

ed in its claims, stands as an excellent example of how to get results from a lumbering government bureaucracy. He effectively pitted all of the major players—politicians, media, and consumer regulators—against one another to get results.

Without a doubt Scott's campaign led the Florida Attorney General's Office to take action against the telemarketer. In August 1993 he wrote Florida Gov. Lawton Chiles to demand stepped up enforcement against telemarketers.

> These Florida public servants do not feel obligated even to return their official-duties telephone calls, let alone to protect the public from telemarketing parasites. . . . The folks who have been victimized . . . and who themselves have been frustrated in their efforts to seek help via your attorney general's office have reached the conclusion that the state of Florida is one big pirate port that welcomes these crooks with open arms. I trust that your personal intervention will serve to spur these officials to perhaps make a token effort to perform the duties that they are paid to perform.

In May 1994, dismayed that the state's problems handling telemarketers seemed to be continuing, Scott fired off another letter to the governor, this time accusing the attorney general's office of covering up for telemarketers and threatening to blow the whistle.

> The time has long been overdue for the Sunshine state to do something substantive. . . . I will avail my evidence to the news networks and TV newsmagazines as well as to other major Florida newspapers until the scale and nature of this consumer holocaust and blight on Florida's reputation is disseminated and properly addressed and remedied. I'm pleading with you once again to personally intervene and see to it that the plug is pulled on this titanic scam.

Classic Motor Carriages, meanwhile, did not appreciate Scott's campaign, which included writing more than fourteen thousand words in his publication blasting the company, and filing at least one affidavit in court accusing the firm of misdeeds. The company's lawyer wrote Scott. Accusing Scott of bias against the company, the lawyer asked him to "pass beyond emotionalism" and see Classic as a business "trying to keep a steady course in difficult economic times and trying to keep people employed." The letter went on to threaten redress, presumably a slander suit, if Scott did not quit trying to interfere with the kit-car company.

Scott did at one point accept advertising from the company in his magazine. He no longer does, he says, because of the complaints about the models. Classic hints that Scott only became a critic after the kit-car company withdrew its ads and placed them elsewhere, a contention Scott hotly denies.

Threats aside, Scott only made more noise. Scott also made few friends in the Florida Attorney General's Office, whose competence his missives regularly questioned. But publicity generated by Scott's complaints and his angry letters most certainly helped prompt the state to haul Classic Motor Carriages back into court. In July 1994 the Florida Attorney General's Office filed another lawsuit against Classic Motor Carriages charging deceptive trade practices and civil theft and asking for damages that could amount to more than $400,000. The company denied wrongdoing.

In a news release announcing the suit, Florida Attorney General Bob Butterworth said: "Many consumers who paid $9,000 to $15,000 for kits did not receive all necessary parts in the promised time or received defective parts. Consumers were unable to obtain refunds and their complaints were largely ignored by the company."

Scott is watching to see whether the latest lawsuit stops the complaints. If not, he'll take up arms again.

Revenge

Dr. Jeff Zuckerman, then a radiology resident in Galveston, Texas, wanted to take his family to Alaska and needed some low-cost plane fares. He saw a newspaper ad for a vacation certificate deal that offered $99 airfares and he jumped at it. He realized he'd been scammed when, after paying three hundred dollars for the certificates, the company told him about the strings: he had to stay two weeks and pay four times the normal rate for his hotel room.

He became angry when the Florida company refused to give him a refund. While thousands of other victims simply give up at that point, Zuckerman decided to get even and he spent hundreds of hours organizing a campaign to do so. Before he was through, he managed to get the telemarketer's real name and home phone number, which surprisingly was listed in the phone book.

He called many mornings at 5 A.M. to demand a refund. He located other victims and encouraged them to call as well. "I never got all my money back, though they sent a nominal fifty dollars to try and quiet me. I kept calling until they threatened me with a lawsuit if I kept it up. They wanted to charge me with harassment," Zuckerman, who has since moved to Fairbanks, Alaska, and set up a private radiology practice, said in an interview in August 1994. Zuckerman resorted to hardball tactics after the company laughed off his efforts to sue it for fraud. "I had a lawyer call them and threaten to take them to court. They said, 'Go ahead and sue us, you're not the first.' "

Realizing that a lawsuit would cost more than it was worth, Zuckerman wrote the Florida Attorney General's Office and got the names of dozens of other people who were ripped off by the firm. He organized them into a complaint machine to pressure authorities and the company. While he's not sure what role his tactics played in its demise, he got a letter from company officials one day saying they had gone out of business.

"I received a number of letters from people who said 'congratulations' and how glad they were that I chose to pursue it. It would have been a lot better to have gotten my money back," he says. Zuckerman still can't believe that state authorities let the company dissolve without repaying victims.

"It's really sickening that they can get away with this. These people are criminals, but nothing ever seems to happen to them. They just move on to another scam. There doesn't seem to be any law to protect consumers. Somebody needs to get the laws changed to close these places down."

Taking on the telemarketer in writing is less dangerous than going one-on-one over the phone. As noted before, phone pros have snappy comebacks to most any objection. When a sale is floundering, they often pass the customer to a more experienced telemarketer who turns up the heat on the buyer. The pros often boast that they can sell anybody, especially the person who is absolutely sure he or she never could be conned by a telemarketer.

Still, many consumers seem eager to spar with the telemarketer, even though the sensible response is simply to hang up. For those who insist on engaging the caller, here is how to do it right, assuming your goal is to irritate the telemarketer and pay him or her back for invading your privacy and irritating you. This excerpt is taken from an undercover FBI surveillance tape. The undercover FBI agent in San Diego was collecting evidence that would later be used to convict the telemarketer of wire fraud, but it works as a primer on how to exasperate a phone pro. The agent rattled veteran telemarketer "Linda Evans" so badly that she tried to get him off the line after fourteen minutes of sparring.

The FBI agent did it by peppering her with questions, picking apart all the lies in her sales pitch. He assumed the name Dale Nelson, supposed owner of Dale's Lawn and Garden, a small business. The deal was the one-in-four prize promotion. Linda tried to persuade him to send $495 for bogus taxes and other charges after implying he would win a new car.

She uses the sales technique known as the catalog rebuttal in which she tries to make Dale feel he will be featured in a major sales campaign. The catalog does not exist. This technique, widely used by phone rooms in Las Vegas and South Florida, has swindled people out of millions of dollars. Readers should remember that the FBI agent knows the scam inside and out, which gives him the advantage. Here's part of the exchange:

> LINDA: Now if it is the car you're getting we're either going to do one of two things. We'll either fly you down to Florida at our expense, of course, and then we'll take photos of you with the car or we could arrange for a photographer to be at a dealership there in your area. Which would be more convenient for you?
>
> FBI: You tell me I got the car and I'll tell you how I'll get it then.
>
> LINDA: What? Its not a matter of winning. You are guaranteed to receive one of these four awards. . . . Okay, now Dale, the bonding agency assumed that this was some big corporation and because of the magnitude of these awards they originally were looking for you to justify this with an invoice of $1,000 but I looked at the account and I figured this was not a big corporation so I had our accounting department contact the bonding agency and after discussing this with them we got them to agree so you won't miss out on this, to reduce this amount. All you need to do is cover the registration, filing of the tax waiver, shipping, handling, documentation, and insurance fees and that would be $495.50. We told them we would pay the balance . . . because we need to get the photos done to get our catalog out.
>
> FBI: I got my pencil here. Let me go over this a little bit. What's your name?
>
> LINDA: Linda. L . . . I . . . N . . . D . . . A.
>
> FBI: And what's your company?
>
> LINDA: P . . . A . . . L . . . M . . . E . . . T . . . T . . . O Park Promotions.

FBI: All right. What's the address? (She gives it and phone number). Just a minute . . . I'm writing this down.

LINDA: Now is that something you'd be able to do at this time?

FBI: Well I don't know. Let me make some notes here first because you kinda went over it fast and just caught me off guard. Okay, let's go over these prizes. (First he reads back her address, then grills her about the value of each prize). What's the watch worth? Well what did it cost you?

LINDA: I can't give you an exact . . . my god!

FBI: And what's the name of the bonding agency?

LINDA: That's our business. You don't need to be concerned about the bonding agency.

FBI: What about the $495? What's that supposed to be for?

LINDA: Like I said for the registration, the filing of the tax waiver, shipping, handling, documentation and insurance.

FBI: What kind of tax?

LINDA: Tax waiver form. I didn't say waiving any kind of tax. I said the filing of a tax waiver form.

FBI: Who does it get filed with?

LINDA: You know what?

FBI: What?

LINDA: I'm going to have somebody from our awards company call you. Because I'm trying to do something here and you know you're just giving me too hard of a time on this.

FBI: Well I'm just asking you questions.

The best way to curb telemarketing calls is to hang up on them. Readers should remember that the most valuable names and phone numbers to a telemarketer are people who buy from telemarketers. So making a purchase or sending back a postcard or calling that 800 number because the prize offer sounds tempting is a sure way to cause your name to be sold to more telemarketers.

Through the 1980s many phone rooms pored over telephone books and other public records and simply dialed every number hoping to make a sale. Some used autodialers that called every number with a computer message, a practice now outlawed in a number of states.

But as telemarketing moves into the 1990s most experts are seeking to refine their lists and avoid "cold calls" to every phone number, which often annoys people and yields a very small percentage of sales for the amount of time and effort expended.

For the legitimate telemarketer these refinements mean paying higher prices for lists of people with interests that suggest compatibility with their product, such as "yuppies" who buy one luxury product and would likely buy another.

The illegal telemarketer also is refining the sales list to avoid wasting time on cold calls. But these efforts are focused almost entirely on "sucker lists," buying the names of people who have previously been large customers of well-known scams. The intent either is to sell them again, or to help them "recover" losses by posing as a government agency and tagging them for even more money.

The best protection against illegal telemarketers is never to buy from them. Legitimate telemarketers will respect the desires of individuals to be left in peace. The Direct Marketing Association will remove names from mailing and telephone lists circulated among its members for anyone who writes to the group. (The Direct Marketing Association, P.O. Box 9008, Farmingdale, NY 11735; (212) 768-7277)

Unfortunately, the telemarketers who are the subject of this book for the most part do not belong to any trade association and would not likely abide by any "no-call" list.

The Federal Communications Commission has toyed with the idea of setting up a national no-call list but the proposal has faltered amid opposition from private industry and concerns over its complexity and cost.

In 1991 the FCC reported 121.5 million phone lines in use in the United States. The agency estimated the cost of setting up a data bank to hold up to ten million phone numbers at $1 million, with an annual operating cost of about $300,000. The Direct Marketing Association, which wants to maintain its voluntary no-call list argues that creating a national list would result in the loss of jobs for "many of the tens of thousands" of people employed in telemarketing, a scare tactic that has a powerful resonance in Congress.

Here are some other tips for recovering money from telemarketers, getting results from regulatory agencies, or just plain raising hell because you are incensed that you were foolish enough to get conned.

• Make sure to file your complaint with as many government agencies as possible, and indicate that you are doing so in the letters.

• Send a copy of your grievance to the advertising department of the newspaper or television station that ran the advertisement for a telemarketer. If the offer was received by mail, contact your local post office or U.S. Postal Service Inspectors. Some newspapers and TV stations will intervene in disputes with advertisers and may be able to get the advertiser to refund money. The media also may drop the ad if many people complain, but don't hold your breath.

• Make sure to send a separate accounting of your complaint to television stations and newspaper consumer reporters in the area where you live and where the company is located. Include enough detail (always type it) to explain the problem, but not too much. Provide legible copies of the sales literature and correspondence from the company. Many areas have consumer-beat reporters who may decide to take up your cause. Nothing gets a quicker response from consumer regulators than media attention, particularly when the story may suggest that the regulators aren't protecting the public.

Remember, the clearer and simpler the package the more likely it is to get results. Reporters like stories made easy for them. Note: the government agencies that make news gathering the easiest for the press are the ones that often get good news coverage.

• Also complain to any other business that had a role in handling a transaction that turns out to be fraudulent, such as the telemarketer's bank, the overnight courier, or any other institution that handled the money. Don't be shy either about contacting the owner of a mail drop and demanding to know why they are serving as a conduit for a scam.

• If (and only if) state laws permit, consider tape recording important conversations with telemarketers. Some states require two-party consent to tape record. Refuse to do business with anybody who gets nervous that you are taping the sales presentation. If you attend a sales briefing, bring a video camera and film any sales presentation that you are serious about. Leave if they refuse to allow taping.

• Don't be talked out of complaining by a telemarketer who tells you he or she has tape recordings of you agreeing to the sale and therefore won't give a refund. Marketers drag out these tapes to intimidate you. In fact, any transaction entered into through fraud can be voided.

• Do your best to find a list of others who have been taken. In states where consumer complaints are public record, write for copies. Get together with other victims and consider seeing a lawyer about the possibility of filing a class-action suit against the telemarketers. Few transactions lend themselves to this approach, though.

• Pressure the telemarketer's local police department to take action. Check also with local authorities to make sure the phone room has an occupational license, and with state authorities (if required). If so, ask for copies of the licensing application, which might contain some personal information about the telemarketer.

Finally, never expect the telemarketer to cheer you up or provide any other psychic benefits. As soon as that occurs, you are headed down the costly road of victimization. Many fraudulent telemarketers seek to build a personal relationship over the phone. They do so for two reasons: they believe their customers are driven to call, or listen when they call, out of loneliness. A few kind words and many customers will defend the telemarketer even when they know deep down they have been cheated.

Take it from Leonard Friedman, the Arizona telemarketer convicted of fraud and sent to prison after marketing breast enlargement creams and other skin-care products. In an interview after his release from prison in the summer of 1994, Friedman said he has reformed. But he still remembers how the racket runs:

> The funny thing is that no matter how much you warn people not to buy, they still buy over the phone. People are lonely and that's why they buy from telemarketers. All you need to do is give them an 800 number they can call back any time so that they have somebody to talk to. It's the loneliness in our society that allows telemarketing to thrive. Most people won't even complain unless you unhook your 800 number, then they get mad. They were buying a friend, a voice, somebody to call when they are lonely. Until you find a way to stop people from being lonely, telemarketing will grow.

16

Civil Wars

Three flights up in the Lower Manhattan building, down the government gray corridors of the New York State Attorney General's Office, they keep the doors to outer offices locked. Before they did so, a thief made off with some typewriters.

Today, the staff struggles to find ways to curb far more serious thefts, notably a boom in illegal telemarketing from Buffalo to New York City that is costing millions of dollars in consumer losses.

"We are drowning," says Assistant State Attorney General Charlie Donaldson, whose dingy office is jammed with more than four dozen file boxes of new cases. "When I came here in 1983, we didn't have 900 numbers, or telemarketing. We had nine people then and now there are just four of us left. It's a combination of inflation and budget cuts."*

Donaldson fights to keep abreast of the phone scammers in between consumer complaint calls and, this day, a visit from a surly window cleaner, who requires him to move more boxes to free the grimy window to the washer's view.

The newest phase of telephone abuse on Donaldson's mind is bogus collect calls accepted by unwitting victims, many of whom have a limited command of English.

"One company has taken more than $1 million in six months calling people and asking them to accept a collect phone call, then billing them for $49.95 for the call," says Donaldson with a hint of disgust. "The local telephone companies will bill and collect for anybody, and people get the bill with an implied threat if you don't pay you will lose your phone service."

Donaldson patiently tells callers that the phone company cannot cut

---

*Interview with Charlie Donaldson, April 13, 1994.

off service over a billing dispute, certainly not one over fraudulent charges. But many people do not understand their rights. They pay the bills, even though they know they did not speak to anybody when they accepted the "collect call." Once they pay, they become victims of yet another telemarketing scam.

"Seeing that envelope from the phone company gives this legitimacy. This company [the telemarketer] tended to prey on the elderly and for-eign-speaking people. We think they used census data to get their leads, but we don't have any idea where they went."

Donaldson, a Harvard law graduate whose office floor is strewn with garbage bags full of recyclable soft drink cans that he donates to the homeless, does his best to track down the telephone marauders.

"I think we do well with what we've got, but we are always playing catch-up," he says with a trace of his native Alabama accent. "Until we finger something as a scam, we don't do anything about it. We're not the Gestapo. We have to get evidence together, and that takes time. By the time we catch up with them, they are gone."

Upstate, telemarketers also are wreaking havoc. Buffalo's sudden emergence as a boiler-room capital in the early 1990s clearly alarmed New York authorities. It's one of the few new major telemarketing zones outside the Sunbelt and the skill its sales agents showed in nailing victims for heavy losses clearly caught law enforcement off guard.

The city houses more than forty sweepstakes telephone rooms, some with ties to organized crime figures, according to New York Attorney General's Office prosecutors. Many of the Buffalo rooms also have con-nections to some of the Las Vegas prize kingpins who have repeatedly been sued by regulators for defrauding their customers. And like their Las Vegas cousins they are moving into the "recovery" scam, hoping to squeeze the last dollars from elderly people who previously lost thou-sands to telemarketers.

"The old classic boiler rooms are back. They are not using high-tech gimmicks, but they can still take people for $12,000," says Donaldson. He says many former mid-level operators stepped in to take over after law enforcement crackdowns snared some bosses. "They grabbed the falling flag and set up their own boiler rooms. They nickel and dime the folks, asking for more and more money until they can't give any more."

Across the country in Arizona there is a similar sense of frustration with the pace of justice when it comes to telemarketers.

"It's so easy to set up a bank of phones. You can do it anywhere, and these guys can make $30,000 a month if they are good," says Jim Nielson, a lawyer with the Arizona Attorney General's Office. "So many of these guys spend the money on fancy cars and walk away."*

The report from the legal trenches is clear: the main weapon of the war against telemarketing fraud—the civil lawsuit—doesn't work very well. "By the time the lawsuit gets to trial, there's usually nothing left in the way of assets, so it's very hard to get restitution to consumers," says Nielson. "A civil judgment is just a piece of paper and the victims never see any significant portion of their money. It's gone."

Adds New York Assistant Attorney General Donaldson: "The only real way to stop this is to put these guys in the slammer."

But very few telemarketers have gone to jail and those who have tend to get light sentences. Ever since the early 1980s, state and federal government agents have tried to tackle telemarketers primarily by filing lawsuits against them.

The idea is sound. Generally, civil suits can be brought more quickly than criminal cases. The standard of proof is lower. A judge or jury deciding a civil case uses a standard of "more probable than not." In a criminal case, the jury must be persuaded "beyond a reasonable doubt."

Most states have laws called "little FTC" acts, which give attorneys general the right to sue to halt a business from engaging in unfair or deceptive trade practices. In most consumer fraud cases, regulators want to force the offender to mend its ways, so consumer protection lawyers often settle for a formal promise from the company not to violate the law. Most states call these pledges "assurances of discontinuance" or "assurances of voluntary compliance." A business, without admitting wrongdoing, simply signs a pledge that it won't violate the law in future, perhaps pays a small fine, and that ends the state investigation. States are supposed to monitor the firms to make sure they keep their word, but most lack the staff to keep a close watch on complaints against firms that have signed assurances.

These civil cases seem at first glance to be a reasonable means to prevent a business from engaging in deceptive sales tactics or to win refunds for aggrieved consumers. They may work with auto dealers tempted to run "bait-and-switch" advertising or other stable merchants who might be tempted to overstate the benefits or worth of their product.

But telemarketers are not like most businesses. Unlike car dealers who occupy huge sales lots and have an enormous investment to protect, they operate out of storefront boiler rooms. They don't even sell to locals

---

*Interview with Jim Nielson, October 23, 1992.

so the threat of public embarrassment in the community carries little weight. They can fold up shop and cross state lines, hide behind layers of dummy corporate fronts, use factors to launder their sales receipts, and find other ways to evade detection. In short, they set out to defraud customers.

Working out of Buffalo, where telemarketers roam from one sales room to another, taught New York Assistant Attorney General Dennis Rosen that filing civil cases and imposing small fines simply doesn't get the attention of the phone con artist.

"Criminal prosecutions are clearly more effective against telemarketers. I'm concerned about the overall deterrent effect. These guys feel that they can keep doing it until they get shut down, and then they just pay a fine. The fine is just a cost of doing business. It's pennies compared to what they are earning," says Rosen.

In late 1993 the New York Attorney General's Office began to work more closely with federal prosecutors. It hoped to see some of the Buffalo-area phone kingpins in jail as a result. Many other states have done the same thing. They seemed to see the light at once, in a collective rush of press releases touting new unions between criminal and civil regulators.

Moving toward criminal prosecutions is a needed step because so many telemarketers are hiring top-flight legal expertise to help them design programs that flout the law, Rosen said in a 1994 interview. "Many telemarketers believe they have tailored their program in a way that doesn't carry any criminal liability. Some have used high-priced lawyers to defend them and help write the sales pitches. They think they have set up a scam that is legal," says Rosen. "The great value of bringing these criminal prosecutions is that it sends a clear message that larceny is larceny whether it's over the phone or with a hand gun."

Interest in criminal prosecutions also has mounted with evidence of organized crime involvement in the boiler-room rackets. Many police and regulators have suspected, but seldom proven, organized crime ties to the shady telemarketing industry. Many police in South Florida feel a number of phone-room operators pay a portion of their take to gangsters in order to avoid a hostile takeover of the business.

This belief got a boost in the summer of 1994 with the criminal case against Anthony Induisi, of Davie, Florida, a Mafioso with a no-nonsense reputation and a fondness for coaching little league baseball. Induisi, forty-five, who is also known as Tony Black, is listed by the U.S. Senate Permanent Subcommittee on Investigations as a member of the Colombo crime family.

Federal prosecutors in Miami charged Induisi with running a number of illegal telemarketing and sports-betting operations in south Florida. Prosecutors told the media that Induisi was a *capo* or captain in the Colombo family. The sixty-six-count indictment, which also charged wire fraud, mail fraud, money laundering, and extortion, made a compelling case that organized crime had muscled in on the boiler-room racket and some of its related enterprises, such as credit-card factoring and money laundering. The indictment cited five telemarketing rooms in the field of travel, overseas employment, a consumer buyer's club, and timeshare-listing brokerage, all of which were allegedly fraudulent.

Induisi became an owner of the overseas employment scam after an associate used "extortion and threats of acts physical violence" to persuade the former owner to sell the operation for $5,000, to be paid in weekly installments. The seller received only $300, according to the indictments.*

Induisi, also a wholesale auto broker, decided to plead guilty to charges of racketeering when prosecutors agreed to drop the charges stemming from an alleged murder plot. Appearing before a federal judge in Miami in August 1994, Induisi supporters rose to laud the man they said spent more than twenty hours a week coaching youth football and baseball and who quietly picked up the tab for kids who couldn't afford to buy athletic shoes or pay registration fees. One woman credited Induisi with steering her fifteen-year-old son away from gangs.

Prosecutors portrayed Induisi as a "lifelong criminal" and argued for a sentence of six years. The judge, citing Induisi's good deeds on the athletic field, cut the alleged mobster's sentence. She gave him five years and three months.

The Induisi investigation took four years to complete and involved several federal and state law enforcement agencies, demonstrating the difficulty of mounting a large-scale criminal case.

Many law enforcers feel similar cases could be mounted, with the same results, in other cities with histories of intense boiler-room activities. They have come to embrace criminal charges, despite the higher standards of proof required to convict, as the best way to crack down on phone cons.

For some, the poor results of using civil powers against the fly-by-night telemarketing industry seemed clear in the 1980s. During a 1987 congressional hearing called to investigate a surge in travel-certificate

*USA v. Anthony Induisi, U.S. District Court Miami, 93-0089-CR.

scams, then FTC Bureau of Consumer Protection Director William Mac-
Leod seemed to acknowledge the limits of pursuing phone pros with lawsuits. He said:

> Because scam artists often close up shop and flee, literally in the middle
> of the night, consumer redress is usually difficult to obtain. . . . Of
> course, even when funds are not available for redress formal law en-
> forcement actions are worthwhile because well drawn injunctions may
> force the worst actors out of the travel scam business and deter others
> from entering it.

In further remarks submitted less than two months later, the FTC official noted that as authorities cleaned up the travel business they could
expect to see con artists move elsewhere.

> Fraudulent telemarketing tends to push certain products or services for
> a short period of time and then move on to different products or services.
> The nature of fraud and deception is to move toward growing, dynamic
> markets—very simply because that's where the money can be skimmed.
> During the period of high inflation the fraudulent operators were en-
> gaged in marketing precious stones and metals. During the energy short-
> ages, fraudulent scams involved oil and gas.

Many of the worst offenders among these phone scammers did just
what the FTC predicted. Most paid no significant penalty during the
1980s. Some began to encounter stiffer resolve among regulators in the
early 1990s, but they simply walked away from scams that stung customers for hundreds of thousands of dollars.

The Fort Lauderdale *Sun-Sentinel* study of telemarketing fraud data
showed that while more than 6,500 companies drew complaints to state
and federal regulators from 1985 to the end of 1992, only about one of ten
faced any sort of legal penalty.*

The telemarketing fraud enforcement actions cited in the study con-
sisted almost entirely of civil lawsuits filed since 1990, suggesting regulators have only started to catch up. Most of the cases plodded through the
courts, taking an average of fifteen months to settle. And the settlements
hardly cheered victims. Despite a few sensational $1 million plus ver-
dicts, most telemarketers were assessed fines of $50,000 or less—income
they could make up in a few weeks.

---

*"Phone Pirates: Hustling the Public," *Sun-Sentinel,* December 13-17, 1992.

The survey uncovered other evidence that suggested many state law enforcement efforts were setting their sights too low in allowing telemarketers to escape with lawsuits. Reviewing cases in eleven states, the study found that schemes which prompted criminal charges in some states and brought prison time for the perpetrators differed little in execution from scams that netted small fines in other states.

Perhaps most maddening, the products pegged by regulators as scams in the mid 1980s—travel certificates for instance—survived well into the 1990s despite repeated civil enforcement.

Passport Internationale, a travel-voucher business that opened in Daytona Beach, Florida, in 1985, shows the pattern. Since 1986, sales tactics used by the travel telemarketer have been the subject of civil enforcement actions brought by five states and the Federal Trade Commission. Passport's 1988 settlement with Wisconsin's attorney general typifies the state actions.

Passport paid Wisconsin regulators six thousand dollars in fines and restitution and agreed in future that it would not misrepresent the value of its certificates or fail to disclose all fees for its trips upfront. The company's executives admitted no wrongdoing.

After easily fending off court challenges from other states, Passport was hit with an FTC lawsuit in April 1992. The FTC alleged that as far back as 1987 owners Michael Panaggio and David Saltrelli fed a hydra of at least thirty-five boiler rooms that sold thousands of travel vouchers nationwide—far more than the company could fulfill.

Passport's telemarketing rooms sent out as many as one hundred thousand postcards each week telling consumers they had been selected for a "spectacular trip to Florida and a luxury cruise to the Bahamas," according to the FTC. The agency determined that after paying off sales commissions and other costs the company kept $219 for each voucher, a good deal less than the cost of the Bahamas leg of the trip. "Thus, Passport can stay in business only if many purchasers do not redeem their certificates for travel," the FTC stated in court filings.*

The evidence persuaded a federal judge in Orlando to issue a temporary order forbidding Passport from engaging in deceptive trade practices. The order also froze Passport's bank accounts. Co-owner Panaggio, in a newspaper interview on the day the court froze his accounts, indignantly denied any wrongdoing. He said Passport had sent 159,000 people on trips since 1990 and expected sales of close to $25 million in 1992. Passport has since filed for bankruptcy.

---

*FTC v. Passport International(e), Inc., U.S. District Court, Orlando, No. 92-275-CIV-ORL-20.

That's the way most FTC cases end. The FTC lacks any sort of criminal power, although the 1994 telemarketing-reform law gave the agency the power to seek criminal-contempt motions against telemarketers who defy court orders to halt deceptive sales practices.

The limited powers mean consumers are not likely to get refunds as a result of an FTC investigation. In October 1993 at a U.S. Senate hearing in Las Vegas to publicize the growing problem of telefunding, Jeffrey Klurfeld, who heads the FTC's San Francisco office, conceded that there were problems with recovering money for victims.

> I think the hallmark of this telemarketing fraud is that often by the time you wish to prosecute, the money has already been expended. It has been secreted. It is offshore. It has basically dissipated. . . . I think that when I look over the landscape of this type of fraud it is almost as if telemarketing fraud metastasizes. Several years ago these telemarketers were in the so-called toner-phoner rooms. Then they evolved into oil and gas scams, then to rare coins, rare stamps. . . . It is opportunistic . . . and the lesson we have learned is often we are too late, although we try to act with dispatch and alacrity.

The tendency to be too late has certainly cheered the con community. Telemarketers failed to pay more than $100 million in federal court judgments between 1985 and 1992, money that was supposed to be used to repay victims, FTC records reveal.

FTC documents show that the agency had won judgments in about eighty fraud cases totalling $197 million, but only about $50 million, or twenty-five cents on the dollar, had been recouped by victims. Another $30 million is held in reserves.

Those numbers are misleading because $29 million of the $50 million disbursed came from the Eagle Oil and Gas case, the massive fraud in the sales of leases that resulted in the former Miami Better Business Bureau chief going to prison and the scam's perpetrator fleeing the country.

In the Eagle case, the FTC recovered the money after it sued law firms, banks, and others it accused of helping Eagle defraud the public. The telemarketing house, which sold more than $51 million worth of bogus oil and gas leases in 1982, paid nothing. However, six of his former sales agents were assessed fines ranging from $1,500 to $225,000. Law firms and others, which had insurance to cover the awards, kicked in even more.

More often, civil prosecutions come too late to leave anything for victims. In thirty-two of the eighty federal court cases, consumers recovered nothing. Some of the cases and their perpetrators have been profiled in this book. Ostrich promoter Steven Tashman and race-track enthusiast James Settembrino both walked away from a $12-million FTC court judgment handed down in the telemarketing of oil leases by Atlantex Associates.

So did the owners of Ion Technologies, a company with branches in Texas and Florida said to have sold more than fifty thousand water purifiers. A court ordered Ion to pay $7.5 million, but it had only $52,500 in the bank. In a 1992 case involving shares in a Nevada gold-mine scheme, the government won a $6.9 million judgment, only to discover that the defendants had no assets.

One phone marketer of facsimile machine franchises, whose assets were frozen by a federal court judge at the urging of the FTC, managed to make thirty-four trips to Atlantic City where he gambled at least $152,750. His assets were supposed to be frozen so that he could repay $100,000 to his former customers. "These blatant violations of the asset freeze have caused harm to consumers and must be remedied," an FTC attorney huffed in court papers.

The low yield of civil suits has drawn fire from time to time from members of Congress who wondered why so much effort was expended in pursuing fines that never get paid.

The FTC greatly boosted spending in the early 1980s to attack telemarketing fraud. The agency in fiscal 1983 spent about $400,000 on telemarketing, up to $2.3 million in 1988 and $4.8 million in 1989. That year, the agency spent 13 percent of its total enforcement budget on telemarketing cases, according to agency records.

Some wondered why spending that much money with so little hope of recovery made sense, and whether money would not be better spent pursuing criminal investigations.

But the civil suit remains law enforcement's primary tool. In October 1993 the nation's state attorneys general kicked off National Consumers Week with a flurry of actions against telemarketing fraud.

"While the smart consumer is our best defense against fraud, we are not going to shy away from vigorous enforcement," declared Minnesota Attorney General Hubert H. Humphrey III, then president of the National Association of Attorneys General. "We want to send a loud and clear message to fraudulent telemarketers everywhere. We will not tolerate scams directed toward our consumers and we will come after you with the full force of the law."

---

*National Association of Attorneys General news release, October 26, 1993.

But an important, if unintended, message came through to anybody who studied his words carefully. Hardly anybody would be given jail time in the aftermath of this national crackdown. The attorneys general association announced more than seventy enforcement actions in ten states. But forty-five of the seventy actions were simply subpoenas or "civil investigatory demands" sent to telemarketers. These legal papers direct the recipient to supply authorities with information about their activities. When these papers arrive from authorities in states a thousand miles away, as they often do, many telemarketers simply ignore them. Most of the queries involved sweepstakes or prize promotions.

Only one of the seventy enforcement actions hyped that day to celebrate Consumers Week was criminal in nature. Nevada Attorney General Frankie Sue Del Papa arrested a Las Vegas telemarketer and charged him with a felony count of theft for allegedly attempting to con a ninety-two-year-old Kansas man out of $1,900. Not surprisingly, the phone man told the old man he must send the money to claim a $100,000 prize. The arrest was the first for Nevada's newly formed telemarketing fraud unit.

The civil wars are likely to continue and may even intensify. New state powers to file civil lawsuits against telemarketers are the centerpiece of 1994's federal telemarketing-reform law, regarded by many in law enforcement as a huge achievement.

The new law giving state attorneys general the power to sue telemarketers in federal court is power the state law enforcers have fought more than seven years to win from Congress.

Tennessee Attorney General Charles W. Burson, the 1994 president of the National Association of Attorneys General, hailed the new law as a major tool in the war against telemarketing. He warned that states will still be hampered by the problems of tracking down telemarketers before they flee or find some way to spirit their profits out of the country.

"That's a perpetual problem to find the money and the individuals at the hub. Sometimes we knock one out or get a dry hole, but we now have more technology to follow the money and to get restitution. We think that getting a court injunction on the front end will make a big difference," says Burson. "I think that in a fairly short period this new law will have a dramatic impact against scams. People can't run to another state anymore," he said in an August 1994 interview.

But Burson tempers his enthusiasm somewhat, noting that while the new law will change the rules the scam game will continue.

"Telemarketing is such a big problem. How they will adjust to this new law, I don't know. But they are so ingenious, I'm not going to say they won't be able to adjust. We are up against some very sophisticated and clever operations."

The civil wars have not only emboldened telemarketers, they seem also to have eroded consumer confidence in the system. No statistics can be drawn upon to support this assertion, but it is apparent to anyone who pores over complaint forms and contacts the victims.

From people taken for $500 or less for an overseas job promised by a Miami telemarketer, to seniors cheated out of $20,000 in donations to phony charities operating out of Las Vegas, the pattern often is the same: discontent with the legal process.

Consumers watch as state authorities accumulate dozens, sometimes hundreds, of sworn complaints all alleging similar patterns of fraud. Some who take the trouble to obtain copies of complaints filed by fellow victims are astounded that any business can so obviously violate the law and get away with it for so long.

They wonder why the state doesn't just swoop down on boiler rooms and lock up the scammers, instead of waiting to accumulate rooms full of sworn affidavits from victims. In the meantime, the scammers shut down, leaving nothing to repay victims. Hundreds of telemarketing rooms that sold all over the country disappeared without a trace in Fort Lauderdale alone during the early 1990s. Many telemarketers didn't bother to answer a state lawsuit, let alone complaints from the public.

To victims, state lawyers often seem to have infinite patience with errant telemarketers. The process can seem even worse, almost unsavory, to outsiders who show up to watch lawyers from both sides present the case against a telemarketer to a judge for settlement. Victims almost never are present because they live out of state and are not likely to make the trip to watch a civil case be decided. Lawyers for both sides banter among themselves as they await the judge's arrival. In South Florida, where these cases are fairly common, the attorney representing the telemarketer can even be a former employee of the state attorney general's office.

Like the victims, the telemarketer often is not present at the hearing, preferring to let his lawyer plead his case. Some lawyers who have enforced laws against boiler rooms for years don't often meet an honest-to-goodness telemarketer face to face. By constantly meeting with the telemarketer's friendly attorney to work out a settlement, which typically includes few if any refunds, regulators tend to lose touch with the damage victims suffer.

In the worst cases, regulators tend to become frustrated and cynical, often blaming the victims for being foolish enough to get taken by a voice on the phone line.

Letting lawyers dominate enforcement also causes state agencies to miss trends as they develop. Many state offices parcel cases out to attorneys, leaving no central repository of complaint data or expertise.

Some attorneys general have realized the need to move toward skilled telemarketing fraud units that know the players and the game—and don't wait until the firm has fled before filing a case against it.

"You need a permanent unit with a technological expert and investigators who understand how these scam networks work," says Charlie Donaldson of the New York Attorney General's Office. "You spend so much time with the alligators, there's no time to look around in the swamp."

Colette Rausch, who heads the telemarketing fraud unit of the Nevada Attorney General's Office, agrees: "Going after these cases takes a specialized unit of investigators with knowledge of telemarketing. We don't have the responsibility to take care of the whole world. We can target our activities and that helps," she notes. "These cases really take a lot of time and resources, but it's got to be done. You've just got to suck it up and do it."

But shifting over to criminal cases is easier to talk about than to accomplish.

Prosecutors say white-collar criminals enjoy a tremendous advantage in the courts. They can afford high-priced legal talent and often succeed in making their business appear legitimate. Witnesses in many cases tend to be elderly, and some are forgetful, further hampering the prosecution. Proving criminal intent also is a challenge.

Many telemarketing rooms house sales agents in separate quarters from the complaint departments or shipping areas, divisions of the operation that might be aware of fraud. Few phone pros want to know anything about the product they are selling—and many never even see it—to minimize the chances they could face criminal fraud penalties.

Owners often disclaim any liability for the sales pitches used by their operators and use a number of subsidiaries to shield them from fraud charges. Many owners hire managers for each shift of their operation and rarely set foot on the premises, making it harder for authorities to link them to the enterprise.

Time after time, authorities are left with cases in which they are certain a fraud was committed, but there is nobody to charge criminally.

Some cases that could be prepared for criminal prosecution fall through the cracks because of poor or inconsistent police work. Police often don't want to take the time and effort to assemble these cases, which so often involve victims who live thousands of miles away.

The enormous number of cases that "fall through the cracks" is a sensitive subject in boiler-room hotspots, from Florida to California, where police are under pressure to solve violent crimes.

One frustrated fraud detective in a Florida police department blames his superiors for putting little emphasis on cracking down on phone cons.

> They don't feel like this is a headline grabber like narcotics. My bosses don't pay any attention to these investigations. Yet these people [telemarketers] are making a fortune. I've worked cases on rooms where they were making $250,000 a week. One scam that we shut down moved to Atlanta and I heard they were doing $386,000 in checks a week. The money is just astronomical. This is just as out of control as drugs are, but feds don't seem to want to do anything about it.

The officer also blames his peers for not being willing to allocate the time it takes to track down victims from out of state. That attitude keeps the subculture of boiler-room pros confident that they will always be able to sell another day. He also gets frustrated by the lenient sentences handed out to white-collar criminals. "I haven't met one of these boiler-rooms guys yet who has reformed. They always get right back into the business. they can just get on the phones for two hours or so a day and make thousands of bucks a week. They don't know how to do anything else. The money is too tempting."

Many states are starting to mix both criminal and civil law enforcement. In late 1993 and early 1994 the Federal Trade Commission sponsored several meetings that brought together both arms of law enforcement with a dedication to fight alongside one another.

FTC Chairman Janet Steiger heralded a 1993 meeting in Atlanta that brought together the attorneys general of eight states, along with the FBI, the IRS, the U.S. Postal Service, and the Securities and Exchange Commission, among others. The effort, she said, "marks a new level of cooperation among an expanded array of authorities to target scams." She promised "a redoubled commitment on the part of criminal authorities to prosecute fraudulent telemarketers."

Steiger said enforcement during much of the past decade had racked up an "impressive" tally, but added: "Despite these steadfast efforts, the number of perpetrators and their victims remain high."*

Some law enforcement agencies believe they simply must have tougher laws, even if the laws impinge on the rights of legitimate business.

"I think that legislators are reluctant to pass strong statutes that would inhibit entrepreneurs. I'm not sure they understand the ill effects of white-collar crime," says Dennis Rosen of the New York Attorney General's Office in Buffalo. "They understand street crime, but this is much worse. Working class peoples' lives are changed for the worse because of what these telemarketers have done. It is much worse than getting mugged and losing a few dollars."†

Rosen says that telemarketing is the "cutting edge fraud in this country and the laws are not equipped to deal with it."

He advocates draconian laws that would outlaw certain sales pitches, such as calling thousands of people and telling each they have won a prize. He also supports "cooling off" periods so that buyers would be able to change their minds and get speedy refunds.

"A lot of these people are just vulnerable and would get taken no matter what laws are passed," Rosen says. "But many people are sending their money to telemarketers because they are saying things that the law should not allow them to say. Elderly people are picking up the phone and a guy is in their house. They try to sweet talk them and when that doesn't work they get abusive. This is almost like a burglary."

Randy Prillaman, FBI Special Agent in Charge of the Las Vegas area, also advocates tough new laws. Testifying before a U.S. Senate committee hearing in Las Vegas in October 1993, he noted that even the FBI's celebrated "Operation Disconnect" did not knock out the phone con. Disconnect was a three-year undercover operation that netted hundreds of telemarketing arrests nationwide in the largest criminal enforcement crackdown to date.

The undercover FBI sting operation targeted many boiler-room operators who had evaded the law enforcement net for years, playing upon their greed with a fake autodialer that promised them huge profits. Not surprisingly most of the arrests were made in sunbelt cities including Las Vegas and South Florida.

Said FBI agent Prillaman:

*FTC news release, November 8, 1993.
†Interview with Dennis Rosen.

Immediately after Operation Disconnect the FBI in Las Vegas and else-where began seeing the telemarketers switch to a slightly different scheme to defraud. Victims throughout the country were being called by telemarketers from Las Vegas and elsewhere and were being told that the telemarketers were soliciting funds for various worthy charities. . . . We have seen solicitations for the homeless, AIDS victims, battered women, and drug awareness and education. While the floods were still raging in the Midwest, the telemarketers were soliciting funds for dis-placed flood victims. Victims are told the proceeds go entirely to the charity and only a small administrative fee is taken out. This adminis-trative fee is frequently the whole contribution.*

The FBI agent noted that the telemarketers switched to charitable solicitations because charities are exempt from Nevada state laws gov-erning the licensing of telemarketers. He offered a list of ten suggestions for controlling the problem, many of which might also thwart the growth of other forms of the phone con.

The list is memorable for its no-nonsense approach and its desire to pro-tect the public no matter whether some charities would object. Some of the goals would be tough to reconcile with court decisions that have taken the position that charitable solicitations are protected free speech. Similarly, for-feiture provisions, which allow law enforcement agencies to confiscate valu-ables from automobiles to houses that are used in commission of a crime, have been subject to abuse, both by state and federal law enforcement.

But the comments seem to provide a useful starting point for address-ing chronic problems such as boiler-room veterans, a number of whom have felony convictions, moving from scam to scam. FBI officials note that more than eighty-five of the several hundred telemarketers identified during the first stages of "Operation Disconnect" had criminal histories, some of them violent. Here is the FBI agent Prillaman's list or suggested rules for telemarketers:

1. States should license and regulate all charities.

2. Persons convicted of fraud should be barred from soliciting for charities.

3. Charitable organizations should be guaranteed a specific percent-age of the money collected on their behalf by telemarketers.

---

*Subcommittee on Consumer, Committee on Commerce, Science, and Transportation, U.S. Senate, March 18, 1993.

4. Customers should be told how much of their contribution goes to charity. (Note: Courts have ruled that states may not impose such a requirement on charities.)

5. The true value of any prizes given in connection with an appeal should be told to the customer.

6. Telemarketing companies should identify their true owners and be subject to audits.

7. The law should prohibit the use of aliases by telemarketers.

8. Telemarketing laws should contain provisions for seizure and forfeiture.

9. Victims' rights and the ability to recover money they contribute should be of primary importance.

10. The owners of telemarketing companies should be held accountable for the pitches used by their sales people.

The agent Prillaman concluded his testimony by noting that while telemarketing fraud can never be eliminated, tough enforcement can make inroads. "To our knowledge, states which have enacted strict laws combined with aggressive law enforcement and/or regulations are not suffering from the growth of illegal marketing," he said.

17

Operation Disconnect

Few telemarketers will turn their backs on technology that promises them big bucks. They love gadgets that boost sales tallies and keep them one step ahead of competitors, and the law. They delight in discovering new tricks to milk their customers for even more money. After all, greed is their greatest motivator.

The VOX 2000 Remote Access Marketing Network was such a device. In the right hands it could revolutionize telemarketing and send profits soaring.

But the VOX 2000 existed only in the mind of an FBI agent who devised the fake dialer as a means to sting illicit telemarketers across the country. Here's how it worked:

The VOX boosters said they had set up automatic dialing machines in major cities throughout the United States. Each of the little devils could make twenty-four thousand phone calls per day, playing a recorded sales pitch to anyone who answered. Customers who were interested in buying could call back a phone number they heard on the tape. The number was *not* toll-free, intentionally so, to eliminate calls from all but the most motivated buyers.

"I've got a system basically set in place that will make your phones ring off the hook," VOX salesman Mike Manson told one boiler-room operator.

The autodialer was tough to ignore. By placing the calling machines throughout the country, VOX users could pick any city to hawk their wares. Best of all, the telemarketing rooms did not have to pay for long distance calls to reach their customers. Because the phone bill can consume 10 percent of a telephone room's gross sales receipts, VOX offered telemarketers big savings.

The mechanical dialers could generate hundreds of calls a day to the boiler rooms, limited only by the number of telemarketers the owner wanted to employ. The dialers also had a number of safeguards to make sure that most of the people who called in were "qualified," that is, they had money to make a purchase.

The phone-in system saved boiler-room owners money in other ways. The telemarketers no longer would have to pay for lists of names and phone numbers of people who might fall for their schemes. Buying sales leads, which can cost several dollars per name, eats up as much as 10 percent of gross revenues in some phone rooms.

"When you're ready to solve your lead-generating problems, WE HAVE THE ANSWER!" VOX proclaimed in its glossy sales literature.

The autodialer, which simply called one number after another, screened out hospitals, police stations, and other institutions that could pose a problem if called and offered a scam deal. The recorded sales pitch also asked potential buyers such questions as did they have a credit card or checking account and were the owner of a business, as a means to qualify them. The dialer also spared telemarketers from having to send out postcards or other mailers to make their sales pitch, also a considerable expense.

Because VOX could prequalify buyers, it promised a higher rate of sales than in most "inbound" phone promotions. Many telemarketers dislike "inbound" sales schemes because so many of the people who respond to call-in ads are not likely to buy, and thus waste the telemarketer's time. Making the customer pay for a long distance call to reach the boiler room also assured that most people who called would be motivated.

VOX assured users that its system of prescreening call-ins would yield a phenomenal sales "closing rate" of 30 percent.

While sales would go up, the phone-room operators would need fewer people because they could predict in advance when most of their calls would come in. Owners hiring banks of telemarketers would no longer pace the floor waiting for the phones to ring. All they had to do was lease the VOX machines and wait for the suckers to call.

The machine even kept track of the numbers of people who stayed on the line to hear the entire pitch, and the numbers that hung up along the way. If too many people hung up in an initial round of auto calls, VOX could replace the pitch, much the same as tabloid newspapers might yank a headline and write a new one in between editions, hoping slow street sales will pick up.

Best of all, though, VOX offered personal service. Its staff worked with clients to develop a recorded sales pitch tailored to any boiler room's needs.

Let's say a telemarketer wanted to call only businesses to pitch them advertising specialties with the "one-in-five" prize scam. Most companies will answer the phone by repeating the name of the business, not "Hello" as would a person reached at home. A computer chip in the autodialer could recognize the word "hello" and disconnect anybody who answered the phone that way, thus assuring that no consumers would be offered the pitch.

Here's a pitch written for the advertising specialties scam, and introduced as court evidence. A female voice came on the line:

> Hello. Please listen carefully. It is our sincere pleasure to inform you that your business has been selected by us as a major award recipient. If you are the owner of the business, push one on your touch-tone phone; if you are not the owner push two now.

If the person pushed two, indicating he or she was not the owner of the business, the computer cooed:

> If the owner is available, I will wait thirty seconds while you notify him of this important call, then when he returns to the phone, have him push the number one to continue.[Once the owner was on the line the message would continue] Thank you. If you have less than fifteen employees, push one on your phone now.

If the person pushed one, the computer voice would launch the pitch:

> Congratulations. By participating today you are guaranteed to receive one of the following awards. Please listen closely. Number one is a brand new Chevrolet Camaro. Number two is a satellite dish that gets seventy-two channels from Santa Link. Number three is a commemorative fourteen carat gold ingot, and number four is a two-and-a half carat diamond and sapphire pendant on a fourteen-carat gold chain plus a beautiful men's or women's watch, and number five a 50-inch Hitachi big-screen television. This will be our only attempt to notify you of your award. . . . We're running a promotion right now where we select businesses like yours to participate. In order to claim your award, you must contact our office within the next twenty-four hours. . . . This program is not available to the general public. This is the only call that you will receive, so please write this down. The number to call is ———. Don't delay. Call now.

The VOX system, manufactured by Sunbelt Diversified in Atlanta, gave the infamous sweepstakes promotion a whole new dimension. Only a handful of states had outlawed the use of autodialers, which meant the system could pitch consumers almost everywhere in the country.

For telemarketers, VOX, with its sales guarantees and technical wizardry, seemed too good to be true.

It was.

Sunbelt Diversified was a front for the FBI. The VOX system peddled by the company existed only on paper. The FBI agent who used the name Mike Manson made the scheme up, choosing the name "Vox" because it was Latin for "voice."* VOX was the centerpiece of "Operation Disconnect," the most ambitious attack on telemarketing fraud in the nation's history.

Before it was over, the VOX scam would result in the arrests of more than three hundred telemarketers in eighteen states.

Then-FBI Director William Sessions unveiled "Operation Disconnect" on March 4, 1993, at a Washington news conference, which did not begin smoothly. Earlier that day word got out of an arrest in the bombing of the World Trade Center, a terrorist act that was dominating news coverage nationally. Some reporters who dropped by at the fortress-like J. Edgar Hoover Building on Pennsylvania Avenue expected to grill the FBI director about rumors of more arrests in the bombing.

But Sessions stuck to the script and issued an account of the three-year undercover operation, which involved eighteen FBI field offices from Los Angeles to Miami.

While Sessions briefed the national press corps, U.S. attorneys in eighteen cities held press conferences of their own to announce local arrests. Forty-eight of the 240 initial arrests were in South Florida. Eleven people were arrested in Dallas.

Sessions began his presentation by calling "Disconnect" a landmark FBI investigation to "beat these con artists at their own game." He explained the sales strategy of Sunbelt Diversified.

> FBI agents posed as sales representatives of a company that leased "one-of-a-kind" computerized automatic dialing systems. They approached the owners of illegal operations to sell them equipment that could reduce their operating costs and increase their profits. And while making their

---

*The FBI knew that the autodialer would be credible to many telemarketers. Such devices do exist, although a number of states have outlawed them as a nuisance. The U.S. Supreme Court in a March 1993 decision upheld the right of states to ban use of the devices. (Hall v. Minnesota, 92-1333).

sales presentation, these agents gathered information about the telemarketers' operations, the products they sold and the victims they preyed on. We also used this information to become willing victims ourselves—and buy the products that were offered.

Sessions said the products ranged from phony overseas jobs to vitamins to costly investment opportunities. Of the ninety-five illegal boiler rooms smashed, the largest single group offered professional services such as loans, jobs, distributorships, and vacation packages. Next came vitamins and skin-care products.

Not surprisingly, half the sales rooms made initial contact with victims through a phone call, either "cold calls" made by scanning the pages of phone books and other public records, or through purchased phone lists. One in four sent mailers out to potential customers and 12 percent relied on newspaper ads to get their message across.

Sessions held up props, including a sapphire and diamond necklace for which agents paid $380 after a telemarketer told the FBI it was worth $1,200. "Some bargain," said Sessions. "The diamonds and sapphires are poor quality, the chain isn't fourteen-carat gold as it was claimed to be. It's worth far less than the $380 we paid."

Sessions said that victims ran the gamut from single women to small businesses, but senior citizens made up the largest category, 34 percent of the total.

In fact, one convicted telemarketer has testified in a congressional hearing that he preferred the elderly because "their memory is poor, they rarely make notes of their phone conversations, and only occasionally ask for written guarantees." Their most notable weakness is that once they recognize the deceit, they are often too embarrassed to relay the events to their offspring, friend, counsel and law enforcement.

"This is an outrage," said Sessions.

Warren Rupp seems more like one of the outrageous characters Sessions spoke of than a hero in the war against telemarketing fraud. For twenty years Rupp manned phones in a number of different costly cons. Three times he was indicted on federal criminal charges: in Nevada, Georgia, and Florida.

Rupp is the type of telemarketer that prosecutors and consumer advocates have warned the public for years to hang up on. He shuttled from state to state, racket to racket, and developed a reputation for being so good on the phone he could make anybody cry.

Rupp was around when it all began in the late 1970s in high-riding sales rooms scattered across Las Vegas. He was both a member of the sales staff and a manager at the now infamous desert boiler room known as 50 State Distributing.

For the right price, Rupp agreed to help the FBI track down others who cut their teeth on the phones at 50 State and its offspring. Since the idea was to "con the cons" as the FBI put it, who better to have on board than Rupp, who could boast of knowing hundreds of phone pros across the country?

Rupp signed on in 1990 in Salt Lake City as what the FBI calls a "co-operating witness," and not exactly pro bono. The FBI paid Rupp more than $110,000 in the three years the operation lasted, $3,000 a month at some points, to snitch on his former comrades.

"Warren looks like a telemarketer," said the FBI special agent who used the alias "Mike Manson" to peddle the VOX autodialer. "He gave us credibility. With my short hair, I look like a cop," Manson testified in federal court in Fort Lauderdale in June 1994.

Rupp played for the hidden microphones, drawing his ex-comrades into admitting that they lied to make sales, and reminiscing about the days at 50 State to loosen them up. The ease with which the FBI operation found the 50 State vets, perhaps better than anything else, testifies to the anemic state of law enforcement efforts directed at white-collar criminals.

"As part of this national operation, various undercover agents involved, including myself, routinely came across and spoke to in an undercover capacity other operators, managers, and salespeople who had worked for 50 State at one time or another," one FBI agent testified in court.

Rupp broke the ice for the FBI teams in a number of sales rooms. He would regale anyone who would listen with tales from the boiler rooms, often the 50 State room, where he was both a salesman and a manager.

Rupp could be engaging. In one boiler room conversation taped by the FBI during its investigation of Cypress Creek Promotions in Fort Lauderdale, Rupp recalled old times in the Las Vegas phone racket. He described a fire one morning at 50 State that brought out nine engines, and shut off electricity so sales agents had to work by candlelight. The smoky blaze didn't concern the greedy management enough to order phone salesmen out. The managers kept saying, according to Rupp: "Don't worry about the smoke, they are going to have it out any minute. Just stay on the phones." Later the bosses regrouped while the building smoldered and said: "We'll get a hotel. They'll hook up phones and they can call from the rooms."

Rupp did so well at 50 State that he found himself assigned a key role in a satellite office in Anaheim, California, one of at least two as the company grew. 50 State then opened another office in Dallas, according to court records.

Like so many of his boiler-room brethren, Rupp shuttled between Nevada, Utah, California, and South Florida, with a few stops in between, running phone rooms. He managed to stay out of jail despite fronting some which were so blatant that they almost guaranteed heat from law enforcement.

The law eventually found Rupp. In January 1989 he pleaded guilty to federal mail fraud charges for his role in Commercial Research International, an Ogden, Utah, boiler room that sold worthless travel certificates under several different names and with claims far more outrageous than most of the Florida dealers.

Using the name "Rainbow's End," Rupp's companies sold twenty-nine-dollar coupons supposedly redeemable for free round-trip airfare to Jamaica or Hawaii. Rupp used four aliases with the company, which switched locations, names, and phone companies three times during the sixteen months it stayed in business.

The scheme was unusually brazen because it used the name of a hotel in Jamaica, falsely claiming it would honor the lodging certificates. The company also claimed some of its vouchers could be redeemed for seven-day Caribbean cruises aboard a well-known cruise line. The firm also sold bogus "flight passes" that they claimed were good for airfare to the Caribbean, Hawaii, or Tahiti. Very few phone rooms attach the names of actual companies, and certainly not a prominent cruise line, on their certificates or ads. Such a move almost guarantees the cruise line will complain to authorities about illegal use of its trademark or name.

While the FBI has declined to discuss Rupp's agreement to provide it with services, court records show that the boiler-room veteran parlayed his Utah arrest into a deal that helped move "Operation Disconnect" forward. In exchange for Rupp's cooperation, the FBI helped him and an associate clear up some other criminal cases filed against them.

Rupp and the associate also had been charged in 1989 with running a boiler room in Pompano Beach, Florida, called National Premium Distributors, which sold travel vouchers for between thirty and sixty dollars to merchants who thought they were buying overseas vacations that they could give away to their customers.

One car dealer in Lakewood, Colorado, paid the men $24,500 for 350 vouchers good for one-week vacations in Hawaii, premiums the dealer gave away to new car buyers, not realizing they were worthless. That scheme netted the men at least $271,000 in five months.

Rupp and the associate ran a similar racket under the name Caribbean Resort Association in Marietta, Georgia, once again peddling twenty-nine-dollar coupons they said were good for round-trip airfare to Jamaica. At least fifteen hundred Atlanta-area merchants purchased the coupons hoping to boost sales with the giveaway.

Rupp's agreement to switch sides kept him out of jail. He received five years probation and was ordered to pay restitution of $125,000 for the Utah charges and $130,000 for the Florida charges. The government deferred sentencing on the Georgia crimes pending the outcome of Rupp's work as an informant. As the undercover operation proceeded, Rupp signed a contract with the FBI. By June 1994 the FBI had paid Rupp more than $125,000 for his assistance, according to court testimony.

Federal prosecutors and the FBI believe Rupp earned his money by guiding the FBI into the dark heart of the criminal boiler-room community. His value was evident in the case against Cypress Creek Promotions and its owner Tim O'Neil, an old friend of Rupp from their days together at 50 State. A U.S. District Court jury in Fort Lauderdale convicted O'Neil and two associates in June 1994 of wire fraud and conspiracy to commit wire fraud. Prosecutors based their case largely on the undercover tapes and testimony from FBI agents. Rupp did not testify, but his presence clearly caused O'Neil to freely discuss his criminal conduct and make dozens of incriminating statements that prosecutors happily played for the jury.

With Warren Rupp on their team, the undercover team of FBI agents had an easy time talking their way into Cypress Creek Promotions in Fort Lauderdale. FBI agent Manson set up the appointment by selling O'Neil, at least partly, on the idea of using the autodialer.

The five-member FBI team arrived at 10:09 A.M. on April 1, 1992. They tested their microphones in the car as they cleared a traffic light near Cypress' office park. One agent yawned and another whistled as they pulled up to the door.

The mission was to get evidence on tape of criminal doings in the phone room. The FBI agents dressed to fit into the casual working atmosphere. Manson, a heavy set ex-Marine jet pilot with dark hair and a quick smile, arrived wearing green shorts. Like the others, he carried recording devices hidden in a briefcase. Each man had a specific duty and they fanned out as they entered the one-story office suites.

Three agents engaged workers in the "front" room in conversation. These less-experienced sales agents, who tended to rely on scripts to make their pitches, proved quite talkative. The FBI agents pumped them for details about the phone room and their sales tactics, supposedly to help them develop a sales pitch that could be recorded and placed on the autodialer. Their real purpose was to get them on tape discussing how they defrauded their customers.

Many of the Disconnect cases followed this pattern. Once the owners of the room had given their blessing to the autodialer, the FBI found the sales force to be cooperative. Many sales workers proved willing to share their illegal sales strategies. Many who boasted of their sales conquests later regretted their comments.

At Cypress Creek Promotions, the FBI team found a frat-party atmosphere. Agents circulated freely chit-chatting about the best happy hour in Fort Lauderdale and trading telemarketing tall tales, and even invited the sales crew out on their boat for a blow-out—all recorded.

The cover of Sunbelt Diversified gave the FBI agents a logical reason to be pumping the sales crew for information. It made sense that the company's representatives needed to learn as much as possible about a phone room's sales objectives in order to tailor the autodialer pitch.

In many cases, Sunbelt employees sat with the front room managers and staff and helped them compose a sales pitch. The tactic put the agents smack in the middle of the boiler room where they could hear the sales crew actually doing the selling. Tapes of these conversations add an entirely new dimension to criminal prosecutions. Federal prosecutors did not need to recreate a sales pitch based upon the recollection of an elderly victim who could be attacked by defense counsel as an unreliable witness.

The exchanges between FBI agents and the sales crews proved devastating to defendants when played in front of juries. The dialogue provided powerful evidence of the state of mind of the sales crews, leaving few people to doubt their criminal intent. Many of the tapes also betrayed the sales agents' utter contempt for their victims, catching them swearing at their customers or laughing as they defraud them.

Operation Disconnect also succeeded far beyond most other infiltrations of the boiler-room industry because it sold a product that required the approval of owners. Some of them rarely visited the sales rooms and took other steps to conceal their ownership in the phone room. The autodialer, for which FBI agents often asked as much as $30,000 in upfront fees, required the highest level of approval, thus getting the FBI together with owners.

FBI agents never collected any money. Once sales rooms agreed to participate, Sunbelt came up with a number of excuses and other stall tactics. Eventually, the phone rooms got fed up with the company and broke off negotiations. But by that time, the FBI had the evidence it needed to arrest the principals and many of their sales crew.

Despite an elaborate brochure printed for use in the sales presentation, the autodialer did not exist. FBI agent Manson paid less than $5,000 for the glossy brochures. He simply altered a brochure a Salt Lake City company had printed for a local high-tech concern. While Sunbelt had corporate papers on file in Georgia showing it had been in business since the mid-1980s, these registrations were phony. In all Operation Disconnect involved just fifty agents in eighteen field offices, by FBI standards a shoestring operation.

In the case of Cypress Creek Promotions, which employed four 50 State veterans in key positions, Manson talked his way into a meeting with boss O'Neil like a phone pro. On his first sales call, he convinced the guy who answered the phone using the alias "Tony" to give him his real name. With a couple more calls, he had an appointment, just like any good salesman.

Mike Manson and Warren Rupp walked into O'Neil's office as the owner took a "heat" call from the eighty-nine-year-old Philadelphia woman named Emma who had lost more than $10,000 and notified police detectives, according to tapes introduced as evidence at O'Neil's trial.

Before the FBI left that day, they had O'Neil on tape not only with Emma, but with another woman as well.

The other woman was a sixty-one-year-old from Vernon, British Columbia, who listed her hobbies as fishing and other sports. She had sent one of O'Neil's reloaders $1,200 with a letter saying that was all she could afford. "Sure hope this is the one I have been waiting for and I can thank you for this. God Bless you," she wrote in the letter.

Four months later, after not receiving the "major award" she had been promised, the woman wrote to O'Neil threatening to go to the police unless she got her prize. And she stopped payment on a number of checks.

O'Neil's lie-laden call to her brought smiles to federal prosecutors, who knew its impact on a jury would be devastating for O'Neil, exactly the type of evidence that Operation Disconnect was expected to reel in.

O'Neil talks the woman, who said she had lost $14,000 to telemarketers, into sending him a money order to replace the checks. She agrees to do so, once she gets the money. O'Neil ends by saying he'll call her back in a week to arrange for her to send the money order.

"You make us money. If I give you a cash award or a nice, nice award, I use that in my advertising. So you're really making me money, but you got something nice for it," he says. After lying to her repeatedly about the company's history and intentions, O'Neil says: "I want you to do me a favor. Don't buy from anybody but Cypress Creek."

Ironically, the woman tips O'Neil off to an FBI investigation, saying her phone calls have been monitored by FBI agents. She mentions a company in Denver and one in South Florida which she knows to be caught up in the probe. Curiously, news of the FBI involvement doesn't seem to worry or interest O'Neil.

Nor does he seem to have any concerns about his old friend Rupp. The transcripts show the ease with which O'Neil was taken in by his old buddy. Their joking over bygone days in the boiler rooms of Las Vegas also leaves little doubt about the criminal nature of the phone business. They talk openly of techniques that work the best at scamming the public. O'Neil reveals several fraudulent facets of his business, then boasts of "having this fuckin' game licked."

Such boiler-room banter, punctuated with many four-letter words, makes a few jurors squirm, but delights prosecutors who are seeking to portray the defendants as unsavory. It's a key advantage. In the Fort Lauderdale trial, prosecutors referred to O'Neil's favorite adjective as "effing" as they addressed jurors, each time driving home the sleazy nature of the phone room.

But while O'Neil opens up to Rupp, admitting that his salesmen are lying, he also insists that Cypress Creek is a legitimate company. He seems indignant as he relates a call from a local fraud detective who opined that Cypress Creek seemed to him to be a "scam."

O'Neil speaks of overcoming his drinking problem and setting out with Cypress Creek with the intent to clean up the ad-specs routine. At the same time, he admits to possible criminal conduct in the past with a boiler room operation that he did not name.

And if I wanted to make a real score. I could have opened for four weeks and take in a quarter-million dollars and been history . . . and believe me with two hundred or three hundred orders out there I ain't gonna get no heat. I know that. I ran a company five years ago when I was a drunk where I didn't ship over four hundred orders. I took the money and ran.

While the tapes whirl, O'Neil goes on to make some telling comments about the state of civil law enforcement by attorneys general, just the sort of comment that the FBI needs to hear to persuade policy makers to continue the fight against the phone fraud menace.

> If a Washington attorney general and Michigan and a Boston attorney and a Louisiana and a North Carolina and an Ohio in the middle all got letters [from complaining customers] it ain't enough to create enough to come down on me, so I took the money and ran when I was a drunk. I ain't doing it now. I wanna do it right. And I'm doing as best I know how. But it's the kind of business that, who the fuck knows. Who knows? You know I've got three attorneys and I pay one a retainer every month.

While Manson and Rupp softened up O'Neil, the rest of the FBI team had a tougher time with Cypress Creek sales manager Bill Clark, also a 50 State veteran, but a suspicious and cynical man who asked many probing questions about the autodialer.

Bill Clark boasted of learning the telemarketing trade at 50 State from the "biggest scammers in the business," but he did not have very fond memories of the place. He recalled disputes over money, a general manager who was tough to get along with, and pressure to make sales that was too hard to stand day in and day out.

Clark also had a good nose for when to leave. He left 50 State about six months before the postal inspectors staged their raid, after five years as a salesman, manager, and customer service employee. Clark joined another Las Vegas ad-specs room but managed to duck out of that place, too, before its owners were arrested, as he recalled, on income tax charges. Just thirty-four, Clark had fourteen years in the boiler-room business—and no arrests—when he walked into Cypress Creek Promotions in 1991 in response to a want-ad in the local newspaper. Clark didn't remember O'Neil, but the 50 State connection got him a job at Cypress Creek where he quickly impressed O'Neil and rose to manager of the front sales room.

The informal telemarketers network, whether through 50 State or other well-known boiler rooms that can supply quick references, has frustrated law enforcement for years, both because so many left 50 State Distributing to open their own boiler rooms and because law enforcers have been unable to infiltrate the boiler-room underground. Operation Disconnect, in part because of Rupp's defection, no doubt has rattled confidence in the network.

Clark gave the undercover FBI team little benefit of the doubt, at least at first. While his comments give no indication that he saw through the scheme, he hurled questions at the FBI agents that proved tough to answer.

Clark had previous experience with call-in telemarketing, the "in-bound" sales schemes, in Las Vegas—and it wasn't pleasant. Clark didn't buy Sunbelt Diversified's claims that the callers would be people with the money and motivation to buy. He said "90 percent" of people who return these calls are a waste of time because they won't buy. He also said that phone rooms that switch to the call-in method after recruiting top-flight telemarketers often are disappointed. Said Clark:

> The calls are so sporadic you go out to another room; you pirate four of the best writers that you can get; you promise them the earth, moon, and the stars; and you get them in there and now the phone don't ring. It's either feast or famine. You either get a lot of calls or you don't get any.

Clark also said that the autodialer pitch "lacked urgency," a critical flaw. People who buy from telemarketers need to be given some sort of deadline, Clark said, and they need to feel they have been singled out for a special award: "They gotta feel like they're special and not everybody can do it. Cause the way we pitch is 'Boy, you got lucky man. The pots and pans are gone and we're down to the finals.' "

Clark conceded that the technique might work for business customers who could be asked to push a button on their phone if they were the owner, but he still doubted the closing rate of 30 percent saying that it would be "tough."

Clark seemed distressed that Sunbelt Diversified would not offer any references other than to say that the firm's autodialer was being used by "several different companies" selling products ranging from vitamins to water purifiers. O'Neil also wanted to know the names of telemarketers who were making fortunes from the auto caller. Clark baited FBI agent Manson. "Just give me one [name of a user]. I know everybody in the industry. I can just call the guy and say, 'Does it work?' "

Manson gave this answer:

> Well, umm, you know, the only problem with that is that we've got a confidentiality agreement that we have signed with our telemarketers, okay? And, basically, what we've said to them is we won't disclose who they are, and they won't disclose who we are, and that's the promise we got with them, okay?

When Clark persists, Manson fires back that he doesn't want to take a chance of losing established clients to satisfy Cypress Creek Promotions, which has yet to commit to more than a test run with the autodialer. Says Manson: "Like I said, I've got clients right now that I don't want to lose, and I'm not going to screw my current client base with somebody that's a maybe, okay? And that's kind of where we are with that."

Within a few days Cypress Creek Promotions got the test run and that provided the only reference O'Neil needed—easy sales that proved too tempting to pass up.

The test stage of Operation Disconnect was perhaps the most inventive phase of the sting. Manson arrived with a taped version of a pitch recorded by a female voice, written jointly by Clark and Sunbelt employees. Manson said the device in San Diego would be turned on for fifteen minutes or about fifty calls using the taped pitch, which would give O'Neil a taste of its sales power.

But the return calls into Cypress Creek came from FBI agents posing as customers, who recorded the transactions. Fourteen agents called in, enough to give the owners a sense that the autodialer could crank away furiously out in California and bring in customers.

Some agents were "lay downs" or easy sales, while others acted tougher to persuade. Clark took a few of the calls and launched into his sales pitch full of lies, misrepresentations, and other deceits that added up to wire fraud. The boiler room was like a drift fishing boat passing over a school of fish. Every angler struck at once, and many happily reeled in their catches.

Four agents sent in $399 after hearing the promises of costly prizes. Three got a letter back, or junk jewelry—a pendant or a watch—all the classic "gimme gifts" and all worth thirty-five dollars or less.

"They said it was like trading a dollar in for twenty dollars when in fact it is quite the opposite," Assistant U.S. Attorney Jeffrey Kaplan said in opening arguments at O'Neil's trial in Fort Lauderdale.

The callers who got away without buying anything asked many questions that prompted the sales crew to lie repeatedly in hopes of snaring them: more vivid evidence of wire fraud at the Fort Lauderdale phone room. And like clockwork, the FBI agents got call backs from Cypress Creek reloaders about a month after the test.

As in many of the nearly 125 boiler rooms that fell under Operation Disconnect, the FBI team returned again for a longer, more rigorous test, racking up even more counts of wire fraud. Each sale can be filed as a count of wire fraud. Each count, upon conviction, can draw a sentence of up to five years in federal prison.

Once it had collected the evidence against O'Neil and company the FBI team moved on to other telemarketing rooms, including several of their neighbors in Fort Lauderdale. When phone room owners called Sunbelt Diversified to check on the status of their autodialers FBI agents posing as Sunbelt employees stalled them. Eventually, the boiler-room operators lost faith in Sunbelt's ability. By that time, it didn't matter, the FBI had the evidence it needed captured on tape. The agents kept their evidence secret until the operation concluded, with FBI Director Sessions' press conference, almost exactly a year after the taping at Cypress Creek Promotions.

The convictions are still coming in from Operation Disconnect. As of August 1994, the sting had identified more than five hundred telemarketing racketeers, and prompted 320 indictments and 230 convictions, a tally certain to grow. The operation also resulted in the seizure of more than $10.5 million in cash, bank accounts, and other articles.

Consumer advocates, cheered though they are by the success, don't know whether the FBI intends to stay in the business of smashing telemarketing rooms. Others wonder about the lasting effects of the series of raids, worrying that the operation took out many of the elder statesmen of the phone racket—the 50 State generation—only to see their lieutenants take over and keep the con game alive.

The next generation of telemarketing kingpins concerns many regulators who fear they will take the racket to high-tech heights, a move that could leave law enforcement even further behind.

Only time will tell if Operation Disconnect unleashes a new apocalypse of phone fraud, much the same as the postal service raid on the granddaddy of boiler rooms did in 1981. But early reports from state consumer regulators are not encouraging. Despite greater awareness among law enforcement of the menace, complaints are not leveling off. Instead, new schemes are popping up in the hope that the FBI won't be able to mount another three-year undercover operation anytime soon.

Former FBI director Sessions, while clearly elated over the splashy sting, warned that the operation would not end the phone pillages. In remarks prepared for his news conference announcing the sting, he said:

> Illegal telemarketing schemes are only limited by the imaginations of their perpetrators and the susceptibility of the consuming public. While Operation Disconnect will ultimately close down a number of illegal operations across the country, telemarketers will move on and continue to use new schemes in new locations to defraud the public.

The FBI director's prediction came to pass quickly. FBI Deputy Assistant Director Fred Veringer, testifying at a U.S. Senate hearing in Washington, D.C., two weeks after the unveiling of Disconnect, said the FBI had heard of a woman being contacted by a telemarketer with a brand new bogus offer. Said Veringer:

> The telemarketer explained to her that he works for Operation Disconnect, our undercover operation. That will show you how fast they pick up on the issue at hand. And for a fee of $424, he can guarantee the return of the money she lost as a result of the illegal telemarketing. The woman did not send any money and immediately reported the incident to the consumer agency who contacted us. This is how fast they quickly adjust and move forward.

But the FBI official went on to make a statement that thrilled consumer advocates in the audience. "I would like to leave this final message for the illegal telemarketers. No longer will it be business as usual. The FBI is in the telemarketing business to stay."

Only time will tell the extent of the FBI's commitment.

18

Future Schlock

Patrick Craig sat in a Florida courtroom, one arm manacled to a secure juror's chair, the other folded in his lap. He was one of more than a dozen criminals awaiting sentencing on the afternoon calendar on a typical hot summer's day in 1994.

Craig, wearing a white golfing shirt and green slacks, hardly looked the part. Save for the handcuffs, he seemed harmless enough, like a kid barely able to fill out his moustache, which appeared a shade lighter than his dark brown, cropped hair.

But Craig was a veteran criminal, the brains behind a telemarketing fraud that netted more than $1.7 million. A high-school dropout, Craig started working the phones at age sixteen. He often boasted, according to prosecutors: "If I can get them on the phone for more than three minutes, I've got them sold."

Craig and a friend opened Galt Ocean Distributors from an oceanfront condo in Fort Lauderdale. It proved so lucrative that they quickly moved to a penthouse.

Between April and July 1992 the young men used the time-honored one-in-three prize scheme: a Lincoln Town Car, $40,000 in cash, or three pounds of gold. Buyers sent money, whatever they could afford, to pay the "taxes." Craig accepted personal checks which he laundered through a local check-cashing emporium.

Arrested on fraud charges, he drew probation, as many do for their first offense. That gave him little incentive to mend his ways, though it did persuade him to leave Florida. Craig moved back to his native Alabama, where he began calling his former victims, posing as an official of a Florida state agency investigating telephone fraud. Craig promised the victims he could get their money back if they sent him $1,000, much more in many cases.

Craig made the mistake of getting pulled over by a Mississippi Highway Patrol trooper in the fall of 1992, which turned up a Florida warrant for his arrest for violating his probation.

Seeking to make an example out of Craig, Florida prosecutors had him returned to the Sunshine State to stand trial. And they piled the charges on, slapping him with fifty-odd fraud counts. A few months shy of his twenty-seventh birthday, Craig pleaded guilty to the charges and drew a ten-year sentence. Because of chronic overcrowding in Florida's prison system, he'll likely serve two years or less.*

More than halfway across the country, Christopher Hess, twenty-one, a Nevada state-registered telemarketer, appeared before a justice of the peace in Las Vegas on a similar charge. Working at Maverick West Marketing, Inc. in Las Vegas, Hess phoned an eighty-one-year-old man and told him he would receive $32,000 if he sent in $1,600 to Maverick.

Hess also claimed to be affiliated with a government agency that shut down bad telemarketers and distributed the proceeds to victims. He, too, got caught. Hess pleaded guilty to a single count of felony theft in May 1994. He was sentenced to three years in prison, which was suspended, leaving four years probation. The sentence also forbids Hess from engaging in telemarketing.

Both men reflect the changing face of the telemarketing fraud epidemic. As the phone-scam progenitors—the 50 State crowd—wear out their welcome with law enforcement, a new generation springs up. Not only are many much younger, they also tend to be more mobile, international, difficult to track—and utterly merciless.

"Most of the people who we have been dealing with lately have been in their late teens or early twenties," says Nevada Deputy Attorney General Colette Rausch, who heads the telemarketing fraud task force in Las Vegas. "We are seeing a lot of young ones. They are mostly sales people who learned the trade and decided to go out on their own because they can make more money. That's the trend."

The recovery scam, which often stings elderly people hoping to recoup $20,000 or more lost to telemarketers, is perhaps the lowest of the long line of mean-spirited con jobs to break out of boiler rooms since the early 1980s. That the scam is a hit with the new wave of young freelancers, who can set up in a hotel room or apartment and be gone long before police catch on to them, worries authorities.

---

*State of Florida v. Patrick E. Craig, Seventeenth Judicial Circuit, Broward County, Florida No. 93-20394. Plea agreement, March 10, 1994.

The small recovery rooms began to rise up as regulators made inroads against large-scale phone parlors. Many of the massive prize scams that operated freely during the 1980s and early 1990s are scaling back to make themselves less obvious targets for law enforcers. Some are actually cleaning up their act slightly, or at least signing agreements with state regulators to refund money promptly to buyers who complain about high-pressure sales tactics. Others have closed in the wake of lawsuits filed by federal regulators. But like 50 State, each prize room that folds sends dozens of graduates out to keep the con alive.

In Buffalo, New York, another sweepstakes and prize scam hotspot, the leaner, meaner telemarketing outfits are worrisome because they are hard to track and discipline, says Assistant New York Attorney General Dennis Rosen.

"They just multiply like a cancer," Rosen concedes in an interview. "When we closed down one room with more than one hundred telemarketers, twenty to twenty-five of them went out on their own. I don't think any of them did the same volume of sales, but they go off on their own and copycat the scam. All you need to do is take the script and some lead sheets and you're in business."

In other areas of the country some authorities worry that the Lollapalooza generation, unsettled and unfocused, will find the temptation of easy money on the phones too tough to turn down. Some areas, such as South Florida, already have seen the results. Phone rooms in fancy suburban areas have hired high school students for summer jobs scamming old people, the unemployed, or young people in need of credit cards or other financial planning tools.

"All of these kids are coming up and seeing this easy money," says one Arizona telemarketer. "The kids get lured in so easily. The wolf of greed stands there as the kids come out the school doors."

In many ways the war on telephone boiler rooms can be likened to the war on drugs. The government measures the success of its anti-drug crusade by checking the supply of drugs on the street. When drugs are plentiful and cheap, enforcement efforts are judged to be failing. By that yardstick the war on telemarketing fraud most certainly is being lost.

Products pegged as scams in the mid to late 1980s—travel vouchers, for instance—still survive. The "newest" phone fraud fads noticed by authorities, the "recovery rooms," have in fact been around for years in one form or another. Other perennials such as overseas employment or precious metals will reappear should the economy sour.

Despite stepped up enforcement by the Federal Trade Commission, the FBI, and other agencies, the federal government cannot seem to move swiftly enough to wipe out the phone-con cottage industry.

Legislators are years behind in attacking the roots of the problem, a lax regulatory climate for business that all but invites illegal manipulation of the nation's banking and telecommunications networks.

Congress acts slowly. Take the laundering, or "factoring," of credit cards, for years a favorite means for the deceptive telemarketer to corrupt the financial system and steal billions of dollars. Visa pointed out the extent of the heist at congressional hearings in July 1987, December 1987, March 1988, and March 1989, by 1989 estimating annual losses of $100 million. Visa came back to testify again in June 1991, stressing that annual losses had climbed to $200 million. Two Visa-member banks reported losses that year from factoring of $2.5 million each. The banks suffered the losses because they had paid the telemarketer for the transactions only to later discover the deals were fraudulent. Because federal law allows a card holder to refuse payment for such charges, the banks had to absorb the loss, which they then pass on to their card holders in the form of higher fees.

Testifying in June 1991, Visa Security Director Dennis Brosan advocated a federal statute to outlaw the practice and impose criminal penalties.

> The federal criminal statutes, such as the mail fraud, wire fraud, and credit card fraud statutes, do not expressly address certain of the credit-card related aspects of telemarketing fraud. . . . Delay will only permit fraudulent telemarketers to rip off more innocent victims.

The credit card companies didn't get a statute that outlawed factoring, with criminal penalties that would deter merchants. Instead, the 1994 Telemarketing and Consumer Fraud and Abuse Prevention Act directs the Federal Trade Commission to write regulations prohibiting the practice, rules which should take effect some time in 1995. Like all violations of the FTC Act, the penalties will be civil, most probably fines, far less than the credit industry wanted.

Other banking schemes that assist shady telemarketers have not been addressed at all, even though they threaten an epidemic of thievery.

Auto-debiting of checking accounts is an example. Two U.S. House of Representatives committees in a joint hearing on June 21, 1991 exposed the growing menace from telemarketers, who had turned to asking customers for their checking-account numbers as many grew wary of giving out their credit-card digits over the phone. The telemarketers used the numbers to prepare sight drafts that were accepted by banks for payment. U.S. Rep. Ron Wyden, of Oregon, made clear the high stakes in an opening statement. He said:

> Even though millions of Americans believe that a withdrawal from their checking account cannot be made without their written consent this deposit draft scam that we are exposing today is allowing personal checking accounts to be tapped without the owner's permission. By the time the consumer gets his bank statement and learns that the money has been taken, the telemarketer can be long gone. . . . Experts tell the subcommittee that even though this new electronic heist is only a few months old, it has already cost consumers hundreds of millions of dollars.

Years after that hearing exposed the problem, auto-debiting continues. Manipulation of the banking system by telemarketers threatens to get worse as some of the phone operations turn overseas for high-tech support systems and new suckers.

International credit-card factoring rings already have begun circumventing U.S. laws, and most consumer regulators expect these schemes to worsen. Others predict that telemarketers will locate offshore, either to rob the U.S. market outside of the reach of American authorities, or to export schlock products to other countries. Already, travel certificates are turning up in the former Soviet Union, as are some investment scams.

"International telemarketing is on the horizon. There will be a huge wave of telephone fraud in eastern Europe," says Eileen Harrington, associate director for marketing practices of the Federal Trade Commission. "They are changing over to a market economy and getting universal phone service, and they are very vulnerable to deception, even more than in this country where people have been getting ripped off for years."

Harrington says some people in these countries "have been waiting for phone service for ten years and the notion that the telephone can be used to con people is beyond what they can imagine. They just are not used to being lied to in this way."

Harrington said demand for telemarketing standards such as low-interest credit cards will zoom in these countries and "anybody with an advance-fee loan scam could make a killing. It is a very tough challenge for law enforcement."

Barry Cutler, of the FTC, testifying in a March 1993 U.S. Senate hearing, worried that the global spread of telemarketing frauds will combine with new technology to help subvert the banking system.

> As we get to the point where with cable television you can show a thirty-minute infomercial in ten different countries in Europe at the same time and use the telephone in the next few years to make an electronic funds transfer, where you do not have the paper trail that you do with the credit cards, checks and money orders, this is the problem that we are getting a handle on none too soon, because pretty soon not only will the problem have expanded globally, but the techniques to follow the money when you are using electronic fund transfers are going to be infinitely more difficult than chasing a check or a credit card charge through the banking system.

Many other consumer regulators expect advances in fiber optics to cause international phone charges to plummet in coming years, opening new vistas for phone vipers.

"We are starting to talk about how to be alert for these things," says Susan Grant, executive director of the National Association of Consumer Agency Administrators. "We're seeing offers for goods that are using international phone numbers, or U.S. phone numbers which are being forwarded out of the country. It's a new global marketplace, and the enforcement problems are crossing borders."

Grant says that few international accords exist setting standards for unfair or deceptive trade practices, or resolving disputes with merchants. "We worry that consumers presented with global shopping won't think about whether they have any recourse when something goes wrong. It's hard enough in the United States when we have sales abuses. International sales are even more complicated. It's a daunting problem."

Another major worry among the regulators is the little-policed information superhighway, which they see as having unlimited potential for wire fraud, from pyramid investment schemes to employment scams.

"We can expect that as people start to use their home computers more, we will see the con artists switch gears. The fraud scheme will be conveyed on computers," says Grant, whose group represents consumer regulators across the country. "This is an unregulated frontier."

While the Internet has a decidedly noncommercial history it is subject to manipulation by con artists. Several state and federal regulatory agencies, including the FTC, have filed civil cases against marketers who used deceptive sales pitches to hawk products on the Internet.

The FTC moved quickly to crack down on one alleged cyberspace con in the fall of 1994, signing a consent decree with Brian Corzine, who used the name Chase Consulting to sell a $99 credit repair program through an online service. The company advised consumers to take steps such as falsifying credit applications, steps the company described as "100 percent legal." They weren't according to the FTC. Chase in signing the consent decree paid $1,917 to reimburse customers and agreed to refrain from using deceptive pitches in the future.*

Not everybody thinks the telemarketing cons will flee the mainland or develop high-tech hocus-pocus to evade the law. Some regulators expect them to gradually abandon states that have become closely connected with phone cons, such as Florida, California, and Nevada, for areas where law enforcement may be even more tolerant.

Many of the Las Vegas boiler rooms have taken this step, setting up satellites in Louisiana and Oklahoma, among other states. One set up shop in Louisiana promising prizes of up to $75,000 to victims who would send in payments for the "taxes," a familiar ploy. The room, where managers rang cowbells every time they racked up a sale, took in more than $1 million in less than a month in late 1993. After scamming the victims with the prize scheme, the sales room passed their names on to a Las Vegas recovery room, where other telemarketers called them and promised to get their money back for a fee of $2,000.

The Louisiana room was raided, resulting in thirteen arrests. But regulators and some veterans in the field are not so sure that other states will prove able to crack down on phone cons.

One Arizona marketer said in an interview he expects to see some of the worst scam artists leave the larger states and head to areas of the country where economic conditions are poor and the telemarketer can become a major player in the local business community. "They are going to be leaving Fort Lauderdale and Phoenix and going to places where they can hire the daughter of the local judge and other relatives of other officials who have never made big money. Telemarketing can pay the whole town real well and that will keep them out of trouble. Rural America is going to be the heir to telemarketing operations," he says.

Wherever they locate, it's a cinch that the phone pros will become a spreading plague among the baby-boom generation, for years the people who perhaps had the least to fear from the phone scam.

*FTC v. Chase Consulting, U.S. District Court for the Eastern District of California, Sacramento, No. CIV-S-94-1446.

More and more, harried forty-somethings can expect to be caught in the middle, trying to protect naive kids and their elderly parents from being conned.

This is the true scourge of the telemarketing racket, as anyone who has tried to untangle telephone transactions on behalf of an elderly relative can readily attest. Similarly, many phone rooms report an upsurge in younger victims, collegiates, and sometimes high schoolers, who have credit cards or checking accounts to plunder. "I would say this is the number-one consumer problem in this country for its monetary impact and the intrusion that it has into people's lives," says Charles Burson, Tennessee Attorney General and 1994 president of the National Association of Attorneys General. "It has more significant impact than any other scam out there. The losses can be devastating."

The losses extend beyond money. Middle-aged children agonize over ways to prevent their parents from being robbed of their life's savings and their self-esteem. For some families, late-night sales calls from ruthless telemarketers have caused emotional rifts not easily bridged.

FBI Deputy Assistant Director Fred Verinder took note of the problem at a March 1993 U.S. Senate Committee hearing, saying: "Personal consequences of these frauds can be devastating." He continued:

> Just recently, the daughter of an elderly victim contacted the FBI to inquire if we could help and do anything to stop the telemarketers from constantly contacting her father. She and her brothers and sisters realized that the father had been defrauded of $25,000 through a contest where he was told that he had won a car. She explained that her father was so convinced by the scam artist that his own children were unable to stop him from continually sending more funds to these individuals. The matter, she explained, was taking a toll on the marriage, taking a toll on the relationship with the children, and depleted his savings. Some victims have lost everything they have, all in pursuit of those tantalizing offers made by telemarketers.

New York Assistant Attorney General Charlie Donaldson said the elderly often side with telemarketers who are draining their bank accounts when their children try to intervene. While nobody has statistics on the phenomenon, some liken it to the tendency for kidnap victims to identify, after a time, with their captors. Consumer regulators tell stories of talking elderly buyers out of dealing with a telemarketer, only to find out later that the telemarketer called back and saved the sale.

Others interviewed report that complaints filed by adult children on behalf of their parents often can be tough for authorities to investigate. "We get complaints from children a lot, but the older people get very upset to have us poking into their affairs," Donaldson says. Elderly parents are embarrassed to admit they were taken and are "more concerned about us looking into their affairs" than about their losses. "People get angry when authorities start messing in their lives," he says.

Donaldson understands a parent's need to maintain self-worth by appearing to be in control of his or her finances and daily living needs.

"Even though I've been practicing law twenty years, my own mother gives me no credibility whatsoever when it comes to finances. Parents think, they changed your diapers, what do you know? I hope that when I'm that old I won't be so blind."

A New Jersey man, who asked that his name be kept confidential, maintained a running log of the hours he spent trying to undo dozens of telemarketing transactions. All of the sales occurred after a family member went to court to obtain power of attorney for the elderly victim, his father-in-law.

The family was shocked to learn that many telemarketers refused to send refunds even after hearing that the old man was not competent to handle his affairs. With a total monthly income of $2,350, the man had fallen more than $8,000 in debt to phone sharks, mostly from Las Vegas.

The New Jersey man arrived at the old man's apartment to help him clean up only to discover mysterious boxes scattered around in the closet. Looking further, he found bottles of fire retardant chemicals, cases and cases of vitamins, and what seemed to be thousands of cheap pens bearing the inscription "Say No to Drugs."

Throughout the apartment he spotted bills for subscriptions to magazines, one of the latest of the telemarketing ruses. The old man was paying about twenty dollars a month for four magazines he never read. Meanwhile, doctors were hounding him to pay medical bills.

Despite the power of attorney, the elderly man gave telemarketers the digits to three credit cards he owned, and all three charged to their limit from playing prize sweepstakes. He also ran up hundreds of dollars in phone charges for calling 900 numbers to find out which prize he had won.

The man expected to win $150,000 any day and thus cared little about the charges. He was so thoroughly in the grip of the con artist that he became angry when anyone sought to set him straight. Hoping to spare his father-in-law's feelings, the younger man backed off temporarily.

"Although he really needs every dollar I can get back for him, he is afraid of jeopardizing his chances of winning (in his mind) if I get in touch with any of the companies," the son-in-law wrote in his computer diary. "Against my better judgment, I agreed not to contact (the company)."

But the more he dug into his father-in-law's finances the more he realized something had to be done, feelings or no. The elderly man had tried to get a bank loan to pay for more telemarketers, but was turned down. He already had taken out a home equity loan, only to forward the funds to fraud artists phoning from Las Vegas.

The younger man realized what he was up against when he began calling the companies to demand that they remove the credit card charges. Most responded only after he threatened legal action and reminded the "customer service" department of the power of attorney.

Several companies tried to justify the swindle by playing him a verification tape of the old man agreeing to buy the products, a standard means to intimidate buyers who demand a refund. "The manner of speaking of the person on the tape was very patronizing and she spoke like she was talking to a five-year-old," he wrote. He spotted the deceptions quite easily, something the elderly man, who became confused easily, could not do. On tape, the old man repeatedly said he did not want to receive a watch, comments the verifier ignored.

"They never told him the chances of winning. They implied that there was an equal chance of winning each one of the three prizes. When he said he didn't want the watch they never told him his chances were 9,999 of 10,000, or greater that he would win the watch."

When the son-in-law confronted a company manager, the firm offered to refund half the money and take the old man off their sales list. He accepted. The Vegas huckster complained bitterly to the young man that he had already paid sales commissions to the telemarketer and would lose money on the deal!

Gradually, the son-in-law got the elderly man out of debt and weaned him from dictating credit card numbers over the phone.

Frank Dowd, a Washington, D.C., research librarian, had a tougher time after his father lost more than $20,000. The father had watched his wife of forty-six years, who suffered from Alzheimer's disease, be taken to a nursing home. He was depressed, in ill health, and a prime target of phony telephone charities. He got more than ten calls and sometimes more than fifty pieces of mail in a day. Couriers came out to his Michigan home and picked up his checks, which were forwarded to telemarketers in Las Vegas.

Dowd managed to get about $5,000 refunded but only after he and a cousin "spent a huge amount of energy and ran up tremendous phone bills." Testifying before a U.S. Senate committee, Dowd said: "These people are relentless. And after they barrage you several times a day for weeks on end your resistance is worn down, particularly in my father's case where he was lonely. He just liked to talk to somebody."

The need to talk to somebody has kept the telemarketing con game alive for more than a decade. How to bond with their prey is the first lesson a phone pro must learn. It might be as simple as remembering the names of the victim's grandchildren or trading upon common political beliefs. In other cases, telemarketers might closely study a client's employment history and past investments before moving in for the kill.

Most of all, though, the marketers must find new ways to make the victims feel special, to tell them they have won the grand prize or a chance of a lifetime.

"Every time consumers get ripped off they say they were talked into it by a soothing, even seductive voice," says one phone pro interviewed. "That's why we would train people to use opening lines that tell our customers what wonderful people they are. They won't hang up after they hear that, and sooner or later they will make a purchase. If you know how to talk to people they will buy anything you want to sell."

Many experts expect a rise in telemarketing schemes that blend the tried-and-true appeal to loneliness and low self-esteem with desires to find others with similar interests and beliefs. That's likely to spur a rise in computer groups, organizations formed to sell and collect goods from antiques to hip art work, and social clubs and investment deals catering to people of similar ethnic background or political views. Also at risk are recent immigrants with a poor command of English, who are unlikely to know where to complain. Many con artists feel members of "affinity" groups are far less likely to complain to authorities than the general public.

Some con artists will respond to stepped-up government enforcement by moving into schemes that by their nature leave victims unlikely to complain.

One such fertile area is selling expertise as "private investigators" who conduct background checks or perform other services, from debt collection to spying. How many people will later admit they were scammed by a company they hired to check out a fiancé's claims, perhaps using illegal means?

Drawing buyers into schemes of questionable legality offers the con artist a cloak. One telemarketing enterprise that turned up in late 1994 with a "confidential" offer seemed to be following this pattern.

The company hawked phony college degrees, saying most of its clients were successful businessmen who never had the chance to attend college or were forced to drop out for lack of money. For sale at about one hundred dollars, bachelor's or master's degrees from six make-believe colleges. If none of those would do, the company's order form contained a blank space for the buyer to write in the name of any college he or she wanted printed on the diploma. "There are no classes, there are no correspondence courses and no tuition," the sales literature read.

The company didn't stop with the degree. It also sold college rings, which could be imprinted with the year of graduation for five hundred dollars. The firm described itself as a seller of "novelty items" for entertainment only, according to sales literature. But the order form also noted that the merchandise was "very realistic in appearance" and it also included a testimonial from an unnamed Dallas company manager who said the phony master's degree he ordered "fooled my whole staff."

While some telephone scams are likely to pick fresh victims from among affinity groups or use a craftier and less caustic pitch, others are taking the opposite tack. They are instructing their new hires to stick with a pleasant sales pitch only if it works; if not, they become aggressive, hoping to bully old people into buying.

Nasty mutations of this style have begun to turn up, some of them seemingly impossible to control. Two such cases out of Florida making national headlines during 1994 not only proved embarrassing for state prison officials, but also painful for victims.

In one case, an inmate at the Palm Beach County Jail, who apparently had plenty of time on his hands and privileges to use a pay telephone, bothered a ninety-one-year-old man with repeated collect phone calls to his home. Inmates are permitted only to call collect, but the elderly man said he accepted the charges out of curiosity.

Apparently working with an accomplice on the outside, the caller demanded that the old man leave $2,000 outside his door. The caller, who used a fake Jamaican accent, said he had a .357 magnum and would kill the man if he failed to comply. Fortunately, the man was able to call the phone company, which installed a locator on the line and traced the calls to the county jail. No arrest was made.

In a second case, Florida corrections officials tried in vain to explain how an inmate serving time for credit card fraud managed to keep the ring alive while in the St. Lucie County Jail. Even after prosecutors learned of the scheme and alerted jailers, they refused to take away the inmate's telephone privileges. That would take a court order, jail officials told the Associated Press on February 2, 1994.

The inmate, who spent two hours or more on the phone some days making deals, used stolen credit card numbers to purchase more than $130,000 worth of goods, ranging from computers to children's clothes to ceramic tile.

On those rare occasions when telemarketers get hauled into court to face criminal charges, they often mount an "I'm-just-a-good-salesman" defense. They might admit to stretching the truth a bit to make a sale, but insist that "puffing the product" is common to advertising and sales campaigns.

"American salesmanship is on trial here," one defense lawyer intoned in opening remarks at a phone scammer's trial on federal wire fraud charges. "Telemarketing is a concept born and bred in America. It's unique to us. We developed it and every single day it is being done."

This line of reasoning trots out the adage "buyer beware" to absolve the marketer of any duty to sell a product fairly and truthfully. The line goes on to imply that government efforts to attack telemarketing fraud waste resources that should be spent fighting "real crimes," such as rape and murder.

While this view seems to be changing in law enforcement, it is not without supporters. The observer can detect it readily in some consumer regulators and police who shrug in disbelief that anyone "could be so stupid" as to fall for a phone scam. Others hint that most victims are motivated by greed and deserve what they get. The cynicism seems to be bred from frustration over seeing scam after scam, year after year, and feeling little support from the public to crack down.

Overcoming this inertia is half the battle against the telemarketing fraud menace. Government must come to view boiler rooms as an organized criminal conspiracy to defraud the public, and deal with it accordingly. Surely, nobody can doubt that the telemarketing con, though mainly a cottage industry of loosely affiliated outlets, steals billions of dollars every year.

Law enforcement must break away from the notions of the past. One fallacy is that telemarketers are best handled by civil authorities. For years in South Florida, criminal authorities generally were reluctant to move against any phone room in the absence of clear evidence that the telemarketer sent no product for the money collected.

The phone pirates knew that so long as they sent their victims something, no matter how cheap or underwhelming, they stood a very, very small chance of getting carted off to jail. They knew they could count on the fact that few law enforcement agencies were likely to put out the time and effort to build a criminal case.

Letting the boiler-room community know that law enforcement is determined to pursue criminal charges against fraudulent telemarketers would make many young recruits reconsider signing up. More states need to follow Iowa's lead and haul telemarketers calling from faraway states into their court system on criminal fraud charges. Iowa also has increased penalties for fraud against the elderly, the most vulnerable of victims.

At the federal level, the critical area for cracking down on nationwide sales schemes, some agency needs to take the lead. The public should not have to rely on the Federal Trade Commission's civil suits as its main line of defense against being fleeced. While the agency has filed more than one hundred lawsuits against telemarketers since the 1980s, thousands of companies have escaped without penalty.

The states need some means to help assure that anybody with fifty dollars and a few phones cannot open up a boiler room without risking some jail time. If the means to that end is licensing laws and bonding requirements, then enact them and police them. Subject state-licensed telemarketers to surprise inspections and require their books and complaint files be open for inspection. Threaten scofflaws with revocation of their license.

Randy Prillaman, FBI Special Agent in Charge of Las Vegas, rattled off a number of ideas in testimony before a U.S. Senate committee hearing in Las Vegas in October 1993.

He said telemarketing companies should be required to identify their true owners and be subject to audits. Owners should be responsible for the sales pitches used by their employees and the use of aliases should be prohibited, he said, adding that victims' rights should be paramount.

Legislators also need to do a better job balancing the rights of legitimate telemarketers against the need to protect the public from ruthless scams. Industry lobbyists too often stave off tougher regulation, creating more chances for phone fraud. Congress seems to have a tough time matching wits with the well-funded telemarketing and business lobbies. Can't they at least grant appropriations to states infested with telemarketers to fund sophisticated anti-fraud units?

State lawmakers in active boiler-room states need to respond far more swiftly as well. The Sunshine State, where many consumer advocates fear the legislature is solidly in the grip of business lobbyists, needs to declare open war on this blight.

Perhaps more than any other state, Florida, whose phone operations have stung the forty-nine other states, owes it to the nation to crack down. That debt may well go unpaid, judging from the resilience of rip-off products such as the travel certificate. More than four hundred travel boiler rooms came and went during the late 1980s. Dozens of others did much the same during the early 1980s, causing millions of dollars in losses.

But Florida travel boiler rooms sell in the 1990s with little to fear. One vacation "cert" palace fed dozens of boiler rooms nationwide that rang up sales approaching $25 million a year in the early 1990s. Late in the summer of 1994, a state legislative committee decided to hold hearings to decide, if indeed, Florida travel certificates are a problem!

And let's not forget the helping hands, that group of upright businesses that comfortably become conduits for scams. Some examples: private mail drops that give a boiler room an instant address and "suite" number; newspapers that print suspect advertising; the phone companies, which will connect service to anyone no questions asked; the overnight courier services and the countless printers and credit processors that keep the fraud network alive.

The Better Business Bureau system, the first line of defense against phone fraud, needs to redouble its efforts. Unfortunately, some bureaus are responding to lean economic times by moving into product endorsements and costly 900 lines that turn off the public and impede the flow of information about scam artists.

That stingy flow of information remains a major problem. No system, public or private, exists to give consumers even the most basic information about the reliability of a company that approaches them by phone. This is inexcusable at a time when the business community can at the touch of a button call up dossiers on millions of Americans. While public education campaigns hold great promise for teaching the public to avoid the telltale signs of a telemarketing scam, nothing substitutes for easy access to free, unbiased data on people peddling these wares. It goes without saying that some victims would have thought twice about making a purchase had they known the reassuring voice on the line belonged to a fraud artist.

Let's not be naive. Even if all of these changes were enacted overnight, there still would be people around to reach out and tap somebody else's bank account. Government lacks the power to alter the dark mental state of those drawn toward a racket that they know can cause so much misery.

Many are talented, intelligent people, but twisted somehow into joining a subculture of reprobates who delight in beating the system, regardless of the consequences for their victims, and without remorse.

"I think that if they made the money legitimately they wouldn't be as happy," says Charlie Donaldson of the New York Attorney General's Office. "They have to prove to the rest of us that they are smarter than we are."

Other regulators interviewed who have fought the boiler-room badguys for the better part of two decades are weary of seeing the traits over and over.

"We can see a gleam in their eye when we ask them how they did it," says Gary Austin, a U.S. Postal Service inspector in Honolulu. "What's pathetic is they get real excited even after they are caught when they talk about their schemes."

Says Austin: "Their thought process is different than most of us. They get a kick out of talking people into things. They just want everyone to buy into a cockeyed scheme."

South Florida prosecutor Scott Dressler agrees that the chances are small of reforming many members of the boiler-room herd. For years, he has seen them steal vast sums only to waste their gains on drugs, drinks, other vices, or life on the edge.

"Oftentimes they have no bank account, or savings or anything to show for it," Dressler says. "These guys are the lowest form of life on this earth. They take people's life savings without batting an eye. They are very bold. When they shake your hand, their other hand is in your pocket."

But without willing victims the con artist would have no way to make a living. Don't join the parade of telemarketing victims who let greed overcome good judgment. Remember: as trite as it sounds, the old adage will always be true: if a deal seems too good to be true, it is!

Appendix A

Thirty-Five Scams

Telemarketers have unleashed an apocalypse of scams, a few of which can cheat almost anyone who is not wary of buying over the phone. Many of these products spread around the country as sales agents leave one boiler room, taking a sales script with them, and set up their own version. Others come and go depending on the economy, unemployment rate, or latest crazes.

Advance Fee Loans: In this scheme, telemarketers promise people with poor credit loans in exchange for an advance payment, or registration fee, usually about two hundred dollars. The loans never appear. These schemes, although illegal in some states, tend to appear when the economy turns sour.

Advertising Specialties (Ad-Specs): Many legitimate companies sell keychains, pens, and other gizmos to businesses, which have them imprinted with the firm's name and give them away to customers. But telemarketing con artists in the early 1980s began selling cheap ad-specs, with the promise of a prize, a scheme that evolved into the phony sweepstakes, perhaps the nation's most nettlesome phone scam. The ad-spec rooms sell an order of cheap pens for about $399 by implying the company owner will receive a valuable prize, such as a luxury car, which turns out to be a ten-dollar watch or other booby prize.

Appointment Setting: A local business phones customers saying they have a work crew in the area and can stop by to perform a service or inspection at a discount price. The appointment is a ruse to gain entry to the house, where the customer will be pressured to buy some expensive, often unneeded, device or repair. The elderly often are victims.

Artworks: Telemarketers hawk supposed "limited edition" artworks of famous artists as investments, some of them bearing fake signatures or bogus "certificates of authenticity." The artworks, which sell for between $500 and $5,000, usually are worth fifty dollars or less. One company, shut down in January 1992 by federal officials, sold more than $11 million in these prints through a network of boiler rooms in cities across the country.

Bogus Better Business Bureau: Several boiler rooms, beginning in the early 1980s in Las Vegas, have filed papers incorporating names that closely resemble Better Business Bureau. One phone room installed a line for the "Better Business Bureau of America," and when customers called, they gave themselves a superb reference. A similar scheme surfaced in Toronto, Ontario, in 1994, when a gemstone scam used an "International Better Business Bureau." The phone was answered in an apartment connected to the scheme and callers were given an enthusiastic reference.

Business Opportunities: Many telemarketing con artists advertise "biz opps" in newspapers, hoping to sucker people who dream of owning their own small business. The possibilities are infinite, but many pitches are for product distributorships. Many states require sellers of business opportunities to register their offerings and provide details of their background and previous sales histories.

Business Phone Directory: A small business receives a bill from a company for about $150 for placing an ad in a directory, which doesn't exist. The return address is a mail drop, often in South Florida. The scam artist hopes the company will simply pay the bill without asking questions.

Campground/Condominium Timeshares: Owners of timeshares buy the right to occupy a vacation property a certain number of weeks a year. Owners of timeshares are approached by telemarketers who pose as brokers able to sell timeshares on behalf of owners, usually for an upfront fee of five hundred dollars or more. One Colorado company in six weeks bilked consumers out of $227,000 with the ruse. These schemes have also operated from Florida in recent years. In a variation, telemarketers sell advance space at campgrounds for persons with recreational vehicles.

Coins: Once a hobby for kids, rare coins became a trendy investment in the 1980s, leading to numerous telemarketing frauds. Many companies began using phony grading systems, which grossly overvalued the coins and lied to customers about the risks of these investments.

College Diplomas: Some "novelty" companies sell extremely realistic bachelor's, master's and doctor of philosophy degrees for about $100. The marketers insist their product is for amusement only, but slyly hint how tough their products are to tell from the true article.

College Scholarships: Phone rooms contact parents of high schoolers nearing graduation and offer worthless material on how to obtain scholarships, often for as much as two hundred dollars. Most of the material is either outdated or too general to be of any assistance. Some offer a money back guarantee, but impose conditions to get a refund that cannot be met.

Credit Cards: Many telemarketing offers peddle credit cards to buyers with poor financial histories. Some of these deals offer the customer a list of "low-interest" credit cards for about one hundred dollars that turns out to be little more than a list of banks that can be had for free elsewhere.

Credit Repair: These schemes target people recently denied credit. The telemarketer purchases a list of thousands of names of people turned down for credit or chronically late in paying their bills (such lists are legal to sell). The marketer claims to be able to fix poor credit ratings for a fee, which has ranged from fifty to one thousand dollars. In fact, only time will heal damaged credit ratings, so buyers get nothing for their money.

Dirt Pile: Telemarketers seek investors, often for thousands of dollars, in unprocessed dirt from a mine, which is guaranteed to contain large amounts of gold or other precious metals. Some of these schemes collect money up front but do not promise any return on the investment for at least a year. By that time, the scam artists and the investors' money are long gone. These enterprises often assemble elaborate sales brochures and testimonials from experts who turn out to be bogus.

Doctors' Office: A Las Vegas company in late 1994 began sending doctors' offices bills for $256.88 for medical supplies never ordered or delivered. The company's address listed on the billings turned out to be a mail drop. The idea is that the company will pay the bills without question.

Fly and Buy: This is a favorite Florida scam that often takes investors for more than ten thousand dollars. The victims answer ads for a franchise or business opportunity in their local newspaper and call a Florida boiler room for more details. At some point, the company offers to fly the client down to tour the factory or facility, where he or she faces a hard sell. Many times, the corporate offices are merely fronts to con the investors. Once clients return home, the firm goes out of business, taking their money.

Free Film: This scam dates all the way back to the early mail order Las Vegas houses that sent cash on delivery (C.O.D.). The buyers in the early 1980s would be told that they got free film for life. They were not told that the processing fees were so expensive that they lost money using the free offer. The free film surfaced again almost a decade later as part of a 900 number promotion.

Gemstones: Boiler rooms, many of them in southern California, sell low-grade stones to investors for a few thousand dollars to tens of thousands, claiming they are excellent, low-risk investments. The gems are vastly overpriced and some of them are sold with fake certificates or appraisals attesting to the inflated value of the stones. In recent years, many of these schemes have located in Canada.

General Partnership: Telemarketers call small investors and sell them units in a general partnership, often some esoteric field from rare-mineral mining to exotic animal breeding. Investors plunk down several thousand dollars and are invited to a general partnership meeting at which managing partners are elected. But the promoter through manipulation of proxies keeps control over the operation and investors lose everything. Many regulators believe such partnerships are a ruse to avoid securities registration laws. Officials advise consumers to investigate the promoters of any such offer carefully before investing.

Nigerian Government Letter: This scam, reported to have started in Great Britain, has suckered people for more than $200 million worldwide. In June 1992 it took the form of an "urgent and confidential" business proposal from Lagos, Nigeria. The recipient is asked to give permission to allow the transfer of $36 million in petroleum revenues to his or her account. Later versions said the money was left over from a contract to refurbish the country's phone system. Either way, the recipient is promised 30 percent of the gross and is asked to fax to Nigeria their bank-account numbers so the money can be transmitted. Instead, the scam artists use the account numbers to drain the sucker's bank account.

Overseas Employment: This scam also turns up in hard economic times, promising unemployed people jobs overseas at salaries that are too good to be true. The marketer collects an advance fee of from four hundred to six hundred dollars as a deposit, usually asking that the money be sent by overnight courier to reserve a job. This scam turns off even some veteran telemarketers because it preys on people recently laid off from their jobs or down on their luck.

Precious Metals: Many of these deals are sold on a leveraged basis, requiring the buyer to borrow money for purchases of metals such as gold, silver, or platinum. Telemarketers often falsely claim that these deals are low in risk, when the opposite is true. A number of these firms charge outrageous commissions that will eat up most of an investment.

Prize Offers: Many telemarketing deals offer some sort of prize to induce people to buy junk products at grossly inflated prices. The most common is the "one-in-five." In this scheme, buyers are misled into thinking they will win one of five great prizes if they agree to purchase. The prizes are listed in an order making it appear to the customer that the least valuable is an award such as a two-thousand-dollar shopping spree. In fact, almost everyone receives what telemarketers call a "gimme gift," usually a cheap watch or piece of junk jewelry. Many customers receive nothing at all. The prize scheme can sting people for tens of thousands of dollars because the phone rooms "reload" customers, selling them over and over with offers of prizes. Many states have laws forbidding a sweepstakes from requiring a purchase to receive an award, but many telemarketers ignore the law.

Radon Test Kits: National news coverage warning of the dangers of radon—a colorless, odorless gas that can seep into the foundations of homes—caught the attention of the boiler rooms, which began selling radon abatement services supposedly approved by the U.S. Environmental Protection Agency. Some swindlers offered to sell the kits, others promised on-site inspections for a fee.

Recovery Rooms: These boiler rooms purchase names of people who have lost large sums, often $20,000 or more, to previous telemarketing offers. They call the victims, often posing as employees or affiliates of a government agency, and promise them they can get their money back if they send the marketer a fee, often about $2,000.

Telefunding: These offers sprang up in 1993 after authorities began cracking down on the prize sweepstakes rooms in Las Vegas. Posing as representatives of charities, telemarketers promised prizes in exchange for donations to charity. Many of the charities are suspect, or have signed contracts with the telemarketers giving them 90 percent or more of the money collected.

Toner Scam: An invoice arrives from an office supply center company, often in California, for about $325 for copying-machine toner. Sometimes these companies call in advance to determine who does the supply ordering and secure a name, then address the invoice to that person. The products never were ordered or received. The scam artists hope that an accountant will see the invoice and pay it without asking any questions. This scam has run mainly from southern California, but several operations have been based in South Florida. The National Office Machine Business Dealers Association in Chicago keeps track of violators.

Travel Certificate: This is a true telemarketing perennial which takes many forms. Often buyers are contacted saying they've been "selected" to receive a dream vacation to the Bahamas, Cancun, or Hawaii. The buyers think they have won a trip, but gradually discover hidden fees and other charges that make the trip a bad deal at about five hundred dollars. Many certificate companies operate on a principle called "breakage," meaning that they sell far more of the travel coupons than they plan to honor. For this reason, buyers of certificates often find it difficult to schedule their trips or face other stall tactics.

Unordered Merchandise: Consumers receive a phone call, mailing, or fill out a coupon clipped from a newspaper promising a free gift. The article arrives along with an unexpected bill. The marketer hopes that many people will pay the bill and may send threatening notices if the bill is not remitted. However, federal regulations allow anyone to keep unordered merchandise received through the mail. Regulators advise that anyone who decides to keep unordered merchandise is wise to write the company a letter saying as much as a precaution against receiving dunning notices.

U.S. Government Publication: A company charges a small fee, usually $9.95, for copies of official publications that can be had for free from a government office. Favorite targets are Social Security and Medicare guides. The practice is legal but many people don't realize they are paying for a free guide.

Vending Machines: While many vending machines sales companies are legitimate, a number of telemarketers have taken up the trade, using false promises to rob small investors of millions of dollars. After putting down several thousand dollars for an "exclusive" territory, for example, an investor discovers several other people have been sold the same routes.

Water Testing/Purifier: Water purifiers have been favorite telemarketing products for many years. Typically, the devices, worth about thirty dollars, are sold for up to five hundred dollars, often in tandem with the offer of a prize. Telemarketers often lie to customers by telling them the devices are approved or endorsed by the U.S. government.

Wireless Cable: By the spring of 1992, boiler rooms selling spaces in the Federal Communications Commission's lottery for cable television franchises had collected more than $50 million from investors sold spaces in the lottery, usually for about five thousand dollars each. Even if the investor wins, which is highly unlikely, it is no guarantee of huge profits. Most boiler rooms greatly exaggerate the chances of obtaining a lease and its worth. The scheme is similar to lease scams for oil and gas drilling on federal land in the early 1980s. Other such scams include cellular telephones or licenses to operate specialized mobile radio systems.

Work at Home: These deals talk people, usually housewives, into sending in several hundred dollars for equipment to set up a business working out of their homes. Some have collected fees for nonexistent "certifying" boards. Others greatly exaggerate the amount of money to be made in enterprises such as sewing at home.

Appendix B

Sample Sales Pitch

Cypress Creek Promotions, an illegal Florida telemarketing company, used this promotion to sell advertising specialty items such as bumper stickers and pens and pencils for from $399 and up. The scam was a "one-in-six" prize promotion in which buyers are led to believe they will receive an expensive prize if they purchase the products. Almost everyone gets the pendant or the watch, for which the marketers pay from ten to sixty dollars.

Federal prosecutors said the pitch was laden with lies and other deceptions. The company listed the "shopping spree" last among the prizes to dupe buyers into believing the least valuable award was worth two thousand dollars. The sales catalogue mentioned in the pitch did not exist. Cypress Creek rang up more than $3 million in sales before FBI agents shut it down. A federal grand jury in Fort Lauderdale convicted Cypress Creek Promotions owner Tim O'Neil on wire fraud charges in June 1994. While it focused on small business customers, the company also sold to members of the general public, often over and over, until they had lost thousands of dollars.

Some customers were called because they filled out a card at a trade show or restaurant to win a prize, apparently not realizing that the slips would be sold repeatedly to boiler rooms. Here's the pitch:

Hi! is this (*name of customer*)? Yeah, this is (*salesperson's phone name*) with Cypress Creek Promotions in Fort Lauderdale, Florida. How are you doing? Good!!! Tell you the reason for the call. A while back you filled out a 3 x 5 entry card at a trade show, a home show or something out there, or somebody might have given your name for one of our promotional award drawing sweepstakes giveaways. Do you recall that? Anyway, we've got some good news for you. Your entry made it all the way to the finals. We are down to six major awards and a handful of people on the whole promotion, and you're one. That's pretty exciting wouldn't you say? (*Get a positive response*)

I'm supposed to go over the awards with you and the other finalists. So get a pen and I'm going to go over the awards.
　　1. A brand new 1992 Jeep Wrangler.
　　2. 12-foot Ranger Bass Boat with an outboard motor. That's always good if you like to go fishing, or you can give it to someone for a gift, whatever you want to do.
　　3. A satellite dish that gets 72 channels from Santa-Link. You know what those are? If you like the movies or sports those are always nice.
　　4. A. Two-and-a-half-karat diamond and sapphire pendant on a 14-karat gold chain.
　　　　B. Priceless Spanish Atocha real coin from the Mel Fisher Collection.
　　5. Diamond and gold man's watch.
　　6. Two-thousand-dollar shopping spree at a local supermarket.

Now I'm sure you're wondering what we want you to do. We're going to ask you to do two things, and I know you can live with both of those. Number one, when you get your award out there, we need you to have your picture taken and send it in. We want to use you in our catalog. Also the manufacturers donate a portion of the awards to us. That's why we do a catalog with the picture because they can get free publicity. Secondly, we are Cypress Creek Promotions. We are an advertising speciality company here in Fort Lauderdale and the reason we work trade shows and conventions obviously is to generate new accounts. The second thing we want you to do is try one of our product lines, with your company name on it. In this case either pens, keychains, or maybe some executive gifts, depending on your business. By showing an invoice for one of the products and giving us a picture, you're going to get one of the major awards.

The good news is we tied this whole thing into an invoice for $399.50. It's not a lot of money like $1,000 or something like that. For whatever product you think you can handle, and like I said, by virtue of your purchases and your photo, you're going to get one of the major awards. Do you have any questions at this point?

(*If he does not have any questions at this point you say*)

So out of pens, keychains, or magnetic business cards, which one do you think you could use the most? (*Let's just say he picks pens.*) That's a good choice. They are neon stick pens. We put your name on them and we want you to pass them out to new customers, and old customers or anybody else.

(*Basically you just tell the guy what he can do with the pens, and when he has any questions he's going to say "I don't know" or whatever.*)

The sequence of events is as follows. The drawing is coming up in a few days so basically in about seventeen days from Tuesday you're going to receive a box out there by UPS. In the box you're going to get your pens and a sealed envelope to match you up to one of the five awards. Also for making the finals we are going to give you something special, a cellular phone or an Atocha coin.

What you do is fill out the paperwork for your awards, send it in, and in a couple of weeks your awards will be delivered. That's the whole thing in a nutshell.

(*If the guy says he's going to go for it, what you do is this*)

Okay—we don't want your credit card. Number one, it's not good for you to give out your credit card. Number two, also it costs us more money to use your credit card obviously because the bank charges us points. In this case you can just write us a business check or a personal check for the $399.50. Which is easier for you? What we need to do, we need a prepaid invoice in here before the drawing date. I need a day or two to do the paperwork. So what do you do? Get an envelope, address the envelope to our company, put your check in it with your business card, and we have Federal Express come out there. The reason we deal with Federal Express is they're a licensed, bonded courier. They're going to give you a receipt. Also we have to sign for the check in our accounting division. So when is a good time for Federal Express to come out there? (*The guy will say 1:00 or whatever.*) Good, I'll tell you what I need you to do. (*Give him Federal Express 800 number.*)

I need you to call Federal Express and schedule the appointment because you know when you are going to be there more than me. Call them up, tell them you have an overnight letter to be picked up at your address. Give them the name and address and check "bill the recipient" because Cypress Creek Promotions is going to pay for the pick up.

(Then make sure he has our name, address and phone number, and any other information written down.)

Do you have any questions? Do you understand everything? On behalf of the corporate offices congratulations!!!!!!!!!!!!!

You sound like a nice guy. Hopefully you'll get the car. Now I have another few minutes of paperwork to process you for this. Like most people, I don't like the paperwork so if you don't want to do it tell me now. *(Then the guy says, "No, I'll do it.")* I'm going down to accounting. Call Federal Express, they're going to give you a confirmation number so someone is going to call you back in about fifteen minutes to get the number. Fair enough. Okay, good. Congratulations, and after you get everything, give us a call collect, let us know everything arrived. Anytime you need more product, give us a call. Because the whole idea is obviously to do business with you in the future. Once again . . . congratulations!!!!!!!!!!!!

Appendix C

Common Customer Objections and Telemarketer Replies

Many people ripped off by telemarketers can't understand how the sales agent came up with glib answers to every excuse they had not to buy. Here's how. Telemarketing rooms write scripts called "objections," which phone-sales agents rely on to overcome a buyer's reluctance. This set was used by a Las Vegas boiler room that sold shower filters by promising customers a prize. The spiel contains several deceptive claims, including implying that the U.S. Postmaster General endorsed the product.

"I must talk to spouse"

I can certainly understand your position . . . and I'm sure your spouse has full confidence in any decision you might have, especially after you've heard all the details. Now of course you can talk to your spouse. And you can explain the promotion, the many benefits of clean water, and the guarantee of a five-thousand-dollar cashier's check or one of those other fabulous bonus awards. However, then you'd also have to tell him/her that you can't take advantage of the offer, because as mentioned due to the tremendous response we have during this limited promotion we have to limit one phone call per person in order to be fair to everyone. Now, if you choose not to participate that automatically releases the bonus gift reserved for you and it becomes available to someone else.

(*Wait for response*) Great, then all I need now is the expiration date on your credit card. I'll hold on while you get it. (*Silence*)

343

"I don't want to do it!"

I can appreciate that ———, although it is unusual. May I, for my own information, ask why not?

(Use appropriate rebuttal and close.)

"I don't want to spend the money"

I can certainly appreciate how you feel. As a matter of fact, many of our current customers felt that same way and when they found out that we weren't asking them to spend money, we're allowing them the *opportunity* to *invest* in a filtration system that could literally save their lives and guarantee them a five-thousand-dollar cashier's check or one of the other three bonus awards, they became enthusiastic owners. Now, wouldn't you like to receive one of those great bonus awards?

Response: Great!!! Then all I need now is the expiration date on your credit card. I'll hold while you get it!!! *(Silence)*

"I've been burned before"

I can appreciate what you're saying and it's a shame that there are companies that take advantage of people. However, don't let me wear the black eye for somebody else. If a person receives a bad meal in a restaurant they generally don't condemn all restaurants. All we ask of you is to give us just 1 percent of your confidence and we'll earn the other 99 percent. Now that sounds fair, doesn't it?

"My credit card is full"

Well, that's no problem. I can take down all the information now and if the card doesn't clear, we'll get right back to you and make other arrangements. That sounds fair, doesn't it?

"I don't give my card number over the phone"

I can certainly appreciate your concern and I'd like to share something with you. You use your credit cards at places like restaurants and department stores and that waitress or store clerk has your credit card information even if they give you back the carbons. Now, you're not concerned about that and you shouldn't be. That's because the *Federal Consumer Protection Act* states that you are obligated to pay *only* those charges you authorize.

"It's too much money"

I can certainly appreciate that. However, when you really think about it, you really can't put a price tag on good health. And by investing in a Krystal Kleer shower filter you're guaranteed one of those four bonus awards.

"How much was that again?"

Well, your total investment for your Krystal Kleer shower filter is $398. Now at this point I must make clear that if your friends or relatives would like to own a Krystal Kleer shower filter, that's great. However, they're not eligible to receive any of those bonus awards. Only the person whose name is on the notification is eligible. And that's your name isn't it?

"Send me some literature"

I can certainly appreciate that, and we'll be more than happy to send you information pertaining to Krystal Kleer shower filter. At this point, however, I should take a moment to reiterate that this is a limited offer, so after you've received our literature and decided that protecting your health is a wise move, you can still own a Krystal Kleer shower filter. However, you will no longer be eligible to receive either a five-thousand-dollar cashier's check or one of the other three bonus awards. And you would like to receive one of those bonus awards, wouldn't you?

"Why do I have to decide now?"

This is a very limited promotion and it runs for a short period of time only. During this time, we get a tremendous response and we have to limit one phone call per household in order to be fair to everyone trying to reach us. Now if you choose not to participate that's fine, however it automatically releases the gift reserved for you and it becomes available to someone else. So while you can always own a Krystal Kleer shower filter, by acting today you are guaranteed to receive either the car, five thousand dollars, or one of the other awards. And you would love to win one of those awards, right?

"I don't have my card. I'll call you back"

Everybody has their card on them. They tell you never to leave home without them. Seriously, when I hear a person say that, what they're usually trying to say is "It's too good to be true," or "It's too much money." So be honest with me, which one is it? (*Wait for answer, then begin rebuttal.*)

OR

That's not a crisis—several of our current customers were in the same situation. All you need to do is simply go get one of your credit card bills or statements. I'll hold on.

"I'm not interested"

Well, I can certainly appreciate that. However, you are interested in good health aren't you? And you would like one of these bonus awards wouldn't you?

"How do I know I can trust you?"

I can certainly appreciate your concern. Let me assure you that you are going to receive everything we've promised you. Now, if you look on the front side of the notification you will see our mailing permit number. We applied for that permit to the Postmaster General of the United States Postal System. After he reviewed our application and investigated our company, we were issued that permit. Our company has been around for several years now and we couldn't continue to use that number if we didn't do good business. So, if the Postmaster General of the United States trusts our company, I'm sure you can, too. So let's go ahead and enter you in our promotion today.

"Do I have to pay for anything before I receive my package and gift?"

We'll bill you now. However, in three to five days you will receive a letter of guarantee stating that you have thirty days to try the unit and that your shower filter and bonus award will arrive within the thirty to forty-five days that I mentioned earlier and since it usually takes thirty days for you to receive your bill you should have the shower filter installed before you actually make payment. Now that sounds fair, doesn't it? Great. Now let's go ahead and get your started on the program.

Appendix D

State Law Enforcement Agencies That Have Jurisdiction Over Telemarketing Fraud

ALABAMA
Honorable Jeff Sessions
Attorney General
State of Alabama
11 South Union Street
Montgomery, AL 36130
(205) 242–7300

ALASKA
Honorable Bruce M. Botelho
Attorney General
State of Alaska
State Capitol
P.O. Box 110300
Juneau, AK 99811–0300
(907) 465–3600

ARIZONA
Honorable Grant Woods
Attorney General
State of Arizona
1275 West Washington Street
Phoenix, AZ 85007
(602) 542–4266

ARKANSAS
Honorable Winston Bryant
Attorney General

State of Arkansas
Tower Building
323 Center Street
Little Rock, AR 72201–2610
(501) 682–2007

CALIFORNIA
Honorable Daniel E. Lungren
Attorney General
State of California
1515 K Street
Sacramento, CA 95814
(916) 324–5437

COLORADO
Honorable Gale A. Norton
Attorney General
State of Colorado
Department of Law
1525 Sherman Street
Denver, CO 80203
(303) 866–3052

CONNECTICUT
Honorable Richard Blumenthal
Attorney General
State of Connecticut
55 Elm Street

Hartford, CT 06106
(203) 566–2026

DELAWARE
Honorable M. Jane Brady
Attorney General
State of Delaware
Carvel State Office Building
820 North French Street
Wilmington, DE 19801
(302) 577–3838

DISTRICT OF COLUMBIA
Honorable Garland Pinkston, Jr.
Acting Corporation Counsel
Office of the Corporation Counsel
441 4th Street, N.W.
Washington, D.C, 20001
(202) 727–6248

FLORIDA
Honorable Robert A. Butterworth
Attorney General
State of Florida
The Capitol
PL 01
Tallahassee, FL 32399–1050
(904) 487–1963

GEORGIA
Honorable Michael J. Bowers
Attorney General
State of Georgia
40 Capitol Square, SW
Atlanta, GA 30334–1300
(404) 656–4585

HAWAII
Honorable Margery S. Bronster
Attorney General

State of Hawaii
425 Queen Street
Honolulu, HI 96813
(808) 586–1282

IDAHO
Honorable Alan G. Lance
Attorney General
State of Idaho
P.O. Box 83720
Boise, ID 83720–1010
(208) 334–2400

ILLINOIS
Honorable Jim Ryan
Attorney General
State of Illinois Center
100 West Randolph Street
Chicago, IL 60601
(312) 814–2503

INDIANA
Honorable Pamela Fanning Carter
Attorney General
Indiana Government Center South
Fifth Floor
402 West Washington Street
Indianapolis, IN 46204
(317) 233–4386

IOWA
Honorable Tom Miller
Attorney General
State of Iowa
Hoover State Office Building
Des Moines, IA 50319
(515) 281–3053

KANSAS
Honorable Carla J. Stovall

Attorney General
State of Kansas
Judicial Building
301 W. 10th Street
Topeka, KS 66612–1597
(913) 296–2215

KENTUCKY
Honorable Chris Gorman
Attorney General
Commonwealth of Kentucky
State Capitol, Room 116
Frankfort, KY 40601
(502) 564–7600

LOUISIANA
Honorable Richard P. Ieyoub
Attorney General
State of Louisiana
Department of Justice
P.O. Box 94005
Baton Rouge, LA 70804–4095
(504) 342–7013

MAINE
Honorable Andrew Ketterer
Attorney General
State of Maine
State House Building
Augusta, ME 04333
(207) 626–8800

MARYLAND
Honorable J. Joseph Curran, Jr.
Attorney General
State of Maryland
200 Saint Paul Place
Baltimore, MD 21202–2202
(410) 576–6300

MASSACHUSETTS
Honorable Scott Harshbarger
Attorney General
Commonwealth of Massachusetts
1 Ashburton Place
Boston, MA 02108–1698
(617) 727–2200

MICHIGAN
Honorable Frank J. Kelley
Attorney General
State of Michigan
P.O. Box 30212
525 W. Ottawa Street
Lansing, MI 48909–0212
(517) 373–1110

MINNESOTA
Honorable Hubert H. Humphrey III
Attorney General
State of Minnesota
State Capitol
Suite 102
St. Paul, MN 55155
(612) 296–6196

MISSISSIPPI
Honorable Mike Moore
Attorney General
State of Mississippi
Department of Justice
P.O. Box 220
Jackson, MS 39205–0220
(601) 359–3692

MISSOURI
Honorable Jeremiah W. Nixon
Attorney General
State of Missouri
Supreme Court Building

207 W. High Street
Jefferson City, MO 65102
(314) 751–3321

MONTANA
Honorable Joseph P. Mazurek
Attorney General
State of Montana
Justice Building
215 N. Sanders
Helena, MT 59620–1401
(406) 444–2026

NEBRASKA
Honorable Don Stenberg
Attorney General
State of Nebraska
State Capitol
P.O. Box 98920
Lincoln, NE 68509–8920
(402) 471–2682

NEVADA
Honorable Frankie Sue Del Papa
Attorney General
State of Nevada
198 S. Carson
Carson City, NV 89710
(702) 687–4170

NEW HAMPSHIRE
Honorable Jeffrey R. Howard
Attorney General
State of New Hampshire
State House Annex
25 Capitol Street
Concord, NH 03301–6397
(603) 271–3658

NEW JERSEY
Honorable Deborah T. Poritz
Attorney General
State of New Jersey
Richard J. Hughes Justice Complex
25 Market Street CN 080
Trenton, N.J. 08625
(609) 292–4976

NEW MEXICO
Honorable Tom Udall
Attorney General
State of New Mexico
P.O. Drawer 1508
Santa Fe, NM 87504–1508
(505) 827–6000

NEW YORK
Honorable Dennis C. Vacco
Attorney General
State of New York
Department of Law—The Capitol
2nd Floor
Albany, NY 12224
(518) 474–7330

NORTH CAROLINA
Honorable Michael F. Easley
Attorney General
State of North Carolina
Department of Justice
P.O. Box 629
Raleigh, NC 27602–0629
(919) 733–3377

NORTH DAKOTA
Honorable Heidi Heitkamp
Attorney General
State of North Dakota
State Capitol

600 East Boulevard Avenue
Bismark, ND 58505–0040
(701) 328–2210

OHIO
Honorable Betty D. Montgomery
Attorney General
State of Ohio
State Office Tower
30 East Broad Street
Columbus, OH 43266–0410
(614) 466–3376

OKLAHOMA
Honorable Drew Edmondson
Attorney General
State of Oklahoma
State Capitol
2300 N. Lincoln Blvd.
Room 112
Oklahoma City, OK 73105
(405) 521–3921

OREGON
Honorable Theodore R.
   Kulongoski
Attorney General
State of Oregon
Justice Building
1162 Court Street, NE
Salem, OR 97310
(503) 378–6002

PENNSYLVANIA
Honorable Ernest D. Preate, Jr.
Attorney General
Commonwealth of Pennsylvania
Strawberry Square
Harrisburg, PA 17120
(717) 787–3391

RHODE ISLAND
Honorable Jeffrey B. Pine
Attorney General
State of Rhode Island
72 Pine Street
Providence, RI 02903
(401) 274–4400

SOUTH CAROLINA
Honorable Charlie Condon
Attorney General
State of South Carolina
Rembert C. Dennis Office Building
P.O. Box 11549
Columbia, SC 29211–1549
(803) 734–3970

SOUTH DAKOTA
Honorable Mark Barnett
Attorney General
State of South Dakota
500 E. Capitol
Pierre, S.D. 57501–5070
(605) 773–3215

TENNESSEE
Honorable Charles W. Burson
Attorney General
State of Tennessee
500 Charlotte Avenue
Nashville, TN 37243
(615) 741–6474

TEXAS
Honorable Dan Morales
Attorney General
State of Texas
Capitol Station P.O. Box 12548
Austin, TX 78711–2548
(512) 463–2191

UTAH
Honorable Jan Graham
Attorney General
State of Utah
State Capitol Room 236
Salt Lake City, UT 84114–0810
(801) 538–1326

VERMONT
Honorable Jeffrey L. Amestoy
Attorney General
State of Vermont
109 State Street
Montpelier, VT 05609–1001
(802) 828–3171

VIRGINIA
Honorable James S. Gilmore III
Attorney General
Commonwealth of Virginia
900 East Main Street
Richmond, VA 23219
(804) 786–2071

WASHINGTON
Honorable Christine O. Gregoire
Attorney General
State of Washington
P.O. Box 40100
905 Plum Street Building 3
Olympia WA 98504–0100
(206) 753–6200

WEST VIRGINIA
Honorable Darrell V. McGraw, Jr.
Attorney General
State of West Virginia
State Capitol
Charleston, WV 25305
(304) 558–2021

WISCONSIN
Honorable James E. Doyle
Attorney General
State of Wisconsin
State Capitol
P.O. Box 7857
Suite 114 East
Madison, WI 53707–7857
(608) 266–1221

WYOMING
Honorable William Hill
Attorney General
State of Wyoming
State Capitol Building
Cheyenne, WY 82002
(307) 777–7841

Here is a list of U.S. government agencies and other offices that can assist victims of telemarketing fraud:

The Federal Trade Commission
Telemarketing Fraud
Washington, D.C. 20580
(202) 326–3128

FTC ConsumerLine on Internet
Consumer.FTC.Gov.2416
World Wide Web
Uniform Resource Locator:
GOPHER://CONSUMER.FTC.G
OV:2416

U.S. Postal Service
Chief Postal Inspector
U.S. Postal Service
Room 3517
Washington, D.C. 20260–6320
(202) 245–4514

Commodities Futures Trading
    Commission
2033 K Street N.W.
Washington, D.C. 20581
(202) 254–6387

To check complaints about a broker:

National Futures Association
Disciplinary Information
    Access Line
(800) 676–4NFA

National Fraud Information Center
c/o National Consumers League
815 15th Street N.W.
Washington, D.C. 20005
(202) 639–8140
Hotline to report
telemarketing fraud:
(800) 876–7060

Index